Making Sense Out of a World Gone Mad

A Roadmap for God's Elect Living in the Final Days of the End Times

Watchman on the Wall

Tantuple Publishing Inc.

Making Sense Out of a World Gone Mad: A Roadmap for God's Elect Living in the Final Days of the End Times

All Scripture references are to the Authorized (King James) Version of the Holy Bible, supplemented with the names of God and Jesus from the Hebraic-Roots Version Scriptures.

Printed in the United States of America

Library of Congress Control Number: 2015901661
Categories: 1. Bible Prophecy   2. Religion   3. Current Events and Issues   4. Politics

ISBN-10: 098609210X
ISBN-13: 978-0-9860921-0-7

Dedication

This book is dedicated to YHWH (pronounced Yahuwah, the
Hebrew name of God) and Yahushua (Jesus) of the Bible
who rescued me from myself some thirteen years ago and set
me on this course and to my best friend, life partner and dear
bride, Marsha.

May this work bring glory, honor and delight to YHWH and
Yahushua and comfort, peace, perspective and insight to the
elect in these very troubled times.

Jonathan, may this book bless you and set you free in the truths in watchman on the wall

Table of Contents

1. Introduction

This book is not for everyone; in fact it is intentionally not a book for most people. My target audience for this book are those people who number among God's elect, a special group of people, chosen by God since before the world began, whose names are written in the Lamb's book of life, who would one day become one of His born again adopted sons and daughters and a true follower of Yahushua, more commonly known as Jesus of Nazareth or Jesus Christ. If you are one of God's elect, this may be the most important book you ever read. The reason is simple. We live at a time in world history unlike any other in the last 6,000 years and the decisions each of us makes over the next year between now and the end of 2016 will impact the quality of our existence for all eternity. These are bold statements, I know. But I ask you to give me the benefit of laying out for you the evidence which I have been led to discover.

The story you are about to read is rooted in my own life story, a story that has been fraught with a number of trials that should have crushed and destroyed me. But they did not. Instead, they profoundly changed and transformed me into the grateful, submitted and obedient servant of YHWH that I am today. Those trials refined my character, taught me wisdom, developed my courage and have given me a life vision that imparts meaning and purpose to everything I do today. In short, I am a man who is blessed beyond my wildest imaginings, hopes and expectations, by the creator of the universe who delights in me, for who I have become. This is the hope I now long to share with you, my readers, so that you too might be encouraged to challenge and examine everything you have ever been told or taught your entire life, as I have done in recent years.

Any reader has a right to know who I am, and why you should heed anything I might have to share with you. I was born in 1954 in Marin County, California, just north of San Francisco, California, across the Golden Gate Bridge. That makes me a member of the Baby Boom generation, and thus, part of a massive population bulge which has transformed America at each of the life stages my generation has passed through. During my lifetime, I have witnessed profound social changes that have occurred since 1960 which very few people have fully noticed or even comprehended, but which I have come to study and understand quite deeply. I happen to have been blessed with a keen intellect, a broad and accomplished education and a dedication to living my life with an unusual degree of honesty and integrity. I have learned a lot, much of it in the past fourteen years, guided on a life changing spiritual journey by YHWH himself.

Then, over the last four years, YHWH led me to discover that almost everything I was ever told or taught all my life was part of a web of lies so pervasive that it defies most people's ability to comprehend it. I am not unique in this experience or discovery. It has occurred to all of us in much the same way and very few people are even aware that it has been done to them. Part of this book's purpose is to reveal what some of the most profound lies are, what the truth is, and explain what implications and conclusions we ought to draw from such discoveries. How one processes such discoveries makes all the difference in whether we grow up, mature, gain real godly wisdom and become truly healthy and whole, or whether we retreat into a world of make-believe and denial that leads to mental illness, despair, addictions and self-destructive behaviors. I now know that my recent discoveries have been no accident. Instead, they were revealed to me by YHWH to lead me to some profoundly important insights which He now wills for me to share with you, my readers. That is the purpose and intent of this book.

1. Introduction

Let me get right to the point and the bottom line. I have significant reasons to conclude that we are living in the time of the great tribulation foretold in Daniel 12 and Matthew 24 of the Bible. In today's era, in which ignorance of what the Bible says and means is celebrated and actively encouraged by all worldly institutions, to keep as many people as possible indoctrinated, mind-controlled, hypnotized, demonized, manipulated and controlled by a set of forces which seek to destroy all of mankind, I must and will presume complete ignorance of the Bible on the part of my readers. I plan to reveal what it says and why we should give it our utmost attention in guiding the most important life decisions we all must make over the next 12 months.

What is this great tribulation I refer to, and why is it significant? The Bible claims to be the inspired and flawless words of God or YHWH, the creator of the universe, who has been, remains, and always will be fully in charge of every circumstance that affects the lives of every person who has ever lived since the beginning of the world. My own life journey, which I plan to share with you here, has proven the Bible to be completely trustworthy and true in every respect, without exception. In contrast, almost every person I have ever known in my life, with a few rare exceptions, has proven himself to be untrustworthy and a liar. Many such people have viciously betrayed and attempted to harm me over my lifetime. Moreover, the Bible fully explains why this happened the way it did to me for a bigger purpose. As a result of this life history, I have come to fully trust the Bible to be YHWH's ownership manual for life, which is exactly what it was intended to be.

The Bible teaches from beginning to end that man is desperately wicked and totally depraved. This depravity is a flaw from our birth that none of us can do anything about. It is the way we were created: we were born to lose in life, is what the Bible claims. It claims that YHWH spoke the world and the universe into existence out of nothing and that YHWH is a personal spirit being so brilliant, all powerful, all knowing, ever-present, all seeing, wise, benevolent, loving, merciful, holy and just that His majesty defies man's ability to comprehend.

3

It goes on to teach that YHWH created man in His image to exercise dominion and rule over the earth as caretakers of YHWH's creation: to multiply and fill the earth, to subdue it and to cultivate it. It further teaches that there are universal moral absolutes of right and wrong that apply to all men and women of all cultures, and that YHWH's holiness demands that for man to live in right relationship with Him, that he must submit his life and will to the will and commandments of YHWH. In the end, this system that the Bible teaches requires that man fear and obey YHWH. Such fear and obedience is enforced with long term rewards and punishments and delayed, but eventual, accountability for our actions to an all-powerful, holy, just and loving God.

What is YHWH trying to accomplish with such a system? The Bible teaches us that YHWH seeks a personal relationship with men and women who are conformed into the likeness of His son, Yahushua, through a spiritual rebirth process (salvation through being "born again" In God's Holy Spirit) and a life-long refining or sanctification process thereafter. It goes on to teach that not all men and women are destined to achieve such a right relationship with YHWH and end up spending eternity with YHWH after death, in harmony with Him, with Yahushua and with other fellow believers, or saints, in a new heaven and earth. In fact, it teaches that most men and woman WILL NOT experience such a right relationship with God, but instead will choose to rebel against Him, will go their own way and willingly choose the path that leads to an eternity of agony and torment, separated permanently from God, in hell, followed by a burning lake of fire and brimstone.

In addition, the Bible teaches that God created spirit beings which exist to oppose and afflict mankind in the form of the devil and demon spirits. Why would a loving, just and holy God do such a thing to mankind? Because God seeks mature relationships with men and women of virtue, nobility, character and courage who will stand up to evil and resist and oppose it. This requires that God must refine and test each one of His chosen people repeatedly to build their perseverance, character and hope in the promises of God. Those whom God

4

has chosen as His people, His elect, since before the world began, will pass the test. Those who were not chosen by God will fail it.

Since the majority of mankind will fail these tests and are not chosen and therefore not part of God's elect, they will not be open or receptive to the appeals of God to obey and submit to His greater will for their lives. Instead, they will rebel against Him and He responds by choosing to have nothing to do with those who reject and defiantly rebel against Him.

All of world history over the past 6,000 years has been driven by spiritual forces and powers which we cannot see, but whose effects we can observe in people's behaviors which are often quite erratic, illogical, self-defeating and self-destructive. Yet they do it anyhow. At several points in world history, mankind has been in steep rebellion against God and exhibited hideous wickedness that has led God to bring destruction upon the wicked: those who engage in actions which are consistently evil and perverse. In the days of Noah, God brought a global flood which destroyed all of mankind and every animal and bird on the earth except for Noah, his wife, their three sons and their wives and the animals that came into the ark, which Noah spent 120 years building, in anticipation of the coming Flood, in obedience to God's instructions. Then, in response to the endless wickedness of the northern kingdom of Israel and an unbroken string of bad kings ruling over them since the days after King Solomon died, God gave a writ of divorce to the kingdom of Israel and brought the fierce and cruel nation of Assyria, under King Shalmaneser V, in 722 B.C. to defeat the northern kingdom and haul its survivors away into exile in Assyria. 136 years later, in 586 B.C., God permitted and used Babylonian King Nebuchadnezzar and his army to defeat the southern kingdom of Judah. Nebuchadnezzar sacked the city of Jerusalem and carried away its survivors to Babylon in exile and captivity for the next 70 years, for much the same reasons as God allowed with the northern kingdom of Israel previously. This history is well documented in the books of the Old Testament of the Bible, or what some theologians prefer to refer to as the pre-Messianic Scriptures (that is, before

Christ). The vast majority of the descendants of the 10 Hebrew tribes of Israel and the 2 Hebrew tribes of Judah never returned to the land of Canaan, but instead were dispersed throughout Europe in three massive waves of human migration in around 500 B.C., about which I will have more to say later.

In the cases of the kingdoms of Israel and Judah, God sent His prophets ahead of time to warn the Hebrew people of their sinfulness, wickedness, idolatry and disobedience against God's commands and to predict what would happen to these two nations if they did not confess, repent and turn from their evil and wicked ways: that God would destroy them. In spite of the miraculous history of the 12 Hebrew tribes who were brought forth out of slavery in Egypt, through the parting of the Red Sea and wandering in the wilderness for 40 years thereafter that are described in the Books of Exodus, Numbers, Leviticus and Deuteronomy, centuries later, the descendants of the 12 Hebrew tribes did not heed the warnings of the prophets whom God sent to warn them, and all of their specific prophecies were fulfilled precisely as the prophets predicted. God's response was to bring the sword, famine and pestilence on the rebellious people of ancient Israel of the Old Testament – first upon the northern kingdom of Israel and later upon the southern kingdom of Judah.

Today, this same process is working its way out around the world as the end of the present age approaches. Every time that God executes His judgments against rebellious mankind, He sends His true prophets as His messengers to warn the people to confess their sins, repent and turn from their wicked ways, and urge God's people to obey God's commandments and fear God, because of His awesome power, which includes the exclusive ability to destroy both body and soul in hell for all eternity. Seldom were the warnings of the prophets of old heeded. And every time, the predicted destruction followed and destroyed those who would not heed the warnings of God's prophets and watchmen on the wall.

1. Introduction

In early 2013, the world crossed a threshold and entered into a three and a half year or 1,290 day period referred to as the great tribulation in end times Bible prophecy that was first predicted in Daniel 12 during the Babylonian captivity in the sixth century B.C. During this period of time, which Jesus tells us in Matthew 24:21-22 will be unlike any other in all of world history before it or after, great trials and tribulation will be experienced by God's elect. His chosen people will experience affliction and opposition at the hands of the wicked. Jesus goes on to explain in verse 24 of chapter 24 of Matthew that the great tribulation will be a time of great deception which will be so deep and pervasive, that if it were possible, even God's elect would be deceived by it. But it won't be possible, because God will reveal the truth to His elect to keep them from harm. Matthew 24 gives us the sequence of events which will occur during these perilous times. First, the tribulation period will occur which, according to Daniel 12:7, will last three and a half years, and which verse 11 defines even more specifically as spanning 1,290 days. Immediately after the tribulation period has ended, verse 29 of Matthew 24 describes four distinct celestial events which will occur:

> *"Immediately after the tribulation of those days shall the sun be darkened, and the moon shall not give her light, and the stars shall fall from heaven, and the powers of the heavens shall be shaken:"*

These events are likely to describe a celestial body coming between the sun on the one hand, and the earth and the moon on the other, a meteor shower and a massive earthquake of global proportions. Matthew 24 then continues to describe what will come next in verses 30 and 31:

> *"And then shall appear the sign of the Son of man (meaning Yahushua or Jesus) in heaven: and then shall all the tribes of the earth mourn, and they shall see the Son of man coming in the clouds of heaven with power and great glory. And he shall send his angels with a great sound of a trumpet, and they shall gather together his elect from the four winds, from one end of heaven to the other."* (parenthetical added)

These two verses describe the gathering up of God's elect, those whom He chose since before the world began, to become His adopted sons and daughters at some point during their lives, at a time and manner of God's choosing and initiative. Let's look at the other passages in the Bible which explain this same event and add further insight as to what we can now expect to occur in late 2016:

> *"And at that time shall Michael (the archangel) stand up, the great prince which standeth for the children of thy people: and there shall be a time of trouble (the great tribulation), such as never was since there was a nation even to that same time: and at that time thy people (God's elect) shall be delivered, every one that shall be found written in the book (the Lamb's book of life). And many of them that sleep in the dust of the earth (the dead) shall awake, some to everlasting life, and some to shame and everlasting contempt (hell)."* Daniel 12:1-2 (parentheticals added)

> *"For if we believe that Jesus (Yahushua) died and rose again, even so them also which sleep (are dead) in Jesus (Yahushua) will God (Eloah) bring with him. For this we say unto you by the word of the Lord (our Adon), that we which are alive and remain unto the coming of the Lord (our Adon) shall not prevent them which are asleep (dead). For the Lord (our Adon) himself shall descend from heaven with a shout, with the voice of the archangel (Michael), and with the trump of God (Eloah): and the dead in Christ (the Messiah) shall rise first: Then we which are alive and remain shall be caught up together with them in the clouds, to meet the Lord (our Adon) in the air: and so shall we ever be with the Lord (our Adon)."* 1 Thessalonians 4:14-17 (parentheticals added)

> *"Now we beseech you, brethren, by the coming of our Lord Jesus Christ (our Adon Yahushua the Messiah), and by our gathering together unto him, That ye be not soon shaken in mind, or be troubled, neither by spirit, nor by word, nor by letter as from us, as that the day of Christ (our Adon) is at hand. Let no man deceive you by any means: for that day shall not come, except there come a falling away (great apostasy of*

8

1. Introduction

the Church) first, and that man of sin be revealed, the son of perdition;" 2 Thessalonians 2:1-3 (parentheticals added)

As I shall demonstrate later, there are substantial reasons to conclude that both of these two events described in 2 Thessalonians 2:3, which must precede the gathering or the rapture, have now been fulfilled.

"Behold, I shew you a mystery; We shall not all sleep (die), but we shall all be changed, In a moment, in the twinkling of an eye, at the last trump: for the trumpet shall sound, and the dead shall be raised incorruptible, and we shall be changed. For this corruptible (body) must put on incorruption (a resurrected body), and this mortal must put on immortality. So when this corruptible shall have put on incorruption, and this mortal shall have put on immortality, then shall be brought to pass the saying that is written, Death is swallowed up in victory." 1 Corinthians 15:51-54 (parentheticals added)

And finally, in the Book of Revelation, which describes seven seal, seven trumpet and seven vial judgments, the seventh and final trumpet will sound, signaling the gathering up of God's elect:

"And the seventh angel sounded; and there were great voices in heaven saying, The kingdoms of this world are become the kingdoms of our Lord, (Eloah), and of his Christ (Messiah); and he shall reign for ever and ever. Revelation 11:15

"And the nations were angry, and thy wrath is come, and the time of the dead, that they should be judged, and that thou shouldest give reward unto thy servants the prophets, and to the saints, and them that fear thy name, small and great; and shouldest destroy them which destroy the earth." Revelation 11:18

The events of end times Bible prophecy laid out here describe events which are now imminent, meaning near at hand and soon to occur. Many signs foretelling that we have entered this stage of world history and God's plan that are prophesied and described in various books of the Bible have been fulfilled during the last half century since 1960. Not everyone is able to perceive that this has indeed happened, because these revelations and insights are only revealed to certain members of God's elect whom God has chosen to reveal them to and to impart to them spiritual discernment. For a person who has not been blessed by God to receive such spiritual discernment, he or she cannot even comprehend that such a thing happens or is possible. As one such man who has been blessed with these gifts by God, I can assure you, my readers, that it is indeed quite possible. In fact, it has occurred many times in my own life over the past fourteen years. This blessing or gift entrusts those of us who have it with a grave responsibility to reveal it to others. This is precisely what my purpose is here and through any other means available to me.

In many eras in the past described in the Bible, God has raised a few men of God who He subjected to extensive trials, sufferings and persecutions and called on them to serve as His watchmen on the wall, whose job it was to warn the chosen people from the 12 Hebrew tribes of Abraham, Isaac and Jacob to confess, repent and turn from their evil and wicked ways, to fear God and to submit their wills and their lives in obedience to the commandments of almighty God. Such men were messengers whom God used to give ample warning to all people who were living in rebellion against an almighty, holy and just God who abhors all sin and will not tolerate rebellion of any kind. These watchmen, or prophets of God, were given the unenviable task by God of speaking into the cultures of their day which were in abject defiance of and rebellion against the creator of the universe, the God of the Bible. Their messages were counter-cultural, politically incorrect, and usually viewed as deeply offensive to those who were living in rebellion and sin against God. As a result, the warnings of these watchmen and prophets were seldom heeded and were instead almost always ignored and dismissed. Frequently, such ancient prophets' messages were suppressed and silenced and they themselves were subjected to extensive ridicule, scorn, dismissals, mockery, injustices, persecution and often even murder to shut them up.

1. Introduction

Today, God has raised up a few watchmen and true prophets to follow in the footsteps and traditions of the great prophets of the Old Testament, which include Isaiah, Jeremiah, Ezekiel and Hosea. In recent years, I have discovered that God has called me to serve Him as one such modern day prophet and watchman on the wall. This book is a part of my obedience to the call God has put upon my life to warn people to wake up spiritually, to turn from sin, evil and wickedness and submit and surrender their lives and their wills completely to the lordship of the son of God, Jesus (Yahushua), who will soon return in late 2016 to gather up the saints (true believers in Jesus), slay the wicked, take dominion, and reign over the earth for a metaphorical thousand year millennial rule in which His resurrected saints will co-reign with Him, and He will pass judgment on the resurrected wicked people of the world, as described in Chapter 20 of the Book of Revelation.

I am completely aware that the majority of people alive on the planet today are unlikely to heed my warnings and advice to them, any more than the people of the southern kingdom of Judah did in response to the teachings and urgings of the prophets Isaiah, Jeremiah and Ezekiel of their day. History from 2,600 years ago in the southern kingdom of Judah, right before Babylonian King Nebuchadnezzar sacked and destroyed Jerusalem in 586 B.C. and exiled most of the survivors to Babylon for the next 70 years, is now repeating itself on a global scale early in the twenty first century. My task as a modern day prophet and watchman on the wall is to blow the trumpet and sound the alarm warning of the second coming of Yahushua (Jesus) as prophesied in the Bible ever since the prophet Daniel first predicted the end times of today during his lifetime, as one of the exiles of Judah to Babylon in the sixth century before Christ, to explain the Bible prophecies and to urge those who are able to listen to get right with YHWH (God) before it's too late and they find themselves destroyed by Yahushua's treading of the winepress of the fierceness and wrath of almighty God, as Revelation 19:15 describes what is coming upon the rebellious and the wicked of our era.

11

The Importance of Knowing the True Names of God and of Jesus

Throughout this book, I will be referring to and quoting from the 1611 King James Version (KJV) of the Bible. I do this because the KJV is the best English translation of the original Masoretic (traditional) Hebrew Old Testament, and the *Textus Receptus* New Testament Greek manuscripts and the one which most tightly conforms to the word for word translation of the original manuscripts of the flawless, complete and inspired words of God to mankind.[1] Additionally, every time the titles 'God,' 'Lord,' 'Jesus' or 'Christ' appear I will be showing in parentheses the proper Hebrew names which appear in the original texts. I am deriving this added insight from the Hebraic-Roots Version Scriptures published by the Institute for Scripture Research which, among other things, attempts to remedy a deliberate deception which goes back at least 400 years to conceal the true names of God and His son Jesus from us. Todd G. Bennett, in his book, *Names: The Father, The Son and the Importance of Names in Scripture,* explains the vital importance of knowing and referring to God and His son by their true Hebrew names by which they originally identified themselves to the ancient nation of Israel, and by which they still prefer to be known today.

God is a personal God and creator of the universe who desires a personal, individual and intimate heart-to-heart relationship with each one of His chosen elect. As such, He knows and refers to us by our given names and He wishes to be known in an identical fashion Himself. For any of us to claim we know and love God without even knowing His true name is patently absurd, and in my own reading of the Bible and in my prayer life, I have largely shifted to referring to God and Jesus this way during the past three years, as I have become aware of this reality and of a long term deliberate plan to suppress their names from man's knowledge.

---

[1] Hendrie, Edward. *The Anti-Gospel: The Perversion of Christ's Grace Gospel.* 2005. pp. 384-385.

1. Introduction

In the original Hebrew text, God refers to Himself by four Hebrew consonants which have been transliterated in the Arabic alphabet employed by the English language into the four consonants "YHWH." Bennett explains in his book his reasoning for concluding that the proper pronunciation of this four letter tetragrammaton is "Yahuwah." The most common academic rendering of this tetragrammaton is 'Yahweh;' but academic and seminary scholars are quite likely to be in error on this matter, as well as on many other topics of Biblical teaching, doctrine and emphasis. Bennett further explains that the name of the son of God, who most of us know as Jesus, Christ, Jesus Christ or Jesus of Nazareth, is actually "Yahushua." At its root, the names of YHWH (or Yahuwah) and Yahushua embody great power and authority and it seems quite apparent that these names were deliberately removed and concealed from most of mankind centuries ago from common translations of the original manuscripts to lead people away from an intimate knowledge of God and His son. Ultimately, the spiritual force behind this concealment can be none other than God's adversary, the devil, otherwise known as Satan, Lucifer, Beelzebub, the Lord of the Flies, the prince of this world, and the father of lies. When the Hebrew name for God is 'Elohim,' rather than YHWH, the Bible is referring to the three persons of the godhead: God the Father, God the Son and God the Holy Spirit, and when it uses the name Eloah, it refers to God the Father only. For those of my readers who number among God's chosen elect, it is my hope and prayer that you too may make this shift to refer to God and to Jesus by their true Hebrew names of Yahuwah and Yahushua in your speech and prayer life so that you may experience a deeper intimacy with God the Father and God the Son.

The Roles of a Prophet and a Watchman on the Wall

Early in the twenty first century there is great confusion among theologians and lay people claiming to be Christians as to whether or not God even calls men to serve as prophets now that the Bible has been written. In recent years, many men have professed to be prophets and made bold predictions of the end of the world, the rapture and the second coming of Christ. The timing of such events have come and gone without their predictions proving to be true. Such charlatans and con artists have thus proven themselves to be false prophets, for whom the Bible teaches us they will experience an extra dose of God's wrath for misleading others. Moreover, their drawing attention to themselves has discredited the true Biblical faith in Yahushua or Christ among a godless world which seeks to deny the existence of God altogether. Thus, it is with great trepidation, trembling and no small amount of fear that I share with you, my readers, that I am convinced that God has called me to serve as one of his true prophets and watchmen on the wall in the end times in which we now find ourselves living. Let me be very clear here: I don't want this to be true. I would much prefer to remain silent and largely anonymous and out of view and keep the revelations which God has shared with me to myself and to a close circle of trusted friends. But I cannot do that and it's important that you, my readers understand why. First, let me define what prophecy is and what it is not.

According to the footnote to 1 Corinthians 14:1 in the *NIV Life Application Study Bible*, "prophesy may involve predicting future events, but its main purpose is to communicate God's message to people, providing insight, warning, correction and encouragement." Over the past five years I have increasingly and intentionally been submitting and surrendering my life and my will to Yahushua as Lord, king and master over every aspect of my life. Every morning in my daily prayers I ask Yahushua to conform my will to His perfect one so that I might bring Him honor, praise, pleasure, delight and glory. As I have done so more completely, I have found that I have increasingly received insights, thoughts and inspirations that I could not possibly have conjured up on my own, but which are brilliant, wise and always consistent with the teachings of Bible Scripture. As such, their only possible source has to be from God. I do not receive dreams and visions and in only three instances over my spiritual walk over the past fourteen years have I audibly heard God speak to me. Yet it is very clear to me that He has repeatedly led me to the writings and books of others, whose insights and discoveries have filled in important missing pieces of the puzzle of what is going on in our world today that I was previously missing, and needed to find, to advance my understanding. God has given me the ability to read, digest and retain large volumes of written material and to connect the dots between ideas, concepts and events which most other people cannot or do not see. My purpose here is not to rehash material, facts and concepts which I have learned from books authored by others. I stand on the shoulders of other authors and researchers who remain giants and my heroes and to whom I am deeply indebted. Without their prior work to build upon, I could not have arrived at the revelations God has led me to, which I plan to share with you here.

The Apostle Paul, in 1 Corinthians Chapter 14, makes it very clear that the gift of prophesy remains active in the community of believers today, as Paul urges his disciples in Corinth to eagerly seek the gift of prophesy more than any other gift, especially over the gift of being able to speak in tongues. Paul's reasoning is quite simple:

> "But he that prophesieth speaketh unto men to edification, and exhortation, and comfort." 1 Corinthians 14:3

Consequently, any person who claims that the gift of prophesy is no longer active in the community of believers today is simply in error. Bible Scripture is entirely trustworthy and anyone who makes claims contrary to what it teaches is simply not reliable or trustworthy as a teacher and should not be listened to.

Another indicator of the reliability of my calling from God as a true prophet and as a watchmen on the wall comes from the book of Ezekiel in two places:

> "And it came to pass at the end of seven days, that the word of the LORD (YHWH) came unto me saying, Son of man, I have made thee a watchman unto the house of Israel: therefore hear the word at my mouth, and give them warning from me. When I say unto the wicked, Thou shalt surely die; and thou

givest him not warning, nor speakest to warn the wicked from his wicked way, to save his life; the same wicked man shall die in his iniquity (sin); but his blood will I require at thine hand. Yet if thou warn the wicked, and he turn not from his wickedness, nor from his wicked way, he shall die in his iniquity; but thou hast delivered thy soul. Again, When a righteous man doth turn from his righteousness, and commit iniquity, and I lay a stumblingblock before him, he shall die: because thou hast not given him warning, he shall die in his sin, and his righteousness which he hath done shall not be remembered; but his blood will I require at thine hand. Nevertheless, if thou warn the righteous man, that the righteous sin not, and he doth not sin, he shall surely live, because he is warned; also thou hast delivered thy soul." Ezekiel 3:16-21

As I read this passage in July of 2013, these words grabbed me by the throat and I found myself weeping over them, whereas verses right before and right after them had no such effect. Chapter 33 of Ezekiel is even more relevant to the events foretold in end times Bible prophecy in the book of Revelation:

"Again the word of the LORD (YHWH) came unto me saying, Son of man, speak to the children of thy people, and say unto them, When I bring the sword upon a land, if the people of the land take a man of their coasts, and set him for their watchman: If when he seeth the sword come upon the land, he blow the trumpet, and warn the people; Then whosoever heareth the sound of the trumpet, and taketh not warning; if the sword come, and take him away, his blood shall be on his own head. He heard the sound of the trumpet, and took not warning; his blood shall be upon him, But he that taketh warning shall deliver his soul. But if the watchman see the sword come, and blow not the trumpet, and the people be not warned; If the sword come, and take any person from among them, he is taken away in his iniquity; but his blood will I require at the watchman's hand. So thou, O son of man, I have set thee a watchman unto the house of Israel; therefore thou shalt hear the word at my mouth, and warn them from me. When I say unto the wicked, O wicked man, thou shalt surely die; if thou dost not speak to warn the wicked from his way, that wicked man shall die in

his iniquity; but his blood will I require at thine hand. Nevertheless, if thou warn the wicked of his way to turn from it; if he do not turn from his way, he shall die in his iniquity; but thou hast delivered thy soul. Therefore, O thou son of man, speak unto the house of Israel; Thus ye speak, saying, If our transgressions and our sins be upon us, and we pine away in them, how should we then live? Say unto them, As I live, saith the Lord GOD (Adonai YHWH), I have no pleasure in the death of the wicked; but that the wicked turn from his way and live: turn ye, turn ye from your evil ways; for why will ye die, O house of Israel?" Ezekiel 33:1-11

These passages from the Bible make it very clear that God's calling on a man to serve as a watchman is a very grave and serious matter, and not one to be taken lightly; nor do I do so. Because we live under the new covenant of grace brought about by the work of Yahushua on the cross, my own salvation is not at risk, but at the same time, my eternal rewards in heaven and the treasures I store up for such rewards later are directly linked to my obedience to God in His calling me to serve as one of His watchmen now. For me to ignore or fail to deliver on any aspect of God's calling on my life is simply not an option for me. I owe my life and my soul to God who saved me from my own depravity and who has blessed my life richly, especially during the last three years, as I will explain later. Thus, it is with a cheerful and obedient spirit that I obey God in this calling, even though if I had any choice in the matter, I would prefer it if God would have delegated this role to someone else far better equipped and more worthy to fulfill it than I am. But God is God, and I am not, and I am perfectly fine with that. So I am being obedient to God's call on my life and don't question it any longer.

Because there have been many charlatans, con artists and false prophets who have in the past made false claims concerning the end times similar to mine, I am very cautious about what I say and don't say, because I wish to avoid misrepresenting God in any way, or of being misconstrued as yet another false prophet. God's Word, the Bible, provides us with extensive signs we can expect to see in the end times. I have personally

17

witnessed quite a few of them at a level that few other people have experienced. I am more than capable of connecting the dots between what I have witnessed in our world and what Scripture says we can expect to see in the end times. Thus, I explain in the pages which follow what those events are which I have witnessed, I connect the dots to relevant Scripture verses, and I urge you, my readers to challenge my scholarship and determine if there is sufficient evidence to indicate that we are indeed living in the time of the great tribulation or not. I offer warnings and advice here on what each of us can and should do about it, if this is indeed the case. But it is not my job to persuade you to take action based on any such conclusions. That is the job of God and His Holy Spirit. My job here is merely to present the evidence and connect the dots for you so that you have a basis for making an informed decision and acting accordingly. Yet I must urge you to consider that the consequences of making the wrong decision here can have profound, serious and eternal consequences that make all other life choices and decisions seem inconsequential, by comparison. In short, this is very serious stuff.

I want to address why it is that I am authoring this book as Watchman on the Wall rather than using my own given name. First of all, this book is about YHWH and Yahushua, and not about me. I don't wish to draw undue attention to myself. John the Baptist taught his disciples that he must decrease so that Yahushua might increase and I see things the same way. Second, the information I am revealing here is very controversial and many other courageous authors who have revealed even a part of what I reveal here have been defamed and viciously attacked and abused by the Jewish Anti-Defamation League (more aptly named the Jewish Defamation League) and other like-minded thought police organizations to suppress and silence the truth and to intimidate others to not even think of exposing the lies of the Jewish conspiracy. I simply do not need to subject myself to such abuse. Third, and finally, I have invested considerable time and effort over the past two years to share many of the ideas contained here over the internet as a blogger, employing the moniker Watchman on the Wall in over 14,000 blog posts I have posted to date. Thus, employing that same pseudonym here permits readers to find my other work more easily and readily and connect the dots between the two.

Recommended Approach to Reading This Book

It is not my intention to draw attention to myself in any way. I seek to draw the reader's attention to YHWH and to Yahushua and their amazing plan for life and humanity, if we will only heed it. I have personally been blessed by YHWH and Yahushua with life experiences and relationships which defy my ability to describe them adequately. To YHWH and to Yahushua belong all the glory and all the honor for these incredible blessings. I am humbled and privileged to be used by God as one of His messengers.

I have written this book with the cynic and the skeptic in mind. Consequently, I make extensive reference to passages in the Bible which are highly relevant to what many of us are witnessing in our world today, but I have no intention of beating anyone over the head with the Bible. In several chapters, I provide you, my readers, with extensive footnote references to numerous other sources, many of them of a secular nature, which populate my own bookshelves, and I urge you to test me on this, by researching as many of them as you are able, and see if you arrive at any different conclusions than I have arrived at. If you read what I have to share here with integrity and an open mind, being willing to have your preconceived notions challenged and provoked with extensive hard evidence which is corroborated from multiple, reputable sources and which fully explains the odd behaviors we are witnessing in our world today, I believe you too are likely to arrive at many of the same conclusions I did when I first discovered this information.

I must warn you that my findings are sharply at odds with almost everything you have ever been told or taught before, and your initial reaction is likely to be one of outright dismissal and perhaps even anger directed at me. In most social circles today, many of the topics I address and expose here will shut down conversation and result in endless denials, mockery, scorn, dismissals and ridicule. I've experienced all this and a lot more in my own life journey. It is not a pleasant experience and I don't enjoy it any more than anyone else. However, God has wired me to seek the truth with an unusual degree of tenacity and persistence. I cannot help myself but to pursue the truth wherever it leads and it has frequently gotten me into trouble with those who seek to preserve a false illusion of truth for their own selfish ends.

Our world today seeks to suppress and silence all truth. This is no great secret; it's quite obvious to anyone with any integrity and honesty. Yet those very traits are quite rare today; they were not nearly so rare when I was growing up, but in the generation of my own children, who are now in their twenties, such traits are seldom, if ever, observed, respected or appreciated. As a result, readers under the age of 40 will seldom be capable of digesting and benefitting from what I have to share here. As unfortunate as this may be, it is the hard truth, which I have witnessed time and time again.

Drawing conclusions and making decisions based on false information is nothing more than insanity, which amounts to a denial of reality. If you have not lived your life dedicated to pursuing the truth at all costs, you will initially find it quite uncomfortable. Yet I urge you to press through your discomfort and look objectively at the evidence and the reasoning I present here and challenge yourself to ask whether your existing worldview comes even remotely close to explaining events happening in our world today that are almost impossible to view as positive developments. Something else is going on that the powers-that-be that rule our world today are not coming clean on and admitting to the rest of us. The risks to us and to our families are too great to trust those who hold positions of leadership who have proven themselves over and over again to be liars, and not very good ones at that. It is time we examined the evidence for ourselves, used sound logical reasoning, and trustworthy sources of authority, to determine what the truth is for ourselves and act accordingly.

1. Introduction

Fiftteen years ago, at age 46, I was an agnostic who sincerely did not know whether God existed. Today I am certain that He does. I came at the Biblical Christian faith with the well-trained mind of a scholar, a detective and an accomplished and competent business management consultant and turnaround financial and general management executive who evaluates problems based on the hard facts, logical reasoning and trustworthy authorities. I have been blessed with some truly exceptional problem diagnosing and solving skills which I hope to benefit you with in the pages which follow. The teachings of the full Bible and of God the Father, God the Son and God the Holy Spirit have miraculously transformed me over the last fourteen years and grown me in maturity and wisdom beyond my wildest hopes and dreams. May my story here inspire you to find the same blessings in your own life and prepare you and your families for what is inevitably coming over the next two years, whether we like it or not.

Watchman on the Wall
Teton Valley, Idaho
February 2015
Updated October 2015

2. Has God Truly Spoken?[2]

The Bible makes the bold and unrivaled claim that it is the pure, flawless and inspired words of God to mankind. Furthermore, it goes on to claim that God can never lie, change or fail. No other book or world religion makes such a bold claim. The books or writings which contain the core teachings of all other world religions claim to be books written by men about God. This chapter examines the evidence supporting the claims of the Bible, which few people, including those who profess themselves to be Christians, have ever examined or properly understood, to reveal that the Bible makes an overwhelming and compelling case supporting its claim to be the source of all objective, absolute and universal truth, inspired by God. If this is true, and it is, then any beliefs held by man about God which deviate from or conflict with the teachings of the Bible in its entirety *have* to be false! Since all major world religions claim exclusivity to objective truth and contain truth claims which conflict with what the Bible says and clearly means, all other world religions, according to the law of contradiction, *have* to be false also. Thus the key starting point to any discussion about the big questions of life, hinges on this anchor of whether or not evidence for the divine

---

[2] I owe a debt of profound thanks and gratitude to Greg Koukl, President of Stand to Reason, a ministry dedicated to teaching Christians how to effectively defend the Christian faith in the public square, whose CD talk entitled *The Bible: Has God Spoken?* from his Ambassador Basic Curriculum Course #1 was the source for most of the concepts and facts presented in this chapter.

inspiration and inerrancy of the Bible reveals that this claim is trustworthy and true.

Biblical faith is not mere wishful thinking. It is trust and confidence which Biblical Christians place on the Bible and act upon because of extensive evidence which forms the foundation for our trust in what the Bible teaches. The writer of Hebrews defines faith thusly:

> *"Now faith is the **substance** of things hoped for, the **evidence** of things not seen."* Hebrews 11:1 (bold face added for emphasis)

In other words, Biblical faith is based on substantial evidence which leads man to discover objective reality as it truly is and as God perceives it. Anyone who is of the truth and who employs intellectual rigor and integrity is likely to conclude, as I have, that the evidence I am about to reveal here is overwhelming and compelling, beyond a reasonable doubt, proving the Bible to be true. This is not to suggest that Biblical truths can be proven with 100% certainty. But it does mean that the evidence is overwhelmingly in favor of the Bible and anyone who suggests otherwise, either has never examined the evidence available for its authenticity and infallibility, or has a deliberate agenda to deny it, in order to deny the existence or nature of God as God reveals Himself to mankind through the Scriptures of the Bible.

What do I mean when I say God has spoken to mankind though His Bible? The Bible claims to be the inspired words of God to man, by which is meant that God has superintended the writings of Scripture, so that human authors, using their own words, personalities, writing styles, research, and resources, still wrote down, exactly as God intended, word for word, the original autographs. That's what we mean when we say the Bible is inspired. The book claims to be the book given by God to mankind, specifically to God's elect. Hundreds of times in the Scriptures it says, "Thus saith the Lord." When the Ten Commandments are being given by God to Moses in

Exodus 20:1 it reads, "And God spake these words saying..."
We read in 2 Timothy 3:16 that "All scripture is given by
inspiration of God . . . " It is actually expired, so that through
the out-breathing of the word of God, the writers of the Bible
recorded exactly what He wanted written.

This concept of inspiration is perhaps best illustrated with a
couple of examples. You can make a dog sit, can't you? Well,
if you can make a dog do such a thing, how hard ought it to be
for God, who is sovereign and all-powerful, whose will is never
thwarted, to get written precisely what He wills to be written,
by a man of His choosing? Secondly, I personally have
experienced God inspiring my own writings many times in
recent years. I know this to be true because I am dumb-
founded by the logical clarity, coherence and wisdom that has
come out of me in these writings of mine; and yet there is no
way in the world I could have conjured up such insights on my
own. No other explanation, other than God having inspired
my writing, reveals how such an amazing thing could have
happened. I will be the first to admit that my own experience
is rather exceptional and not at all a usual occurrence with most
people, yet God only used some 40 godly men to write the 66
books of the Bible. In short, He didn't need to use many men
to write His Bible through inspiration: just a few who were
completely submitted to doing God's will, as He willed for it
to be done. Moreover, even though it is common for men to
make mistakes, when they are under the inspiration of a
sovereign God, what kind of a limitation is to for God to use
fallible men to write precisely what He wills, free of errors?
Such a thing poses no limitation for God; after all that's what
it means to be God: what God wills, He gets.

Turning to the evidence for the Bible being a book written
through inspiration by God to man, let us examine six marks
which provide compelling evidence of the Bible's supernatural
origin.

2. Has God Truly Spoken?

Bible Has Predicted Historical Events with Hair-Splitting Accuracy

The Bible is the only volume ever produced by man in which detailed prophecies related to the rise and fall of individuals and empires are given with hair-splitting accuracy. The book of Daniel is an excellent example, which gives prophecies so detailed, that critics now looking back on it, seeing its fulfillment in history, claim it must have been written after the fact, because it is so detailed and accurate. They claim it must have been written after it happened, because that's the way it reads. We have roughly 300 prophecies, 60 main ones, which were fulfilled in Yahushua's life alone. Even more startling, today, eight end times prophecies, documented in Appendix G, have been fulfilled with similar hair-splitting accuracy over the past decade, which were first predicted between 2,000 and 2,600 years ago. Clearly, Bible prophecy and its accurate fulfillment cannot be accounted for by mere human intervention or action. The only plausible explanation for this amazing feat is that the Bible is not a human book, but is a supernatural book, authored, or more accurately inspired, by God.

Bible Has a Supernatural Unity

The Bible consists of 66 books, written by 40 or more authors, over a 1,500 year time span, by Luke, a physician and historian, David a king, Joshua, a general, Matthew a tax collector, John, a fisherman, and Paul, a Pharisee, written under a diversity of conditions: on battlefields, in the wilderness, in jails, in palaces, on a diversity of controversial topics including:

- Where did man come from?

- Who is God?

- What is the goal of man?

- What is man's problem?

- What's the solution to man's problem?

- Where does evil come from?

- What is right and wrong?

- Do human beings have value?

- What happens to us when we die?

All of these subjects are dealt with in this one book, the Bible. Now, if you were to take just a handful of authors at one period of time, not separated by time or culture or ideology, and you were to ask them to respond to just one or two controversial issues, you would expect to get a wide disparity of responses and very little agreement. This is the way human beings are when they are asked to respond to these kinds of things. Yet the Bible reveals a very different kind of picture to those few people who have read the Bible from beginning to end and have a fairly good grasp and recall of its contents. The Bible addresses the big issues of life consistently and coherently throughout, which makes sense out of man's dilemma and reveals a gradually unfolding plan of salvation and redemption for the fallen state and nature of mankind and for God's elect, in particular. Reading the Bible from beginning to end, a diligent reader can discern a tremendous unity throughout Scripture. A plan is unfolded that no one writer understands completely, but each one adds a little piece, that is consistent with all the others, so that when these pieces are put together, we see with clarity, if we number among God's elect, the plan of God which reveals a supernatural unity. Nothing else, but a supernatural inspiration and superintending of its contents adequately explains such a unity, coherence and consistency.

Bible Answers the "Big Questions" of Life

The Bible answers the big questions of life, noted above, in a way that is consistent with the way we experience and perceive the world, and in a way that is internally cohesive. These big questions of life are the kinds all people ask at some time in their lives. Sometime in their lives they reflect on these issues. What the Bibles does, is give answers. In fact, most religions give answers to the big questions, but seldom do the answers of those other religions fit the world the way we know it to be. Eastern religions solve the problem of evil by claiming that the whole world is an illusion. Everything around us is illusory and good and evil are no different: they're an illusion too; it's called "maya." This is completely absurd! "Why is there all this pain and suffering in my life?" you may ask. Their answer: "You have no pain and suffering in your life: it's all just an illusion. Change the way you think and pain and suffering will end." What is the meaning of life? "For you to evaporate back into the impersonal godhead." Those explanations simply ring hollow and certainly seem incoherent and inconsistent with life as I have known it, during the 61 years I have been alive on this planet.

But the Bible does something different: it takes evil seriously. It says, "Yes, man is special, he is unique, he has great dignity and nobility." And sometimes we see that reflected in our behavior or in that of wise, noble, virtuous people we admire, respect and revere. Christianity makes sense out of that by explaining that we are made in the image of God, although imperfectly. At the same time, we know there's something desperately wrong with human beings: we're broken, twisted, selfish, sinful and depraved. The Bible makes sense out of this as well without denying its reality. It not only identifies the source of the nobility and the cruelty of man, but it gives God's born again elect a solution to the problem that plagues all of mankind: the problem of guilt.

The solution to guilt is not denial, although in today's twisted world ruled by Satan and the non-elect, that seems to be the prevailing norm that is not working. The solution to guilt is confession, repentance, forgiveness and reconciliation with YHWH who chose some of us to be His elect since before the world began, and wrote our names in the Lamb's book of life, so that one day He would save us from ourselves and our own spiritual lifelessness. So here you have a situation where the Bible answers the big questions of life, but it answers those questions in a way that conforms with the world as we experience it. There is a truthfulness to the Bible and its teachings that we understand, even though we may often not like them.

Bible is an Accurate Record of History

The Bible is historically accurate. This is important for two reasons. The first reason is that if God is acting through the events of history, as the Bible claims in multiple places that He is doing, and those events are being recorded in His book, for the Bible to prove trustworthy and of supernatural origin, it ought to get God's history right. And it does. We can go back to the Bible and find the cities that are recalled there, or the individuals and events described in the Bible and find evidence in the archeological record or in secular historical records that corresponds with and confirms the veracity of what the Bible claims and this is not just done with isolated incidents; it is done all the time and in rather dramatic fashion. This is true even though the evidence is often suppressed and silenced by the world's secular authorities today, in order to undermine the credibility of the Bible. Dramatic finds in recent times include the discovery of coral-encrusted chariot wheels and human and horse bones on a land bridge sixty feet underneath the surface of the Gulf of Aqaba, the discovery of what appears to be the remains of Noah's ark on Mount Ararat in modern day Turkey and the discovery of the ruins of the Assyrian capital city of Nineveh, all of which were aided by reference to the accounts in the Bible, used as a guidebook to those sites. Whenever the Bible is used as a historical reference, just like any other accepted work of antiquity, such as the writings of Tacitus or Josephus, or any of the others, the Bible comes out with flying colors, as being precise and historically sound and accurate.

The other reason that it's important for the Bible to be historically accurate is based on what kind of history it reveals. Under any honest yardstick, the Bible proves time and time

2. Has God Truly Spoken?

again that it is a good historically accurate document, confirmed by other accounts, including eye witness testimonies. Given that track record of reliability and accuracy, we then read in the Bible about a man, Jesus of Nazareth, who taught as no one ever taught, gave the greatest moral teachings the world has ever seen, healed the sick and cast out demons, calmed the storms and raised the dead, predicted his own death and subsequently raised himself from the dead in three days as He had previously predicted and this man claimed to be the son of God Himself. Now if the Bible is historically accurate, which it has proven itself to be, and these are the events it recalls, the words of this man have tremendous authority unlike those of any other man who has ever lived. This man is no ordinary man. This man is man is other-worldly. It's convincing evidence to all but the most headstrong cynic that He is who He claimed to be: God come in the flesh to bring truth and salvation to the spiritual sheep whom God the Father gave to Him. So the Bible has tremendous historical accuracy that seems to have a supernatural imprint on it, because of the events that are described, and that are well attested to from other legitimate historical sources, that are supernatural events.

Bible Transforms Lives

When people apply the teachings of the Bible to their daily lives they thrive, not because of anything they did differently, but rather because when we submit and surrender our lives to the lordship of Yahushua, that God's Holy Spirit, working in and through us, changes us in profound ways that we could have never done before, on our own power alone. Our lives manifest a transformed life. We become more truthful, loving, kind, just, moral, compassionate, patient, humble, self-controlled, wise, forgiving and filled with grace. We increasingly take on the character of Yahushua. This change is not something unique to our American culture. It applies in people's lives across the globe from Europe, to China, to the jungles of South America. It doesn't matter if you're rich or poor, black, white or oriental, intelligent or foolish, high strata or low strata, or what country you come from. This is because

Christianity and the truth of the Bible touches the hearts of all human beings who number among God's elect. The Bible supernaturally transforms lives because Christianity and the Bible are universally, objectively and absolutely true.

Bible is a Fighter

The hard truth is that the Bible has been under an all-out assault to discredit it from its very beginnings 3,500 years ago and this has been no more true than it is today. The Bible has survived through time and relentless persecution. Jesus promised us in Matthew 24:35 that,

> *"Heaven and earth shall pass away, but my words shall not pass away."*

And Paul wrote to Timothy that

> *". . . the word of God (Eloah) is not bound."* 2 Timothy 2:9

These truths concerning the Bible's staying power have been demonstrated to be the case for thousands of years. In 1778 Voltaire, the French revolutionary and Freemason, boasted that "In one hundred years Christianity will be swept from existence and passed into history!" Well that certainly didn't happen, did it? In fact, 50 years after Voltaire's death, the Geneva Bible Society used his printing press and his house to print Bibles! If the Bible had not been the supernatural book of God, men would have successfully destroyed it long ago.

Confidence that we Have the Inspired Original Words of God to Mankind

Some skeptics and cynics, whose real aim is to undermine the credibility of the Bible to discredit it, have attempted to do so by claiming that even if the original Hebrew and Greek documents were inspired by God Himself, it's been nearly 2,000 years since the last book of the Bible, the Book of Revelation, was written and lots of changes and distortions can creep in during such a time. They disingenuously infer that the Bible has been corrupted, when in fact they know it hasn't been, or they simply don't have a clue how the integrity of the Bible we have today has been maintained. Most skeptics and cynics falsely assume that the Bible has been translated from Hebrew to Greek to Latin to German to English and that in each step in the translation process, errors and distortions have crept in, such that today we can have no real confidence that our English translation of the original Hebrew and Greek manuscripts has any integrity to it. Yet such a notion is simply not supported by the facts.

This notion usually comes from people's experiences in elementary school in which one person writes down a brief story and tells it to the first person in the classroom and by the time this same story has been relayed 20 or 30 times between students in the classroom, the story told at the end is barely recognizable compared to how it first began. And this is how many people falsely assume that the Bible has been significantly distorted through multiple translations from one language to another. But that's not how it works at all. The original Hebrew and Greek manuscripts of the Old and New Testaments, respectively, were translated ONCE into the English 1611 KJV of the Bible we are using here as our source document, and was not produced from 20 or 30 transformations of the original documents at all.

The next objection raised by some cynics and skeptics is that the original autographs have been lost; we don't have them. All we have are copies or fragments of copies of the original autographs inspired by God and written by the authors of the various books of the Bible, and thus we can have no confidence that the source documents used to translate the Bible into English haven't been corrupted prior to our translating what we do have into English. This objection too is a red herring when we examine the science of textual transmission.

In the time in which the books of the Bible were written, they had no way to replicate books of the Bible other than through manually creating copies of the originals and these copies were made all the time by students studying and learning the Bible in their original Hebrew and Greek texts. Portions or entire books of the Bible in these copy forms have been preserved, cataloged and reproduced in several key libraries around the world which are available to Biblical scholars and translators. Now as you might expect with any manual copying process, not every copy of the same book of the Bible exactly matches every other copy that has been preserved and catalogued. Here is where the disciplines and principles of textual transmission come in handy, using several common sense rules of logic to deduce what the original autograph that was inspired by God Himself must have said.

Let's say we have 30 copies of a particular book of the Bible produced over the course of several hundred years. Clearly those copies made closer to the time when the original autograph was written are likely to have fewer distortions and changes than those made hundreds of years later. Thus, the science of textual transmission favors older copies over more recent ones. Next, for copies of roughly the same generation, Biblical scholars look for consistency of the text. If 15 copies are identical, but one has some spelling errors, those spelling errors are easy to fix. Likewise, if one copy has a few words added, but the remaining copies are all identical in text and spelling, common sense would suggest that the outlier copy ought to be dismissed to the extent that it is different than all the others. Using this analytical process, Biblical scholars are able to reconstruct the original text of a number of documents from antiquity with an extremely high level of confidence.

There are two factors that scholars focus on when reconstructing original documents of antiquity. One is how many copies they have and the other is how old each of the copies is. Obviously, the more copies scholars have and the older they are, the greater confidence they have that they can accurately reconstruct the original. So how does the Bible compare with other documents of antiquity in these two regards? Extremely well it turns out. Most ancient documents have only one or two handfuls of copies that still exist: on the order of five or ten copies. Homer's Iliad is the one with the most copies: 650 copies of the ancient Greek epic. Many of these copies have an 800 to 2,000 year or more time gap between the date of the copy and when the original was written. In spite of these challenges, scholars of works of antiquity are very confident that they can reconstruct what the original looks like. In contrast, we have 5,366 manuscript portions of the Greek New Testament (and many more thousands of manuscript portions of the Old Testament Hebrew text).[3] Some portions are small fragments, some entire books or collections of several books, or whole Bibles. The dates when these copies were made go back to the third and fourth centuries, some fragments go back to the beginning of the second century, and one, called the John Ryrie Papyri, a fragment of the gospel of John, was written around 120 A.D. It was found in Egypt. The gospel of John was written around 85-90 A.D. This means that we have a portion of the New Testament that goes back to within 30-35 years of the original autograph. There are some more recent discoveries of manuscript copies, held in the British Museum, that go back to the middle of the first century when most of the books of the New Testament were first written.

The inescapable conclusions we can draw from this hard evidence of antiquity, when scholars lay them side-by-side and examine their contents, is that 98% of them are in total agreement. The remaining two percent have only trivial differences. While it is true that there are approximately 300,000 individual variations in the text, most of them are spelling errors that are easily corrected. Of the remaining two percent of the variations, virtually every one of these 6,000 remaining textual variations yields to rigorous examination. The final conclusion of Biblical scholars and experts in textual

---

[3] *The Bible: Has God Spoken?* Gregory Koukl. CD. 2003.

transmission is that our New Testament is 99.5% pure. Of the 20,000 lines of the New Testament, only 40, or 0.2% are in doubt: 400 words. None of these discrepancies affect any serious doctrine. Such a result is truly remarkable by any measure. It is one more sign that God has supernaturally superintended the text and preserved it for us. So the original Hebrew and Greek manuscripts of the Bible have not been altered or changed; they just haven't; and this is the universal conclusion in academia by scholars who have spent their entire careers studying these sorts of things.

Interpreting the Bible

A final common objection today to any claim one may make concerning what the Bible teaches is for a cynic or skeptic to assert, "Well that's your interpretation of what it means, but I have a different interpretation. What makes your interpretation any more right than mine?" This is really a very dishonest objection. In truth, this objection is usually offered to shut down communication so as to suppress and silence the truth of what the Bible really is teaching.

Whenever anyone reads a book or anything else written by another person, a well-educated person of honesty and integrity does not try to put his own spin on what is written to make it conform to his preconceived notions and prejudices of what he wants it to say. Instead, such a person seeks to understand the intent the author is attempting to communicate to his readers. Most writings have only one meaning intended by its author, and the Bible is no different than any other writing in this regard. Much of the Bible is historical accounts and personal correspondence and is intended to be read that way, as opposed to inventing our own interpretation because a reader doesn't like the obvious implications to himself and his future behaviors that the Bible is clearly revealing. In fact most verses are quite clear as to what they say, mean and how they apply to our lives. For example, John 3:36 reads,

2. Has God Truly Spoken?

"He that believeth on the son hath everlasting life: and he that believeth not on the Son shall not see life; but the wrath of God (Eloah) abideth on him."

Now how many ways can anyone legitimately interpret this passage? Some things in the Scriptures are difficult to understand, to be sure. Other things we think we understand, but may not. But there are some things that are impossible to misunderstand. Most of the important things Scripture teaches are pointedly clear, as in this example. Usually, when someone objects to one's interpretation of a passage in Scripture, he has read and understood what it both says and means, but when he gets to its application to his life, he doesn't like what he concludes from reading it, and so attempts to go back and try to distort what the words say or mean, taken in the context of what was written both before and after a passage or a verse in question and what the author's clear intent was, and what doctrinal matter was being discussed. Again, it's a fundamentally dishonest way to dismiss what the Bible clearly says. Usually such a person will not offer any alternative explanation, he will merely dismiss your understanding of the words, or quote some other verse, completely out of context and twist the words to try to make them say precisely the opposite of what the words clearly mean. You won't have an honest dialog with a confirmed skeptic or cynic, so you would do better to walk away and have nothing to do with such a dishonest person.

Summary

Virtually everything we have ever learned in our lives, that we know with any degree of certainty, we have learned through second-hand knowledge from a reputable authority. Somebody who we trust has given us the information; we haven't learned it first-hand. Spiritual truth is not any different in this regard. When dealing with eternal issues, any sensible person ought to back up his conclusions with an authority that has impeccable credentials. In this regard, the Bible is in a class by itself. It claims to be the pure and inspired words of God to mankind that are 100% true and trustworthy and which never contradict themselves and then backs it up with the six compelling pieces of evidence we have just examined which, when taken together, prove beyond a reasonable doubt that the Bible is everything it claims to be. Moreover, in all of history, no one has ever successfully disproven any claim made by the Bible. Many have tried and deceived many into believing otherwise, but the truth is that the Bible has yet to be proven as anything other than what it claims to be. Thus, the burden of proof falls on the skeptic and the cynic to prove that the Bible is not what it has proven to be time and time again.

If this is true, and it is, then any sane, honest person of intellectual integrity, ought to start by examining every claim the Bible makes and placing his trust in every word of it, until proven otherwise. Yet this is seldom done, even by those professing themselves to be followers of Christ. According to the Pew Research Center, less than five percent of all those professing to be Christians admit to having read the Bible from beginning to end, yet they profess to be followers of Christ. This evidence alone distinctly suggests that they are not at all what they claim to be. This is a topic and conclusion we shall return to later.

Is the Bible the invention of men about God? Or is it God's unique communication of absolute truth to mankind for our salvation that no other belief system can hold a candle to? The evidence is crystal clear: reason, hard evidence, history and critical analysis all tell us that the Bible is everything it claims to be: the true and inspired words of God to mankind, and that anyone in his right mind ought to devote him or herself to reading and mastering everything it teaches. This is the fundamental premise on which the rest of this book is founded. Trust in its teachings is fully justified, and is backed by hard evidence, logical coherence and trustworthy authority, that no other source can come even remotely close to matching. By comparison, all personal philosophies concerning spiritual matters and God which deviate one iota from what the Bible says and clearly means are empty and

2. Has God Truly Spoken?

completely meaningless against this unassailable standard of objective, universal and absolute truth.

3. God's Divine Nature and Purpose

Most of humanity has a seriously distorted view and understanding of the divine nature of YHWH, or the God of the Bible, and His attributes. Similarly, most of the world is deeply confused concerning the answers to the the most fundamental questions of life, including:

- Where did we come from?

- What is the nature of man?

- Does God exist?

- If God exists, what is His nature?

- Is there any real purpose or meaning to life, can we know what it is, and if we can, what is it?

- What happens to us when we die?

What is important to understand is that the confusion we witness in our world over these profoundly important questions of life is no accident. In fact, it is intentional and planned by YHWH in order to conceal the truth from those from whom He seeks to conceal it, while making the truth apparent to others, whom God has chosen since before the world began, to be His elect, His chosen or set-apart-ones. Even within circles of people who purport to be followers of Yahushua (i.e. Christians) today, you will find people who violently object to the doctrine of election and begin branding anyone with the audacity to assert such a claim as a close-minded, ignorant Calvinist or worse. Throughout this book, I am going to try to reject and side-step such counter-productive labeling and teach by my example that the path to the truth is found by going to the source of all objective truth, knowledge and wisdom, while keeping an open mind and letting the inspired and flawless Word of YHWH, the Bible, reveal what it says to us with no hidden agenda or preconceived notion of what we may want the truth to be. Instead, let us discover it together.

Many of the world's religions which seek to answer the six questions posed above embody conflicting worldviews or belief systems which teach claims which purport to be true, but which are inherently in conflict with truth claims from other religions or worldviews. To add further confusion to this mess, in the Christian religion alone, I've seen it reported on the internet that there are approximately 33,000 separate and distinct Christian denominations or sects, most of them professing to be grounded in the teachings of the Bible, yet each clearly professes to have some special insight on that which is true. So something more must be going on here than first meets the eye. And there is. One of the most basic laws of logical reasoning, the law of contradiction, states that when two truth claims are in conflict with one another, they cannot both be true; one of them has to be false. I plan to employ this principle of logical reasoning extensively throughout this book, and in so doing, illustrate that many truth claims cannot possibly be true, since they violate the law of contradiction, or fly in the face of the evidence of hard facts, and/or trustworthy authority, that ought to cause us to challenge our pre-conceived notions of reality. Usually, such contradictions do not have this effect upon our thinking and over time, our tolerance for such absurdities dulls our critical thinking skills and causes us to believe a set of claims which cannot possibly both be true. When we act on such false beliefs, we harm ourselves and those around us. My goal is contribute to reducing these unfortunate errors and wake up as many people as I can in the process.

In 2015, the world's culture is very uncomfortable with any claim which purports to be exclusive or to exclude some other points of view. Virtually every view is tolerated in our culture, provided that it is not articulating the truth claims of Biblical

Christianity. This too is no accident. It is deliberate, intentional and has been permitted by YHWH in fulfillment of a bigger plan that He has laid out in His Bible for mankind, in particular, His elect, to discover.

Where did We Come From?

In 2015, the vast majority of the world's population believes that mankind is an accident of evolution and that life sprang from non-life out of the primordial ooze roughly 4.5 billion years ago, and from simple single-cell organisms, evolved over time, and through the process of natural selection, to the highly complex organisms we know as man today. This view was first made popular by Charles Darwin in 1859 with the publishing of his book, *The Origin of the Species*. In the late 1960s, I was taught this theory of evolution in high school biology class and by age 18, left my Episcopal Church upbringing and became an agnostic, hanging off of this one theory for the next 28 years of my life as the basis for my "not knowing" if God existed or where I came from.

The other primary explanation for where we come from is Creationism, as described in the first chapter of the Book of Genesis of the Bible. This explanation of where we come from starts with an eternal God, YHWH, who has always existed, and will always exist, who spoke the universe into being out of nothing. The Biblical story of creation points man to the amazing, brilliant, all-powerful, all-knowing, ever-present, all-wise, purposeful nature of God who created man in an imperfect likeness of His perfect image and placed him in a world untarnished by sin that is characterized in the Bible as paradise: the Garden of Eden.

Frankly speaking, my sophomore year biology class teacher was required by state law to make passing mention of the theory of Creationism, but by the late 1960s, he made no bones about conveying to all of us who were his students that he regarded such an explanation as hopelessly naive, uninformed, uneducated and unsophisticated. And I bought his views for the next three decades without ever thinking about or challenging them.

The implications of these two competing worldviews of Scientism or macro-evolution on the one hand, and Creationism on the other, are profound for us as individuals and as a society and are sharply in conflict with one another. If the religion of macro-evolution is true, it implies the absence of a creator or an eternal God who defines a set of universal and absolute moral rights and wrongs guiding human behavior. If such a theory is true, then man does not intrinsically embody any inherent dignity, virtue and transcendent purpose beyond the mere satisfaction of his bodily needs and wants for food, shelter, clothing and sex and the laws of natural selection and survival of the fittest reduce morality to something resembling the philosophy that "might makes right." If, on the other hand, Creationism is true, then there is an eternal and all powerful God who rules the universe, moral universal and absolute truths concerning right and wrong *do* exist, and man does have intrinsic worth, purpose, dignity and virtue well beyond that of the animal kingdom, which ought to guide our every thought and conduct. Clearly, how a person and how a society, culture or civilization comes out on this debate between macro-evolution and Creationism is profoundly important for the nature and direction of that society, culture or civilization.

Later, I will lay out the secular arguments, reasoning and evidence which I have discovered for why macro-evolution cannot possibly be true. But for purposes of this discussion, let us examine what the Bible teaches mankind concerning the nature and purpose of God, revealed to us by the creation story.

The Bible professes to be the inspired and infallible words of God to mankind. It has never been successfully proven to be otherwise. It professes to be a love letter from God to His people and an owner's manual for life. If it had been proven otherwise, one might reasonably dismiss it as a fraud. But since it has not been so proven, the wise man ought to be open-minded enough to see what it says, and test its teachings against life and against the way the world works, to see if it might explain things, before dismissing it outright. Yet few men ever do such a thing. Perhaps this is because most men have little interest in that which is wise or that which is true. There is something very basic and primal at work here, defined by the inherent depraved and sinful nature of man, with a heart bent on rebellion against God, which we are all born with.

The creation story first of all tells us that God is. He has always existed, thus making Him eternal. Mankind, as finite beings who live an average of 70 to 80 years and then die and are no more, struggle to conceive of such a thing. Yet this is what the Bible claims in Genesis 21:33:

> *"And Abraham planted a grove in Beersheba, and called there on the name of the LORD (YHWH), the **everlasting** God (El)."*

Moreover, throughout the Bible, it refers to the eternal or everlasting God and to eternal life promised to those who believe in God and who submit and surrender their wills and their lives to His son, Yahushua (Jesus) as Lord, master and king over their entire lives. Clearly, a finite God is in no position to promise eternity or everlasting anything to anyone.

The creation story tells us that YHWH speaks the world, the heavens, the land, the seas, the sun, the moon, the stars, the fish, the birds and all land dwelling creatures into existence after their own kind (species).

> *"And God (Elohim) said, Let us make man in our image, after our likeness: and let them have dominion over the fish of the sea, and over the fowl of the air, and over the cattle, and over all the earth, and over every creeping thing that creepeth upon the earth. So God (Elohim) created man in his own image, in the image of God (Elohim) created he him; male and female created he them. And God (Elohim) blessed them, and God (Elohim) said unto them, Be fruitful, and multiply, and replenish the earth, and subdue it: and have dominion over the fish of the sea, and over the fowl of the air, and over every living thing that moveth upon the earth."* Genesis 1:26-28

So according to the creation story, mankind has great dignity, value and purpose whom God designed to be fruitful and multiply and subdue and rule over the earth. Moreover, God made special provision for man. In Genesis Chapter 2, God planted a garden in Eden with every tree that was pleasant to the sight and good for food, along with the tree of life and the tree of knowledge of good and evil (verses 8 and 9) and put the man whom he had formed there to dress it and to keep it (to cultivate it), according to verse 15:

> *"And the LORD God (YHWH Elohim) commanded the man, saying, Of every tree of the garden thou mayest freely eat: But of the tree of the knowledge of good and evil, thou shalt not eat of it: for in the day that thou eatest thereof thou shalt surely die. And the LORD God (YHWH Elohim) said, It is not good that the man should be alone; I will make him an help meet (helper suitable) for him."* Genesis 2:16-17

Shortly thereafter, in verses 21-25, God made a woman, Eve, out of one of the man's (Adam's) ribs. Ever since that time, God has designed that in holy marriage a woman and a man would leave their parents and cleave to (join) with each other as one flesh in sexual union and unity with one another. Prior to the fall,

> *" . . . they were both naked, the man and his wife, and were not ashamed."* Genesis 2:25

So what is important to understand is that God, by His very nature, is relational and longs for a close, personal intimate relationship with man. The triune God the Father, God the Son, God the Holy Spirit, three persons in one God, live in perfect harmony with one another and it is in their triune nature that God created man in their image.

God is a God who longs to bless man, as He blessed the first man and woman in the Garden of Eden, a veritable paradise, lacking in nothing. Creating man in His image, God recognized that it was not good for man to be alone so He created woman from the flesh of man so that they would function as one body, in harmony with one another in complementary roles. So God demonstrates in the creation story His benevolence and love for man and His dedication to man's well-being.

Finally, we can see that God is purposeful and strategic in the creation story. He deliberately creates the man first and gives him a work to do (be fruitful and multiply and subdue the earth and rule over it), a will to obey (God's — in the form of don't eat from the tree of the knowledge of good and evil), and a woman to love (Eve). Those are the roles God designs for man. For woman, God designs her to be man's helper suitable for him.

What is the Nature of Man?

Throughout the Bible, we read story after story of the nature of man's depraved heart and wicked and rebellious ways, in disobedience to God. By only the sixth chapter of Genesis, the first book of the Bible, God was so fed up with the wickedness and corrupt ways of man that He resolved to destroy all of mankind except Noah, his wife, their three sons and their sons' three wives. So God brought the Flood that drowned all living things on the earth except for those in Noah's ark. Later, He destroyed Sodom and Gomorrah for their rapacious homosexuality and violence. In 722 B.C., after enduring wicked king after wicked king ruling over the ten Hebrew tribes of the northern kingdom of Israel, God used the Assyrian army to defeat Israel, slaughter many of its wicked and sinful inhabitants, and haul the remnant off into exile in Assyria. 136 years later, in 586 B.C., God found it necessary to do the same thing to the two Hebrew tribes of the southern kingdom of Judah at the hands of the Babylonians, who hauled many of the survivors off into exile in Babylon. Finally, in end times Bible prophesy, we are told that we can expect a period of lawlessness and rebellion against God unlike anything ever before witnessed, prior to the second coming of Yahushua (Jesus) who will slay the wicked in the winepress of the fierceness and wrath of almighty God, we are told in Revelation 19:15.

3. God's Divine Nature and Purpose

In many places throughout the Bible, man is described as rebellious, wicked and deceitful beyond all measure. In response, we see a God who is long suffering and patient, but who is also holy and just and by his very nature must punish sin, which always inflicts harm and destruction upon its victims. Thus the Bible portrays a God who watches, waits and seethes in anger and wrath at the injustices perpetrated upon their fellow man by the wicked, but who eventually comes to the limits of His long-suffering patience and destroys the unrepentant, headstrong, rebellious sinner. So when provoked beyond all reason, God becomes angry and filled with wrath, by virtue of His holy and just nature, which abhors all sin and evil.

You would think with all the sinfulness of man that YHWH would have given up on mankind long ago. Yet He has not. In fact, His holy, just and loving nature toward man caused Him to come to earth, in the form of a man, His son Yahushua, who lived a blameless and sinless life, testified to the truths of God during his three and a half year ministry on earth, and then bore the sins of all of God's elect: past, present and future, on his shoulders and paid the ultimate price of humiliation, death and separation from God the Father for three days, so that his righteous nature might be imputed to those of us who surrender our lives and our wills to Him as our Lord and Savior in all things, so that we might be transformed into the likeness of Yahushua over our remaining lifetimes, and live in harmony with YHWH, Yahushua and the rest of the saints for all eternity in a world without pain, suffering or evil ever again. By Yahushua paying the price of death we all deserve to pay, we who believe and trust in Him are reconciled into a right relationship with God the Father and God the Son through God the Holy Spirit living in and working through us, to permit us to do that which we could not do on our own: surrender our lives to Yahushua as Lord over our lives. That is a loving God who longs for a personal and intimate relationship with each of His elect.

What is the Nature of God?

Thus far, we have established that the Bible teaches and claims that YHWH most assuredly exists and that His nature is eternal, brilliant, all-powerful, holy, just, long-suffering, patient and loving. But there's more.

In Isaiah 55:8-9, YHWH tells us,

> *"For my thoughts are not your thoughts, neither are your ways my ways, saith the LORD (YHWH). For as the heavens are higher than the earth, so are my ways higher than your ways, and my thoughts than your thoughts."*

In other words, it would be a gross error to assume that mankind can begin to fully comprehend the thoughts and ways of YHWH. We are His creatures and He is the creator of the entire universe which operates in accordance with all the intricate laws of nature which He established in the first place!

In the Book of Proverbs, the Bible's book of wisdom, we learn in Proverbs 1:7 that:

> *"The fear of the LORD (YHWH) is the beginning of knowledge: but fools despise wisdom and instruction."*

Fear, reverence and awe of YHWH are common and recurring themes throughout the Bible, indicating clearly that YHWH is not to be trifled with, nor will He have anything to do with those who choose to rebel against Him, reject Him or choose to have nothing to do with Him. As Romans 1:18-32 explains, YHWH will turn His back on unregenerate sinners and let them destroy themselves in the perversions of their own lusts and wickedness. This is because it is impossible and fruitless to persuade the wicked sinner of his own sin beyond a certain point of depravity from which there is no return.

YHWH's nature is such that He cannot lie, change or fail. He is the same yesterday, today and forever. He is the embodiment of truth, honesty, holiness, justice, courage, integrity, honor, strength, wisdom, power, love and gentleness. Here is how Proverbs 6:16-19 describes some of the things YHWH abhors:

46

"These six things doth the LORD (YHWH) hate: yea, seven are an abomination unto him : A proud look, a lying tongue, and hands that shed innocent blood, An heart that deviseth wicked imaginations, feet that be swift in running to mischief, A false witness that speaketh lies, and he that soweth discord among brethren."

In short, YHWH's holiness requires that He abhors all forms of sin. All sin damages or destroys our relationships: with YHWH and with each other, and relationships of integrity are what YHWH values above all else.

What is often not comprehended or appreciated about YHWH is that He orchestrates each and every circumstance in each of our lives, even though we may not be aware of it. This principle is explained by the following five proverbs:

"The preparations of the heart in man, and the answer of the tongue, is from the LORD (YHWH)." Proverbs 16:1

"The LORD (YHWH) hath made all things for himself: yea, even the wicked for the day of evil." Proverbs 16:4

"A man's heart deviseth his way: but the LORD (YHWH) directeth his steps." Proverbs 16:9

"There are many devices in a man's heart; nevertheless the counsel of the LORD (YHWH), that shall stand." Proverbs 19:21

"Man's goings are of the LORD (YHWH); how can a man then understand his own way?" Proverbs 20:24

Thus, as much as we may wish to believe and convince ourselves that we are completely free agents, free to choose and act precisely as we alone exercise our will, the Book of Proverbs, the book of wisdom from YHWH himself, reveals otherwise. As such, nothing ever happens to us by random chance and there are no such things as mere coincidences. What appear to be coincidences are, in reality, always part of a pattern of circumstances which YHWH is permitting in our lives to teach us something, and often, to get our attention.

What is the Meaning and Purpose of Life?

Many forms of false religion, organized or otherwise, seek to teach and deceive us that YHWH's ultimate aim for each of us is to be happy. This is sheer nonsense and not at all supported by the teachings of YHWH's Word, the Bible. Instead, in many places throughout the Bible, YHWH teaches us that He seeks to refine and mature those who number among His elect into the character and likeness of His son, Yahushua, through trials, suffering, affliction, opposition and persecution.

In Romans 5:3-4, the Apostle Paul writes,

> "... we glory in tribulations also: knowing that tribulation worketh patience; And patience, experience; and experience, hope:"

Frequently, the Bible refers to the refining of precious metals, such as silver and gold, in which the metals are heated to a high temperature to melt them, causing the impurities or dross to rise to the top to be scooped off, leaving pure metals suitable for the silversmith or goldsmith to create something of beauty, without impurities:

> "And I will bring the third part through the fire, and will refine them as silver is refined, and I will try them as gold is tried: they shall call on my name, and I will hear them: I will say, It is my people: and they shall say, The LORD (YHWH) is my God (Elohim)." Zechariah 13:9

> "And he shall sit as a refiner and purifier of silver: and he shall purify the sons of Levi, and purge them as gold and silver, that they may offer unto the LORD (YHWH) an offering in righteousness." Malachi 3:3

> "Take away the dross from the silver, and there shall come forth a vessel for the finer. Take way the wicked from before the king, and his throne shall be established in righteousness." Proverbs 25:4-5

Yahushua promises all of His followers that we will suffer if we are truly His:

"And the brother shall deliver up the brother to death, and the father the child: and the children shall rise up against their parents, and cause them to be put to death. And ye shall be hated of all men for my name's sake: but he that endureth to the end shall be saved." Matthew 10:21-22

"Think not that I am come to send peace on earth: I come not to send peace, but a sword. For I am come to set a man at variance against his father, and the daughter against her mother, and the daughter in law against her mother in law. And a man's foes shall be they of his own household. He that loveth father or mother more than me is not worthy of me: and he that loveth son or daughter more than me is not worthy of me. And he that taketh not his cross, and followeth after me, is not worthy of me. He that findeth his life shall lose it: and he that loseth his life for my sake shall find it." Matthew 10:34-39

In other words, the path of an adopted son or daughter of YHWH is a path of challenges, opposition and affliction which refines our characters, tests our faith and matures us into reflecting the character and the emotional and spiritual maturity of Christ in our interactions with others. This is not because YHWH is a killjoy. It is because there is no other way to transform the heart of a wicked and depraved sinner, which we are all born into, into a true saint who routinely exhibits the fruit of the Spirit taught in Galatians 5:22-23:

"But the fruit of the Spirit is love, joy, peace, longsuffering, gentleness, goodness, faith, Meekness, temperance: against such there is no law."

This fruit, is the output of a life refined by trials. There is no other way to get there, but through trials, tribulations, suffering and discipline.

Throughout the Bible, YHWH tells us that what is of greatest value to Him is maximizing His glory, not man's. He seeks a personal relationship with His elect, His chosen ones, chosen by Him since before the world began, but on His terms and not ours. YHWH expects to be feared, honored, revered, respected, appreciated, obeyed and delighted in by His people. This brings YHWH the honor, praise and glory which He seeks from His people. Conversely, YHWH has no interest in having any form of a relationship with a rebellious sinner who rejects the very notion that YHWH even exists, in spite of all the evidence in His creation of His majestic nature. YHWH simply will not tolerate the wicked and the foolish. Instead, He chooses to turn His back on such petulant children and let them choose the path that leads to their own destruction and eternal torment and agony in hell, permanently separated from YHWH: a choice all sinners make, led by their own rebellious natures.

In summary, YHWH's entire plan for humanity has always been to refine, test and mature those whom He chose to become His adopted sons and daughters of the truth and of the light so that we might fully appreciate the magnificence and goodness of YHWH throughout all eternity and bring Him glory for it. In order to accomplish this outcome, YHWH created Satan and knew beforehand that one third of the angelic host would rebel against Him and follow Satan as demon spirits to afflict the souls of men and women throughout the last 6,000 years. He allowed the world to be ruled by the prince of the air, and the father of lies, Satan, and his allies for the last 6,000 years to afflict those of us who are of His elect, to test and refine us and in so doing, transform our hearts and characters into the likeness of His son, Yahushua in preparation for the day in which He gathers all of us to Himself in new resurrected bodies, just like that of Yahushua after He rose from the dead.

All along, YHWH has planned for this era of mankind, ruled by Satan, to one day come to an end. Just as YHWH created the earth and all that is in it in six days, and then rested on the seventh day, YHWH has planned all along that the era in which YHWH and His son were not visible and present would last 6,000 years, to demonstrate to man repeatedly in the events of world history that every time man abandons YHWH, mankind makes a royal mess of things, thus demonstrating the wisdom of our depending upon YHWH and Yahushua in all things. At the end of the first 6,000 years of mankind on earth, YHWH plans to put an end to the rule of Satan and wickedness and to usher in a metaphorical thousand year millennial kingdom in which His son, Yahushua, returns to rule over the world, co-reigning with His resurrected saints, meaning every adopted son and daughter of YHWH since the Fall until the gathering described in Matthew 24:30-31. 2 Peter 3:8 reveals to us this Biblical timeline YHWH has had in mind all along:

"But, beloved, be not ignorant of this one thing, that one day is with the Lord (YHWH) as a thousand years, and a thousand years as one day."

God rested on the seventh day, the sabbath, a day designed by YHWH for man to rest from his weekly toil and contemplate the blessings of YHWH and give thanks to Him. So too, the coming metaphorical seventh millennium since creation is intended by YHWH to bring glory to Him and rest to His people: His resurrected adopted sons and daughters who put their faith and trust in Him and in His son Yahushua over the past 6,000 years.

In these end times Satan is trying to revolt once again, and YHWH will destroy him and any of his allies and throw Satan and the contents of hell into the burning lake of fire and brimstone to burn in torment for all eternity. The existing heaven and earth shall pass away and YHWH will usher in a new heaven and earth where all of YHWH's adopted and resurrected sons and daughters will live in peace, harmony and joy with Him and His son Yahushua for all eternity.

The day ushering in the start of this metaphorical one thousand year millennial kingdom, ruled by Yahushua and His resurrected saints, is now very near. As of this writing, it is likely to begin to occur roughtly a year from now: by the end of 2016. In the coming chapters I will reveal the evidence and analysis I am using to arrive at my rather startling conclusion, which I believe YHWH has chosen to reveal to me as one of His watchmen on the wall in these end times, so that I might share what He has revealed to me with others. If I am correct in my conclusions, and I believe that I am, it has profound implications for how each of us ought to invest our lives between now and the second coming of Yahushua in 2016. I will be discussing these implications in some depth in the last chapter of this book and offering my own perspective on what YHWH's elect can and should be doing to prepare for that event, and how we can protect ourselves during the remaining months of the great tribulation.

4. Principles of the Bible: God's Roadmap to His People

The Bible makes some pretty audacious claims and then goes on to prove them to a special group of people, whom God has chosen ahead of time. The purpose of this chapter is to reveal and explain the most essential principles which anyone needs to properly comprehend the vital importance of this supernatural book, which is unlike any other in all the world.

The Bible Claims to the the Flawless and Inspired Words of God to Mankind

Every world religion other than Biblical Christianity is founded upon the writings and teachings of men who claimed to be wise teachers or prophets who spoke on behalf of an unseen and invisible god. The Bible is unique in its claim to be the flawless, infallible, inerrant and inspired words of God to man. Many men and books claim things which prove, in the end, not be true. But the Bible, in its 3,500 year existence, has never been successfully disproven in ANY regard: not one jot or tittle has ever been successfully proven to be in error or a lie. Similarly, no other worldview or belief system is rooted upon the person and work of its founder, other than the Bible, in the form of Jesus Christ (Yahushua). Every other world religion can exist apart from the personhood of its founder, as a collection of philosophies and ways to conduct one's life. Biblical Christianity is unique, in that without the deity and work of Jesus Christ, its teachings become meaningless and useless to men seeking to make sense out of the big questions of life addressed in the prior chapter.

Let's examine the truth claims made in the Bible first, and then examine their implications, which are truly profound.

Proverbs 30:5-6 tells us:

"Every word of God (Eloah) is pure (flawless): he is a shield unto them that put their trust in him. Add thou not unto his words, lest he reprove thee, and thou be found a liar." (parenthetical added)

2 Timothy 3:16-17 reveals:

"All scripture is given by inspiration of God (written by the Spirit), and is profitable for doctrine, for reproof, for correction, for instruction in righteousness: That the man of God (Eloah) may be perfect, thoroughly furnished unto all good works." (first parenthetical added for clarification)

Jesus, who claimed to be the son of God and then proved it by the events and miracles in His own life, fully endorsed and validated the Bible as trustworthy when He told us:

"For verily I say unto you, Till heaven and earth pass, one jot or one tittle shall in no wise pass from the law, till all be fulfilled. Whomsoever therefore shall break one of these least commandments, and shall teach men so, he shall be called least in the kingdom of heaven: but whosoever shall do and teach them, the same shall be called great in the kingdom of heaven." Matthew 5:18

When Yahushua (Jesus) was being tempted by the devil, who encouraged Yahushua to turn stones into bread so He could eat and relieve His fast in the wilderness, Yahushua referred to the teaching in Deuteronomy 8:3:

"But he (Yahushua) answered and said, It is written, Man shall not live by bread alone, but by every word that proceedeth out of the mouth of God (YHWH) (meaning what is written in all of Scripture)." Matthew 4:4 (parenthetical added)

Finally, the Apostle Paul teaches us in Romans 12:2:

4. Principles of the Bible: God's Roadmap to His People

"And be not conformed to this world: but be ye transformed by the renewing of your mind, that ye may prove what is that good, and acceptable, and perfect, will of God (Eloah)."

So there are some of the most pertinent claims made within the Bible, in which it purports to contain the flawless, perfect and inspired words of God to mankind, which answers all the big questions of life and a whole lot more for those who have the eyes to see and the ears to hear.

Now let's examine the implications of this truth claim. If the Bible is what it claims to be, that no other book has successfully claimed and proven for thousands of years, does it not follow that a wise man or woman ought to invest his or her life in reading and studying every word of the Bible, from beginning to end, in order to see what it says and teaches? A reasonable person would certainly arrive at such a conclusion. And yet studies by the Pew Research Center and other polling organizations have consistently reported that only 5% of those who profess to be true followers of Christ have ever read the Bible from beginning to end! If this is not something that every reader finds simply incredible, such a reader is not thinking clearly and rationally (which is a very common problem in 2015). Furthermore, in my own life experience, I would venture to guess that the true percentage of alleged Christians who have read the Bible from cover to cover is more likely to be less than 1% of that group of professed Christian believers. Such a finding is pathetic and deplorable, to say the least. It reveals that the world is incredibly ignorant of what the Bible actually says. And yet the Bible has vitally essential information for daily living that is seldom taught in our world today, to the harm of world civilization, such as it is, in the 21st century.

Moreover, throughout the last 3,500 years since the Bible began to be written and taught to man, billions of people's lives have been transformed for the better by its brilliant teachings and godly wisdom which true believers in Christ (Yahushua) have placed their trust in and followed, in submission and obedience to a God and to Jesus, His son, who claims to be loving, kind and has nothing but the best interests of mankind in store for us, if we would only heed His protective guidance, delivered to us in the form of His commandments to us. In short, the Bible claims that the promises of God in the Bible to His people, are only available to those who truly love God, who have a personal relationship with Him, and who trust and obey Him in all things. Interestingly, some of the most brilliant men and thinkers of the last 2,000 years have proven to be Biblical Christians who submitted their lives and their wills to the lordship of Jesus in all things and experienced the life transformation for the better which the Apostle Paul wrote of in Romans 12:2 quoted above.

My own personal spiritual and life journey and experience over the last fourteen years or so confirms all of this. I am part of the less than one percent of all professing followers of Christ (Yahushua) who have read the Bible from cover to cover. Moreover, God has blessed me with some powerful gifts of reading comprehension and recall which allows me to remember many passages I have read and find them again when I need to refer to them, to remind me of what God has actually said, as opposed to what flawed and sinful men may claim it says. I have placed my trust in the Bible as what it claims to be and have attempted to live my life to the letter of what it says, to the best of my flawed ability, for those fourteen years or so, and I have experienced the life transformation of which the Apostle Paul speaks. I am a new man in Christ (Yahushua), living my life fully submitted and surrendered to Him, as the Bible teaches me to do. In the process, I have learned that everything I once held to be true, proves to be part of a preposterous set of lies I intend to expose and reveal later in this book.

The Bible is Unintelligible to Most People

The Bible claims, and has proven itself to be, a holy and supernatural book. The word "holy" is defined in *Noah Webster's 1828 American Dictionary of the English Language* as follows:

"Properly whole, entire or perfect in a moral sense. Hence, pure in heart, temper or disposition; free from sin and sinful affections."

That same source defines "supernatural" this way:

"Beyond or exceeding the powers of the laws of nature; miraculous . . . Hence supernatural events or miracles can be produced only by the immediate agency of divine power."

The Bible reveals that its words and meaning cannot be fully comprehended as its divine author God (YHWH) intends without the reader first possessing God's Holy Spirit living inside his or her heart, in what Jesus defines as being "born again" in the Spirit of God:

"Jesus (Yahushua) answered, Verily, verily I say unto thee, Except a man be born of water and of the Spirit, he cannot enter into the kingdom of God (Eloah). That which is born of the flesh is flesh; and that which is born of the Spirit is spirit. Marvel not that I said unto thee, Ye must be born again. The wind bloweth where it listeth, and thou hearest the sound thereof, but canst not tell whence it cometh, and whither it goeth: so is every one that is born of the Spirit." John 3:5-8

The Bible was written by men of God who were filled with God's Holy Spirit, guiding them to write that which God wished for them to write. Similarly, God's chosen people, His born again elect, are able to comprehend this same intent of its divine author, God, in the same way.

This teaching of the Bible has rather profound implications based on what it does not say, as much as what it does say. It implies that those who are not born again, cannot fully comprehend the intent, thoughts, ways and teachings of God in the Bible. This explains why Christianity has developed some 33,000 different denominations or forms of organized religion, which, as I shall reveal later, do not remain faithful and true to the full teachings of God, Jesus and the Bible, and so are all false and apostate, led by men, and a few women who, while they may falsely believe that they are born again in God's Spirit, clearly are not, because they teach in error and contrary

57

to what the full word of God, the Bible, teaches. In fact, this attribute of teaching that which contradicts or conflicts with the Bible in any material way, is a telltale sign of a false teacher or a false prophet, with which the Bible teaches God's elect to have nothing to do. Such a Biblical teaching is seldom obeyed in the community of false, apostate, organized religion of any form today. Whenever a person witnesses this in people, their claim to be true followers of Christ is likely to be false and a fraud. Some may know it; but I believe most such people are self-deceived, because all they have ever known is what their brand of false organized religion told them was the truth, even though it conflicts with what Scripture says in one or more material ways.

In addition to teaching doctrines which are contradicted by one or more passages in the Bible taken honestly and with integrity in the full context of the Bible passages referred to, how else can we discern if we, or anyone else, is what they claim to be: born again in the Spirit of God?

1 John 4:1-6 give us some very useful guidance in this regard:

> *"Beloved, believe not every spirit, but try the spirits whether they are of God (Eloah): because many false prophets are gone out into the world. Hereby know ye the Spirit of God (Eloah): Every spirit that confesseth that Jesus Christ (Yahushua the Messiah) is come in the flesh is of God (Eloah): And every spirit that confesseth not that Jesus Christ (Yahushua the Messiah) is come in the flesh is not of God (Eloah): and this is the spirit of the antichrist (false Messiah), whereof ye have heard that it should come; and even now is already in the world. Ye are of God (Eloah), little children, and have overcome them: because greater is he that is in you (Jesus and God's Holy Spirit), than he that is in the world (the devil). They are of the world: therefore speak they of the world (elevating worldly interests in sex, money, power, fame and status over God), and the world heareth them. We are of God (Eloah): he that knoweth God (Eloah) heareth us; he that is not of God (Eloah) heareth not us. Hereby know we the spirit of **truth**,*

and the spirit of error." (parentheticals for clarification and bold face added for emphasis)

Note the emphasis and importance the Apostle John places upon the spirit of truth. This will be a recurring theme throughout this book, for reasons that will soon become distinctly clear and evident.

Yet another largely fool-proof method that permits anyone to discern who is truly born again in God's Spirit, and who is not, regardless of what they may claim (which is often a lie), is to watch their behavior and words and compare them to the contrasting verses of Galatians 5:19-21 revealing the acts of the sinful nature versus the fruit of the Spirit revealed in Galatians 5:22-23:

> *"Now the works of the flesh are manifest, which are these; Adultery, fornication, uncleanness, lasciviousness, Idolatry, witchcraft, hatred, variance, emulations, wrath, strife, seditions, heresies, Envyings, murders, drunkenness, revelings, and such like: of the which I tell you before, as I have also told you in time past, that they which do such things shall not inherit the kingdom of God."* Galatians 5:19-21

> *"But the fruit of the Spirit is love, joy, peace, longsuffering, gentleness, goodness, faith, Meekness (humility), temperance (self-control): against such there is no law."* Galatians 5:22-23

Anyone who fails to pass these tests has revealed himself to be someone other than who he claims to be and ought not to be trusted concerning anything which the Bible does or does not teach. We see this manifested in endless attempts in American culture to claim that the Bible needs to be "interpreted" in some manner by those who are qualified, through seminary education or something equivalent, to make such judgments. This is absolute hogwash and finds no support for it anywhere in Scripture! If you have the Holy Spirit dwelling in your heart, God will reveal His intent and meaning in every verse of Scripture you read, reflecting the degree of spiritual depth and maturity you already possess. As a person matures in his or her faith, God will reveal deeper and deeper levels of meaning in the same verses which He previously did not reveal to a person when he was in a less spiritually mature state. The Apostle Paul speaks of feeding his newer converts to the true faith of Jesus Christ spiritual milk, which he contrasts with the metaphor of solid food suitable for the more mature believer, and this is what he means by these terms.

Not Everyone Is Able to Become Born Again

In light of the prior section which revealed that a person needs to be born again in God's Holy Spirit to fully and properly grasp the intent and meaning of the Bible's divine author, God, the reader is justified in asking, "So what does it take to become born again in the Spirit?" Generally, anyone asking this question assumes that any person can make the choice anytime he or she likes to become born again in the Spirit, but nothing could be further from the truth.

The Bible teaches a doctrine of election, in which God, since before the world began, chose (or elected) some people to become His elect, who would one day during their lives, at a time and method of God's choosing and initiative, cause His Holy Spirit to come into that person's heart, and God would then orchestrate events in that person's life so he would hear the word of God preached, he would believe it (through the guiding of God's Holy Spirit) and in the believing of it, would become saved and from that point forward would become a true believer in Christ, which the Bible otherwise refers to as a saint, God's elect, or one of God's born again adopted sons and daughters in the true faith in Jesus Christ.

This doctrine of election is one seldom taught inside any form of organized religion today for several fairly obvious reasons. Organized religion in America today is big business and it has little or nothing to do with leading lost and hurting souls to salvation and from the fiery pits of hell, but rather its emphasis is on the external trappings of success, as measured by the number of participants who show up every week to church and the volume of money collected in the form of tithes and offerings from those same attendees. Generally, if a church is growing in numbers of heads and offering dollars, they deem themselves successful and "doing God's will," and conversely, if their numbers of heads and dollars are stagnant or in decline, they will deem themselves to be unsuccessful and will seek to modify and water down their messages to make them more palatable to a wider audience. In the process, no one gets saved, but that's because in reality, the spirit of Satan rules those forms of organized and false religion.

Additionally, almost all those inside false religion today do not number among God's elect, and at some level deep in their hearts, they know this and resent it. They go to church to delude themselves into thinking that they are saved, when in fact they most assuredly are not and remain headed for the hell we are all born heading to at birth. In order to deceive themselves that they are saved, these people seek to suppress and silence certain "inconvenient" teachings in the Bible that they are offended to hear, and in the doing, they lead others inside those same churches astray, as well.

I have witnessed this very phenomenon from the wife of an elder of a small non-denominational church I attended shortly after I arrived in Idaho over three years ago. Even though the pastor of that church taught the doctrine of election quite openly and accurately, this woman openly and loudly announced that she refused to believe it, thereby undermining her husband's and her church pastor's teachings and witness. What was the truth? The truth was that this woman was in Biblical error (contradicting the teachings of the Bible) on several points and no one in that church had the knowledge or the courage to bring appropriate Biblical correction to her, out of fear of further offending this rude and brash woman. She abused her informal power as a wife of one of the church's four elders to intimidate others into silence. This illustrates how even smaller forms of organized religion have become infiltrated and corrupted by false teaching and psychologically manipulative and controlling behaviors of those who do not number among God's elect at all.

61

If one opens any Bible concordance to the words "elect(ion) and "chosen" and reads all pertinent verses that their concordance references on these two words, one will find all the teachings of the Bible on the doctrine of election. Here are a few of the most compelling verses to prove this teaching is fully backed by Scripture:

> *"According as he hath chosen us in him before the foundation of the world, that we should be holy and without blame before him in love:* **Having predestinated us unto the adoption of children by Jesus Christ** *(Yahushua the Messiah) to himself, according to the good pleasure of his will,"* Ephesians 1:4-5 (bold face added for emphasis)

> *"For by grace (meaning unmerited favor) are ye saved through faith; and that not of yourselves: it is the gift of God (Eloah): Not of works lest any man should boast.* **For we are his workmanship, created in Christ Jesus** *(Yahushua the Messiah)* **unto good works, which God (Eloah) hath before ordained that we should walk in them."** Ephesians 2:8-9 (parentheticals added for clarity and and bold face added for emphasis)

> *"As it is written, Jacob have I loved, but Esau have I hated. What shall we say then? Is there unrighteousness with God (Eloah)? God forbid. For he saith to Moses, I will have mercy on whom I will have mercy, and I will have compassion on whom I will have compassion. So then it is not of him that willeth, nor of him that runneth, but of God (Eloah) that sheweth mercy. For the scripture saith unto Pharaoh, Even for this same purpose have I raised thee up, that I might shew my power in thee, and that my name might be declared throughout all the earth.* **Therefore hath he mercy on whom he will have mercy, and whom he will he hardeneth."** Romans 9:13-18 (bold face added for emphasis)

These verses from Scripture are sobering indeed for all of us. They reveal to all of mankind that God, the sovereign God of the entire universe, who spoke it into existence, does whatever He chooses and we, His creation, are at His mercy to experience either grace or wrath, as God, and God alone, decides. Anyone heeding these words of God ought to be humbled and chastened by them. Man simply is not as special as we often choose to think we are. We simply need to get over ourselves and appreciate the might, power and wisdom of an almighty, all-knowing, holy, just, ever-truthful, unchanging, never-failing God.

For those who discover that they are not yet born again in God's Spirit, all is not lost. God also has complete control over the timing and method by which He reveals Himself and His Word to those who number among His elect. God's spiritual sheep, His elect, often behave like God's spiritual goats, His non-elect, prior to our being born again in God's Spirit. This is because man's nature is desperately wicked and there is no good thing in us, apart from the power of God's Holy Spirit working in and through us.

The ways God reveals himself to His elect is usually rather brutal and shocking. In my own experience, I was led to hear the gospel preached at a men's retreat in late 2000 and for seven months I knew I was in trouble and went looking for a loophole in the Bible which would permit me to continue rationalizing a choice I had made in my life which I knew to be contrary to God's commandments. I never found this loophole. Instead, God confronted me with another ethical dilemma I could not ignore, I chose rightly, and then He crushed me and broke me and brought me to the end of myself out of answers and facing the sin I was ducking head on. Only then did I capitulate, throw in the towel and submit and surrender my life to the lordship of Jesus, having little idea what was in store for me in the 14 plus years that have followed, much of which entailed many trials, great suffering and excruciating emotional pain that matured and refined my character and my courage, preparing me for these times in which we are now living.

My point in sharing a bit of my own story is to reveal that a true born again experience is seldom a response to an altar call or the result of praying the sinner's prayer so common in today's various forms of organized and false religion. The real deal of conversion is seldom so neat, tidy and clean. It is often messy and quite painful at first, but as one who has emerged out the other side of it, I can assure you, my readers, that it is well worth the agony to grow us up and mature us into the men and women God designed us to become since before the world began and to assume the unique roles He designed for us to assume in His perfect plan of history.

The Bad News of Man's Depraved Nature

Since the Age of Enlightenment of the 1500s to 1700s in Europe, western philosophers have sought to counter the teachings of God's Word, the Bible, and falsely claim that man is inherently good, when all the evidence in our wicked, deceitful, treacherous and evil world today proves conclusively that the Bible has been 100% true all along. Here's what God has to teach us about the inherent nature of man:

> *"The heart is deceitful above all things, and desperately wicked: who can know it?"* Jeremiah 17:9

> *"For all have sinned, and come short of the glory of God (Eloah);"* Romans 3:23

> *"As it written, There is none righteous, no, not one: There is none that understandeth, there is none that seeketh after God (Eloah). They are all gone out of the way, they are together become unprofitable; there is none that doeth good, no, not one. Their throat is an open sepulchre; with tongues they have used deceit; the poisons of asps is under their lips: Whose mouth is full of cursing and bitterness: Their feet are swift to shed blood: Destruction and misery are in their ways: And the way of peace they have not known: There is no fear of God (Eloah) before their eyes. Now we know that what things soever the law saith, it saith to them who are under the law: that every mouth may be stopped, and all the world may become guilty before God (Eloah). Therefore by the deeds of the law there shall no flesh be justified (declared innocent) in his sight: for by the law is the knowledge of sin."* Romans 3:10-20

"For the wages of sin is death (both physical and the eternal in hell); but the gift of God (Eloah) is eternal life through Jesus Christ our Lord (our Adon Yahushua the Messiah)."
Romans 6:23 (first parenthetical added for clarity)

Later in this book, I will be revealing the full depth and breadth of the global conspiracy in all its vile ugliness and wicked deceit and depravity which will prove beyond a shadow of a doubt that the Bible, and only the Bible, has things right when it comes to the nature of man: we are all desperately wicked, selfish, deceitful and sinful, having no interest in the things of God. The Bible further reveals that the things of God are evident to all of us, as revealed to us by God's creation and through His revealed words of the Bible, and so we are all without excuse, the truth of God having been written on every man's heart. Yet in spite of all of the undeniable evidence for the existence and nature of God, the vast majority of mankind rebels against God, denies His existence, mocks His Word, the Bible, in an endless barrage of mockery and scorn and mistakenly thinks that there will be no long-term consequences for their foolish actions and choices. Nothing could be further from the truth. The Bible goes into great detail as to what these consequences will look like and for anyone paying attention, they are simply horrifying. Yet man, in his depraved state and nature, will not heed the obvious warnings and will spurn God and choose to do whatever seems right in his own eyes.

In Romans 1:18-32 the Apostle Paul spells out man's wickedness and foolishness and reveals to all of us what God's response is to wicked and foolish men and women:

"For the wrath of God (Eloah) is revealed from heaven against all ungodliness and unrighteousness of men, who hold the **truth** *in unrighteousness; Because that which may be known of God (Eloah) is manifest in them; for God (Eloah) hath shewed it unto them. For the invisible things of him from the creation of the world are clearly seen, being understood by the things that are made, even his eternal power and Godhead;* **so that they are without excuse;** *Because that, when they knew God (Eloah), they glorified him not as God (Eloah), neither were*

*thankful; but became vain in their imaginations **and their foolish heart was darkened.** Professing themselves to be wise, they became fools, And changed the glory of the incorruptible God (Eloah) into an image made like to corruptible man, and to birds, and fourfooted beasts, and creeping things. Wherefore God (Eloah) also gave them up to uncleanness through the lusts of their own hearts, to dishonor their own bodies between themselves: Who changed the **truth** of God (Eloah) into a lie, and worshipped and served the creature more than the Creator, who is blessed for ever, Amen. For this cause God (Eloah) gave them up unto vile affections: for even their women did change the natural use into that which is against nature: And likewise also the men, leaving the natural use of the woman, burned in their lust toward one another; men with men working that which is unseemly, and receiving in themselves that recompense of their error which was meet (suitable). And even as they did not like to retain God (Eloah) in their knowledge, God (Eloah) gave them over to a reprobate mind, to do those things which are not convenient (right); Being filled with all unrighteousness, fornication, wickedness, covetousness, maliciousness; full of envy, murder, debate, deceit, malignity; whisperers, Backbiters, haters of God (Eloah), despiteful, proud, boasters, inventors of evil things, disobedient to parents, Without understanding, covenant-breakers, without natural affection, implacable, unmerciful: Who knowing the judgment of God (Eloah), that they which commit such things are worthy of death (temporally and in hell eternally), not only do the same, but have pleasure in them that do them."* (parentheticals added for clarity and bold face added for emphasis)

If this passage does not describe America and the world in 2015, I don't know what does. The vast majority of mankind worldwide today professes to be wise, have rejected all aspects of God, tacitly condone and embrace the homosexual acts described in this passage as natural, normal and healthy, and are practicing virtually every one of the wicked and sinful acts described at the end of this passage. And what does God's Word tell us will be the ultimate consequences for their rebellion? Eternal death, agony and torment in the fires of hell, which these same fools dismiss as mere fairy tales designed to frighten and keep them from doing as they wish, and to hell with any consequences! Anyone with half a brain and any common sense and adult life experience knows that such foolish choices can only end in tragedy.

Shortly after God brought me to my knees, desperate, out of answers and dependent upon Him, He chose to give me a premonition of hell. It was the most terrifying experience I have had or will ever have. I was gasping for air, hyperventilating, with my heart racing rapidly and no matter what I did in each gasp, I could not get enough oxygen. I was burning in the flames of hell and in agony; and for the first time in my 47 year life, I realized that I could not die so that the agony would cease, I could never again rest, and that eternity meant that the torment would never end. That experience literally scared the hell out of me, and I sincerely hope that the telling of my own story, has the same effect on some of you, my readers. From that experience alone, I know hell to be very real and worthy of every effort to avoid. I state this without qualification.

Thus, the Bible clearly teaches that we are all born with a sinful nature which is deceitful, wicked and selfish, and that in our wretched condition, we are born separated from a right relationship with God, and in our depraved and rebellious condition, God has no use for us and refuses to have anything to do with any of us. In this condition that we are all born into, all of us are destined for an eternity in that terrifying hell of torment I just described, unless something happens to us before we die. Just so we are clear about what I am saying here: this is very bad news for all of us! Yet God tells us that this is the condition of all of mankind. In light of this revealed reality from God, are we all completely screwed forever? Or has God left at least some of us a way out of man's universal problem of sin? The good news is that for some of us, He has. The rest of the bad news is that for most of humanity, He has not. Thus, which side of the fence we each sit on, as determined by God, makes a great deal of difference!

The Good News of the Gospel of Jesus Christ for God's Elect

Once God had established the very bad news that all men are sinners, with a bent to do evil, in rebellion against God and therefore choosing to spend all eternity in torment and agony in the fires if hell, you would think that perhaps He would have gotten man's attention, wouldn't you? Yet, from all the mockery, scorn, ridicule, dismissals and denials of God, Jesus, and the Bible in America and our world today, it ought to be clear to every last one of us that there is something hideously wrong here and that man, left to his own devices, is on a path to his own self-destruction. For God to get some men's and women's attention, He has to permit most of us to freely choose to make a mess of ourselves to prove to the few that God has chosen as His elect, that the path we were all born into is a path to our deaths – both our physical deaths, and even worse, our eternal deaths in the fires of hell.

So from the very outset of time, before the world began, God devised a brilliant rescue plan for some of us, but not all of us, as is falsely and endlessly taught in our wicked and deceitful world. God's perfect holiness demands that He not permit unrepentant sinners to pollute His heaven. So how does God admit at least some sinful people into His heaven, while at the same time not defiling the place? God's answer was to reveal to His elect their guilt for breaking God's moral laws and that they deserved eternal punishment in hell for it, and then offer them a way out, a pardon, if you will. But this chance for a pardon comes with a catch: anyone offered this deal for a pardon by God must die to himself and his selfish ways and be reborn spiritually with God's Holy Spirit leading him or her so that they have the power to choose to cease sinning and rebelling against God – not perfectly, but rather that they *try* hard not to, out of love for the grace and love of almighty God that He first showed them. The pardon also requires that the saved sinner believe God, Jesus and the Bible and seek to come to know God and Jesus intimately and personally and in such

68

a loving, safe and affirming relationship of trust with the all-powerful God, to submit and surrender their lives and their wills to the lordship of Jesus, God incarnate, in all things.

In short, the price that any of God's elect must pay to be able to count on being saved, born again in the Spirit, and having the promise of being raised one day in resurrected bodies just like that of Jesus, to live with God, Jesus and other believers in joy, love, peace and harmony, without pain, suffering, lies and wickedness ever again is not an easy one. It requires any true believer in Jesus to give up chasing the lures of a world which are intent on promoting that which are, in the end, meaningless and without lasting value. These worldly pursuits include the pursuit of sex, other physical pleasures, money, power, fame and status which the ruler of this world, Satan, promotes endlessly as the path to true happiness, which in reality, is a hideous lie straight from the pits of hell to deceive all of humanity and keep us on the pathway to hell we were all born into.

Thus, God came to earth in the flesh in the form of His son, Jesus (Yahushua), who lived a sinless life, taught mankind the thoughts and ways of God, leading by His own example as a role model for us all, performed miracles which proved who He was: the son of God, and then died a painful death on the cross, bearing all the sins of all of God's elect, past, present and future, upon his shoulders, paying the price of death that we deserved to pay for our sinful actions, so that His righteousness and holiness might be imputed to God's born again elect, and we might be reconciled into a right and respectful relationship with almighty God (YHWH) of the Bible.

Romans 10:9-10 explain all that must occur for anyone to be saved:

> *"That if thou shalt confess with thy mouth the Lord Jesus (Adon Yahushua), and shalt believe in thine heart that God (Eloah) hath raised him from the dead, thou shalt be saved. For with the heart man believeth unto righteousness; and with the mouth confession is made unto salvation."*

What does this really mean? To confess means to make a specific, verbal statement of fact. To confess the Lord Jesus means that you surrender your life and your will to the perfect will of Jesus as your lord, king and master over every aspect of your life from that day forward, with no hedges, and no holdbacks. To believe in your heart speaks to much more than mere intellectual assent that you think it true that God raised Jesus from the dead. It means that you are prepared to live your life in conformity with such a belief for the rest of your life. As such, the allures and enticements of this world, which is perishing and passing away, no longer hold the same attraction they once had for you.

In my own life experience, I am not sure I have ever met anyone who is truly born again in God's Spirit (thus proving that they number among God's elect), who was not brought kicking and screaming to the foot of the cross of Jesus. That certainly was what it took to get my attention and commitment: God had to break me and humble me first, and indeed, He did just that and it was not at all pleasant. It was quite painful and nothing I would have ever signed up for voluntarily, until I had no other option and no other place to go. Many forms of false organized religion encourage people to respond to an altar call or pray the sinner's prayer and once they do so, their charlatan church leaders tell the gullible and the naive that they are saved and "good to go" in the kingdom of God. In my experience and extensive observation, this is seldom the truth. Usually, it is a hideous lie, designed to deceive the hurting person and hold them in bondage and captivity to the lies of Satan that enslave most of the world today.

Having said this, the good news of the saving grace and mercy of God through the propitious death of Jesus on the cross, as payment for our sins, is almost too good to be true. But in this case, it is true and is the best news in all the world and in all of life for God's elect.

So what can we expect if God truly has saved us as explained here? Is it likely to be a bed of roses and a life free of affliction, pain and suffering henceforth? Unfortunately, that is not the case at all, and false organized religion deceives many people into believing just the opposite of what the Bible teaches us on this subject. Jesus teaches us that if we become one of His true followers, that we will experience much opposition, affliction, pain, suffering and persecution in this life for following Him, God and the Bible as we seek to follow the example Jesus left for us of how to live righteously (in right relationship with God) for the kingdom of God and for God's glory, and not our own. Here are a couple of teachings from Jesus on this point:

> *"Think not that I am come to send peace on earth: I came not to send peace, but a sword. For I am come to set a man at variance against his father, and the daughter against her mother, and the daughter in law against her mother in law. And a man's foes shall be they of his own household. He that loveth father or mother more than me is not worthy of me: and he that loveth son or daughter more than me is not worthy of me. And he that taketh not his cross, and followeth after me, is not worthy of me. He that findeth his life shall lose it: and he that loseth his life for my sake shall find it."* Matthew 10:34-39

> *"If the world hate you, ye know that it hated me before it hated you. If ye were of the world, the world would love his own: but because ye are not of the world, but I have chosen you out of the world, therefore the world hateth you. Remember the word that I said unto you, The servant is not greater than his lord. If they persecuted me, they will also persecute you; if they have kept my saying, they will keep yours also. But all these things will they do unto you for my name's sake, because they know not him that sent me."* John 15:18-21

How often do you hear or read about any form of false, organized religion (and they are all false today) teaching this to their flocks? Seldom, if ever, is the truthful answer. The reason for this ought to be obvious, as I've shared previously. Organized religion of all forms in America is big business today and has almost nothing to do with saving souls or maturing people in Christ. Instead, all forms of organized religion are about making money and exerting power over others. This is because all forms of organized religion deceive people into thinking they are saved, when in fact they are not, making people feel good about themselves so that they will show up and give offerings and tithes to the institutional church to cover its financial overhead, which consists mainly of debt service on a mortgage on a church building and the salaries and benefits of full and part time clergy and church staff. To keep this money engine humming, most churches have permitted themselves to be corrupted. They teach messages which purport to teach the Bible, but seldom do so accurately and completely, because if they did so, they would teach messages such as the one here that they know would be likely to chase many paying customers away. So instead, they water down the messages to teach half-truths, which purport to be from the Bible, but are not messages of integrity which teach the full word of God. Half-truths have the same effect as bald-faced lies: they deceive their listeners, to their harm and destruction, and this is the business of all of organized religion worldwide in 2015. As a result of this unfortunate dynamic, every church of organized religion is filled with self-deceived, spiritually dead people today who do not read their Bibles for themselves and passively absorb pleasing messages, manufactured by psychologically manipulative frauds and charlatans, who pretend to be faithful men of God, true to the full teachings of the Bible, but who most assuredly are not that at all!

The Best Kept Secret in All the World: We Live in a World at War

Few adults, with any life experience of 50 years or more would argue with the observation that life is hard and fraught with challenges, trials and adversities. King Macbeth, in William Shakespeare's play, "Macbeth:" says it this way:

> *"Life is a tale, told by an idiot, full of sound and fury, signifying nothing."*

The character of Macbeth here is articulating the view of the atheist who, without objectively examining all the evidence for

72

his claims, concludes that God cannot possibly exist, that there is no meaning to life, and that once life is over and we die, there is nothing more and we cease to exist. People who embrace such an uninformed view, often subscribe to the life motto, "Let us eat, drink and be merry, for tomorrow we die." It is an immature and rather foolish life philosophy of selfishness and hedonism, in which its adherents pursue pleasure, and seek to avoid pain, at all costs. Their life philosophy is best summarized by the statement, "I just want to be happy."

There are others who recognize that life is hard and who view things with a sense of despair and deep cynicism, as articulated in the pessimistic statement:

"Life is hard; and then you die."

Even true Biblical Christians and followers of Christ know that life is not a bed of roses and that we seldom live happily ever after, as almost all fairy tales end, appealing to our deepest yearnings and longings. Something is not right with our world, and we all know it. Yet few people grasp what is at the root of this opposition in life and a sense of meaninglessness and purposelessness. Once again, God reveals the answer to this vitally important question through His Word, the Bible. God reveals to us that we live in a world at war, a war waged not in the physical realm, but in the spiritual realm: in a dimension beyond our material, three dimensional world, in which spiritual forces of good and evil are at work to fulfill the perfect plan of God for all of humanity, for His good purposes and ultimate glory, and not necessarily our own immediate comfort. And yet through it all, God (YHWH) remains fully in control of all events in each of our lives and in all of the events of world history for the past 6,000 years of man's existence.

John Eldredge, in his book, *Waking the Dead*, talks to this reality that there is indeed a spiritual battle raging underneath the surface of all of life and that we all have a unique role to play in this epic story of humanity. Eldredge contends, and I agree, that to live our lives fully, a large part of our life ought to be devoted to figuring out what this unique and heroic role is that God has planned for us since the beginning of time, and then living out this divine purpose for our lives as faithfully and completely as we can. In fact, while Eldredge fails to make the distinction between God's elect and non-elect, he asserts that:

"The story of your life is the long and brutal assault on your heart by the one who knows what you could be and fears it."[4]

The one Eldredge refers to here is the devil, who goes by a number of names: Satan, Lucifer, Beelzebub, Lord of the Flies, the father of lies and prince of this world, being among them. The Bible teaches us that the devil is very real and that he is a fallen archangel who became so enamored with himself that he foolishly tried to usurp the place of God and that a war raged in heaven for control and that he, Lucifer, and one third of the angels in heaven who joined his revolt against God, were thrown to earth where the devil and these fallen angels, who are demon spirits, roam the earth seeking humans to devour and destroy out of Satan's jealousy because God made man one level below God to rule and have dominion over the earth and all that is in it, and not Satan. The Bible teaches us that Satan is filled with jealousy, pride and hatred toward all of mankind and since he cannot defeat God, he has chosen to do the next best thing and try to destroy all of mankind and keep all of us on the pathway we were born into, heading for eternal death, damnation and torment in hell, where he knows he is ultimately headed too. Here is how the Bible describes these events:

"And there was war in heaven: Michael and his angels fought against the dragon; and the dragon fought and his angels, And prevailed not; neither was their place found any more in heaven. And the great dragon was cast out, that old serpent, called the Devil, and Satan, which deceiveth the whole world; he was cast out into the earth, and his angels were cast out with him. And I heard a loud voice saying in heaven, Now is come the salvation, and strength, and the kingdom of our God (Eloah), and the power of his Christ (Messiah): for the accuser of our brethren is cast down, which accused them before our God

---

[4] Eldredge, John. *Waking the Dead.* 2003. p. 34.

> *(Eloah) day and night. And they overcame him by the blood of the Lamb (Jesus), and by the word of their testimony; and they loved not their lives unto the death. Therefore, rejoice ye heavens, and ye that dwell in them. Woe to the inhabiters of the earth and of the sea! for the devil is come down unto you, having great wrath, because he knoweth that he hath but a short time. And when the dragon saw that he was cast unto the earth, he persecuted the woman which brought forth the man child. . . . And the dragon was wroth (angry) with the woman, and went to make war with the remnant of her seed, which keep the commandments of God (Eloah), and have the testimony of Jesus Christ (Yahushua the Messiah)."* Revelation 12:7-13 and 17 (parentheticals added)

The woman represents the true nation of Israel, the 12 Hebrew tribes descended from the patriarchs Abraham, Isaac and Jacob of the Old Testament, and the remnant of her seed are true Biblical Christians since the days of Christ through to today. In other words, God's true elect, as evidenced by their becoming true born again Biblical Christians at some point in their lives, can expect intense opposition and affliction from the devil and his demon spirits, working through those who number among God's non-elect, to bring pain, suffering and tribulation to God's people.

What is vitally important for all of God's people to recognize and appreciate is that God remains fully in control over all world events throughout all time and over all his creation, including over the spiritual powers of darkness, Satan and his demon spirits. So why would God permit His chosen elect to experience affliction and pain at the hands of Satan, demon spirits and the wicked people who Satan controls? Throughout all of Scripture, God reveals that it is to refine, test and mature the characters of His adopted sons and daughters in order to mold and transform us into the likeness and character of His son, Jesus.

The first time I read Eldredge's quote above I was stunned. It was as though Eldredge was writing directly to me and me alone. I had given my life to Jesus (Yahushua) five years earlier, had read much of the New Testament and thought I was pretty far along in my understanding and comprehension of the true faith of God until I read this. But when I read this, I knew. I knew it was all true! Over the next six years, I would find myself engaged in an all-out war with the devil and his army of demon-infested wicked and deceitful liars and fools. Through it all, the God of the Bible (YHWH) revealed to me who I really was and who He created me to be since before the world began. I was to become not just a mere follower of Jesus; I was to become the modern day prophet and watchman on the wall in the final days of the end times that I now find myself living out in submission to the will of almighty God, YHWH and His son and my Lord, Yahushua (Jesus).

The journey to get here has, in many ways, been a hideous and treacherous one. I would never have chosen this for myself, and I am sure God fully knows this and that is why, at least in part, He revealed it to me the way He did: in small gradual steps and pieces that I could absorb and digest one bite at a time. Throughout it all, God's Word gave me guidance in the stories of the Bible that spoke more than to just my mind; they spoke to my heart and revealed to me that I possess a heart much like that of King David and several prophets of the Old Testament, notably Jeremiah, Ezekiel and Hosea, in whom God took great delight.

In the final days of the great tribulation, it follows the pattern of the Bible that God would raise one or more modern-day prophets, who He would use much as He used the Old Testament prophets Jeremiah, Ezekiel and Hosea, to warn the people of the ancient kingdom of Judah of their rebellious spirits, sexual immorality, idolatry, witchcraft, lies, betrayals, murders and strife all rooted in the sins of the people and urge the people to confess and repent for their sins and plead with God for mercy, which if they did not, would otherwise lead to their destruction. The people of ancient Judah failed to heed the many warnings of those prophets and great men of God, who were persecuted mercilessly to try to suppress the truth and shut them up, and in the end, the wicked people of Judah were destroyed, precisely as God had revealed to His prophets

He would do so, if they failed to repent. Those who fail to study history are doomed to repeat it. History is now repeating itself and reflecting the ways of God which He has revealed to His people long ago.

In this context, the Bible teaches that the great tribulation which we are now living through will be fraught with strife, affliction and wickedness, as Satan, the enemy of God and of God's true remnant, wreaks havoc on earth. This is in order to prove once and for all to mankind that without God, mankind is doomed to its own self-destruction.

Fear of God is a Prerequisite for all True Knowledge and Wisdom

The Bible teaches repeatedly of the importance of fearing God, who professes to be omnipotent (all powerful), omniscient (all knowing), eternal, unchanging, the source of all truth, holy, just, loving, filled with grace and mercy, but intolerant of fools and sin. Here is how a few key verses state this truth:

> *"**The fear of the LORD (YHWH) is the beginning of knowledge**: but fools despise wisdom and instruction."* Proverbs 1:7

> *"**The fear of the LORD (YHWH) is the beginning of wisdom**: and the knowledge of the holy is understanding."* Proverbs 9:10

> *"And fear not them which kill the body, but are not able to kill the soul: **but rather fear him which is able to destroy both soul and body in hell.**"* Matthew 10:28

> *"Saying with a loud voice, **Fear God (Eloah), and give glory to him**; for the hour of his judgment is come: and worship him that made heaven, and earth, and the sea, and the fountains of the waters."* Revelation 14:7

False teaching of organized religion of almost all forms teaches the naive and the gullible that God is love and that's really all you need to know; the implication being that God is an indulgent, impotent dufus and little more than that. Nothing could be further from the truth, as proven throughout Biblical history.

It is true that the Bible does state that God is love in 1 John 4:16, but to fully comprehend what the Apostle John was teaching here one must examine the entire verse and what it actually says:

> *"And we have known and believed the love that God (Eloah) hath to us. God (Eloah) is love; and he that dwelleth in love dwelleth in God (Eloah), and God in him."*

Thus, when we don't play fast and loose with Bible verses (which is quite common today), but examine every verse in the full context in which it was written, to whom, and for what purpose, we get a very different understanding, if we are seeking to comprehend the intent of God, as He inspired John to write these words. What God was saying was that God loves each and every one of His adopted born again sons and daughters who love, respect and revere Him. To love God is to obey Him in all things, Jesus teaches us in John 14:23-24:

> *". . . If a man love me, he will keep my words: and my Father will love him and we will come unto him, and make our abode with him. He that loveth me not keepeth not not my sayings: and the word which ye hear is not mine, but the Father's which sent me."*

Thus, in truth, according to what the Bible says and teaches us, God has the power to redeem and save us from our depraved human natures and make us one of His own born again adopted sons and daughters, but He also has the power to bring an end to our lives any time He chooses and to throw us into the fiery pits of hell in eternal agony and torment. Now there is a power and a being worthy of our fear and reverence! Furthermore, from the initial verses from the Book of Proverbs, God informs us that all real wisdom and knowledge originates with Him. Thus, we can know with confidence that those who do not fear God, as evidenced by their denial of or rebellion against Him, have no true knowledge or wisdom. The

Bible refers to such people as fools: they are stupid beyond belief and it shows in their foolish words, choices and behaviors. The Bible defines a fool as someone who is morally deficient. We think of a fool as a stupid person. Now we can see that a person's moral deficiency and rebellion against God is what makes him profoundly stupid.

Now that we are in the midst of the great tribulation, we can observe an increasing level of foolishness, wickedness and gross incompetence in those with whom we have to interact, as we go about our daily lives. I don't know about you, but my bride and I most certainly have noticed this in recent months, and we know that things have to get a whole lot worse in these respects between now and the end of 2016 when Yahushua (Jesus) returns in His second coming, for the reasons I have just explained here.

How God Inspired the Writing of the Bible

Many people I have encountered struggle to comprehend how God might have authored the Bible through the inspiration of godly men who authored the 66 books of the Bible. It really ought not to be that difficult to comprehend, if one has a proper understanding of who God is and the limitless reach of His almighty power.

Can you, as a man or woman make a dumb dog sit? Of course you can. So why is it so hard for mankind to comprehend how God might influence the thoughts and ways of the forty plus authors of the books of the Bible to induce them to write precisely what God intended? This requires absolutely no leap of faith at all! Moreover, on a number of occasions I have personally experienced God inspiring the words of my own writing. I am distinctly aware of it when it happens, because the writing becomes almost effortless for me and the result is always concise and contains insights of brilliance which I know for a fact I could not possibly have conjured up on my own power. Just because you may not have had this experience does not mean that it is outside the realm of human experience. It merely means that you were not as richly blessed as some others were. We all have different gifts and different blessings from almighty God. Yet we can all indirectly receive God's blessings from His having inspired the writings of the authors of the Bible so that we might come to have a glimpse of the thoughts and ways of God, which are so far above the thoughts and ways of man that we struggle to understand the brilliance, sovereignty and majesty of God.

The Entire Bible Needs to be Viewed as the Gradual Unfolding of God's Perfect Plan for Mankind

Every passage in the Bible can be viewed as teaching the redemption story of God for His people: His born again elect whose names are written in the Lamb's book of life since before the world began. God predestinated some of us to become His adopted sons and daughters and He predestinated others to be used for ignoble purposes to bring pain, suffering and affliction upon God's people to grow us up, mature us, and transform us into the likeness of His son Yahushua (Jesus). Many events in the Old Testament or pre-Messianic Scriptures foreshadow a more perfect unfolding of God's plans and ways which appear in the New Testament writings. If one understands how Scripture holds together in such a tight and beautiful tapestry of foreshadowings, one cannot help but stand in awe at the brilliance and majesty of almighty God. Even though we cannot see Him, the results of His creative genius are everywhere, if we have the eyes to see and ears to hear Him and delight in His obvious goodness and love for His elect.

The Old Testament Hebrew laws were given by God to mankind through Moses, not to turn us into legally obsessed nuts, but rather to prove to mankind, over the next 1,500 years, that we could not possibly obey all 613 laws on our own power and in our own strength. Then, with the first coming of Jesus and His propitious death on the cross, He paid the price we all deserved to pay for our sins and His righteousness was imputed or credited to us so that we might be saved and live in right relationship with Jesus and the Father throughout the rest of eternity. In so doing, God ushered in His new Messianic era, the era of grace. In both Old and New Testaments, God reveals to mankind what He intends to accomplish through mankind in minute detail hundreds, and often thousands, of years before He orchestrates all things to fulfill His prophecies with hair-splitting accuracy. He gives mankind more than full warning of what's coming every time before He reveals Himself in powerful and rather dramatic ways to mankind, and He repeats the patterns of history over and over again so that we are all without excuse as to what He is up to and what He expects of us. In light of this reality, anyone would be a fool not to cling to His every word, contained in the Bible. Yet few of us do. It's truly tragic. Yet the future need not repeat the patterns of the past; some of us can learn from the errors of our predecessors and make different and wiser choices that will not lead to our ultimate destruction. Those who study Biblical history, need not repeat it, if they diligently seek to know God by reading and studying and obeying His Word, the Bible.

The Kingdom of God is Rooted in Two things Above All Else: Truth and Love

The Bible, from beginning to end, teaches mankind two attributes of the essential nature of God, those being truth and love. These attributes of God are so central to comprehending Him and enjoying a personal and intimate relationship (unique to each one of us) with Him that I will be devoting the next chapter to these subjects and to explaining what they really are, and why they are so vitally important.

For now, I merely wish to assert that anyone who fails to exhibit the twin attributes of dedication to the truth at all costs, and a sacrificial love for his or her fellow man, is merely going through the motions of claiming to be a follower of Christ, and therefore a Christian, but who most assuredly is not. This assertion of mine ought to make 99% of Christendom seriously squirm in their seats, knowing that my truth claim here probably applies to them. If it does, here's what Yahushua (Jesus) told His followers to expect, as part of His Sermon on the Mount:

"Not every one that saith unto me, Lord, Lord (Adonai, Adonai), shall enter into the kingdom of heaven; **but he that doeth the will of my Father which is in heaven.** *Many will say to me in that day, Lord, Lord (Adonai, Adonai), but have we not prophesied in thy name? and in thy name have cast out devils? and in thy name done many wonderful works?* **And then I will profess unto them, I never knew you: depart from me, ye that work iniquity.** *"* Matthew 7:21-23 (bold face added for emphasis)

In the next chapter, we will explore what it means to know Jesus and to be known by Him. Regrettably, the verses here apply to the vast majority of those who profess to be Christians today, but in reality are self-deceived frauds, most of them trapped inside the walls of false organized religion.

5. The Centrality of Truth and Love in God's Kingdom

Jesus (Yahushua) told Pilate in John 18:37:

> "... To this end was I born, and for this cause came I into the world, that I should bear witness unto the **truth**. Every one that is of the **truth** heareth my voice." (emphasis added)

Yahushua tells is in John 14:6:

> "... I am the way, the **truth**, and the life: no man cometh unto the Father, but by me."

In short, God is the source of all truth and truth is reality, as perceived by God. This distinction is critical because, as I shall show throughout the remainder of this book, almost everything we all have been told or taught is a hideous lie. If we place our trust in those lies, and believe them to be true, we often end up making some hideous choices and decisions which end up harming us, and we remain clueless about the source of our problems and the pain our own actions have brought upon us. As a result, we keep making decisions which harm us over and over again. This amounts to a form of insanity: living in denial of objective reality and doing the same things over and over again, expecting a different outcome.

One of the frauds perpetrated upon modern day American society is the bankrupt philosophy of moral relativism, which posits that there are no absolute moral truths: that what is your truth does not necessarily pertain to me and vice versa. But can this absurd notion really be true? No, it can't. No one can really live this way and here's why: if someone tells me that my moral truths may be my truth, but not theirs, try stealing their stereo and see what happens. Anger and outrage will be the inevitable result, because we all know instinctively that stealing is wrong.

Furthermore, if there are no moral absolutes, then is the statement "there are no moral absolutes," not a violation of that very assertion or truth claim? It most certainly is. As such, the truth claim of moral relativism falls flat on its face: it commits suicide and is self-refuting by virtue of being contradictory of its very claim. As such, it has to be false! Nevertheless, millions of Americans, most of them young people who have been deliberately indoctrinated and dumbed-down by a corrupt and deceitful public education system over the past 40 years, attempt to live this way and then wonder why their entire lives, especially their relationships with other people, are in shambles and not working. It is because they are living incoherent lives disconnected from objective, universal, moral truth and from reality as God perceives it. Their own distorted perceptions of reality are not relevant, as soon as they have to start interacting effectively with those around them.

Jesus, the son of God, and God incarnate, claims that He is the only way to salvation, heaven and a right relationship with God the Father. Jesus and the Bible, in numerous passages, makes it quite clear that those who routinely lie are not of God, but in fact serve the father of lies, and prince of this world, Satan. Proverbs 6:16-19 reveals the very things God hates the most:

> "These six things doth the LORD (YHWH) hate: yea seven are an abomination to him: A proud look, **a lying tongue**, and hands that shed innocent blood, An heart that deviseth wicked imaginations, feet that be swift in running to mischief, **A false witness that speaketh lies**, and he that soweth discord among brethren." (emphasis added)

In Revelation 21:8, God reveals the qualities of those who will end up in the burning lake of fire, the ultimate destination of those who end up condemned to hell by God by virtue of their failing to place their trust in Him and His son, Jesus Christ:

> "But the fearful, and unbelieving, and the abominable, and murderers, and whoremongers, and sorcerers, and idolaters,

and all liars, shall have their part in the lake which burneth with fire and brimstone: which is the second death."

In short, God hates lies and liars. There is no equivocation here. Yet how often do we hear false teachers in our world today teaching us that God loves everybody and has a wonderful plan for our lives? If you asked almost any group people in America today whether this was true or not, I am certain that over 90% would agree with this statement. And yet it is a bald-faced lie, which is seriously misleading most self-professed Christians into believing that they are saved and going to heaven when they die, when there is no Biblical basis to support such a belief and plenty of Biblical support to refute it! The implications of this conclusion are simply staggering! It implies that the majority of Americans who claim to be Christians today are delusional and deeply deceived. And the truth is, that they are, and time is running out to remedy this.

One common lie advanced by the enemies of God is that He changes, and thus lies. Yet the Bible clearly refutes this false teaching:

> *"For I am the LORD (YHWH),* **I change not;** *therefore ye sons of Jacob are not consumed."* Malachi 3:6

> **"God (El) is not a man, that he should lie;** *neither the son of man, that he should repent: hath he said, and shall he not do it? or hath he spoken, and shall he not make it good?"* Numbers 23:19

> *"That by two immutable things,* **in which it was impossible for God (Elohim) to lie . . .** *"* Hebrews 6:18

In contrast, God's Word, the Bible, distinguishes God (YHWH) from His greatest adversary, Satan, the father of lies, when Yahushua states:

> **"Ye are your father the devil,** *and the lusts of your father ye will do. He was a murderer from the beginning,* **and abode not in the truth, because there is no truth**

in him. **When he speaketh a lie,** *he speaketh of his own:* **for he is a liar, and the father of it.** "John 8:44

So, from a Scriptural point of view, objective truth is an essential attribute of God. In contrast, Satan, God's and man's greatest adversary, is a liar and a thief who comes to destroy all of mankind, if he can. The good news is that he can't. Christ has already defeated him on the cross of Calvary. All Satan can do now is lie and deceive and he remains an expert and cunning foe in that regard.

The second central attribute of God, Jesus and the kingdom of God is agape, or sacrificial, love. Agape love in Scripture "is a purposeful commitment to sacrificial action for another." It is not telling someone what they may want to hear that is not true, which is a common error and deceptive way the word "love" is applied in today's popular writing and conversation. Jesus defined the essence of real love to His disciples this way:

> *"Greater love hath no man than this, that a man lay down his life for his friends."* John 15:13

In the Greek language, phileo and eros love pertain to brotherly and erotic love, respectively, but when the Bible refers to love, it is most often referring to agape, or sacrificial, love which looks out for the long term best interests of another, ahead of one's own wants and comforts. The ultimate manifestation of such love is the love of Jesus when He suffered and died on the cross so that those of us who number among His elect, might believe on Him, surrender our lives and our wills to His lordship in all things, and be saved from the eternal condemnation of hell that all of mankind is born into and will, in the end, endure without the saving grace of Jesus' atoning sacrifice on the cross in our place for our sins, so that His righteousness might be imputed to us so that we might be reconciled into a right relationship with God the Father, and His son Jesus, for all eternity.

In personal relationships, especially intimate ones and friendships, it is impossible for them to function effectively without both the truth and agape love. In 2015, few relationships are genuine and grounded in either one of these two essential traits of God and of Jesus. This is the root cause of why America and our world are spinning out of control today: we have lost our way, having rejected the truth and love of God and a personal and loving relationship with Him and replaced them with a preoccupation with self and all its ugly accompaniments: selfishness, pride, greed, lust, hatred, anger, bitterness, jealousy, rage, abuse, disrespect, fraud, treachery and deceit. Truth and love have been sacrificed on the altar of short-sighted selfishness and personal gratification at the expense of genuine relationships: the only thing of any lasting meaning and value.

Throughout the rest of this book, I will be returning to this dual theme of truth and love as the defining marks of a true and authentic follower of Yahushua. By this standard from God's Word, the Bible, any honest person has to freely admit that well over 99% of those Americans who today profess themselves to be Christians fail miserably and seldom, if ever, exhibit to any material degree either one of these two defining attributes of Jesus and of God. As such, these individuals are quite likely facing a serious and shocking discovery when they find themselves confronted with Jesus' rebuke and dismissal, as He promises many in Matthew 7:21-23:

> *"Not every one that saith unto me, Lord, Lord (Adonai, Adonai), shall enter into the kingdom of heaven; but he that doeth the will of my Father which is in heaven. Many will say to me in that day, Lord, Lord (Adonai, Adonai), have we not prophesied in thy name? and in thy name have cast out devils? and in thy name done many wonderful works? And then will I profess unto them, **I never knew you: depart from me, ye that work iniquity.**"*

To know Jesus (Yahushua) is to love Him. To love Him is to obey His commandments. Which ones? Not just the fun ones, but rather all of them! Here's how Jesus himself put it:

> *"**If ye love me, keep my commandments.**"* John 14:15

> *"... **If a man love me, he will keep my words:** and my Father will love him, and we will come unto him, and make our abode with him. He that loveth me not keepth not my sayings: and the word which ye hear is not mine, but the Father's which sent me."* John 14:23-24

> *"**If ye keep my commandments, ye shall abide in my love**; even as I have kept my Father's commandments, and abide in his love."* John 15:10

> *"Greater love hath no man than this, that a man lay down his life for his friends. **Ye are my friends, if ye do whatsoever I command you.**"* John 15:13-14

> *"**These things I command you, that ye love one another.**"* John 15:17

In other words, to truly follow Jesus requires us to lay down our lives for Him, and surrender and submit our wills to His perfect will for our lives forever. This may seem like no big deal when things are going well for us, but Jesus makes it very clear that all true followers of His will experience many severe trials and afflictions by virtue of our choosing to serve and follow Him:

> *"Behold, I send you forth as sheep in the midst of wolves: be ye therefore wise as serpents, and as harmless as doves. But beware of men: for they will deliver you up to the councils, and they will scourge you in their synagogues; And ye shall be brought before governors and kings for my sake, for a testimony against them and the Gentiles. But when they deliver you up, take no thought how or what ye shall speak: for it shall be given you in that same hour what ye shall speak. For it is not ye that speak, but the Spirit of your Father which speaketh in you. And the brother shall deliver up the brother to death, and the father the child: and the children shall rise up against their parents, and cause them to be put to death. **And ye shall be hated of all men for my name's sake: but he that endureth to the end shall be saved.** But when they persecute you in this city, flee ye into another: for verily I say unto you, Ye shall not have gone over the cities of Israel, till the Son of man*

be come (meaning until Jesus returns in His second coming). The disciple is not above his master, nor the servant above his lord. It is enough for the disciple that he be as his master and the servant as his lord. If they have called the master of the house Beelzebub (the devil), how much more shall they call them of his household?" Matthew 10:16-25

"Whosoever therefore shall confess me before men, him will I confess also before my Father which is in heaven. But whosoever shall deny me before men, him will I also deny before my Father which is in heaven." Matthew 10:32-33

"Think not that I am come to send peace on earth (a common false teaching today): **I came not to send peace, but a sword. For I am come to set a man at variance against his father, and the daughter against her mother, and the daughter in law against her mother in law. And a man's own foes shall be they of his own household.**" Matthew 10:34-36

"He that loveth father or mother more than me is not worthy of me: and he that loveth son or daughter more than me is not worthy of me. **And he that taketh not his cross, and followeth after me, is not worthy of me.** *And he that findeth his life (living for himself) shall lose it: and he that loseth his life for my sake shall find it."* Matthew 10:37-39

"If the world hate you, ye know that it hated me before it hated you. *If ye were of the world, the world would love his own: but because ye are not of the world, but I have chosen you out of the world, therefore the world hateth you. Remember the word I said unto you,* **The servant is not greater than his lord. If they have persecuted me, they will also persecute you;** *if they have kept my saying, they will keep yours also. But all these things they will do unto you for my name's sake, because they know not him that sent me. If I had not come and spoken unto them, they had not had sin: but now they have no cloak for their sin. He that hateth me hateth my Father also. If I had not done among them the works which none other man did, they had not had sin: but now they have both seen and hated both me and my*

Father. But this cometh to pass, that the word might be fulfilled that is written in their law, **They hated me without a cause.** *"* John 15:18-25

Anyone reading these passages with any honesty and integrity about him or her ought to be stopped cold by them. Jesus is not promising His followers and true believers a life of prosperity, riches and ease. In fact, He is promising us quite the opposite! He is promising us a life of trials, tribulations, suffering, pain, affliction, mockery, scorn, ridicule, hatred, opposition, false accusations and persecution for being true to Jesus and teaching and modeling to others what Jesus teaches and models to us in the Bible. This teaching from Jesus is seldom taught in any form of organized and false religion today for obvious reasons: if it were taught accurately and faithfully in churches today, the pews and seats would empty and so too would the flow of money in the form of tithes, offerings and donations, and at its heart, organized and false religion is all about superficial measures of growth in attendance and giving, and not much else. As a result, the messages of all false teaching churches are inevitably watered down, diluted, corrupted and reduced to little more than "feel good" messages which leave its lazy and Biblically ignorant sheeople believing that they are Christians and thus are saved, when in fact it is highly unlikely that they are that at all! This is not at all truthful, and about as unloving as it gets: these churches know the truth and suppress and silence it to keep their members on the pathway to eternal torment and agony in hell, into which we are all born. But worse, these poor people are being misled, deceived and defrauded to believe that they are saved, setting them up for a very rude awakening on Judgment Day when Jesus tells them,

"... I never knew you: depart from me, ye that work iniquity. " Matthew 7:23

Where will those false teachers be on that day? Nowhere to be found. Yet the Bible teaches that the harshest punishments are reserved for such false teachers:

5. The Centrality of Truth and Love in God's Kingdom

*"But there were false prophets also among the people, even as there shall be false teachers among you, who privily shall bring in damnable heresies, even denying the Lord (Adon) that bought them, **and bring upon themselves swift destruction.**"* 2 Peter 2:1

God and Jesus seek a personal and intimate relationship with each one of God's elect. No genuine relationship between two persons is possible without the truth and sacrificial love, in which we put the best interests and needs of another ahead of our own. Given our carnal, sinful, depraved and selfish natures, none of us is capable of either of these two character traits unless and until God's Holy Spirit resides within us and we are born again in the Spirit and fully submit and surrender our lives and our wills to the will of Jesus as lord, king and master over every aspect of our lives. As such, no person is truly capable of genuine, loving relationships with others until he has first experienced the love of God in his own life. First, God reveals to us that He loves us. Second, we love Him back in gratitude for what He has first done for us and our love is evidenced by our loving obedience and submission to His son, Yahushua.

"We love him, because he first loved us." 1 John 4:19

Third, we learn to love ourselves as God loves us: in grace, mercy and responsibility to ourselves so that we no longer endure abuse and disrespect from others. Finally, God fills our hearts to overflowing with thankfulness and gratitude to Him, which spills over into our pouring our hearts into our compassionate love for others who are safe, good and healthy for us to love. In this sanctification process, which usually takes years, if not decades, we learn to love others as God loves us.

That perfect love from and for God drives out fear for anything other than a healthy fear, respect and reverence for God Himself.

*"Herein is our love made perfect, that we may have boldness in the day of judgment: because as he is, so are we in this world. **There is no fear (of hell) in love; but perfect love***

casteth out fear: because fear hath torment. He that feareth (hell) is not made perfect in love." 1 John 4:17-18

Moreover, the truth sets us free from the bondage and captivity of the lies of Satan and permits us to live our lives in freedom to become everything God designed us to be from before the world began: delighted in by God the Father and created by Him to do good works which He has predestinated for us to do since before the world began.

> *"Then said Jesus (Yahushua) to those Jews which believed on him, If ye continue in my word, then ye are my disciples indeed;* **And ye shall know the truth, and the truth shall make you free.** *They answered him, We be Abraham's seed, and were never in bondage to any man: how sayest thou, Ye shall be made free? Jesus (Yahushua) answered them, Verily, verily, I say unto you, Whosoever committeth sin is the servant of sin. And the servant abideth not in the house for ever: but the Son abideth ever.* **If the Son therefore shall make you free, ye shall be free indeed."** John 8:31-36

In short, until or unless the Spirit of Yahushua lives (abides) in us and we in Him, we are not yet fully alive and thus are incapable of discerning the truth and of truly loving others as God has designed those of us who are God's elect to love one another. In such a state, we remain dead in our transgressions (sins) and not yet fully alive and free to become all whom God (YHWH) designed us to be. Without truth and genuine love, we are completely screwed and remain hell-bound sinners, one and all.

92

6. The Reality of the Spirit Realm

Life is difficult for most of humanity, most of the time. Moreover, most of us go through life largely dazed, confused and in a fog, without real clarity on what life is really all about most of the time. The reason for this is quite intentional on God's part. Proverbs 25:2 explains,

> *"It is the glory of God (Elohim) to conceal a thing: but the honour of kings is to search out a matter."*

In other words, God intentionally conceals His truths from all of humanity, so that He might delight in revealing Himself and His truths to those of us who are blessed enough to number among His elect: His born again adopted sons and daughters with whom He seeks a personal, unique and intimate relationship, as a loving and noble father longs for with each of his children, in whom he delights.

So why does life seem to be so hard and filled with opposition and affliction most of the time? John Eldredge reveals the answer in his book, *Waking the Dead*. It is because underneath the surface of life, the world is, and always has been at war; a war between forces of good, led by YHWH (God), Yahushua (Jesus) and angelic spirits, who are opposed by the devil (a.k.a. Satan) and one third of the angels who were expelled from heaven with the head of the angelic host, Lucifer, who have been cast to earth and who function in the spirit realm as demon spirits today. Satan's goal is to thwart God's perfect plan for His elect, by keeping all of us deceived and enslaved to his endless lies, so that we might never find the path to the truth and to true, eternal life that is only found in submission and surrender to Jesus as lord over our entire lives.

93

The Bible teaches us that Satan was defeated once and for all when Jesus sacrificed His life on the cross out of His deep and abiding love for God's elect. Love and truth defeated the hatred and lies of the devil once and for all in that moment. But it did not put an end to Satan and his demon spirits. Instead, that event stripped Satan of his ability to prevail over God's elect, while permitting Satan to enslave and torment God's non-elect and use them to oppose and afflict God's elect to build our characters and our faith in Jesus. Since Jesus' death on the cross, the most potent weapon of Satan, also known as Lucifer, the father of lies, the prince of this world, Beelzebub, Lord of the Flies, Belial and Baal throughout the Bible, is the power of deceit and lies. Yet God promises in His Word to reveal Himself and the truth to those of us who diligently seek His face and seek to know intimately the true nature of God in all of His glory, brilliance, power, knowledge and wisdom.

In contrast to Satan's use of endless lies to deceive the vast majority of humanity who make up God's non-elect, God and Jesus teach God's people the truth through a faithful reading and study of God's Word, the Bible, and our obedience to it. The Bible claims to be the source of all truth, knowledge and wisdom for all of mankind. As a result, whoever is not one of God's people is without knowledge and wisdom and is seriously handicapped as a result. The truth is the most powerful weapon in the world; especially in the spiritual realm, where much of the spiritual war between the forces of good and evil is played out.

We live in the physical and material world which most of us can measure and perceive through the use of our five senses of sight, hearing, touch, smell and taste. The Bible teaches us that there is a spiritual realm or another dimension, which is more powerful than the material one, which most of us cannot directly see or otherwise prove out with our five physical senses. Yet it is no less real. Those of us who know what to look for, have developed an awareness of when we are being opposed and afflicted by spiritual forces we cannot see which manifest themselves in treachery, deceit and demonic attacks from others which are clearly directed at opposing and crushing us, if they can. In other words, strange and destructive behaviors from others allow us to deduce the operation of spirit beings in the spiritual realm, who are seeking to oppose us.

The Bible clearly reveals the reality of this spiritual battle to us in Ephesians 6:11-18:

> *"Put on the whole armour of God (Eloah), that ye may be able to stand against the wiles of the devil. For we wrestle not against flesh and blood, but against principalities, against powers, against the rulers of the darkness of this world, against spiritual wickedness in high places. Wherefore take unto you the whole armour of God (Eloah), that ye may be able to withstand in the evil day, and having done all, to stand. Stand therefore, having your loins girt about with truth, and having on the breastplate of righteousness; And your feet shod with the preparation of the gospel of peace; Above all, taking the shield of faith, wherewith ye shall be able to quench all the fiery darts of the wicked. And take the helmet of salvation, and the sword of the Spirit, which is the word of God (Eloah): Praying always with all prayer and supplication in the Spirit, and watching thereunto with all perseverance and supplication for all saints;"*

Until we fully comprehend this spiritual reality, which we cannot see, but whose effects we most certainly **can** see, most of life simply makes no sense. Once we begin to comprehend this spiritual reality, everything in life begins to make much more sense, although we may often be distressed by what we discover. Usually, we discover that most of life is made up of an endless array of lies, deceits and illusions which harm and oppose us and which keep us from finding true joy, love and peace which, if we are truly honest with ourselves, we would admit are all the things we all long for more than anything else in life. Such a goal is entirely attainable; but not on our own power alone, and it is seldom defined in terms which the world misleads us into thinking is the path to true happiness − which it never is.

Thus, 1) life is seldom what it first appears, 2) we are engaged in a spiritual war raging underneath the surface of life, and 3) most surprising of all, we all have a unique role to play in the epic story of humanity, which in reality, is God's story of the history of man. For God's elect, a major task of life is figuring out what this unique and heroic role is which God has predestinated for us, and then live it out fully, as God has designed for us in advance. I'll have much more to say concerning this seldom-taught Biblical truth later on.

The reality is that the devil, heaven, hell, angels and demon spirits are very real and play a far more influential role in our daily lives than most of us fully realize. Why is this so seldom understood? Because if you knew that you were being opposed by an enemy who sought to destroy you, you would be far more vigilant and able to defend yourself from his wicked schemes and treachery. As in all forms of warfare, misinformation, lies and deceit are employed by the enemy of mankind to keep us deceived and in a fog while he and his demon spirits wreak havoc in each of our lives and in those personal relationships that mean the very most to us in order to make us miserable. His most effective lie of all is that he and hell do not even exist. Nothing could be further from the truth!

To fully comprehend how Satan wages war against us, it is important to understand how God has designed His economy. God is, has been, and always will be, fully in control of His creation, including the actions of His created being, Satan. God allows Satan and his demon spirits to operate in the world today, but only under a tightly regulated set of rules proscribed by God. In particular, God does not permit Satan to afflict a person unless God has first authorized Satan to do so, and He will never permit Satan to afflict a person unless that person has provided legal grounds to be so afflicted. Legal grounds are certain types of sins which the person has committed, which Satan then uses to fly up to God and petition Him to permit Satan to afflict the sinner with his demon spirits, to permit him to take control over the sinner's life and hold him or her in bondage to their sins and the lies Satan uses to confuse them with. These demon spirits come in a variety of forms which produce distinctly different deviant and dysfunctional behaviors in their respective victims, which are almost always related to the particular life circumstances of each demon-infested person.

The types of sins which give Satan legal grounds to infest a sinner's body and life with demon spirits consist of three principle areas: 1) sexual immorality, 2) engagement in the occult, and 3) curses of inheritance, the first two of which are prohibited by God in His flawless words of the Bible. Since the 1960s, America has witnessed a sharp increase in all three of these pathways to demonic infestation, which has been quite intentional and has been orchestrated to bring about a complete collapse of American culture and society.

America in the 1960s witnessed the Vietnam War protests and with it a Baby Boom generation which experimented extensively with sex outside of marriage, use of hallucinogenic drugs and an affinity for rock and roll music. All three of these activities provide pathways for demon spirit infestation, and most assuredly had that effect upon the majority of those who chose to pursue the Hippie movement and its attendant lifestyle. As much as the majority of people in America today think it is no big deal to engage in sex outside of marriage, God, who never changes, defines all sex outside of marriage between one man and one woman for life as sin and contrary to His will. In Genesis 2:24 God explains,

> *"Therefore shall a man leave his father and his mother, and shall cleave (join) unto his wife:* **and they shall be one flesh.** *"*

When two people engage in sex with one another, and thus become one flesh under any circumstance other than in holy matrimony between them, it is sin which allows demon spirits from one partner to easily pass to the other. Thus, in highly promiscuous societies, as is quite common on the continent of Africa, the culture of those societies becomes heavily laden with and influenced by demon spirits and their confusing and destructive influences, as people interact with one another. America has increasingly become such a culture since the 1960s, for this same reason.

Hallucinogenic drugs are spiritually dangerous because they open up channels whereby a drug user may experience and communicate with the spiritual world directly, and in so doing, commune with the spirit world in the form of sorcery, witchcraft and divination, all of which are occult practices forbidden by the Bible. The only Spirit being with whom God approves our interacting is His Holy Spirit, which He chooses to put inside the hearts of all of His elect born again believers. Interactions with all other spirit beings are likely to be with demon spirits, which often results in the person who engages in such practices becoming infested or controlled by them.

Rock and roll music as a genre evolved from the occult and demonic music of the Louisiana Bayou, and serves as a form of occult ritual which lowers the inhibitions and ability of its listeners to avoid becoming influenced by the beat, intensity, music and dark lyrics of much of that music genre.

In the 1970s, forces aligned with the devil introduced the demonic ideas and philosophies of feminism, best captured in the motto of the National Organization of Women that "women need men about as much as fish need bicycles." Young women of the 1970s and beyond have been bombarded by the media and entertainment industries with messages appealing to a young woman's pride that she was somehow inferior to a man if she married him, stayed at home and raised her children and supported her husband in his role as the primary bread winner for the family, in spite of the fact that this has been God's design for mankind from the very beginning. Millions of American women bought into the lies and flatteries of the demonic notions of feminism and the result has been an explosion in promiscuity, marital infidelity, divorce, fatherlessness and single parent families, usually producing seriously wounded and often angry children, who act out their emotional and psychological wounds in our culture and society, to the harm of everyone.

Since the 1990s, sexual deviancies of homosexuality, lesbianism, bisexuality and transgenderism have been actively promoted as normal, natural and healthy by Jewish-led global elites through our public schools, media and entertainment industries. Every one of these forms of sexual immorality and perversion have resulted in demon infestation of those who engage in such behaviors with very powerful, angry and violent demon spirits that have wreaked havoc in those people's lives and in American society at large.

Since the 1980s, an endless array of eastern religions and New Age practices have been actively promoted to Americans as a path to healing and enlightenment, when in reality all such spiritual practices are rooted in the pagan religion of ancient Babylon from which they sprang. New Age teachings and practices in particular, are of the occult and seek to teach naive and gullible youth to connect and commune with spirit guides and practice transcendental meditation techniques which clear the mind and open them up to infestation by these spirit guides, which in reality, are nothing more than demon spirits invited into a person by incantations and other forms of sorcery, divination and witchcraft, forbidden by God in His Bible.

In spite of these dark and evil forces that have been at work in America since the 1960s, almost no one writes or talks about any of this openly. Why not? Because almost all Americans have been deeply deceived and brain washed to believe that the devil, demon spirits and hell do not even exist, and much of the blame for this must be laid at the feet of all forms of organized religion today. The sad truth is that all forms of organized religion are, and always have been, ruled by demonic forces intended to confuse and deceive people trapped in those fraudulent forms of religion. The Bible foretells of this happening in the last days right before the second coming of Yahushua (Jesus) will occur at 2 Thessalonians 2:3A:

> *"Let no man deceive you by any means: for that day (the second coming of Christ and of the gathering) shall not come, except there come a falling away first . . . "* (parenthetical added).

This "falling away" refers to all forms of organized religion teaching false doctrines and falling away from the true teachings of YHWH and Yahushua in the Bible. This prophecy has already been fulfilled and is operating now to deceive many naive, gullible and lazy people who choose to play fast and loose with what the Bible teaches, because in reality, they do not number among God's elect, but rather are God's spiritual goats – His non-elect, who are deceived into thinking that they are saved, when in fact they are not and on the last day, Matthew 7:21-23 will be fulfilled in their lives:

> *"Not every one that saith unto me, Lord, Lord (Adonai, Adonai), shall enter into the kingdom of heaven;* **but he that doeth the will of my Father which is in heaven.** *Many will say to me in that day, Lord, Lord (Adonai, Adonai), have we not prophesied in thy name? and in thy name have cast out devils? and in thy name done many wonderful works?* **And then I will profess unto them, I never knew you: depart from me, ye that work iniquity."**

To know Yahushua (Jesus) is to love Him. To love Him is to obey His commandments He tells us in John 14:15 and John 14:23-24:

> *"If ye love me, keep my commandments."* John 14:15

> *". . . If a man love me, he will keep my words: and my Father will love him, and we will come unto him and make our abode with him. He that loveth me not keepeth not my sayings: and the word which ye hear is not mine, but the Father's which sent me."* John 14:23-24

Which commandments must we obey? All of them, including the challenging and not so fun ones, such as those commanding true followers of Jesus to have nothing to do with evil and to expose wickedness whenever and wherever it appears, as in Ephesians 5:11:

> *"And have no fellowship with the unfruitful works of darkness, but rather reprove (expose and rebuke) them."*

In other words, genuine members of God's elect will evidence their born again status in Christ by obeying this commandment (and all other commandments) and speak out boldly against that which is evil all the time. Yet where have all forms of organized religion been since 1960 in the face of the wicked and sinful developments and deviancies which are now the norm in American society? The answer is obvious to anyone with any honesty and integrity: eerily silent and providing little, if any, real leadership to their flocks. In short, all forms of organized religion are frauds today and have evidenced their apostasy (falling away from the true faith of Jesus of the Bible) by their endless failures to boldly oppose evil in our culture when it appears. There are many reasons for this, which I will address more thoroughly in Chapter 11, but for now suffice it to say that the apostasy of all forms of organized religion today has actively suppressed and silenced the truths of the reality of the spirit realm and the very real spiritual dangers of engaging in activities leading to demon spirit infestation, possession and control, in particular, sexual immorality of all kinds and engaging in magic, spiritualism and the occult.

The implications of my conclusion here are profound. It means that the vast majority of Americans alive today are infested with one or more demon spirits which act to confuse and deceive their host bodies and lead those people to lie, deceive and betray others, thus creating a very hostile and dangerous world for those of us who number among God's chosen elect and born again adopted sons and daughters of YHWH. In light of the apostasy of all forms of organized religion, probably less than 1% of all Americans who claim to be Christians today really are. The corollary to this is that over 99% of all Americans professing to be Christians are likely to discover that they are subject to the prophecy of Jesus in Matthew 7:23 and will one day hear the words from Yahushua (Jesus),

"I never knew you: depart from me, ye that work iniquity."

Meanwhile, not one pastor in all of America will ever have the honesty to warn anyone in his flock that the evidence from their lives strongly indicates that they are not saved and will not end up in heaven with God and Jesus when they die. Instead, every last one of them will tell members of their churches what their itching ears want to hear, in fulfillment of end times Bible prophecy once again:

> *"This know also, that in the last days perilous times shall come. For men shall be lovers of their own selves, covetous, boasters, proud, blasphemers, disobedient to parents, unthankful, unholy, Without natural affection, trucebreakers, false accusers, incontinent, fierce, despisers of those that are good, Traitors, heady, highminded, lovers of pleasures more than lovers of God (Eloah); having a form of godliness, but denying the power thereof: from such turn away (have nothing to do with them). For of this sort are they which creep into houses, and lead captive silly women laden with sins, led away with divers lusts, Ever learning, and never able to come to a knowledge of the truth."* 2 Timothy 3:1-7 (parenthetical added for clarity)

> *"For the time will come when they will not endure sound doctrine (this time has now arrived); but after their own lusts shall they heap to themselves teachers, having itching ears; And they shall turn away their ears from the truth, and shall be turned unto fables."* 2 Timothy 4:3-4

The Apostle Paul, writing to the Thessalonians in his second epistle to them explains that in these end times, God will send (and thus now has already sent) a strong delusion on many, including the vast majority of people trapped inside the cults of all forms of false and organized religion, so that they will believe a lie (remember, all lies are from the father of lies, Satan himself), and so be condemned (to hell) for repeatedly rejecting the truth and for delighting in unrighteousness or wickedness, as God and His flawless and inspired words of the Bible define those terms. Thus, seeking to confirm these truths with anyone stuck inside organized religion of any form today will not result in any such confirmations. Instead, it will inevitably result in anger and hostility from such people, directed at anyone who would dare to prick their pride and suggest that they might be deceived and still on the pathway to hell that we are all born into as a result of our depraved and sinful natures.

6. The Reality of the Spirit Realm

So how can you, my readers, discern whether what I am teaching here, which is admittedly very controversial, is the truth, as God perceives it? My advice is very simple: In all things, go to the Bible, read it for yourselves and test everything I teach here against the standard for all truth: the flawless and inspired words of the Bible to God's elect.

7. My Story

For you, my readers, to understand the story of the end times that this book is aimed at telling, you need to understand my story which illustrates the many Biblical principles I have already unveiled in the preceding chapters. Remember, I have discovered who I am, and the calling that YHWH (God) has on my life, only recently. That calling is to serve as one of YHWH's true prophets and a modern day watchmen on the wall, blowing the trumpet and sounding the alarm of the coming storm foretold in the Book of Revelation.

The life stories of the prophets of the Old Testament, especially those of the prophets Jeremiah, Ezekiel and Hosea, are life stories fraught with pain, suffering, affliction and opposition, which were orchestrated by God to prepare those messengers from God by refining their characters with the fires of adversity and testing and building their trust (faith) in YHWH (God). This too is my story. I have changed the names of most of the people here in order to focus attention on the numerous bizarre and demon-inspired behaviors of people I encountered and to avoid revealing their true identities, but the facts I relay here are unaltered from what actually happened. My personal story reveals that something very odd is at work in our world today that only the Bible can adequately explain.

I was born in 1954 in Marin County, California. I was born a month prematurely to a mother who was an overly controlling, castrating barracuda who bitterly complained that I came out of the chute "willful." My father was fairly passive man, a World War II veteran who served as an officer on a submarine in the Pacific during the war, which he never spoke about. I am quite certain that his war experience left him emotionally wounded and scarred, and for much of his life, he medicated himself with alcohol to numb his emotional pain. Both my mother and father came from upper middle class east coast families. When my father was fifteen and a half, his mother, who was 18 years younger than his father, left her husband, and moved from Connecticut to the San Francisco Bay Area in Marin County. My father went to work as a messenger boy for the Bank of America in San Francisco, supporting himself, his mother, and his younger brother. So he never had a chance to fully grow up himself. My mother grew up in a very stiff and formal family that trained any humanity she might have had out of her. She was essentially raised with a silver spoon in her mouth and was ill-prepared to become a mother; especially a mother of a son who she deemed willful and therefore uncontrollable, when she herself had obsessive needs to try to control everything. My mother never emotionally bonded with me and I never bonded with her. Our relationship was always one of mutual antagonism and as far as I was concerned, the less I was around my mother, the better.

As a child, I grew up small and scrappy for my age, not taking crap from anyone, no matter how much bigger than me they were. I was also a voracious reader, and by around eight years old, I was reading every book I could get my hands on concerning America's founding fathers and heroes. I strongly identified with such men and resolved to follow in their footsteps and try to become like them: men of honesty, virtue, nobility, courage, leadership and vision. Today, I realize that those longings were ones God placed in my heart.

My younger brother Paul was born three and a half years after me and he quickly became the fair haired son, and I the black sheep of the family. As he grew older, at my parents' encouragement, Paul teased me rather unmercifully and in shame and anger over it, I lashed out at him on more than one occasion. I realize how hideously unfair and wicked it was of my parents to encourage such behaviors from my brother. But I also realize that I grew up in a dysfunctional household, as 95% of American households are today. In that toxic and dysfunctional family, I was assigned the role of "Indicated Patient," who becomes the family scapegoat and takes the brunt of the rest of the family's frustrations and hang-ups.

By the time I was about 12, I discovered a couple of notable things about myself. First, I had a hunger to learn and began to become interested in school. Second, I joined the Boy Scouts and almost immediately decided that I was going to become an Eagle Scout, which only about one out of every 50 Scouts ever achieves. I discovered that I had a tenacious drive to excel at whatever I put my mind to. Scouting was a way for me to get out and go camping and do things outdoors away from my parents, which made it all the more appealing. By age 15, I earned my Eagle Scout recognition and went on to lead the Boy Scout troop I was a member of. In my senior year of high school, I founded an Explorer Post devoted to rock climbing.

As a sophomore in high school, I ran for and was elected student body Treasurer in partnership with a friend of mine, Ralph Abernathy, and together we served in that capacity for the next year and a half. That early financial management experience was to shape some key career choices for me later on.

My family went through the motions of observing Christmas and Easter, but I never had any sense that either of my parents had any interest in things that were of a spiritual nature in the least. To get me out of the house on Sunday mornings, my parents sent me off to the local Episcopal Church near where we lived. But my parents and younger brother never had anything to do with church, God or the Bible, and so for me church was merely an obligation where grownups intoned the same boring prayers every Sunday, that had no real impact in their lives. As a teen, I was baptized and confirmed and served as an acolyte in the church until I was about 18, when I determined that church was little more than a social control mechanism that I did not want or welcome. In addition, my high school biology class convinced me that evolution explained how we got here, so the creation story seemed to me to be a nice fairy tale that had no relevance to my life. For the next 28 years, I became and lived my life as an agnostic: I didn't reject God, I simply didn't know if God existed or not, and didn't give it much thought, to tell the truth.

During my summers as a teenager, I went to summer camp to get away from my parents. The feelings were mutual, and I knew it. For three summers, starting when I was 16, I worked as a ranch hand on a couple of different cattle ranches, where I mucked out cattle barns, fed horses and beef cattle hay and silage, dug fence post holes, set fence posts and strung barbed wire fence, mowed, raked, bucked and stacked hay bales in barns, logged fence posts and concluded that living a life by my brains was much more desirable than wearing out my body on such manual labor. For this reason, and to escape being trapped inside my dysfunctional family system indefinitely, getting a good education was my path to financial independence from my parents.

I graduated from high school in 1972, as the Vietnam War was coming to a close, and went to college at the University of California, Davis, located about 70 miles away from where I grew up, majoring in economics and taking extensive course work in world history, political science, psychology and philosophy, seeking to get a broad liberal arts education. I worked hard in college, but had a good time socially, and made a number of close friendships. I graduated from U.C. Davis in economics with Highest Honors and Phi Beta Kappa, and Phi Kappa Phi academic honors distinctions in 1976.

I had initially been thinking about going on to law school, but after taking a couple of Legal Aid Society internships and seeing what lawyers actually did, I concluded that the court bureaucracy would bore me to tears. Moreover, I concluded that to earn a decent income as a lawyer, I would have to sell my soul to the devil and become an ambulance chaser. Alternatively, if I wished to defend the poor and the downtrodden as a Constitutional lawyer, as I dreamed, I would never be able to afford to raise a family and provide for them the sort of financial comforts I had enjoyed growing up. So I decided to take 2-3 years and try my hand at business and see if that was more to my liking, and if it was, to go on to business school at one of the top business schools in the country, since I had the academic accomplishments and abilities to get admitted to such a school.

I went to work for Arthur Andersen's Systems Consulting Division, which later became Accenture, out of their San Francisco office. On one assignment, I was sent out of town to Idaho Falls, Idaho for a client project for nine months and while there, I fell in love with the area and the Grand Tetons, Jackson Hole, Wyoming and Yellowstone Park. 34 years later, that place was to draw me back to where I now live with my new bride today. At the time, I was dating a woman, Barbara, who I married the following year (1979) right before we headed off to Boston, Massachusetts, for me to attend the Harvard Business School for the next two years. I graduated with an MBA degree from Harvard with second year honors and just having missed earning first year honors by one class, having competed with the best and the brightest at the top business school in the country and come out near the top. I was pleased with my performance and picked up a mastery of business strategy, finance and organizational behavior in my arsenal of academic disciplines that I was proficient in.

I returned to work for Arthur Andersen for four more years, where most of my work involved designing and implementing large, complex business information systems for major corporations and banks. From 1985 to 1988 I worked for a smaller, more entrepreneurial operations consulting firm, PRTM, which specialized in providing operations consulting and interim management services to rapidly growing high tech companies in the Silicon Valley. While there, I developed my skills and interests as a change agent, guiding companies through rapid and significant change initiatives and discovered that I was quite good at it. However, I frequently encountered clients who lacked the will and political courage to do what was required to bring about the changes needed for their companies to overcome their challenges and become more successful, and I thought I could do a better job of it than they were doing. In 1988, I left consulting and joined ABC Controls, Inc. in the San Francisco Bay Area as its CFO, to partner with their new CEO in turning it around and selling it on behalf of its private owner. Having never closed a set of books, or been through an audit or managed an accounting, treasury and IT operation, my first 15 months on the job were akin to my drinking water from a fire hose, as I learned how to master my new role as a Chief Financial Officer of a relatively small ($28 million in sales) manufacturing company.

My CEO and I successfully turned around and sold ABC Controls for our owner at an attractive price in 1990 and in 1991, I followed my mentor and former boss as his CFO and VP of Finance and Administration at XYZ Corporation. XYZ made semiconductor capital equipment, and was a busted management-led leveraged buyout in need of a turnaround, with the dream of taking it public in an IPO (Initial Public Offering) somewhere down the road. Frankly, when I joined, I assumed that the IPO was a pipe dream and little more than wishful thinking, because the company was in serious trouble with a dysfunctional management team and culture. Nevertheless, we successfully turned XYZ around and in 1996, my CEO and I took the company public in an IPO on the NASDAQ stock exchange. I remained with the company as its public company CFO for another 5 years to get my public company CFO ticket punched on my resume, before venturing forth to do it again with a bigger and more successful company later. The day XYZ went public, a day that was a highlight in my entire financial management career, I remember thinking to myself, "Now what? Is this it? Is this all there is?" It seemed rather empty and lacking in real meaning and purpose to me. I had achieved everything I had set out to do early in my career and had exceeded what I could have imagined then. Yet something was missing and I didn't know what.

My relationship with my parents was always a strained one and after we returned from business school in Boston and work in Chicago, several times out in public with my parents proved to be less than pleasant. Both my parents seemed to take twisted pleasure in belittling or dismissing me or anything I did, and so I chose to avoid spending any time with them. My father contracted recurrent lung cancer in 1991 and died in early 1992 and during his illness I only visited him once, which was very awkward and uncomfortable for me. We simply had no relationship with one another and my mother could not have been colder and more unwelcoming of my visit to see him. Within six months of my father's death, my mother was diagnosed with recurrent breast cancer. I went to visit her and told her that if the shoes had been reversed, I certainly would have hoped that she could bury the hatchet between us and offer me her love and support through a frightening time in my life and that I was there to offer that to her. Roughly seven months later, my daughter, and her only granddaughter, was born and we invited her to come over to our home to meet her new granddaughter. My mother had shown no interest in my two sons, but was thrilled with my daughter and for the next nine months or so, we had my mother over for dinner almost every Sunday for her to spend some time with us, and particularly with her granddaughter.

My mother died of her cancer in late 1993. Her final action was to disown me completely, in the process leaving her entire estate to my brother Paul. Her final message to me was unmistakable: she clearly wished I had never been born and she wished to harm me as much as she could. Her final action was clearly designed to inflict a brutal emotional blow upon me and I have to admit it hurt me deeply. The money was not the issue for me. But her action confirmed her endless actions of rejection which she had displayed to me all my life were part of a lifelong pattern of hers. It further revealed a dishonesty and woeful lack of integrity on her part, in coming over to my home and seemingly enjoying our kindness to her, only to discover that it was all a fraud and a scam on her part. My own mother's treachery and duplicity truly sickened and disgusted me.

Later, I learned from an aunt of mine that shortly before she died, my mother told my aunt that she found it hard to grasp how someone as angelic as my daughter, could have sprung from someone as evil as I was. I knew then, as I do now, that my mother's vile comment was completely unjustified and unwarranted, and merely served to confirm an earlier therapist's comment and observation to me that my own mother was a controlling, castrating barracuda. Those were strong words, but my mother's hateful final actions revealed them to be true. In reality, my mother proved herself to be the one who was evil in the end. Today, I believe the reason why my mother rejected me from the time I was born was because the demon spirits in her knew that there was something different and special in me that was part of who I was from the very beginning, that she could not control, and it drove her nuts that she could not do so; though she certainly tried!

In late 2000, I left XYZ and joined a troubled recruiting software company in Brisbane, California as its CFO and SVP of Finance and Administration, hoping to do for that company, what I had been able to do for XYZ, but hopefully with greater financial rewards in it for me, so that I might retire by the time I was in my mid-50s, if I chose to. The same week I joined my new company, an investment banker friend of mine, Mark Farthing, hosted me as his guest at a weekend men's retreat.

This retreat was something Mark invited me to, billing it as a fun weekend in which we would be listening to a few talks on the big questions of life such as, "why are we here?" and "what's the purpose of life?" using the Bible as our guide to see what it had to say on these topics. He assured me that there would be good food, good wine, recreation, good cigars and interesting people I might meet. I wasn't interested in the cigars, but everything else sounded appealing and so, as an agnostic, who had never contemplated these issues, and who had no idea that men got together and discussed these sorts of things, I agreed to give it a try, with no preconceived notions of what I might experience.

The first of the speakers at that weekend was Henry Jackson, who gave a talk in which he contended that he who controls the filters through which you view the world, controls your life.

I immediately became annoyed because I was convinced that no one controlled my life and I couldn't possibly see why I needed Jesus in my life to be right with God and I argued with him about it. The next guy to speak was a lawyer and federal magistrate from San Diego by the name of Ron McCormick, who explained that we all are judged for our performance throughout life, so what makes us believe we won't be judged by God at the end for the things we have done in this life? And he pointed us to 1 Corinthians 3:13-15:

> "Every man's work shall be made manifest: for the day shall declare it, because it shall be revealed by fire; and the fire shall try every man's work of what sort it is. If any man's work abide which he hath built thereupon, he shall receive a reward. If any man's work shall be burned, he shall suffer loss: but he himself shall shall be saved; yet so as by fire."

Hearing and reading that in a Bible someone had loaned to me, I became very concerned. While I had conducted my professional life with the utmost honesty, integrity and character, there was something in my personal life which was not so reputable that no one knew about.

The final speaker, Ron Giles, who was a business entrepreneur from Atlanta, Georgia, gave a talk in which he explained and pointed out to all of us that as men, we all experience a declining level of energy throughout our lifetimes, at the same time that most of us experience an ever-growing set of responsibilities as we age and that during the first half of our lives, we have more energy than we have responsibilities that usually allows us to overcome life's early challenges on our own power, but that in the second half of life, starting around age 40, our responsibilities begin to exceed our energy level and unless we have the supernatural power of Jesus in our lives in that second half of life, we are likely to find ourselves overwhelmed with problems we lack the ability to resolve on our own power. At the time I heard this talk, I was 46 years old and I knew instantly that I was in big trouble, because I could see the wisdom of Ron's words.

At the end of the weekend, I was very uncomfortable and didn't want to talk to anybody about it. I knew that many of the other men in that room had figured out some important lessons about how life really works, about which I was clueless. I hated that! I had always been near the top of every class in school, and now I felt as though I had nothing to offer and was downright stupid. I resolved that day to figure out what some of those other men had already discovered and, in the process learn what true wisdom looked like. That weekend began a journey that has profoundly transformed my life, in ways I could never have imagined fifteen years ago.

I subsequently joined Mark Farthing in a men's Bible study group being led by his friend Ted, who had orchestrated the men's weekend retreat I attended. The group met once every three weeks in Ted's home. That first year, Ted led a thematic Bible study in which he provided a list of topics we could choose from, and each man was asked to pick a topic, study the Bible to learn what it had to teach on that topic, and then share his discoveries with the other men in the group. I chose a topic that was gnawing at me: a man's responsibilities to his wife and kids. For roughly 12 years off and on, I had been having an inappropriate relationship with a woman friend who was also married, and while I knew that I was breaking the seventh commandment, "Thou shalt not commit adultery," I had compartmentalized my life and justified my sinful actions as acceptable in God's eyes, because my illicit relationship felt so affirming to me. So I began to search my Bible looking for the loophole or exception clause that would permit me to continue in my sin, and still be right with a God I was just beginning to become familiar with. I never found that loophole, and the more I searched for it and came up empty, the more convicted I became that I was guilty of sin and that I was leading a double-minded life. When I read what my responsibilities were to my wife and kids, as God commands of me in Ephesians 5:25-33 especially, I felt trapped and even more convicted than before.

In May 2001, the dot com bubble was bursting in the stock market. I had been with my new company for about seven months and had put together a turnaround plan, which included our trying to raise $25 million of additional outside capital from the venture capital community to buy us time to execute our turnaround plan. We had hired investment bankers to help us compile a private offering memorandum and prepare an investor road show, and had presented our investment story and opportunity to about 20 different venture capital firms and were waiting to receive expressions of interest back from each of them when I discovered that our sales pipeline had shrunk dramatically; so dramatically that at best, we were likely to only book 50% of the sales order dollars we had planned on for the quarter ending June 2001.

Raising investment capital is a very challenging undertaking under almost any set of circumstances. The goal of CEOs and CFOs of emerging growth companies who have not yet turned the corner to breaking even or generating positive cash flows is to create a large amount of interest in a company's investment prospects; so much so that there is more interest than there are shares available to buy and so generate a favorable price per share that will hopefully be higher than the price of the last round of funding, so that existing investors' interests are not diluted by the new round of investment. The goal of all investors is to pay as little as possible for an attractive investment opportunity and get as large of a percentage of the company's outstanding stock post money, and as many board seats as they can negotiate, because it's all about legal power to control the company's direction subsequently. Thus, fund raising becomes a high stakes poker game and many things can go wrong.

One thing that is often the kiss of death is that management puts forth a business plan and a set of financial projections and during the fund raising time period, materially falls short of that plan, which seriously undermines the credibility of existing management. When such a thing happens, prospective new investors have little or no interest in putting money into the company and are more than happy to wait things out and see

114

what develops as the company comes closer and closer to running out of cash to fund its operations. As this process continues, management has less and less leverage and is forced into considering very unfavorable terms for any new financing. This is precisely the set of conditions that I instantly knew we were facing with this very bad sales outlook.

When I brought these irrefutable facts to the attention of my CEO, he didn't want anything to do with the truth and wanted to keep telling our prior investment story. I felt morally obligated to inform our largest investors, who sat on our board, of my findings and conclusions, which I did, much to the annoyance and irritation of my CEO, and I discovered evidence that he was seeking to undermine and discredit me in the performance of my CFO duties. In response, I resigned from the company to avoid misrepresenting myself and potentially exposing myself to any claims of fraud.

I had never been unemployed before. My wife Barbara was not at all supportive of the actions I had taken. Moreover, I had foolishly been corresponding with the woman with whom I was having my inappropriate relationship via company email, and I had good reason to believe that my former CEO was keeping tabs on my email correspondence and was aware of my moral lapse and might very well use that information to blackmail me in some way and/or to blackball me from locating another CFO position in the San Francisco Bay Area ever again. My guilt over my affair and my well-founded fears over what rich and powerful investors might do to damage my future employment prospects led me to confess my affair to my wife Barbara. She took the news rather stoically and I promised her that I would put a permanent end to my illicit relationship, which I then did.

I called Ted, the leader of my men's Bible study, and told him that I had really screwed up my life and didn't know what to do. He suggested that I stay after our next study a day or so later and we could talk further about it. That evening, in Ted's home, I told him that I was out of answers, desperate and broken. He told me the only thing he could offer me was to ask me if I wanted to invite Jesus into my life. I told him, "yes," not fully understanding what I was signing up for, but knowing I was out of answers and at the end of myself. Ted led me in a prayer that night, in which I gave my life to Jesus.

Afterwards, Ted gave me perhaps the best piece of advice I have ever received. He urged me not to get involved with organized religion too soon, because they come in a variety of forms and flavors and could potentially do me more harm than good right away. He knew my mother-in-law was deep into a very liberal strain of the Methodist Church, and mentioned that one in particular, to be wary of. Instead, he urged me to pick up the Bible and read it, and question and challenge everything in it that did not make sense to me and ask other men further along in their spiritual walk, whom I respected and trusted, to explain to me what I didn't understand. I took Ted's advice to heart and for the next four years I never set foot inside any form of church or organized religion. I read my Bible, and participated in Ted's men's Bible study every three weeks and in his men's retreats once a year.

I wish I could tell you that from that point forward, my life prospered and was free from affliction, but quite the opposite occurred. God had in mind some major chastising, refining and disciplining to do to me over the next several years, spanning over a decade. Within a week of my accepting Jesus (Yahushua) into my life I became so depressed and paranoid that one morning at 6:00 a.m. I told Barbara I was going to go kill myself and ran out of my home and to the edge of San Francisco Bay where I realized I had no plan and didn't really want to kill myself. So I sat down by the water's edge, grabbed two stones the size of my fists, and began to scream and pound the sides of my head with the stones until the Marin County sheriff's deputies, whom Barbara had called, found me, slapped handcuffs on me, and threw me into the back of a patrol car and shut the door.

Sitting there, I began to have a premonition of hell that quite literally scared the hell out of me. I was gasping for breath as I felt my whole body burning in flames, I lost my vision, my heart was racing and I knew that I was in hell and for the first time in my life, it dawned on me what eternity in hell was all about: no rest — ever. Death was not an option to make the pain and the terror stop and it was without end, 24 hours a day forever. I cannot tell you the horror and the despair I felt at that moment. I have never experienced anything half as horrible or terrifying in my entire life! Today, having had this hideous premonition, out of love for my fellow man, I would do almost anything to spare just one soul from this hideous destination that most of mankind is heading toward.

The sheriff deputies transferred me from the patrol car to an ambulance and I remember being hauled out of the ambulance and strapped to a four post canvas platform, getting a shot and then a sheriff deputy began to interview me. I woke up 13 hours later in the mental health outpatient facility of the local hospital. They called Barbara and she came over to the hospital and explained to me what had happened, that they had checked me out for a concussion, and that I was OK, but they wanted to confine me in a mental health ward for a week or more. The psychiatrist assigned to my care was downright creepy and I didn't trust him one bit. I vigorously resisted all medications or other treatments they wanted to subject me to, since I made my living using my mind and wasn't about to let people mess with it.

Barbara and my brother and his wife came to visit me every night and bring me some food from outside the hospital. While there, all I wanted to do was read the Bible. I was largely clueless where to begin, so I just opened the Bible and started reading it. I later learned that my Methodist mother-in-law, when learning that I had found Jesus said, "Praise God!" and yet in the next breath remarked, "Oh, my God, he's a fundamentalist!," meaning that I actually believed what the Bible said, thus making me one step removed from a backward Neanderthal, in her eyes.

As I read the Bible in the hospital, I was confused and suffering a great deal over my guilt over my affair. At one point, I must have read the Book of Revelation, because I concluded from my reading that I must be the Antichrist. I know how absurd this sounds now, but I was dead earnest then, and it scared Barbara and my brother Paul a great deal. It was only later that I fell upon the teachings of Psalm 103, which brought me immense relief:

> *"The LORD (YHWH) is merciful and gracious, slow to anger, and plenteous in mercy. He will not always chide: neither will he keep his anger for ever. He hath not dealt with us after our sins; nor rewarded us according to our iniquities. For as heaven is high above the earth, so great is his mercy toward them that fear him.* **As far as the east is from the west, so far hath he removed our transgressions from us.** *"* Psalm 103:8-12

I was dumbfounded by my good fortune! My wife Barbara exhibited no sign of forgiveness toward me, but the God of the universe had, and that was good enough for me!

My time spent in the mental health ward of the hospital was not at all pleasant. No one was friendly and I felt very out of place and sensed that I could not trust anyone. I sensed I was not at all safe. After about seven days, I was released from the mental health care ward and entered into a partial care program for 4-6 hours a day affiliated with the hospital for 4 months or so. It was completely worthless.

After that, I spent a number of months at home during which I played endless hours of my sons' video games, as a way of gaining some sense of accomplishment as I got better at them. I experienced little interaction with or care from Barbara or my kids. It was a lonely and miserable time. Twice, I connected the hose of my shop vacuum to the tail pipe of my car, fed it into the open window of my car, stuffed the remaining hole with towels and turned on the car in the closed garage and got into my car hoping to asphyxiate myself and end my life. Both times, I couldn't go through with it, but when I later admitted it to my brother and psychiatrist, they insisted that I commit myself to a second mental health care facility.

7. My Story

This second facility was in Vallejo where the doctor assigned to me, Jim Locklear, was a Seventh Day Adventist who was the first person in roughly nine months who didn't completely dismiss my newfound interest in the Bible. Moreover, he was kind to me. And so I began to put my trust in him. He and one other health care professional recommended that I undergo ECT or electro-convulsive therapy, commonly known as shock treatments. I was afraid, but felt that nothing else offered any real promise of my getting over my severe depression, and so I was moved to another facility where Jim had access to the required treatments and I underwent eight ECT treatments under his care. I don't remember much about that period of time because ECT muddles a person's short-term memory while he is going through treatments, but the good news is that they worked.

I returned home and recovered my strength and my memory and by the fall of 2002, I was eager to try my hand at returning to work, beginning with some volunteer work for a non-profit doing financial modeling and consulting work for them. By the end of 2002, it was clear to many that the CEO of the non-profit needed some significant coaching on how to perform his job effectively and I proposed that I provide full-time CEO coaching services to him, while serving as a consultant to his organization, which was struggling. I began doing so in early 2003, and was performing at the same peak level of performance as I had been prior to my resigning from my prior company a year and a half earlier. That alone was a miracle. Meanwhile, my troubled relationship with my wife Barbara did not improve.

Three months into my CEO coaching role, the board of the non-profit organization asked me to assume my client's position as CEO to help them get to the bottom of some serious financial irregularities, which proved out to be far more serious than had been previously understood by the board and in June of 2003, I had the unpleasant task of informing the 50 or so employees that we were closing the non-profit's doors and putting the company in an assignment for benefit of creditors, in what amounted to the equivalent of a bankruptcy proceeding, and I was out of a job once again.

By August of 2003, I had located new work as an interim executive trying to save a struggling software company in the SF Bay Area on behalf of its owners: a Jewish husband and wife team who proved to be seriously abusive and morally deviant individuals who, in the end, took advantage of my good intentions and willingness to help bridge them to a new round of financing I was trying to help them secure. I was driven out of the company after committing more money than I should have to try to save it, losing all I had put into the company on my behalf and on behalf of my family in the process. It was a maddening, humiliating and embarrassing experience, but one God orchestrated to begin exposing me to true evil.

I went to discuss what happened with Ted, the man who had first led me to Christ, and rather than listen to me tell my recent story, he merely asked me how things were going on at home. This exasperated and angered me. I was doing all I knew how to do to provide for my family and Barbara was not supportive of my efforts, nor at all encouraging, and yet, Ted implied I was failing at home in some way, without offering me any useful diagnosis of what might be wrong or where I was falling short. All he offered me was the question, "You've gone in the ring and gotten bloodied a couple of times, care to go for another round?" His comment was not kind or helpful and it hurt and stung me greatly. What was I missing? What was I not getting or doing wrong? It seemed to me that everywhere I went, I was facing opposition. It felt that way, because I was, but I didn't understand why or where it was coming from at the time.

About that same time, an acquaintance of mine learned that I had been reading the Bible for the past four years and not attending any church, and he asked me if I thought it might be time to give church a try. His question seemed reasonable to me and so the next Sunday I went to his church to see what it was all about. My acquaintance saw me enter and wouldn't permit me to hide in the back corner and watch from a removed location. Instead, he invited me to join him and his wife right in the middle of the church building and introduced me to a number of couples around us. It felt welcoming. I didn't realize it then, but I was in desperate need of some new friends who might share my Biblical faith that was still fairly new to me. But I knew what the Bible said and taught and I was committed to finding a church which taught what the Bible teaches in its entirety. This church thing was entirely new to me, so I invited the new pastor out to lunch and introduced myself and sought to get to know him better. By the end of our lunch, I was asking him how I might connect more with his church community than just showing up for Sunday services. Shortly thereafter, he introduced me to a couple who led a weekly Bible study in their home, which I began to attend. I also learned of a men's support group that met once a week at the church and started to attend that too, and pretty soon, I knew just about everybody in that church and almost everybody began to know me as well.

After about a year, a buddy with whom I had become friends through the men's support group, sent me an email directing me to a website he thought I needed to see, although he feared it might not offer me much help. By this time I knew Vince's story and he knew mine, and in my story, he recognized a set of behaviors I was describing of what was going on in my home with Barbara that was eerily reminiscent of Vince's continuing struggles with his ex-wife, who was seriously character disordered. The website provided a profile of a sociopath. As I read the profile, my jaw dropped to the floor. My wife Barbara routinely exhibited 95% of the behavioral traits described in that profile. The contents of that website appear as Appendix A. As I studied what it said, I came to realize that the woman I thought I had married and been married to for 25 years, was not at all the person I mistakenly thought she was. I was familiar with the term sociopath and its near-synonym, psychopath, but really had never studied what they amounted to. I had no reason to before. Now I did.

Sociopaths and psychopaths have no conscience. That results in their experiencing no genuine feelings of regret or remorse for hurting others. They seek out victims to enslave in a psychological and emotional web of lies and treachery that leaves their victims dazed and confused about what's happening to them, and there are few genuine resources of help available to the victims of sociopaths and psychopaths. Such character-disordered personalities are almost always pathological liars who accuse their victims and those seeking to expose them for the very moral and often legal crimes they are most guilty of having committed. Such people are incapable of assuming accountability for their own actions that are harmful to others, and they endlessly scapegoat others to avoid detection and responsibility for their actions. Worst of all, the profile revealed that this disorder is not treatable by conventional medication or talk therapy, because the subjects themselves do not accept that they are ill, nor do they wish to change.

As I read the profile and thought about what I then knew about spiritual matters, I realized that the condition is not treatable because it is a spiritual disease and not a physical one. I have never heard of any sociopath or psychopath being cured of their condition. Today, I am not convinced that it is even possible: in short, once a psychopath, always a psychopath, because there is no cure and God has no intention of redeeming them.

As a result of my friend Vince revealing this information to me, our men's support group was shut down and much later I learned that the lead pastor had directed Vince to have nothing further to do with me and that the pastor and three to four other men in the church were "managing" my situation. I was highly annoyed that anyone, pastor or otherwise, would have the audacity to suppress and keep the truth from me, especially anyone in a Christian church setting, but I chose to overlook the offense and move on with my life.

Meanwhile, I was openly telling my story, including my affair and bouts with depression and ECT, with a number of people in my church and at my pastor's referral, was investing in spiritual direction with a pastor at another church who was trained in that discipline. At first, I wasn't sure why I was there, but merely trusted my pastor's judgment that I could benefit from it. The first hour long talk session concluded with Joann urging me to get and read John Eldredge's book, *Waking the Dead*. I have talked about this book previously. It changed my whole outlook on life. Eldredge's main points in his book were that 1) life is difficult, 2) underneath the surface of life is a battle raging for our hearts between forces of good and evil, and 3) that, at least for God's elect, God has designed a unique and heroic role to play in the epic story of life, known as His story (history). Eldredge contends that a big part of our life is about figuring out what this unique and heroic role is that God has designed for each of us, and then living out that role fully in a spirit of adventure.

In his book, Eldredge writes, "The story of your life is the long and brutal assault on your heart by the one who knows what you could be and fears it." The "one" he was referring to was the devil, and I was awestruck by his observation. He was describing my entire life! All my life I had experienced opposition and affliction and now I understood why for the very first time! As troubling as that might have been for me, it was quite liberating. I hadn't just been imagining things. Someone I could not see hated me and was opposing me because of my good and noble heart. Now it all began to make perfect sense! At the time, I had no clue what my unique and heroic role in God's epic story was to be, but I knew it was true and I was determined to discover it and live it out fully. I have since done just that. Today, I have discovered it, and I am living it out fully each and every day and being blessed by it.

The second book Joann directed me to was equally impactful upon my thinking. It was David G. Bonner's book, *Surrender to Love*. In it, the author claims that in contrast to how most of us believe God must feel about us every time He thinks about us, God takes delight in each one of those of us who number among His adopted sons and daughters, every time He thinks about us. Given my past sin, this was quite a mind-bending concept to encounter and embrace as my own. It was a liberating teaching in light of the fact that every time I went home I was encountering a sociopathic wife who was demeaning, disrespecting and belittling me and reminding me repeatedly of my past marital infidelity for which I knew God had already forgiven me and for which she had not, because it suited her to use as a way to entrap me in feelings of anger and guilt. I have since given copies of this book to others who I have discovered struggle with the concept of a benevolent God who loves and accepts us in our imperfections which He already knows all about, and loves us anyway! It has similarly blessed them, as it has blessed me.

In early 2006, a close friend's father who was an effective coach and mentor to his son, and with whom I had been fortunate enough to spend some time when my friend and I were college roommates at U.C. Davis, died and I found myself much more grief-stricken by Peter's death than by the death of my own father fifteen years earlier. As I thought about it, I realized that it was because Peter had served more as a coach and older mentor even to me, than my own father had, and that Peter had figured out how to be an effective and strategic father that I remained clueless about. At the time, I had two young teenage sons at home and realized that if I didn't get myself educated and equipped to raise my sons into becoming well-adjusted young men who would become difference-makers in their generation, I was on a path to repeat the errors of my own father. I resolved not to let that happen. So I began a search for all that has been written on fathers effectively and purposefully fathering sons into manhood.

Within two weeks of launching my search, I was commuting to work one morning and heard a guy being interviewed on a Christian radio talk show about his book, *Raising a Modern Day Knight*, and as I listened, the author, Robert Lewis, discussed how manhood in America was in a tailspin and that men today have no clue what it means to be a man. Everything he was talking about resonated with me at a primal level. This guy had insights that were precisely in line with what I was looking for and what I had experienced in my own life. I called the radio station and ordered the book and a CD containing the week-long set of interviews with Robert Lewis promoting the ideas in his book and listened to it over and over when it arrived. The book gave me a number of insights and ideas on what I could do to help guide and steer my two sons toward a healthy vision of authentic manhood, which I knew to be seriously lacking in Marin County and the church community that I was a part of at the time.

I asked a friend of mine, Tom Jacobs, to read the book and see what he thought. He was equally impressed with it and so we resolved to approach the men who led our church's men's ministry group to impart our vision to offer this fathering of sons material to the teenage boys of the church, which was very clear to me was desperately needed. The response we received from those men was mixed and less than enthusiastic. They simply didn't get it. As I drove home from our evening meeting that night, it dawned on me that they didn't get it, because you cannot teach what you don't possess. We men couldn't teach teenage boys what it means to be an authentic, godly man of integrity and character, until we invested time in educating and equipping ourselves with such insights and knowledge. I remembered Robert talking in his CD interviews about a set of teaching materials that he had developed and offered to the men in his church in Little Rock, Arkansas, which he called Men's Fraternity. So as soon as I got home I went on the internet and found Robert's Men's Fraternity website, viewed a video clip of Robert presenting Men's Fraternity materials and immediately ordered the first year course entitled, *The Quest for Authentic Manhood*, composed of 24 weekly presentations on issues related to healthy manhood.

When the DVDs arrived, Tom Jacobs came over to my house and we watched 2 or 3 DVDs together and they had the same impact on both of us: they grabbed us by the throat and heart as something desperately needed by every man we knew, which offered the potential to heal men, their wives and families in a county that has an 80% rate of divorce and in which many other marriages were in shambles and headed for serious problems in the future, my own one included. Tom and I went back to the leaders of our church's men's ministry and proposed that Tom and I host or facilitate a pilot offering in the fall of 2006 to see what sort of response and reception the materials might generate from the men of our church community. One of the leaders was somewhat dismissive of the concept, wondering aloud what any hick from Arkansas might have to offer to "sophisticated" Marin County. I was a bit appalled by this man's arrogance in a church setting, but held my tongue and said nothing. The men agreed that if we could garner the support of our three pastors, that they would support our pilot idea.

Tom and I scheduled meetings with all three pastors shortly after that meeting and each one agreed to go along with our idea, but protested that they had so much on their plates already, that they couldn't invest much time in it themselves. I wondered to myself: if a healthy church requires healthy men, as I knew it did, why on earth was this not one of their top priorities?!? In fact, why was the health of marriages and families in their church not their #1 priority? Much later, I was to discover the answer; but at the time, it completely baffled me.

As the launch date approached, Tom and I told ourselves that it might just be the two of us watching another DVD each week for 24 weeks. We concluded that if a dozen men showed up and stuck with it for the full 24 weeks that would amount to success. Three dozen men ended up participating in our pilot program and the next year we re-offered it and roughly 50 men participated in it, after hearing from the first group of men how helpful the teaching material and experiences processing this information out with other men was. I personally learned a ton about the issues pertaining to how to effectively engage with one's wife, and made many new friendships with other men who were learning the same things as I was. In later years, we offered the second and then the third years of Men's Fraternity, which greatly expanded our repertoire of understanding of how to live lives of purpose and meaning that brings satisfaction to any man who dedicates himself to living out the Biblical principles Robert Lewis taught there. I reached out to other churches in Marin County to expose them to the availability of these valuable materials and another four churches picked up on our lead and offered Men's Fraternity to their communities of men, reaching a total of roughly 150 men throughout Marin County. Yet there was a problem.

At one point in the first year of Men's Fraternity, Robert Lewis properly teaches that the Bible teaches that God has designed distinctly different roles for men and women in marriage and in society and He led us to those Bible verses which teach about the importance of men understanding the psychological and emotional needs differences between men and women and learning how to meet the core needs of our wives so that they might thrive and become all whom God has designed them to be. Similarly, but in more subtle form, Robert revealed that men have core emotional needs which also must be met by their wives for their marriages to thrive and for men to become all whom God has designed them to be. When this teaching first surfaced, Josh Hambro, the associate pastor who was keeping an eye on our men's ministry, almost put a halt to any further presentations of Men's Fraternity materials. Only because I had viewed all coming DVDs before we began and knew what was coming, was I able to assure Josh that there was nothing in the materials that were coming that he would find objectionable. I went so far as to acquire a second set of DVDs for Josh that he could view on his own, to satisfy himself that there was nothing objectionable in the materials to come, and he relented. Yet in our reoffering of the first year materials the next year, Josh interrupted the process once again and revealed to all of us his grave concerns about what were obviously teachings consistent with what the Bible teaches, and he informed us that when it came to encouraging women to assume positions of leadership in his church, that his paycheck was conditioned upon his supporting that agenda of his denomination.

I walked away from Josh's interruption quite dumb-founded. That church professed to teach that which the Bible teaches, yet here was a clear example of that not being the case in the least! Moreover, I was waking up to the reality that my own marriage was in shambles because my wife was unable and unwilling to respect and support me as her husband and head of our household. Her secret agenda was becoming clearer to me: her goal was to wrest power and control from me at every turn and to undermine me every chance she got in the proper raising and disciplining of our three children. Yet here was a church that represented itself as teaching faithfully what the Bible teaches, but was in fact acting in ways that suppressed and silenced important truths and teachings from the Bible which conflicted with the church's adoption of the feminist agenda that my wife and mother-in-law clearly embraced. One of my younger friends from Men's Fraternity did some surfing on the net and uncovered a couple of doctrinal position papers on the denomination's website which clearly revealed a dishonest and aggressively hostile attitude toward the teachings of Ephesians 5:22-24 which states:

> *"Wives, submit yourselves unto your own husbands, as unto the Lord (our Adon). For the husband is the head of the wife, even as Christ (the Messiah) is the head of the church: and he is the saviour of the body. Therefore as the the church is subject unto Christ (the Messiah), so let the wives be to their own husbands in every thing."*

This arrogant pastor, who clearly prided himself as having a PhD in theology, was aggressively dismissing the authority of these three verses, claiming, that these were three of the most abused verses in all the Bible! First, he provided no evidence to support such a ridiculous and ludicrous claim and second, even if that were true, it in no way negates the truthfulness of these verses as reflecting God's will for mankind. It was clear to me that radical feminism had infiltrated and corrupted the entire denomination and was resulting in the distorted, deceitful and harmful teaching that I was seeing evidence of in my local church, which was harming marriages and families in the church and in the local community. Especially given the dysfunctionality that was resulting in my being emotionally and psychologically abused in my own home by my wife and children by this sort of foolish and wicked thinking, I was going to be damned if I would tolerate such overt dishonesty from the church I was attending, without bringing challenge and correction to it, as the Bible clearly teaches that I am to do, in many places.

I sought a meeting with the associate pastor Josh, to discuss these disturbing matters with him directly. He was highly guarded, which raised my suspicions, so I sent him an email laying out my questions in advance of our meeting, as a courtesy to him, and to be completely above-board. Instead of having the decency and integrity to meet with me openly, Josh forwarded my email and list of questions to the lead pastor, who sent me a very strong email directing me to schedule an appointment with him through the church secretary. I was annoyed and irritated at his obvious attempts to manipulate and control me, and for several weeks I ignored his request, but finally decided to meet with him. When I did, he expressed outrage at my daring to question his authority with his superiors (something I had indeed done) and then proceeded to subject me to an abusive tirade in his office in which he told me that I didn't know anything and that I needed to sit down, shut up and learn from others more informed than I was. What he was also conveying to me, in no uncertain terms, was that he and the rest of the church leadership would never permit me to host or facilitate any further Men's Fraternity offerings at his church, thereby marginalizing me and reducing me to the status of a permanent second class citizen in his church. I knew instantly that I had to resign from and leave his church. I would not tolerate such untruthful, unloving, manipulative and controlling power plays being pulled on me by anyone. The fact that a senior pastor of any church would have the brazen audacity to pull such a Nazi Gestapo-like intimidation routine on me made a complete mockery out of the gospel of Jesus. Where was the truth? Where was there any love in his brazen behavior toward me? They were nowhere to be found.

So I began to attend another church, near my home where several other men I knew attended and which was one of the other four churches which offered Men's Fraternity in our county, which I knew I might be able to tap into. By the late summer of 2009, I left the first church and joined the second one which initially, welcomed me with open arms and invited me to serve as one of their hosts and facilitators for their Men's Fraternity offerings.

During the year 2009-10, the Men's Fraternity offering went without a hitch and blessed a number of men who chose to participate in it at that church and I settled into becoming quite at home and comfortable in that church community. One of the church elders began to host a men's gathering at the church once a week in the evening, which was targeted at community outreach to men who were troubled and were casualties of life that needed some serious help, but many of which possessed addictive or character-disordered personalities not really amenable to effective help. The leader of the group had no clue that what he was doing which, while perhaps well-intentioned, was ill-considered and likely to lead to more harm than good over the long run, and was destined to generate lots of frustration among men seeking to offer help to others, who were clueless how to do it under well-defined conditions that had a chance of making a difference in the lives of down and out men of various ages.

In the fall of 2010, several of these seriously disordered men showed up at an evening offering of Men's Fraternity which I was facilitating or hosting. Three of these men were so rude and/or disruptive to our group discussions in which we were processing out what we had just viewed from the DVD presentations by Robert Lewis from Men's Fraternity, that I felt I needed to take each one of these three aside individually to see if I could build a friendship with each of them and provide some one-on-one coaching and mentoring that they clearly needed.

The first man, Russell, was the husband of a woman who had just been elected a deaconess of the church. The Bible is crystal clear that all bishops and deacons of any church must be men, and never women. Here's what the Bible has to say on the qualifications of a deacon:

> *"Likewise must the deacons be grave, not doubletongued, not given to much wine, not greedy of filthy lucre; Holding the mystery of the faith in a pure conscience. And let these also first be proved; then let them use the office of a deacon, being found blameless.* **Even so must their wives be grave**, *not slanderers, sober, faithful in all things.* **Let the deacons be the husbands of one wife**, *ruling their children and their own houses well. For they that have used the office of a deacon well purchase to themselves a good degree, and great boldness in the faith which is in Christ Jesus (Yahushua the Messiah)."*
> 1 Timothy 3:8-13 (boldface added for emphasis)

Thus, this second church twisted and distorted the words of God to justify permitting women to serve as deacons by finding a professor of Greek at the local seminary who claimed that the Greek words translated into "husbands" and "wives" here could be translated into "spouses." Yet anyone of any honesty and integrity, looking at the full context of these verses, can come to no other honest understanding other than what I have stated previously: a deacon ought always to be a man, and a man only! So demon spirits had previously crept into that church undetected, and had corrupted some of its teachings.

Russell claimed at our first Men's Fraternity offering that his wife was not at all who she appeared to be and after making this provocative disclosure, asserted that, in contradiction to what Robert had just said on the DVD we had watched, he never found it did any good to talk about any of his challenges or issues with others. So why was he even there? Apparently he was there merely to be rude and disruptive to the other men there. And he was.

A few weeks later, Russell phoned me to ask me if I thought he was in the right to be concerned that his wife seemed to be having inappropriate communications with the head deacon of the church (who was a man). I told him that it was not up to

131

me to make that determination, but that if he had such concerns, he needed to man up and confront the head deacon and tell him in no uncertain terms to stop messing with his woman. This is entirely in keeping with the roles of men, which the Bible and Men's Fraternity teach. Russell told me he couldn't possibly do that because if his wife found out she would divorce him and clean his clock financially. I rolled my eyes at this; Russell was telling me that his wife wore the pants in his family and controlled him. It was apparent to me that his financial comfort was more important to him than a functional marriage was.

He insisted that I keep what he had shared with me to myself, which I initially agreed to do, out of respect for his privacy. But as I reflected further on it, I realized Russell had, in essence, done the equivalent of pulling the pin on a hand grenade and handing it to me saying, "Here, hold this for me," while he ran away. I now possessed knowledge that might indicate that the spiritual health of the entire church community was in jeopardy by two deacons who might be having an inappropriate relationship with one another. The church deacons were entrusted with the moral and spiritual health of about 20 couples assigned to each of their cares. I had no idea if the allegations had any merit to them, but what I did know was potentially explosive and that I had a moral obligation to inform a church leader of what I had come to know, but wished I didn't.

I called and arranged to meet with one of the associate pastors and informed him of what Russell had discussed with me. The pastor failed to indicate that he understood or was at all concerned about the severity of what I was revealing to him. All he told me was to urge Russell to come speak to one of the pastors, otherwise his hands were tied and he could do nothing out of respect for Russell's and his wife's privacy. In other words, the spiritual health of the church body he was entrusted to protect, was of less concern to him than keeping a secret and a lie of one of the deviant members of his church. It was not an argument I was was going to prevail on, so I said nothing and vowed to try to persuade Russell to speak up.

Unfortunately, Russell refused out of fear for the the financial repercussions to him, and he repeatedly dodged my attempts to sit down with him over coffee or lunch to process out with him the serious ramifications to our church community of his cowardice.

Finally, giving up on Russell, I revealed to the head deacon over coffee, that Russell had concerns with him that he needed to be aware of, so that he might address directly with Russell whatever the truth really was. The head deacon agreed to contact Russell directly and clear the air. He revealed to me that he and his family and Russell and his family were friends and had even gone on vacation together. So Russell should have had the sort of open relationship with the head deacon to express his concerns directly with him, and leave me out of it. The head deacon called me back to inform me that he and Russell had talked at length by phone and had cleared the air and that all was good between them. He assured me that it was all over. It wasn't. Within an hour, Russell called me and proceeded to read me the riot act for violating his confidence and privacy. I attempted to explain the very compromising position he had placed me in, but he had no interest in listening, only in verbally abusing me. I informed Russell I would not tolerate such abuse and would hang up on him if he persisted. He continued his abusive harangue, and I hung up on him, as I had warned him I would do if he persisted.

The second guy, John, was repeatedly dismissive of the personal challenges of other men in our Men's Fraternity group, which is inconsiderate, insensitive, arrogant and rude of any man in such environments that are seeking to provide a safe place for men to talk about their life struggles and problems with other caring men. John obviously did not care. Moreover, he positioned himself with the rest of us as someone who obviously thought he had his act together much more than the rest of us, which I knew to be a lie from the way he interacted with his wife and young son, whom he always referred to as "junior." Life was all about John. That much was very clear. He had told a group of us a year earlier that prayer just didn't work for him after he had prayed that his father wouldn't die and he died anyway.

John obviously had no relationship with God, and much of Men's Fraternity teachings are grounded in the teachings of the Bible, yet John was confident that all he needed to do was bring Men's Fraternity to the unchurched men of Marin County on his own. I had gone out of my way to invite him to a men's retreat, at considerable generosity and expense on my part, giving me a something of a moral right to speak into his life a bit. So I engaged in several email exchanges with John to try to bring some much needed correction to his arrogant attitude and his Biblical error. He couldn't hear it, became offended, and left our Men's Fraternity group, from which the rest of us benefitted by no longer being subjected to his dismissive and demeaning comments directed at the rest of us. He went to my first church and joined their Men's Fraternity offering, joining a small group run by my friend Tom Jacobs.

The third man, Tom, was a guy who, over time, revealed himself to me to be a very troubled guy who had been raped when he was 10 years old by a friend of his older brother. Tom had kept this hideous trauma secret from everyone for 28 years. At age 38, Tom was twitchy, seriously disturbed, and living with his demon-infested mother in her two bedroom apartment. He was attempting to make a career change, was single, desperately wanted to get married, buy a home and start a family and was in no mental frame of mind to successfully accomplish any of that. His own family of origin was deeply dysfunctional and of no genuine help to him. Tom was between a rock and a hard place and had been taking anti-psychotic meds which he had come off of on his own and its effects were quite evident to someone such as me who knows what to look for in people's behaviors which evidence serious emotional and psychological challenges.

At one point, Tom was dating a girl who was the daughter of a couple in our church who were about my age. Ed, one of the men leading the men's ministry at the church, who was a physician and should have known better, was actively encouraging Tom in doing so. As the father of that daughter, I would have been livid to know that one of the church's lay leaders was perfectly willing to put my own daughter in jeopardy out of ignorance, or worse, out of malice. So I wrote Tom and copied the other members of our Men's Fraternity group and told him point-blank that he was one sick puppy and was in no condition to be dating anyone at that time. I copied the other men so that they would know exactly what I was advising Tom and would not be foolish enough to offer advice to Tom which might be contrary to mine, that would merely further confuse and harm both him and potentially others.

One evening, Ed took me aside and rebuked me for violating Russell's privacy and for offending Tom in front of other men via the email I sent him. I took real exception with Ed's correction. He stridently asserted that I was under an obligation of confidentiality that I had violated with Russell, analogous to a physician's patient privacy considerations. Where in the Bible does protecting the spiritual health of an entire church community get trumped by a character-disordered man's manipulative and controlling tactics that are rooted in selfishness, cowardliness, lies and secrecy between dysfunctional spouses? The simple answer is, nowhere does it teach such a thing. Ed was simply in the wrong and I had done all I had done with pure motives and great love for my fellow man. I spoke the truth to three men who were offended by the truth. Jesus embodies speaking the truth in love in all things and I had done just that. I had nothing to apologize for, and I did not back down or agree with Ed.

Around November 1, 2010, Jeff, the lead pastor at the church, invited me to join him for coffee one morning. We spoke cordially for about an hour and only at the end of it did Jeff reveal to me that my wife, Barbara, had called him complaining to him that I was being overly controlling with our family finances (which I was not). I was rather annoyed with Jeff's lack of candor and integrity at the outset of our coffee meeting, but chose to overlook his offense. But it was less than honest of him and not at all the way I wished to be treated. I informed Jeff that Barbara's calling him was part of a pattern of hers of undermining and deceitful behaviors which she had engaged in several times before with leaders of my first church and even Gary, the associate pastor of his church a year before, in which I had challenged Gary to test me and my integrity and invited him to contact several friends of mine who could and would vouch for me that Barbara was being undermining, deceptive and disrespectful toward me in my home and marriage.

I had given Gary a list of five to eight men and I invited him to call as many as he liked. He did nothing with the list I had provided to him. I informed Jeff of my conversation a year before with Gary and informed him that before I would entertain or tolerate any further discussion on the topic of Barbara's complaints that I would like him to talk to my friend Tom Jacobs who had tried (unsuccessfully) to mentor both Barbara and me previously and found Barbara to be unable and unwilling to meet any commitments she made to try to heal our dysfunctional marriage. Jeff agreed to do so, and I called Tom to ask him to speak with Jeff on my behalf, which Tom agreed to do.

Meanwhile, Brian Lord, a friend of mine, and I had got together over coffee every week over the course of three to four years to share our lives with one another, covering subjects such as our respective challenging marriages to disrespectful and undermining wives and our mutual interests in American politics, business, men's issues and Biblical Christianity. During the fall of 2010, a woman who had overheard several snippets of our far ranging conversations introduced herself to us as Susan Rice and began to share with us some of her past experiences as a political activist. On one such encounter, she relayed to me that in her travels she had met an Ernst Zündel, who had authored a number of articles in his native Germany and in Canada proving that the holocaust never happened. Susan told me that Zündel had hired materials scientists to test the walls of the alleged gas chambers at Auschwitz for evidence of Zyklon-B gas residues and discovered that no such residues could be found. I listened to what Susan had to say, but frankly walked away assuming that she must be some sort of a wacko. So I remained skeptical, but kept an open mind. Yet Susan had planted a seed in my mind and understanding that would bear much fruit and insight later.

Additionally, in the second half of 2010, I was experiencing intensifying harassment and being subjected to a hostile workplace environment by the CEO of the company where I had been serving as its CFO for the prior two years. My CEO was a personal friend and ally of one of the struggling high tech company's deep-pocketed private equity investors who had repeatedly engaged in a game of chicken with the company's other private equity investors to gain an ever-increasing ownership interest in the company through devious and immoral tactics, with which I did not agree, and with which I was not cooperating. In response, the CEO was doing all he could to isolate me and make me feel unwelcome there, in the hope that I would voluntarily resign, but he was pushing the limits of what was legal, and had gone well beyond what was morally right, and he knew it. By Thanksgiving Day weekend, I was about at my limit and prayed several times at length that God would bring me a way to confront my CEO and put an end to his abusive tactics.

That same weekend, I viewed a DVD documentary entitled, *Agenda: Grinding America Down*, produced by Idaho state legislator Curtis Bowers, which I had stumbled across on Amazon.com. The documentary provided extensive and compelling evidence that America has already largely been taken over by Communists who have had a track record of producing the most effective killing machine ever devised by man. Bowers had been a graduate student at U.C. Berkeley in 1992 when he infiltrated and observed a weekend long planning session of the American Communist Party on the U.C. Berkeley campus who were laying out a program of infiltrating and corrupting America from within. At the time, Bowers discounted most of their plans as highly unlikely to occur. But by the 2008 Presidential election, Bowers realized that virtually all of the plans of the American Communist Party had been achieved by then, just 16 years later! Bowers went on to illustrate how a number of seditious and destructive political movements had coalesced into a monstrous network of incestuous relationships designed to infiltrate and corrupt America from within, which were targeted at America's three main pillars of historical strength:

- America's patriotism

- The strength of the traditional American family

- America's Christian morality

As I viewed the film and reflected back on my life since the 1950s, I could see how the traditional American culture in which I had grown up had been gradually and hideously transformed into something I barely recognized by 2010. I realized that my role as husband, father and head of my household had been intentionally eroded and viciously attacked to make me impotent and ineffective and that there were no social institutions who were dedicated to doing anything about this at all. Everything that was once viewed as noble, virtuous, pure, heroic and good, which I fully embraced as my own values, heavily influenced by my character-building experiences as an Eagle Scout in my teenage years, were now viewed by America's decaying and dying culture as hopelessly old fashioned, evil, dangerous and mentally unbalanced.

On Monday, December 1, 2010, I received a daily devotional email from Rick Warren of Saddleback Church teaching that God has a plan for our lives way better than our own. I had had it with my CEO by then, who claimed to be a Catholic who went to mass every Sunday with his wife, but who was clearly dishonest and immoral in his business dealings. So I forwarded the devotional to him with a cover note in which I stated that it was quite clear to me that our company was floundering because we weren't doing business God's way, but rather his way. I informed him that I stood ready to show and coach him how to lead our company God's way, but that we could not continue operating as he had been leading the company for the prior 18 months. When the CEO came into the office, he was clearly annoyed and wanted to meet with me. When we met, he informed me that we could no longer work with one another and that he was terminating me with no severance, on the spot. I gathered up my personal effects and left feeling liberated from a toxic and dysfunctional environment which had been sucking the life out of me. Over the next few weeks, God inspired me with new ideas almost every morning, and I knew beyond a shadow of a doubt that He was delighting in me and leading me to new insights and revelations of the truth because I had put my trust in Him and followed His leading to bring much-needed correction to my former CEO and to walk away from what had become a toxic and emotionally unsafe working environment for me.

About a week later, the associate pastor of my second church, Gary, approached me and asked me if we could meet together at 7:00 p.m. one night at the church. My suspicions were aroused by the timing he proposed. The prior time we had met over the issues with Russell and his wife, it was at 9:00 in the morning in his office. Something smelled fishy, but I agreed to meet with him about eight days later. Within 24 hours of my agreeing to that meeting, a friend, Jeff Taft, sent me an email telling me that he could see that I was on fire for Christ, as was he, and that I needed to flee organized religion and he referred me to two books: *Pagan Christianity?* by Frank Viola and George Barna, and an electronic essay entitled, *The Wheat and the Tares*, by Harold Camping. I strongly sensed that God was using Jeff to warn me of something coming up in my meeting with Gary and so I got the books and read them prior to the meeting.

Author Frank Viola, in *Pagan Christianity?* challenges all forms of conventional organized religion and reveals that most of the modern forms of church services are rooted in the practices of the early Roman Catholic Church, which materially departed from the first century church of the Book of Acts which met in people's homes, where teachings from Scripture were jointly offered by a group of more spiritually mature men, who taught men, women and children in an informal circular discussion format. Viola teaches that Roman Catholicism was the result of merging the pagan religions of Babylon, Greece and Rome with Biblical teachings to arrive at a form of church that was centered around a building, with full-time paid clergy, and which adopted many of the trappings, ceremonies and ritual displays of wealth and power that were all directed at elevating the clergy who sat on the dais while the lay people were seated in rows looking forward and entertained by the ceremonies in the front of the surplus Roman government buildings which were given to the church. Viola calls for a return to more informal home church communities and practices. I readily saw what Viola was saying and I agreed with him.

Harold Camping was an 89 year old civil engineer with a degree from U.C. Berkeley in the 1930s who had founded a Christian radio ministry called Family Radio in Oakland, California, who had predicted that the rapture, prophesied in the Bible, would occur in 1994. Obviously he was wrong about that, but he was claiming that he had figured out his prior errors and had arrived at a new date of May 21, 2011 when the rapture would occur and Camping had authored and posted a number of downloadable books on various topics related to end times prophesies. Jeff had urged me to read one of these books which contended that all true Christians should flee organized religion of all forms, and that God was in the process of separating the wheat from the tares (weeds), as the Bible teaches He will in the end times, as Jesus returns in His second coming.

Both books caught my attention and prepared me for what was to come next. Around this same time, I called Tom Jacobs to see if he and Jeff Souza had connected on my behalf. Tom informed me that they had just recently done so, and he confirmed to Jeff that Barbara had indeed demonstrated no genuine commitment to heal our marriage in the mentoring sessions Tom and his wife Elizabeth had led and attempted to guide the both of us through. Notably, Tom made no mention of another agenda and discussion that was held without my knowledge in that same meeting.

On December 20, 2010, I arrived at the church building at 7:00 p.m. where Gary was rearranging flower pots in the front lobby. He suggested that we proceed to the library, which was in the back of the church. This struck me as odd, since his office was in the front of the church just off the lobby and this is where he and I had met previously. As I arrived at the library door, I observed that the two men heading up the men's ministry of the church were there waiting for us with sheaves of paper in front of them. I clearly was walking into an ambush, and was immediately annoyed and turned on Gary and angrily asked him what the hell was going on? He urged me to sit down, offered up a perfunctory prayer and then proceeded to reveal to me that he and Jeff had both met with my friend, Tom Jacobs. This shocked and surprised me and caught me off balance.

Tom had represented himself to me as a loyal and faithful friend with whom I got together over coffee or a meal once a week for the prior six years. I had indeed urged Jeff to meet with Tom on my behalf to confirm Barbara's deceptive and combative spirit and behaviors. But this was the first time anyone had revealed to me that Gary had inserted himself in the process. Clearly, Tom had intentionally withheld pertinent information from me and had deceived and betrayed me when I asked him if he had met with Jeff on my behalf. To avoid creating a misleading perception, had Tom had any honesty, integrity and decency to him, he would have openly disclosed to me Gary's presence and the second agenda that was discussed in their meeting that I was about to learn of.

I was angry at Tom and Gary's obvious deceit and treacherous behaviors and called Gary on it right away, informing him that his little Gestapo tribunal that night was illegitimate, sinful, unbiblical and downright wrong and I glared across the table at all three of those cowardly frauds. Gary falsely countered my objection by claiming that they were conducting themselves Biblically in accordance with Matthew 18:15, with which I was quite familiar. Gary was lying and improperly applying that passage to my set of circumstances. I seriously doubt that Gary had a clue that I knew what I knew. Here's what Matthew 18:15 properly teaches:

"Moreover, if thy brother shall trespass against thee, go and tell him his fault between thee and him alone: if he shall hear thee, thou hast gained thy brother. But if he will not hear thee, then take with thee one or two more, that in the mouth of two or three witnesses every word may be established. And if he shall neglect to hear them, tell it unto the church: but if he neglect to hear the church, let him be unto thee as an heathen man and a publican." Matthew 18:15-17

In my case, only Ed had approached me with advice and counsel which was unbiblical and was actually contrary to what the Bible teaches concerning my telling the truth and bringing correction and rebuke to men who were part of Men's Fraternity who were disruptive, arrogant, and inconsiderate to others in the group. The Bible teaches in many places that the wise and the godly mature follower of Christ, motivated by a spirit of love for his fellow man, is commanded to bring correction and rebuke to those who are conducting themselves in a contentious and divisive manner, as those three men I had been counseling had been doing. The motive in doing so is to restore a person into right relationship with God, the teachings of the Bible and a man's fellow believers and that had been my intent and motive all along. In short, Gary's claim that they were following Matthew 18:15 was a bald faced lie and made a complete mockery of the real purpose and meaning of that Bible passage. Gary, Don and Ed quickly discovered that I knew it too.

Gary resumed his planned monologue and condemnation of my perfectly legitimate conduct by informing me that in his meeting with Tom Jacobs, Gary had characterized me as being unmanageable and disruptive and according to Gary, Tom fully agreed with him on that. Tom had never so much as suggested such a thing **ever** to me in our six year alleged friendship! I interrupted Gary, informing him that I was not going to sit still and tolerate a one-sided lynching that had no basis in fact or Biblical truth and demanded to know immediately what the bottom line was and where their farce was headed. Gary dodged, ducked and weaved and in response I stood up, glared at all three men in righteous and justified anger and repeated my prior assertion that their little ambush was illegitimate, unbiblical, sinful and wrong and informed them that I was resigning from their church on the spot, and walked out of the library and the church fuming mad.

I found it incomprehensible that three men, who claimed to be followers of Christ and the Bible, could ever do such a wicked and treacherous thing to such a good, noble and courageous man as myself. Could they not see the parallels between their conduct, and what the scribes and Pharisees did to Jesus in the dead of night on the night He was betrayed?!? It was as obvious to me as the nose on my face! Yet all three of them lacked the integrity and character to stand up and demand that such a fraudulent proceeding be halted! Their hypocrisy and fraud reeked of treachery, deceit, cowardice and corruption! I was so very grateful that God had used Jeff Taft to warn me over a week earlier and be prepared to leave all forms of organized religion, when I was confronted with that godless ambush from those alleged church leaders.

I went home, and within 30 minutes Jeff Souza called to inform me that he and Tom Jacobs had both been asked to be there at the meeting which I had walked out of, and he asked me to return to the church to finish the discussion. I refused. What Jeff had just disclosed to me was that things were even worse than I had initially perceived them to be! The plan was to have not just three, but five men oppose and try to intimidate me into compliance with their fraudulent proceeding. It was quite clear that they had previously charged, tried, found me guilty in absentia, and were merely there to deliver their sentence to me. Apparently, these cowards were so spineless that they feared the wrath and fury of a lone good and righteous man when confronted with their fraudulent and coercive tactics, which clearly were of the devil. Gary foolishly followed up my departure by sending an email and bogus "covenant agreement" which the three of them foolishly thought I would ever agree to. This is what he sent me:

> Watchman, I want you to know from the bottom of my heart that I did not intend to set you up tonight nor upset you. I invited two men that have known you since we were introduced prior to you and Tom coming to our men's retreat a few years ago. I do apologize for what happened. I also want you to fully understand that you are loved and the meeting was meant to help. I have attached what I wanted to say and what we wanted to accomplish. I heard what you said on your way out the door, but I want to encourage you to reconsider. Your brother in Christ,

> Gary Lathrop, DMin
> Executive Pastor, XXX

This was attached:

> I want to begin the meeting with the acknowledgement of what the Lord has done in your life. God desires to get our attention and some people go through life and this never happens. However, it is clear that you have a passion for God and that has in turn, has led you to Men's Fraternity and a desire for men, especially in Marin County, to experience the same zeal for the Lord that you do.

> You and I met one-on-one sometime in the fall of 2009 and I shared my concerns with you over inappropriate behavior in your family. While not condoning anything that Barbara had done to you, I told you that if you wanted her to follow your leadership and show the kind of love and respect that you demanded, you would first have to model that, including forgiveness. You chose that day to basically tell me I did not know what I was talking about and we left on pretty rocky terms. You followed this with a lengthy email giving me the names of about a dozen guys who would tell me exactly the same thing. I

chose to not communicate with any of them if that was the case.

Nearly a year passed before you called to set up an appointment and you came in and shared with me what I perceived as a change of heart and that you were going to no longer wage war in your home with Barbara or the children. I felt that you had turned a corner; one that I felt you had to see for yourself and turn on your own. I truly felt we were getting somewhere.

Within the past three months, information has come to me that seems to indicate that this was not the case. I discovered that you broke confidence with one of the men after a parking lot conversation. You came in and we talked again at length over this. You made assumptions about his wife and another man in the church that proved to be wrong and you continued the string of broken confidence. You confronted two other men that have come forward to say that you have inappropriately confronted them.

After a gathering of leadership about three weeks ago to weigh the issues and determine a course of action, we agreed to encourage you continue to be involved in your various Men's Fraternity groups and that Ed maintain the leadership and closely monitor the situation. He shared with me just this past week that he had a meeting with you in which you defied his leadership and raised your voice at him for confronting you.

In the meantime, Jeff and I met with Tom since you have directed me to him on more than one occasion. We met at Jeff's house and briefly outlined for him our observations of you. After sharing about our encounters with you and our few meetings with Barbara, Tom shared with us from his vantage point. Please clarify if I get any of this wrong with Tom.

Tom shared that we were pretty much on target with our assessment of you: lack of maturity in handling of your faith, inability to heed Godly counsel, inability to listen, lack of humility, lack of patience and generally always willing to see the speck in your brother's eye and not seeing the log in your own. While we acknowledged your passion and zeal to become the man you were created to be, especially in your connection to Men's Fraternity, you have used it as a virtual club to beat both other men and your wife.

The revelation that day for me was Tom's assessment and comments to help me more clearly understand Barbara. I have always felt that the truth was somewhere between the two of you. I was never getting the whole picture from either one. I believe that I now understand what she brings to the table, but since she is not a member of our church, I do not have any authority over her.

I had asked Tom to be present today since he is a man you respect, but he was unable due to family commitments.

I drew up the following covenant to help guide us through this ordeal.

Covenant between Watchman and XXX:

- The pastoral staff and leadership of our men's ministry want to be an encouragement to you.

- We appreciate your love of Christ and your passion to follow him.

- We want you to understand that you are welcomed at XXX and that the XXX leadership is concerned for you and your family.

- We want you to be a part of every aspect of

church life (worship, Bible study, Sun nights, Wed nights and the men's groups).

- However, we see the following areas that detract from your leadership and ministry effectiveness and need growth: maintaining confidentiality; listening skills; receiving Godly counsel and the ability to demonstrate love, respect, kindness, gentleness and patience to men in the church and to members of your family.

- Based on the foregoing, we ask that you agree to the following for the indefinite future:

  ○ You have full freedom to meet with any of the men listed here: Ed Mickle, Don McCulloch, Jeff Orleans, Tom A, Jim B, Bill C, John D, Craig E, Don F, William G, Jerry H, Rudy J, Jerry K, Bruce L, Gary Lathrop and Jeff Souza.

  ○ You will refrain from serving in a leadership capacity and will not assume authority to speak to any other man privately on behalf of the church including counseling related to Men's Fraternity at XXX.

  ○ You agree not to single anyone out to counsel, especially men who are new to the church or who are deemed young in their faith by our XXX leadership. If you have a question regarding this, consult with Gary, Ed or Don.

  ○ You may receive Godly counsel, primarily from God's Word and any of the men listed above throughout this time.

- You are not to send emails to anyone related to XXX except men on the above list.

- We would ask your permission to communicate with your counselor and would further designate Ed as the primary communication point.

- We will plan to meet again at three-month intervals or as often as either deems necessary.

This agreement will serve as the covenant between Watchman and XXX.

This is what a modern day lynching at the hands of the leadership of harlot apostate churches looks like! It makes a complete mockery out of Jesus and the Bible. The fact that this could ever occur in any church setting reveals how fraudulent all forms of organized religion and our American culture have become.

The following day, Tom Jacobs called me to ask what had happened and to cover his tracks and try to disavow his role in the fraudulent ambush of the night before, to which he had been invited, but declined to attend (out of embarrassment, shame and cowardice on his part, I suspect). He claimed that some of what Gary attributed to him never occurred, but by then Tom's treachery and betrayal was clear to me, and I made it very clear to him that I was appalled and deeply hurt by his betrayal and failure to disclose the full facts of his conversation with Jeff and Gary previously. It was becoming apparent to me that my entire friendship with Tom over the prior six years was not at all real and genuine and that Tom was part of a fairly broad and deep conspiracy of allegedly Christian men in Marin County who had secretly colluded with one another to oppose and afflict my attempts to bring healing to my own marriage and to the lives and marriages of other Christian men in Marin County.

That same day, Brian Lord loaned me a book of his on spiritual warfare which we had been discussing for several weeks prior to the ambush. The book, *He Came to Set the Captives Free*, by Rebecca M. Brown, M.D. was to change my life forever.

God used Brian to lead me to another set of insights which became critical to my discoveries over the next two to three years, much of which came to me through books God led me to read, and circumstances which occurred to me at strategic points in my life, to permit me to assemble a remarkably complex jig saw puzzle in my mind of how the world and life really work, as opposed to how we have been deceived into thinking they work. It was to become a remarkable discovery of the truth, revealed to me by God's loving and brilliant hand that has truly set me free!

Several days later, on Christmas Eve, I met with Jeff Souza in his office out of a courtesy to him, but my mind was made up: I was done with his church for good, and perhaps with all forms of organized religion too. My meeting with Jeff was disappointing. He explained that he was fully aware of Gary's plans for the night of my ambush, yet clearly Jeff had no more character and integrity than the other frauds of that night to put a hard halt to it. As the leader of his church, Jeff had the ultimate accountability and responsibility for all actions taken by members of his church, and I was not about to let Jeff off the hook for it. At the time, I was emotionally crushed by the treachery and betrayal which I had experienced in recent days. Many of those I had trusted within the community of Christian men in Marin County had revealed themselves to me to be treacherous and malicious frauds who claimed they were Christians, but whose conduct revealed just the opposite, and no one was offering me any coaching or insight to figure out what was really going on and why. It was a very lonely time for me. Meanwhile, my wife and children showed little or no compassion for what I was facing and trying to make sense out of.

On January 3, 2011, after actively participating in Ted McGuire's men's Bible study sessions in his home for the prior ten years, I received the following email from him, the night before our next scheduled Bible study in his home:

Watchman,

I am writing this email to you because I have no choice other than to do so. I am, as so many are, aware of the conflict and pain which has been brought about within the Body as a result of your actions and behavior.

Many have attempted to speak to you, help you and encourage you to acknowledge how destructive your words and deeds have been, not only to your family but others within the Body who have faithfully prayed for you.

Notwithstanding the attempts by many to try to reach you, show you, and make you aware of your destructive behavior, it has been met by ridicule, anger and bitterness.

I am required to ask you to withdraw from the Tuesday evening bible study and encourage you, once again, to acknowledge that you are in deep, deep trouble spiritually and emotionally. I am not basing my decision to ask you to withdraw upon rumor or innuendo, rather by observation and conviction after much prayer.

You are in trouble my Brother, deep trouble. You cannot continue to ignore the counsel of the many, many men who have tried to get you to see this fact. Should you continue to do so, I fear for your soul.

Those are your decisions however, and mine is to tell you that until you make significant changes in your behavior and heart, I cannot, in good conscious (sic) welcome you into the fellowship we share in my home on Tuesday evenings each month.

I have spoken to Mark Farthing and Dr. Jeff Orleans with regard to this decision and asked them if they would be willing to meet with you, not to debate or argue, but rather to pray should you wish. I too, will be willing to meet with you to pray Watchman, for your soul, family and heart.

I, along with others, over the last year or more have resisted obeying what I am commanded in Matthew 18, but can no longer do so. When, and if, you can demonstrate that you have been able to rebuild the broken relationships you have with family, friends and church, thus demonstrating the "fruit" which is a result of surrendering your heart to Christ, we will welcome you home with open arms and rejoicing.

Ted

Ted McGuire and Jeff Orleans were both very wealthy businessmen, prominent members of my second church, and probably two of the largest financial contributors to that church community. Consequently, Ted's letter to me, which effectively excommunicated me from his Bible study group, was clearly part of a much broader conspiracy of allegedly Christian men in Marin County, aimed at crushing me emotionally, psychologically and spiritually, by isolating me and secretly afflicting and opposing my every effort to speak the truth in sacrificial love to others.

I forwarded Ted's email to at least four other men who were part of Ted's Bible study group, asking them what they made of it. None of the four had any insights to offer to me that were at all helpful. I did later talk with Mark Farthing, who had originally introduced me to Ted and his Bible study meetings, and Mark admitted to me that he didn't necessarily agree with Ted and Jeff's actions. It was clear that I was the victim of a coercive power play on Ted's and Jeff's parts which I did not fully understand. But that was soon to change.

During December of 2010 and January 2011, I acquired and began to devour several books many of whose authors and titles I became aware of through the DVD, *Agenda: Grinding America Down*, which I had first viewed during the

Thanksgiving weekend in 2010.[5] These included the following books:

The Unseen Hand: An Introduction to the Conspiratorial View of History, by Ralph Epperson

None Dare Call it Conspiracy, by Gary Allen

The Naked Communist, by W. Cleon Skousen

The Naked Capitalist, by W. Cleon Skousen

The Illuminati: The Cult that Hijacked the World, by Henry Makow

Illuminati 2, by Henry Makow

The Secrets of the Federal Reserve, by Edward Mullins

He Came to Set the Captives Free, by Rebecca M. Brown, M.D.

Much of what the *Agenda* DVD spoke of, I had studied in college in my studies of world history, political science and economics. Thus, I was somewhat familiar with the role and functions of the Federal Reserve System and Bank and with the accidental view of world history that is always advanced in university level textbooks. Moreover, in my own life, I personally had experienced the endless assaults of feminism on my role as a husband and father in my own family. Something was opposing me and I didn't fully understand it, and how it worked; but I was determined to figure it out, because over the prior decade, I had been unwittingly running into several figurative buzz saws that ripped big gashes in my forehead and knocked me down and I was bound and determined not to let it happen to me again.

As I read the first wave of books, I discovered the existence of the global conspiracy, which revealed to me that most of what I had ever been told or taught in school or heard or read in the media or conventional books was part of an elaborate network of lies and deceit at the highest levels of leadership in America.

---

[5] *Agenda: Grinding America Down*. Curtis Bowers. DVD. 2010.

As I read about the fraud and deceit employed by wealthy Jewish investment bankers on Wall Street in collusion with prominent Senators and other politicians in Washington, I began to realize that every major building on the campus of the Harvard Business School was named after and honored various co-conspirators who pushed through the fraudulent, unconstitutional and illegal Federal Reserve Act in the dead of night on December 23, 1913. This Act granted the private Federal Reserve Bank a legal monopoly to print Federal Reserve Notes out of thin air and loan them to the federal government in exchange for charging the American taxpayers with the privilege of unending interest.

As an economics major in college, who invested a 30 year career as a business management consultant and turnaround chief financial officer (CFO) for troubled high tech companies, I had far more opportunities than most to discover this colossal fraud and con job perpetrated upon the American people. But until I began to read these books and connect the dots with other new data points I was gathering, it never dawned on me that the entire American economy was built on a house of cards and is little more than a colossal Ponzi scheme! Moreover, the preeminent business school from which I earned my MBA, Harvard, was clearly funded by and at the epicenter of this colossal conspiracy which exists to this day, stronger and more pervasive than ever before. And yet throughout my two year graduate study at the Harvard Business School, I remained completely clueless of a conspiracy so dark and so secretive, that even in my privileged position, I was given no visibility into its very existence.

Connecting the dots here, I realized that I had been ignorant of the nefarious and malevolent forces behind the leadership of the Harvard Business School because there was something different about me. That difference was my honesty, integrity and moral decency. There were others like me at the school. But I now realize that we were a very small minority and that the majority of graduates from the Harvard Business School are fully in on the scam of the global conspiracy which secretly rules our world today and is actively working to create their vision of hell on earth in which the rich and powerful, largely Jewish global elites rule a global police state, which they refer to as the New World Order, ruled by satanic Communism, enslaving the mass of humanity in suffering, murder, premature death and eternal damnation.

In late January of 2011, I came across Chapter 17 of Rebecca Brown's book, *He Came to Set the Captives Free*, in which the author's friend, Elaine, who had been a high priestess in the American Satanic Brotherhood and a bride of Satan before Rebecca had rescued her from Satanism, revealed that she had been taught, and then she later taught others in the craft, an eight point program they universally used to infiltrate and corrupt any denomination of Christian church. According to Elaine, Satan's goal was to make every Christian church like the church of Laodicea described by Jesus (Yahushua) in Revelation 3:15-16:

> *"I know thy works, that thou art neither cold nor hot: I would thou wert cold or hot. So then because thou art lukewarm, and neither cold or hot, I will spue thee out of my mouth."*

Churches full of passive, lazy, apathetic people who never bother to read or study the Bible, who *"having a form of godliness, but denying the power thereof..."* as is so well described in 2 Timothy 3:5, are *no* threat to Satan.

Here's that eight point program Satanists use to infiltrate and corrupt any church:

1) Profession of Faith

The Satanist must pretend to be saved in order to gain credibility with church people. In churches which have altar calls, the person will go forward, usually with tears, and pretend to "get saved." The one thing they cannot do is pass the test of the spirits given in 1 John 4. They cannot look you square in the eye and say, "Jesus Christ who is God, who came in the flesh, died on the cross and three days later rose from the grave and now sits at the right hand of God the Father. This Jesus is my Lord, Savior and

Master." Oh, they can lie and say "Jesus saved me." But which Jesus are they talking about? They can also read or repeat a confession or profession of faith in Jesus Christ. They can and do read Scripture. If you ask them if Jesus Christ who came in the flesh is their Savior, they can lie and say, "Yes." But they cannot, with their own mouth, make the declaration given above.

2) Build Credibility

Satanists build credibility within Christian churches in many ways, depending upon the particular church. They are regular attenders. They can be counted upon to always be ready and willing to help in any project. They also get to know the church and its members to discover who is truly committed to Christ and who is not.

Money is a big tool. If the church is a large and wealthy one, they give regularly, gradually increasing the amounts they give until they are one of the main benefactors of the church financially. In smaller churches where the members are mostly poor, they do not flash around a lot of money, but gradually and carefully increase their giving until many of the programs within the church become dependent upon their financial support. The Satanic Brotherhood provides the money they give, and money talks. Unfortunately, this is true even in most Christian churches. Rarely will you find poor people on the board of directors or elders of any church.

3) Destroy the Prayer Base

The single most important goal of the Satanists is to knock prayer out of the church. The Bible contains many Scriptures about prayer. A strong and healthy church is a praying one. Often, a powerful Satanist will get himself established as a leading contributor and elder of a church and orchestrate competing programs that meet at the same time as church-wide prayer meetings, aimed at pulling church members away from participating in unified church-wide prayer groups and prayer sessions or meetings. Many times, smaller discipleship groups may be formed in their place in which the Satanist sees to it that the people chosen to lead the smaller groups are fellow Satanists, thus destroying the prayer and power of the church.

4)   Rumors

Once the prayer base of a church has been destroyed, the Satanists are free to do just about anything they want. One of the easiest things is to use rumors and gossip to inject destructive lies into a church body, thereby easily destroying the credibility of a pastor and true Biblical Christians. One common ploy is to coax a church leader to the home of a member of the church of the opposite sex to help or counsel them, only to be easily framed. Many pastors' careers have been destroyed by just such set-ups.

5)   Teach and Change Doctrines

Satanists particularly covet teaching positions within churches, where they can do tremendous damage by misleading many.

A number of pastors and ministers of large large and wealthy churches in America are Satanists. They have far-reaching influence and get away with distorting the truth and misleading others because those who profess to be followers of Christ are too lazy to study their Bibles to check out what they are saying and to bring rebuke and correction to error.

There are three basic areas Satanists teach most about:

a)   Prayer. They make prayer a very complicated, ponderous, boring and repetitive ritual, rather than a relaxed, casual and sincere appeal to and conversation with God with whom the one praying has a genuine, tender, trusting and loving relationship. One Satanist I knew, who portrayed herself as an experienced and accomplished prayer warrior, endlessly recited chapter and verse out of the Bible, going on and on, without any pause or opportunity to interject or to interrupt her. On some occasions, she made derogatory or demeaning statements about others participating in the prayer session. A second Satanist, who became an elder of the first church I was a member of, ended every sentence of his stultified prayers with the words "Lord God." Both the words "Lord" and "God" are merely titles, not God's true name, Yahuwah (YHWH), by which God prefers to be known, thus making his prayers ritualistic and not at all the sort of dialog with the one true God which He desires. I suspect that this elder was a Freemason, and that unbeknownst to others around him, he was secretly praying to the god of Freemasonry, namely Satan, and not to God (YHWH) at all!

b) One of the most destructive satanic doctrines of today is the health and wealth message, which teaches falsely that if a person is right with God, then he ought to experience health all the time and be wealthy, and that if anyone is not experiencing both of these blessings, that they are not right with God in some way. The Bible is replete with Scriptures showing that this teaching is a bald-faced lie! Here is one prime example of this:

> *"Yea, and all that will live godly in Christ Jesus (Yahushua the Messiah) shall suffer persecution."*
> 2 Timothy 3:12

c) The love doctrine: "We can't judge anybody." Satanists protect themselves by this false teaching. Passive, uncommitted nominal followers of Christ go along with it because they don't want to step on anyone's toes. They just don't want to be bothered, because if they did, their quiet little well-planned and prosperous lives might not be so quiet and prosperous any longer.

6) Break Up Family Units

Satanists within Christian churches work hard to separate families. They start all sorts of programs for preschool, school age and teenage children and offer different programs for women and men to keep the parents separated as much as possible too.

Children need to listen to the sermons and join in prayer meetings just as much as the parents. The Bible teaches throughout that children learn best by joining in with parents and other adults to learn the ways of God and respect for their elders entrusted with their care. Once programs separate children from the main church services, they learn to have no respect for God, church, teachers or adults, all of whom are just too boring and irrelevant to their lives.

Husbands and wives are under constant attack by Satan. In this day of the demonic philosophy of feminism pervading our culture, easy divorce and endless enticements to be promiscuous, couples need time together in God's Word to stay unified to Biblical principles which are counter-cultural. Separating them within the church and for such things as retreats and Bible studies is a major contributor to driving wedges between husbands and wives.

7) Stop All Accurate Teaching About Satan

One of the most effective lies of all is to convince everyone that Satan, demons and hell do not even exist. At the very least, as long as people remain ignorant about Satan and his activities, he is relatively unhindered in anything he chooses to do. Satanists are always commanded to prevent any teaching about Satan within the churches they attend.

One simple incantation by a high Satanist will assign a demon to every person attending the church in which he is involved. The purpose of the demon is to stand guard and the instant anyone says anything about Satan, to beam thoughts into the person's mind that he or she should not be listening to anything about Satan.

Beware, the very church members who complain the loudest about any teaching about Satan and his tactics, will probably turn out to be Satanists themselves, according to former Satanist Elaine.

8) Direct Attacks by Witchcraft Against Key Members of the Church

This is another reason why prayer is so important. Any pastor and church leaders or members who are really taking a stand for Yahushua, and against Satan, will come under tremendous attack by witchcraft.

They will be afflicted by all sorts of physical illness, difficulties in concentrating, confusion, fatigue, difficulties in praying and the like. The leaders of any church must be continuously upheld in prayer and interceded for by the members of the congregation. Once such a prayer base is lost, the pastors and leaders face these attacks alone. Often they are overcome. This is why the Apostle Paul asked his fellow Christians to pray for him at the end of almost every letter he wrote.

As I reflected on this list of tactics used by those who secretly serve Satan or the devil, I realized that Ted McGuire, Jeff Orleans, their wives and number of their friends had first attended the first church I had been a member of, and had thoroughly corrupted and polluted it, using many of these very tactics, and had then moved to my second church, where they had followed the same pattern to defile and destroy it. Being slick at sin, these wealthy and powerful global elites wreaked considerable damage among the residents of Marin County, while projecting the image of being accomplished and moral leaders in the community. These practitioners of Satan worship were the source of the figurative buzz saws I had been repeatedly encountering in my life for the prior decade. Suddenly, everything began to make perfect sense to me. I cannot tell you what a sense of relief, peace and freedom this brought to me, in spite of the continuing afflictions, trials and opposition directed my way.

After a month of having nothing to do with any form of organized religion, I decided to relent and attend a Calvary Chapel church about half an hours' drive away from my home. After having been so badly burned by two forms of organized religion which had later proven themselves to be ruled by demon spirits, I resolved not to do anything more than attend Sunday worship services and made no effort to become further involved in that church community. I found the teaching sound, relative to what the Bible says, but it struck me as a form of "Christianity light," even though I couldn't pinpoint why I sensed that. The pastor was a talented young man who whole-heartedly endorsed and championed the offering of Robert Lewis' Men's Fraternity in his church, which I perceived to be a very healthy and good thing.

During the first half of 2011, I chose not to pursue another CFO role. I sensed that I was done with that portion of my career and that God was strongly leading me to dig deep in my reading and research into the workings and reality of the global conspiracy and its obvious connections to end times Bible prophecy. Three different men, Jeff Taft, John Nabors and my therapist Donald Anderson, each urged me to read and comment on the writings of Harold Camping on the end times prophecies contained in the Bible.

Camping was predicting that the rapture foretold in Matthew 24:30-31, 1 Thessalonians 4:13-17 and 1 Corinthians 15:51-55 would occur on May 21, 2011. Initially, I resisted delving into this. My understanding was that no man knows the day and hour of Christ's second coming, and besides, if I was a born again Christian, thus proving that I was one of God's elect, what difference did it make? But after Dr. Anderson urged me to look into it, thus making three men who did not even know one another, who all were urging me to examine Camping's ideas further, I concluded that God must be leading me to look into it. So I read a number of Camping's downloadable books in early 2011. While I was unable to see anything which conflicted with what the Bible said, Camping made a number of claims concerning numerology, critical for his predictions, which I did not find supported anywhere in the Bible.

7. My Story

One claim Camping made that I found quite interesting, and likely to be true, was that all forms of organized religion had become apostate, meaning that they were teaching false doctrines which conflicted with what the Bible, in its entirely, teaches. Camping's claim appeared to have been confirmed by my own unpleasant experiences with organized religion in the form of the two Marin churches I had once been a member of, until I discovered their respective frauds.

My marriage to my wife remained highly dysfunctional. We continued to have little in common with one another and Barbara made no gestures to reconcile our broken marriage, in spite of my repeated attempts to initiate marriage counseling with her. In February 2011, as I attempted to nurture an ongoing relationship with my 19 year old son Nathan, who was attending San Francisco State University and living in the city, he informed me that he and I had nothing in common and that he had no interest in any kind of a relationship with me. This was after I had invested the prior 19 years being his biggest fan and encourager and a good and caring father to him.

He threatened me that he would call 911 and accuse me of stalking him if I ever came around the house he was renting with several friends of his in San Francisco, again. I now realize that he was indoctrinated and brain washed by his public school education and his sociopathic grandmother and mother, and that his interest in heavy metal rock music had led to his becoming infested with one or more demon spirits who hate the Holy Spirit, who is clearly in me. I am certain that Nathan was encouraged by his mother to pull the 911 trick, since she too has used such a ploy multiple times to pit the legal system against my Biblical headship of our home, marriage and family. In hurt and anger, I accused Nathan of being a Nazi and told him that if he ever made good on his threat, that he and I were through forever. I have neither seen nor communicated with him since then. I seriously doubt I will do so ever again.

Harold Camping's May 21, 2011 rapture date came and went with no rapture occurring. Listening to Camping on the radio on Monday, May 23, 2011, it was clear that he was a false teacher. Two weeks later, it was reported that Camping had suffered a stroke which incapacitated his ability to talk on the radio. Clearly, God was chastening Camping for his false teachings. Nevertheless, it occurred to me that God used Camping to bring the subject of end times prophecy into the limelight and to challenge a number of people's thinking about the subject and where we were in God's prophetic timeline. In the process, I became educated on the prevailing views of a number of well-known pastors and theologians that the rapture would occur before the great tribulation begins, which I have since discovered to be in error, as well.

In late 2010 extending through the spring of 2011, I joined and served on the executive board of a new non-profit organization, Protect Kids Foundation, whose mission was to keep LGBT (Lesbian, Gay, Bisexual and Transgender) indoctrination out of public schools, focusing initially on California's schools, but eventually extending nationwide. California's Proposition 8 had been declared unconstitutional in the summer of 2010 by Vaughn Walker, a homosexual federal judge in San Francisco, and I had written a thought piece and sent it out as an email attachment to a number of friends of mine, in which I lambasted the court decision as dishonest and in conflict with common principles of law. One of my friends forwarded my thought piece to his wife, Linda, who was impressed enough with what I wrote that she asked me if I would consider joining her new board. Linda and I were both evangelical Christians, and the other two board members were Mormons.

Our first test case was the City of Vallejo which was forcing all public school children from kindergarten to 12th grade to submit to LGBT anti-bullying indoctrination every year, as a result of a settlement agreement made by the ACLU with the school district after a lesbian high school student was confronted by a teacher for kissing another female high school student on campus, and the parents of the lesbian student sued the school district for bullying their daughter. Linda and I joined a number of Vallejo churches and parents, who were

162

outraged that the school was forcing this indoctrination on their children with no opt-out provision or prior notice to parents, to prepare for and attend several school board meetings to demand a cessation to the indoctrination.

The indoctrination consisted of showing one of three blatantly gay promotion films to every student in the school district once a year. As I watched the openly lesbian school board member on the board panel and the interim school superintendent, it was very clear to me from their darting, glaring eyes and tight lips that they could barely contain their animosity, hatred and disdain for any parent who opposed their kids being subjected to their deliberate and intentional lies of the LGBT lifestyle.

Shortly thereafter, an openly gay Jewish state legislator from San Francisco, Mark Leno, introduced LGBT anti-bullying legislation into the Sacramento legislature and so Linda and I went to the state capitol and spoke before a couple of committees which heard testimony on both sides of the issue and approved the proposed legislation to be voted upon by the full Assembly and state Senate.

Observing the committee hearings, it was patently obvious to me that the whole production was a complete charade and that the liberal California legislature was going to ram their LGBT indoctrination agenda through and get it passed regardless of what the California voters wanted, what was right, or in the best interests of California's public school children. Observing the dishonest, manipulative and controlling proceedings almost made me sick to my stomach. The wicked perverts were clearly in charge.

Our executive board met by conference call once a week and it began to become apparent that the two Mormon men on the board were undermining Linda's competent public advocacy opposing the proposed LGBT indoctrination legislation, and they were reneging on a prior promise they had made to her to include her on the paid staff of the foundation, once sufficient funds were raised for that purpose. The two Mormons were failing to listen to Linda's objections and obliquely revealed that they were secretly and underhandedly seeking to fund the foundation through the Mormon Church and their Mormon contacts and cut Linda out of any ongoing role in the foundation. Both Linda and I resigned from the board, once we realized that our alleged partners were less than honest and decent with her.

In addition, the Mormon who was the founder of the non-profit falsely alleged that he had reimbursed me twice for a $400 bill I had paid to print foundation brochures and business cards, and that I had improperly cashed and deposited both checks, when the truth was I had yet to receive a single reimbursement from him. After checking the facts with my bank, I asked him for evidence of his claim and all he sent me were the alleged copies of the fronts of both checks. When I asked him to provide me with evidence of my having endorsed one or two checks, he sent a copy of a back of a check which was completely illegible. It was very clear that this wealthy Mormon lawyer was attempting to rip me off and to this day I have yet to be reimbursed for the $400 I paid, based on his verbal assurance that he would reimburse me from foundation funds. Knowing what I now know about the deceitfulness of the Mormon Church and its members, this doesn't surprise me, but the brazenness of this man's deceit, which was clearly directed at stealing from a true Biblical Christian, was quite overt.

As part of my involvement with the Protect Kids Foundation, I attended a couple of seminars on American history, the Constitution and the Biblical principles which formed the core framework for America's system of government in the first half of 2011. While there, I met and befriended a woman, Jennifer Rowley, who was active in her local Tea Party organization in her area and and a member of a local evangelical church. We exchanged email addresses and shared politically-related email blasts with one another for the rest of the year. I introduced her to the *Agenda* DVD and began to share with her what I was discovering concerning the global conspiracy and its obvious links to end times prophecy in the Bible.

Interestingly, both of the seminars we attended on American Christian history failed to mention anything concerning the global conspiracy that God was clearly leading me to. I found this a bit bewildering, if not dumb-founding. The people leading those history seminars were closely affiliated with the Tea Party movement and yet none of them acknowledged one bit of what was becoming clear to me was the key to understanding why America's political system was in the obvious mess it is: the world had been hijacked by a satanic cult and no one was talking about it! Jeff Taft and Jennifer Rowley seemed to fully grasp its significance, but almost everyone else I sent periodic email blasts to, in order to wake them up to what I was discovering, remained almost universally silent, which I found rather dumb-founding.

In the spring of 2011, an acquaintance of mine, Fred Marks, asked me to get involved with a men's ministry he sought to bring to Marin, called "Leading from the Heart Men's Ministry." He told me that he had invested some time in what he referred to as "deep emotional work for men," and was impressed with its leader, Larry Bowles. I agreed to attend one of Larry's workshops with Fred and another guy from Marin, Justin Luther.

The three of us drove to Bear Lake in southern California and went through a three day workshop led by Larry. I was initially quite put off and offended by Larry's pride, arrogance and presumption, and was tempted to just go to the local library for three days and wait for the other two to be done with it, but decided since I was there anyway, I would see it through. The workshop was designed to permit men to go back in their pasts and visualize the hurts and wounds in life that they had experienced, confront them, get the trauma out of their systems through what amounted to primal scream therapy techniques, and release the pent up trauma from their bodies and spirits. Other men were invited to act as stand-ins for people in each participant's life as they were visualizing what had happened to them in the past.

I didn't find the processes particularly useful. I had invested considerable time and effort in talk therapy and Men's Fraternity in the past and felt I had a pretty good handle on what my personal wounds were, had grieved over them, and had moved on. My most difficult issue was living with an intractable and deceitful wife who refused to work on her own character deficiencies and endlessly blamed me for all of our relational strife. I was being faithful to the teachings of the Bible not to initiate a divorce from her, out of my love for and obedience to God, but I was seeing no end in sight to a spiritual war that had been going on for years. However, by the end of the first workshop, Larry had demonstrated that he was reasonably competent Biblically, and so I decided to give him another chance.

Over the remainder of 2011, I participated in several more workshops with Larry, Fred and others, seeking to find a group of men who might be real and committed to working out their own "stuff;" and we all have "stuff." At one workshop with Fred, we all went through an exercise in which Larry asked us to think back to our relationships with each of our parents and in one part of it, Larry had an attractive woman friend of his play the role of our mother and, one at a time, we went into a cabin where she was seated and she invited us to sit down next to her and she put her arms around us and she asked us to share with her what we would have most liked to hear from our mother, if she could hear us. Then she played that message back to each of us and I must say, it felt very nurturing and comforting; something with which I was wholly unfamiliar. But when we debriefed about our own take-aways from that exercise, Fred, who was 72 years old and attempting to position himself as a leader and facilitator of this group work, joked that he had quipped to the woman as he left, "So baby, what are you doing later tonight?"

For what was intended to be a Christian men's workshop, Fred's quip was degrading to the gal and way out of line. Moreover, Fred and I were sharing a room at the retreat house and one night he shouted at me to wake me up, because I was snoring and the next night, he insisted that I go find another room to sleep in because my snoring had disturbed his sleep the night before. There were no other beds for me to sleep on and yet Fred seemed to be oblivious to the selfishness of his request. One of the other guys offered to sleep on the floor on couch mattresses and made the bed he was previously using available for me to sleep on, but Fred's two actions at that workshop led me to suspect that he was not at all the Christian man he claimed to be.

At yet another workshop which I attended with two other men from Marin in the late summer of 2011, as we were returning home, one of the other two guys, who was single, but who prided himself on having gone to Bible college and claimed to be a devout Christian man, made the comment, "I sure could use a good lay right now." The other man, Chris, on the journey home from southern California, proudly showed me the design of the latest of seven tattoos that his wife, Sally, was planning to get. By this point, I had listened to a graduate course on spiritual warfare on CDs taught by Rebecca Brown, M.D. and I knew that tattoos and body piercings provide legal grounds for demon spirits to infest a person. Chris and his wife were going through a rocky time in their marriage and she was threatening to leave him, because she "just wanted to be happy," and claimed she wasn't happy being married to him.

A number of men at the various workshops led by Larry Bowles revealed in their process work that earlier in their lives they had gotten women in their lives pregnant, who had gone on to abort their babies. Rebecca Brown's teachings on spiritual warfare teach that abortion amounts to child sacrifice and almost inevitably leads to demon spirit infestation. As I began to reflect on my experiences with this group of men, I began to conclude that most of the men attending the workshops were suffering from demon spirit infestation and Larry's work was doing nothing to address or even acknowledge this reality.

I had introduced Jennifer Rowley to the Leading from the Heart workshops and in September 2011, she participated in a workshop for women in southern California which Larry led.

After she returned, she called me and told me about it. She had quite a dramatic experience. The deep process work revealed to her that her mother had thrown her against a wall at six months of age and broken her leg, while all her life, the family false narrative was that she had fallen out of her basinet and broken her leg. She also discovered that she had been raped as a little girl, although she wasn't clear who did it.

From her college days, Jennifer was aware of a book entitled, *Primal Scream*, which explained a lot of the methods and techniques Larry Bowles was employing, and integrating what I learned from that book, with the teachings on spiritual warfare from Rebecca Brown, I began to become suspicious and concerned about the safety of the work Larry Bowles was leading. Shortly thereafter, events revealed to me that my concerns were fully justified.

Fred Marks and Larry Bowles planned to offer a Living from the Heart workshop for women in Marin which Larry Bowles asked Jennifer to participate in as a staff support person since, she had already been through it. Jennifer agreed to do so. Fred suggested that my wife Barbara might benefit from the workshop and I agreed, but doubted that she would have any interest in it, based on numerous past attempts at marriage counseling on my part, in which Barbara repeatedly demonstrated that she was not really serious about or committed to reconciling our broken and dysfunctional marriage and family.

Instead, she consistently used those as opportunities to emotionally browbeat me with endless lies and false allegations about me. With my knowledge and support, Fred and his wife met Barbara over lunch and attempted to persuade her to join Fred's wife, Maria, and about five other women who were planning on participating in the workshop. Much to my surprise, Barbara agreed to give it a try. Barbara knew about Jennifer, but had never met her and she insisted on meeting with Larry Bowles and me before the workshop began.

When we met, Barbara made it clear that she didn't like the friendship I had struck up with Jennifer and wanted me to have nothing further to do with her and Larry Bowles crossed the line with me and suggested that Jennifer's and my friendship was inappropriate in some way. First of all it was not. Moreover, by this time I had very few friends I could trust, and I valued my friendship with Jennifer, who shared my interest in the Tea Party movement and my recent discoveries concerning the global conspiracy and its links to end times prophecy. Barbara had no reason to fear my doing anything inappropriate with Jennifer and she knew it. What she was really up to was seeking to isolate me from healthy people and friends, so she could more effectively enslave me in an emotional and psychological prison and hell at home. I made it very clear to Barbara and Larry what I knew what the real agenda was and angrily left the meeting. Larry clearly had orchestrated the meeting to pull a bait and switch agenda on me, and I was seriously annoyed with him over it.

Jennifer called me on her drive from Rocklin to Marin and we agreed to connect after the workshop for us to have coffee and catch up. She had a cookie exchange party the night that the workshop ended, and was expressing concern that she had no time to cook anything and so I offered to cook a batch of cookies for her and pass them off to her when we met. She gratefully accepted my offer. Barbara went to the workshop the first night and I heard very little from her about it. The next day, I called Jennifer to arrange for a time and place for me to hand off the cookies I had baked for her once the workshop ended a day later. Jennifer did not return my call, which in and of itself was odd for our friendship since I left her a message of why I was calling.

When the workshop was scheduled to end, I drove to the location where the workshop had been held and Larry Bowles was packing up his car. The workshop was already over. Larry informed me that Jennifer had left a day or so before while offering me no explanation, hiding behind his ruse that everything that transpired in his workshops was confidential and not to be shared with anyone who was not there. I smelled a rat in Larry. No truly Christian man would keep another

Christian man in the dark they way he was doing with me. Not hearing from Jennifer, which was highly unusual, and then hearing Larry give his evasive explanation, I became concerned for Jennifer's physical safety, and having the cookies with me, I drove 2 hours to Jennifer's home in Rocklin to deliver the cookies and see if she was indeed all right. She was not at her home, so I left the cookies on her doorstep, left her a message of what I had done, asked her to call me back and returned to Marin.

Over the next week or two I pieced together what had happened. I confronted Barbara when I got home and she revealed that she had confronted Jennifer in front of the other women in the group the first night of the workshop and asked Jennifer to have nothing further to do with me. After I called the Sacramento Sheriff's Department where Jennifer was retired from as a sheriff's deputy, seeking some way of contacting Jennifer, I got a call back informing me that she was OK, but did not wish to speak with me. Jennifer had represented herself to me as a godly Christian woman throughout our friendship. Yet her callous disregard and lack of courtesy for how she was treating me now made a complete mockery of anyone claiming to be a follower of Christ. It was heartless, selfish and insensitive of her, in response to my heeding my protective instincts of friendship which led me to be concerned for her safety. As a former cop she, of all people, ought to have understood this.

I attempted to speak directly to Larry Bowles on the phone, but he dodged and would not take my calls. I discovered that Fred Marks was fully aware of Jennifer's abrupt departure from the workshop, but failed to show me the common decency of informing me of what was going on either, knowing full well that my own wife was seeking to disgrace and harm me behind my back. All four of them were clearly colluding and conspiring to harm me and I was annoyed to no end by their collective duplicity and cruelty. Not one of them was honest or who they represented themselves to be. All four of them were complete frauds and liars. I resolved to have nothing further to do with Larry Bowles, Fred Marks or Jennifer from that point forward.

During the fall of 2011, God led me to discover a book entitled, *A Greater "Miracle" Than the Ten Lost Tribes Discovered... − The Dead "SIX MILLION" Uncovered... !*, by Brian Alois Clèraubat, which provides clear and convincing evidence that the claim that the Germans gassed six million Jews to death in the camps or in mobile gassing vans from 1942 − 1945 is a complete hoax and fraud! The author did an outstanding job of research and made his case simply and persuasively, with a full explanation of who was behind it and what the real motive and agenda was.

The essence of the proof for this startling finding is actually quite simple. The *World Almanac and Book of Facts* for 1934 and 1945 reported that in 1934 there were 15.6 million Jews worldwide, and in 1945 there were 15.2 million Jews worldwide.[6] So where did the alleged 6 million Jews gassed by the Germans disappear to?!? Clèraubat went on to document the massive volumes of railroad ties and fuel needed to cremate six million bodies, how long it would take and how much ash would be generated from such an endeavor during a war effort which was consuming every piece of material available and the absence of uncovered or buried ash that would even remotely make such a thing credible, and revealed that the true record withers under any serious scrutiny that has any integrity and honesty to it at all.

Furthermore, the author chronicled 200 instances, listing the year and the country or principality that expelled the Jews over the past 2,000 years for their consistently seditious and immoral acts which were degrading and defiling their moral, Christian host nations. Appendix D provides a restructured version of this list. The author further documented extensively the stories of numerous brave people who have courageously

---

[6] Clèraubat, Brian Alois. *"A Greater "Miracle" Than the Ten Lost Tribes Discovered... − The Dead "SIX MILLION" Uncovered... !"* 2007. pp. 196-197.

sought to expose the truth of this hideous lie to the rest of the world over the last 70 years, and how they have had their lives, their honors and their fortunes destroyed by rich and powerful Jewish interests who were hell-bent on suppressing and silencing the ugly truth of the Jewish lie. Included was the story of Ernst Zündel about which Susan Rice had first told me over a year earlier. Everything Susan had first told me concerning the lie of the holohoax had proven itself to be true.

My new discovery concerning the holohoax left me with my head spinning. What was I to do with such information? Whenever human beings encounter information which challenges the very root of their core beliefs, it is not uncommon for them to experience cognitive dissonance. Such discoveries are such a shock to our mental outlook, that we either choose to deny the hard evidence and logical reasoning and dismiss the new evidence as though it could not possibly be true, or we experience a period of time in which we gradually adjust to our new understanding of reality as it objectively is, and begin to think through the full implications of our discovery. The latter was my experience.

For about three months, I chose to keep this new information to myself and let it sink in. I fully realized that I would be inviting similar reactions to my news as I experienced when Susan had first revealed it to me, when or if I chose to begin talking about it. I knew full well that I could not, and would not, suppress this truth, but when I did, I intended to be ready and well prepared to confront the vicious, cruel and wicked backlash I was bound to receive.

I resolved to learn more about "the Jewish question" which is so taboo everywhere. The more I dug and read, the more God led me to understand that the Jewish people are not at all who they claim to be and do not at all believe what they claim to believe either. In fact, I have come to comprehend that the Jewish religion, rooted in the Babylonian Talmud and Jewish Zohar Kabbalah of the occult is at the heart of the world's suffering and ills today. Anyone with half a brain knows that this is not a popular view to hold in our world today. Yet I now know it to be the truth, because God revealed it to me with hard evidence and simple logical reasoning and He did it for a very important reason: He wills for me to share it with others, as I am doing in this book.

Throughout the first quarter of 2012, my wife Barbara became increasingly sullen and non-communicative and resisted having any form of a civil relationship with me in our home. By this point, our third and last child, Megan, had left home for college at U.C. Davis and Barbara and I were empty nesters. Barbara and I had little in common and it was very clear to me that she had no interest in reconciling our hideously dysfunctional marriage. I fully comprehended what I was dealing with by then: a demon-possessed sociopath whose main aim in life was to enslave me in an emotional and psychological prison of lies, deceit, false allegations and undermining, in the hope that I might respond in some sort of self-destructive way. Months before, I had asked Barbara to leave our bedroom and go sleep in one of the kids' bedrooms and she had done so, living in our son Robert's bedroom in extensive disorder and clutter. Most of her time at home was devoted to sitting passively in front of the television, walking our dog, or hanging out with her one and only equally dysfunctional and character-disordered friend, Susan, of whom I strongly disapproved, because I knew that Susan was a bad influence on her. I made no bones about this, and Barbara knew it. Proverbs 13:20 teaches us that

> "He that walketh with wise men shall be wise: but a companion of fools shall be destroyed."

Susan, Barbara's friend, was undeniably a wicked fool. So the conditions for the perfect storm were set up and in motion.

On March 31, 2012 my daughter was home for a week long break from college. The day before, Megan had demonstrated disrespectful, obnoxious and abusive behavior and disdain toward me and I was not pleased about it. I fumed all day about what to do about it and realized that Megan was, with her mother's obvious encouragement, seeking to challenge my authority in our home and that I could not tolerate such a thing from continuing, because it would only enable and encourage more of the same from her. She was 19 and an adult and if she chose to be disrespectful toward me, she would have to find some other place to live during her summer break from school which was approaching. I went out to dinner by myself that evening, as I often did once a week. While there, I had a half bottle of wine and a full dinner with coffee and desert and returned home around 9:00 p.m. Barbara and Megan were sitting on the couch in our family room watching television and I walked in and informed Megan in no uncertain terms that if she wished to continue to be disrespectful to me in my home that she was not welcome there any longer and would have to make alternative living arrangements for the coming summer break. She sullenly said nothing. I went to read in our living room.

At about 10:30 p.m. I was disturbed from my reading by loud rock music wafting down the hall from outside the bathroom which my daughter and wife shared. When I walked down the hallway, Megan had planted her laptop on the hallway floor and she was sitting on the lid of the toilet, waiting for my reaction. It was clearly a set up. She was testing me. I told her that she was just as much of a wicked sociopath as her mother and grandmother were and she stood up, turned her back on me and grinned out of the corner of her mouth. I angrily pushed her on her right shoulder with my open palm, which did not cause her to lose her balance and told her "I hope you eat shit and die, Megan!" I was furious. Megan, with four years of high school drama under her belt, started screaming and cowering hysterically. I stormed into Barbara's room where Barbara was and ripped a demonic poster off the wall, stormed to Megan's room and did the same thing and then to my son Nathan's former room and tore the demonic posters off his wall, realizing that my home was infested with demon spirits that Barbara and my three children had foolishly invited into our home. Barbara proceeded to call 911 and file a domestic violence claim with the county sheriff's department and within five minutes, I had half a dozen sheriff's deputies traipsing through my home.

Domestic violence laws in California are so preposterous today that if anyone dials 911 and claims domestic violence, someone has to go to jail. This is all quite intentional and by design of the satanic cult of global elites who rule our world today. Their aim is to destroy the authority of the father and husband in the home and destroy marriages and families, so that the State takes the place of God. The sheriff deputies smelled alcohol on my breath and falsely accused me of being intoxicated, which I most assuredly was not, but with half a dozen cops invading my home and my privacy, I didn't have the presence of mind to demand an alcohol intoxication test. By virtue of my having touched Megan, the cops gave her the option of having me arrested, which she chose to have done to me. Furthermore, Barbara demanded a seven day restraining order barring me from communicating with her or Megan and barring me from coming within 100 yards of them or my home.

I spent the next seven hours on the concrete floor of the drunk tank of the Marin County jail, in spite of the fact that the cops told me I would only be in there for four hours. I posted bail at 7:00 a.m. the next morning and called my friend Juan Valdez to ask him if he would pick me up and drive me to our church in Hayward that Sunday morning. On the drive there, I wept in front of my friend and his mother, Julia, who were both very kind and supportive to me.

The evil collusion, conspiracy, deceit, treachery and cruelty of both my wife and daughter was initially almost incomprehensible for me to grasp. I had been a good father and provider to my three kids and to Barbara for 33 years. For the first three years of her high school years, Megan would call me at work to see when I was coming home almost every day so that I could "help her with her homework." She didn't need my help. She was a straight A student. She merely wanted to snuggle on the couch with her dad with his arm around her and feel my love and protection. Afterwards, she frequently asked me to come give her a back rub as she fell to sleep in her bedroom. Those were tender moments between a good, noble, righteous and strategic father and the daughter he loved. And in return, she viciously turned on me and colluded with her mother to drive me from my home, with the full and tacit encouragement of the legal system and the fraudulent Christians of Marin County.

I called my brother Paul and friend Dan Taft for help, moral encouragement and perhaps a place to stay until I had figured out my next steps. Neither one was willing to get involved or help me. That really floored me. My own brother and my best friend for 40 years since we were 18 in college and for whom I had been there when his youngest son committed suicide two years prior, chose to abandon me at a very hard time in my life. It was a pathetic display from both of them of human selfishness, depravity and disloyalty. I was disgusted with both of them. I enlisted another acquaintance to help me retrieve my car and a few personal effects from my home so I could live out of a motel for a while, which ended up being for about a month.

Once Barbara slapped a restraining order on me, we were through. For years she had defied, disgraced, defamed and demeaned me every way she possibly could and had enlisted our three children in a wicked family conspiracy which she and her 90 year old mother had led. The Bible, at 1 Corinthians 7:15-16, clearly teaches God's born again elect:

> *"But if the unbelieving depart, let him depart. A brother or a sister is not under bondage in such cases: but God (Eloah) hath called us to peace. For what knowest thou, O wife, whether thou shalt save they husband? or how knowest thou, O man, whether thou shalt save thy wife?"*

While Barbara had manipulated the legal system to drive me from my home, she had clearly departed from me relationally years before. Her restraining order was a declaration of war against me, and for the first time in our 33 miserable years of marriage, I was free to move on and initiate legally what she had already initiated in fact.

Barbara proceeded to hire an attorney who appeared to have bribed the Marin County deputy DA to file misdemeanor

176

battery charges against me for merely pushing my daughter on her shoulder with my open palm. Barbara incurred a $15,000 legal bill for filing a few court papers related to replacing the temporary restraining order with a five year one. Clearly, there was more to the $15,000 than the costs of preparing a simple court document of two or three pages.

I had to hire a criminal attorney to fight off her false allegations that I was in any way a violent man (I am not) or that I was a suitable candidate for "anger management" classes (I was not). Eventually the DA offered a plea bargain whereby the DA would drop the battery charge in exchange for my agreeing to a five year restraining order. Knowing that any restraining order bars a person under such an order from owning or possessing a firearm to defend himself, I refused and demanded a jury trial in order to expose the ridiculous battery charge made against me for what it truly was. The domestic violence commissioner hearing my case sought to avoid such a circus at all costs and ordered that Barbara's application for a five year restraining order filed in the divorce court where I had filed for divorce be transferred to her domestic violence court instead. It was painfully obvious to me that the entire legal system was wicked and corrupt beyond anything I could have possibly imagined.

On July 26, 2012, Barbara, her attorney, the deputy DA and Megan lined up on one side of the courtroom, and I sat opposed to them, and we went through the charade of a hearing, whose outcome was clearly pre-determined. I presented a letter from my therapist and psychiatrist, which clearly documented that I was the victim of a seriously dysfunctional family system and which urged the court not to grant the restraining order as it would only further humiliate and injure me unjustly. I came prepared to explain that Barbara is a sociopath and that she and my daughter were colluding liars.

It didn't matter. The globalists behind the scenes had clearly targeted me because they knew I was uncovering the truth of the global conspiracy and openly talking and teaching about it and vigorously resisting it. They just made matters worse by persecuting me in this fashion, and only steeled my resolve to expose them and their wicked tactics all the more. The commissioner granted Barbara all she asked for: a five year restraining order against me, barring me from communicating with or coming within 100 yards of Barbara or any one of my three grown children for five years. The globalists stripped me of my ability to physically defend myself against their abuses and the DA recommended to the court that "in the interests of justice," the bogus battery charge be dropped, which the commissioner agreed to. The corrupt legal system of Marin County had done its dirty work.

In May 2012, I rented a room in a two bedroom apartment from Joseph Peachtree, a Kenyan church deacon from XXX church, who I previously had gotten to know a bit. Anytime I would see Joseph and ask him how he was, he would always play sugary sweet, smile, look up at the sky or ceiling and say, "Oh, I am blessed, Brother Watchman!" Yet I quickly discovered living with him that in reality, he was a swindler, a con artist and a sociopath to boot.

One evening, he asked me what I would advise him to do because an elderly couple in his church (the one which had deceitfully ambushed me 18 months before) wished to donate their old Saab automobile to him and Saab was no longer in business. He claimed he didn't want to hurt their feelings and when I told him that he wasn't responsible for other people's feelings if he elected not to accept their offer, he abruptly cut me off and told me that that was not what he was asking me about and stormed out of the room and holed up in his bedroom for the rest of the night. The next evening, I confronted Joseph and informed him that I did not appreciate being treated by him in such a rude and disrespectful manner and that he owed me an apology. He couldn't do it and could not accept that his behavior toward me was destructive of a healthy relationship between us. He clearly was not a church deacon whose conduct was beyond reproach. He was quite the opposite, in fact!

The qualifications for becoming a deacon in any church are clearly spelled out in 1 Timothy 3:8-12 as follows:

> "*Likewise must the deacons be grave, not doubletongued, not given to much wine, not greedy of filthy lucre; Holding the mystery of the faith in a pure conscience. And let these also first be proved; then let them use the office of a deacon, being found blameless. Even so must their wives be grave, not slanderers, sober, faithful in all things. Let the deacons be husbands of one wife, ruling their children and their own houses well.*"

Yet Joseph's behaviors toward me evidenced to me that he was nothing more than a con artist and a sociopath; the precise opposite of traits which a church of any integrity ought to expect of its deacons. Clearly, God was exposing me to multiple sociopaths in my life at this time and was revealing to me their common behaviors in order to build my powers of spiritual discernment in this area.

Shortly after I had moved in with Joseph, he had asked to speak with me over his challenges in working with the INS to permit his alleged fiancé in Kenya to come to the United States and marry him. He asked me if I would lend him $1,500 or $2,000 which he told me that the INS required of him to have in a bank account during his application process. I agreed to loan him the money for 90 days without interest as a favor to him with this understanding of the facts in mind. Later, after Joseph revealed to me his less-than-honest character, I challenged him on whether he still had the money I had loaned him in the alleged bank account and when he confirmed my suspicion that he didn't have it, I told him that in lieu of repayment I would apply the monthly rent I owed him against the loan balance he owed me to pay it off. Joseph was not pleased, but I gave him no choice in the matter.

In early August 2012, God awoke me at 2:30 one morning and inspired in me the thought, *"Let them which be in Judaea, flee into the mountains,"* a verse I was very familiar with from Matthew 24:16. The passage continues,

"Let him which is on the housetop not come down to take any thing out of his house: Neither let him which is in the field return back to take his clothes. And woe unto them that are with child, and to them that give suck in those days! But pray ye that your flight be not in the winter, neither on the sabbath day: For then shall be great tribulation, such as was not from the beginning of the world to this time, no nor ever shall be."
Matthew 24:17-21

I asked God where I was to go and He gave me a vision of Jameson Lake, a place in the Sierras where I had backpacked to and camped at almost every year since I was 12 years old, and which bore many fond past memories for me and my former friend Dan Taft and his family. In fact, two years earlier, we had scattered Dan's younger son's cremation ashes at the far end of this lake. All my backpacking and camping gear was held hostage by my wife in my home, but God made it clear to me that He had given me the financial resources to buy replacement gear and that He wanted me to go immediately.

That morning I drove to Berkeley, purchased enough gear and food for ten days and drove to the Sierras, where I rented a motel room and packed for my trip into the wilderness. The next morning, I called and left messages with four or five close friends of where I was, and where I was going, and headed off to Jameson and Rock Lakes, with which I was intimately familiar. I thought then that perhaps Jesus was going to rapture me from that location. Clearly God was leading me there for something.

I ended up spending ten days camping, fishing, picking and eating wild berries and reading my two Bibles I had brought with me to try to make sense of why I was there and what was coming. The first night after it grew dark, I heard crashing in the bushes near my camp and turning my head lamp in that direction, I saw two red eyes staring back at me. I grabbed the machete I had with me and shouted out, "In the name of Jesus, get out of here; I am a son of God and you are trespassing on hallowed ground!" The animal or demon spirit (I suspect it was a bear) turned on its heels and scrambled away. But for the next two hours, I feared that what I heard was one or more black operations commandoes who were trying to sneak up on me and strangle me to death with a wire or something similar. So I stood rigid over my campfire with my machete in my hand ready to strike and waited for the attack, which never came.

After two hours crouching, tense and ready to spring on my attacker, it dawned on me that if it was God's will for me die in the wilderness at the hands of anything or anyone, there was nothing I could do to stop it. Similarly, God revealed to me that He had not brought me there for me to disappear or die after all He had put me through up to that point in my life. There was more to the story to be written. That much I knew.

The next morning God put it in my head that he wanted me to strip down to my hiking boots and walk naked down the trail to Rock Lake and to fully immerse myself in the lake as a form of baptism. I repeatedly asked God if He was sure He wanted me to do this; that it seemed pretty weird, and what if I encountered someone on the trail? God made it clear to me that this was precisely what He wanted me to do, and so I obeyed. As I came out of dunking under the surface of the lake, I felt as though I was cleansed and reborn in some mysterious way.

After this, I dressed, returned to my camp and began reading the King James Version of the Bible I had brought with me, starting with the four gospels and then the beefier books of Daniel, Romans, Revelation and a few others. I was quite familiar with the New International Version of the Bible, but had learned that the KJV of the Bible was the most reliable and trustworthy word-for-word translation of the original Hebrew and Greek manuscripts into English that we have available to us. I discovered a new level of depth and understanding as I read those books in the KJV of the Bible that I had read a number of times before in the NIV. It was as if the stories and teachings with which I was already familiar were revealing new and deeper meanings to me out of the KJV of the Bible. In particular, I was fervently seeking to understand what end times prophecies in Bible Scripture actually say and mean.

While there, I had no way of knowing what was going on in the outside world. There was a large forest fire nearby that filled the sky with smoke and during my ten days there in the middle of summer, I saw very few parties of other people and I deliberately kept my distance from those that I did see. I feared that God had called me there to protect me from some form of calamity that was occurring in the outside world. One afternoon, half way through my 10 day sojourn, I heard a familiar voice shouting my name. It was Jeff Taft, one of the people I had called right before I disappeared into the wilderness, who was coming to check on me and bring me some more food.

I cannot describe what a blessing Jeff's showing up was to me! I shared with him all that had happened to me and how I had burned most of my freeze dried food after the first meal I ate tasted like foul chemicals. I knew it was no coincidence that the campsite I was in had huckleberry bushes and wild raspberry plants surrounding it, and every morning and evening, more of the wild raspberries ripened and were available for me to eat. I knew confidently that God was revealing to me that He was providing for my every need. God similarly provided the additional food which Jeff and brought and left with me.

I walked back with Jeff to the parking lot at the trailhead where he showed me that a local sheriff's deputy had left his card on the windshield of my car, revealing that a missing person's report had been issued on me and that officials were concerned that I might be at risk of harming myself or others. I asked Jeff to contact the deputy when he was able to get cell phone coverage and assure him that he had found me and that I was perfectly all right, which Jeff agreed to do for me.

After ten days in the wilderness, my food was running out and Jeff had revealed to me that there was no evidence in the San Francisco Bay Area that revealed why God might have commanded me to flee to Jameson Lake so suddenly and without warning. I now believe that God was testing my faith: the trust I was prepared to place in Him, and that I passed His test.

Largely out of necessity for food, and annoyed that someone had filed a missing person's report against me and falsely accused me of being "at risk" to myself or others, I decided to return to civilization, clear my name, sort out my remaining financial matters with my roommate Joseph, and flee California for good. It was now clear to me that everywhere I turned, I was being betrayed and manipulated by wicked people who claimed to be one thing, but who were clearly not at all who they pretended to be. I was sick of it!

Upon my return to the Bay Area, I stayed with Jeff Taft for a night and the next morning, found a business card left on my car windshield from the local Napa County sheriff's office asking me to contact them. I happened to be visiting my friend Jerry at the Santa Rosa jail and in so doing, I had parked my car in the parking lot of the Sonoma County sheriff's office. So I walked over to their lobby, revealed who I was, and after waiting for half an hour, was interviewed by two sheriff's deputies concerning the missing person's report which was still showing outstanding on their systems, even though Jeff had reported back to law enforcement that he had encountered me in the wilderness and that I was fine. I asked the deputies what it was going to take to get the missing person's report canceled and my name cleared that I was not an "at risk" individual. They assured me that our conversation was sufficient and that they would see to it that the missing person's report was cancelled.

Later, I returned to Marin to learn that my roommate Joseph Peachtree and Kent Russo, who had no business getting involved, were behind the filing of the missing person's report and that my wife Barbara had been in on it in some way too. I was visited by a second pair of detectives from the San Rafael police department at my apartment the next day, who were investigating the same missing person's report, and I had to go through the same explanation and conversation with them that

I had been through with the Sonoma County sheriff deputies the day before, and once again I asked in exasperation what it was going to take to make this bogus missing person's report go away?

I didn't trust the system at this point and went to the city police department to see what had been written and whether I could file my own counter-statement revealing that those who had filed the report on me were in no position to file such a report and to ask what I could do further to make that report go away? All I encountered was evasion and non-answers, but they assured me that the report was no longer active and it was clear to me that this was all I could hope to accomplish to protect myself and my reputation. My take away from all this was that law enforcement in California and Marin especially, was deliberately incompetent and not safe at all for me to remain under.

I informed my roommate Joseph that I expected him to repay me the remainder of the loan that I had not yet applied against rent I owed him, which totaled $1,050. He didn't have the money, so I told him I would approach his church's pastor, Jeff, and ask his church to see to it that I was properly reimbursed for his misrepresentations to me, as one of the church's deacons.

He didn't like it, but he had no choice. I spoke to Jeff over the matter and asked for his help and he agreed to take it to his church elders for approval. He later called me back to confirm that it was agreed to and that I could pick up a check later that week. I informed Jeff that I would be leaving Joseph's apartment as soon as I received the check. Several days later, once I had received the check, I packed all I had in my possession in my car and headed to Napa to stay with Jeff Taft that night and the next morning, headed out of California for southeastern Idaho, guided by a book entitled *Strategic Relocation*, by Andrew Skousen, who recommended Star Valley in Idaho as one of the safest places in the country to strategically relocate to.

184

7. My Story

I cannot describe the joy I felt as I left California and headed across the Nevada desert that afternoon. The clouds were billowy and white over the dry and barren hills and were absolutely beautiful. On a couple of occasions I found myself weeping with joy and gratitude knowing with certainty that God was with me on my journey. I left behind virtually my entire life of over 58 years and all but a handful of people I chose to remain in contact with. I was following a plan Jeff and I had laid out together and he was planning on joining me later once I scouted out suitable places to live, but God was guiding my every move and I was at peace; more so than I had been in a very long time.

Upon arriving in Star Valley several days later, I began to do my due diligence on the area. I visited a local real estate agent who was very helpful in explaining that most of the valley was heavily Mormon, and as I drove around, I got the distinct impression that I would be a fish out of water and feel pretty isolated living there. I chose to keep driving north and arrived in Teton Valley, which was not entirely new to me. 34 years earlier, as a young consultant with Arthur Andersen's Systems Consulting Division (what is today Accenture), I had worked on an out-of-town assignment in nearby Idaho Falls for nine months and discovered the Grand Tetons, Jackson Hole, Wyoming and Yellowstone Park, and had fallen in love with them. To get to the Tetons and Jackson Hole, I had had to pass through Teton Valley on the way. I knew instantly that this was where God intended for me to spend the winter and located and leased a home in the country that was perfect for my needs and came fully furnished. The fact that everything came together so seamlessly demonstrated to me that this was where I was supposed to be, living in the shadows of the western slopes of the Grand Tetons.

I soon discovered a non-denominational church in town and on the first Sunday I walked in, a 32 year old young man, Mason Black, a visitor who was a friend of the pastor, spoke of his recent two week journey to Israel and mentioned the word "Talmud." My ears perked up immediately and I sought him out, introduced myself to him and we ended up spending about 45 minutes comparing notes with one another and both became excited about our common interests and insights.

Later that afternoon, I drove 70 miles to where Mason and his extended family lived to observe him lead a small informal para-church group in singing worship songs and leading a Bible study. I resolved to continue joining Mason, his brother and his wife, Mason's wife and three young kids, his mom and dad, and several other people who lived locally who had been studying and learning under Mason's evident teaching gifts once a week, with the intention of watching, listening, learning and supporting Mason in whatever way God led me to do.

Additionally, I made an effort to introduce myself to and get to know the 46 year old pastor of church #6 that I had found in Teton Valley, Ralph Bunche. I was very open and candid with him about who I was and the divorce I was going through, and equally candid with him about my knowledge of the global conspiracy and its obvious links to end times prophecy and I sought to learn his life story.

Everyone has a story, and Ralph was no different. He and Mason Black had gotten to know one another as fellow staff members at Calvary Chapel in Pocatello a number of years earlier, and Ralph had recently completed seminary studies at John MacArthur's Master's Seminary in southern California. He revealed that he had successfully raised money from personal contacts of his, which undoubtedly began with his father Ralph Bunche's NFL contacts, and it appeared to me from the new, modern and spacious look of his church that someone with deep pockets was underwriting both it and him.

Ralph had majored in psychology at Utah State University, were he attended on a football scholarship. He was hoping to follow his adopted father into the NFL, but was injured in the summer before his senior year, and that ended his hopes for a football career and led to his going through a tough period of time seeking to figure out what he was going to do with his life instead, and in the process, claimed he became a follower of Christ.

186

On our fifth weekly get together, Ralph's and my conversation took a decidedly different turn. Ralph clearly had an agenda that morning and intended to ram it through, and I found his brazenness rather extraordinary. First, he informed me that he wanted me to accept his and his church's ministering to me, in light of the divorce I was going through, even though by then he clearly knew that I was not seeking such support. Moreover, I found his suggestion rather impertinent, coming from a man 12 years my junior and quite a bit less experienced than I was.

Second, he made it clear to me that he in no way wanted me to share with others in his church anything about what I knew concerning the global conspiracy. In other words, he was telling me to suppress and silence the truth.

He further made it clear that he viewed himself as a wise teacher and discipler of followers of Christ, didn't much care if his church grew or not, and that as long as he was in charge as pastor, people were free to leave and go elsewhere if they had a problem with that. It became clear to me that Ralph was a very controlling and manipulative individual with a thin skin, an arrogant attitude and a willingness to run over others to get his way. This was not a man of God, as he would soon reveal even further.

Shortly thereafter, Ralph began to preach and teach a pre-tribulation rapture, which by then I had figured out was a false teaching not at all supported by what the Bible says. The Bible teaches that the rapture, or gathering of God's elect, consisting of both the dead in Christ, and then those who are living who are born again followers of Yahushua will be transformed into resurrected bodies and gathered up into heaven with Yahushua during the end times before the wrath of God is poured out upon the wicked, as described in the Book of Revelation.

Over the prior two years, I had read a number of books on the topic of end times Bible prophecy and come to realize that many prominent self-professed theologians falsely taught that this event would occur before a period of time foretold in Daniel 12 and Matthew 24 referred to as the great tribulation. Yet as I read the Bible, especially during my 10 days in the wilderness that summer, it became quite obvious to me that this was a complete fraud and that in fact, the Bible teaches the precise opposite of this: namely that the gathering or rapture will occur AFTER the great tribulation is over.

I could see precisely why these frauds, deceivers and false teachers were pushing this false teaching: it fills church pews and offering plates by delivering a "feel good" message that those professing themselves to be followers of Yahushua need not experience discomfort, sufferings and trials, even though this is precisely what the Bible teaches God's elect.

I asked around his church after his teaching on the pre-trib rapture and found that only one other person seemed to be at all alarmed by Ralph's false teaching. One fellow I had developed some rapport with showed me a textbook from the mid-1800s he had that showed a graphical timeline of end times prophecy events in which the rapture was shown occurring right before the tribulation period began. So this heresy clearly has been floating around for over 150 years; there is nothing new about it at all. Yet it blatantly flies in the face of what the Bible teaches and says.

So I sent Ralph a private email the next week and asked him how he could possibly arrive at such a conclusion based on the text of Bible Scripture and admonished him that the Bible teaches that false teachers will be subject to extra severe judgment on judgment day for misleading others. Not surprisingly, Ralph dodged and did not address my question and merely invited me to come to his next adult Sunday school teaching where he would address a number of questions related to his prior teaching. So I went to listen.

Matthew 24:15-31 is where we get the clearest timeline and sequence for the great tribulation and rapture. First, in verse 15, Yahushua (Jesus) reveals that at the end of the current age of world history there will be an event, referred to as the "abomination that causes desolation standing in the holy place," which signals the start of the great tribulation. Yahushua describes that this time period will be more distressing than at any other time in all of world history and so deceiving, that if it were possible, even God's elect would be deceived (Matthew 24:21-24). Then in verse 29 it says quite clearly, that immediately after the end of the great tribulation, four dramatic celestial events will occur: the sun will grow dark, the moon will not give off its light, the stars will fall from heaven and the earth shall be shaken. Verse 30 then begins, "And then . . . " and goes on to describe the gathering of God's elect from the four corners of the earth. This is the event in end times prophecy commonly referred to as "the rapture." The conclusions that any honest reader of this passage ought to derive from it are painfully obvious.

First, God's elect will be brought *through* the tribulation (defined as a period of troubles, suffering and trials), and not rescued *from* it! The Bible often repeats patterns and in this instance, this aspect of God bringing His people through trials and tribulations is repeated over and over, the best example being how God brought Noah and his family through the Flood which destroyed all living creatures who were not with Noah on the ark. He didn't rescue them from it.

Second, it is only *after* the tribulation is over that the events leading to the gathering or rapture are described with words which can only be construed honestly as events occurring in sequence. In this context, the gathering occurs *after* the four celestial events which occur *after* the great tribulation is over.

How much more clear can it be?!? It cannot. The only explanation left is that anyone advancing a belief in a pre-tribulation gathering or rapture is deceived and is not at all likely to be one of God's elect, whom Yahushua tells us by deduction, from verse 24, will not be deceived, while the rest of the world will be.

Ralph's explanation for this contradiction was that there will be *two* raptures: one for God's elect right before the tribulation begins, and a second one at the end for those who become God's elect during the tribulation. There are two distinct problems with this claim.

First, there are no words in the Bible to support such a preposterous two rapture view. And second, it reveals a serious error in understanding who God's elect are, compared to what Scripture teaches. God's elect are not just born again followers of Christ, although everyone who is an authentic born again follower of Christ is proven to be one of God's elect, by virtue of having been truly born again in the Spirit. The elect are those people, chosen or elected by God, since before the world began, to become one of His adopted born again sons or daughters at some time in their lives, at a time, and in a manner of God's choosing, and at God's initiative – not man's. Therefore every person alive in the world today is either one of God's elect, or one of God's non-elect, and their status with God never changes.

So Ralph's claims wither upon careful thinking and examination. He went on to explain that he and the other three elders of his church were in the process of developing a statement of faith for their church that they were going to ask every member of the church to attest to, that would include a belief in the rapture. He clarified that a person would not have to attest to a belief in a pre-trib rapture, but that everyone entrusted with teaching in his church would be required to acknowledge and teach a pre-trib rapture. In other words, anyone who did not wish to be treated as a second class citizen and pariah in his church would have to subscribe to Ralph's heresy and false teaching.

I had heard enough, and informed Ralph via email that I would not be participating in his church any further. I had also been attending and participating in a Bible study at the home of one of the other three elders in Ralph's church, which I continued to attend for another month or so until, in reply to one of the numerous email blasts I was sending out to a group of about 40 contacts of mine, I received the following email from this elder's wife:

Watchman,

I am very concerned with where you are going with all this. First of all the Word tells us to pray for Israel and His people. Also this hatred you have for a number of groups is so unlike Christ it scares me. We are to be praying for all of His creation, gays, Hollywood movie producers, Jews and x-wives. He did not give us the right to decide who is worthy to be saved and who is not. I know there are many, many people who are not easy to love, but we are commanded to love them and to hold them up in prayer.

There has (sic) been horrible atrocities that have happened against almost every nationality, horrible, horrible things. We know these things are going to happen the Bible tells us so, but the way your mind is working, you are not letting the Lord work through your life the way He wants to. He wants to make you like Him and the Bible tells us He is love. I am going to pray that your computer breaks so you will stop feeding these feelings you have toward so many people.

And I have told you before, no matter what you have against the Jews to say that the Holocaust never happened is ludicrous, and ignorant to say the least, I already told you I personally know victims of the Holocaust. The Jews are not the only ones to claim it happened.

Do you think that God grieves any less for all those who have been murdered Jew or no Jew?

And anyone who accepts Christ IS His elect, to think that God picks and chooses only certain people is wrong, the Bible says he died for all mankind.

Please don't dismiss what I am saying because I don't have the education that you have remember pride is another sin, I am speaking truth to you, please before it's too late for you to turn back ask God to give you His love, cause you don't have it. And get a JOB.

This is the text of the email I had included her on which had provoked her above reply to me:

Dear friends,

Through a new friend of mine, I discovered a new source of truth and book concerning the identity of true Israel this morning that prompted me to compose and send to you this thought-piece. I truly hope you will take the time to read and think about what I have to share here quite carefully and thoughtfully. I believe it to be very important to our futures.

Did you know that:

1. 90% or more of those who are Jews are not descended from the ancient Hebrew tribes of Abraham, Isaac and Jacob?

2. The descendants of white Europeans are the true descendants of the 12 Hebrew Tribes of ancient Israel?

3. Evangelical Christian pastors who are teaching naïve, gullible and uninformed Christians that America must bless the modern state of Israel for America to be blessed and avoid God's curse are teaching falsehood?

4. That God's true Chosen People are not the modern day Jews, but instead are God's elect, chosen as individuals by God since before the world began to one day, at a time and method of God's choosing and initiative, become one of His adopted sons or daughters?

5. Sociopaths always prey on the pity and sympathy of the naïve and gullible in order to avoid detection and exposure as the criminals they truly are?

6. Most of the world's Jewish-Freemason global elites qualify as sociopaths (that is, they have no consciences)?

7. The holocaust (claiming the death by gassing of 6 million Jews under the Nazis in WWII) is a preposterous lie and fraud, perpetrated by these sociopaths and designed to conceal from the world's attention the truth that Jewish-inspired Bolshevik Communists murdered 66 million white Russian non-Jews under Lenin and Stalin to consolidate their political power and eliminate all potential sources of opposition to their tyrannical rule?

8. 70 million Chinese, 4 million Vietnamese and 2 million Cambodians died similar hideous deaths under the brutal totalitarian Communist regimes of Mao Tse-Tung, Ho Chi Minh and Pol Pot, respectively, for the same reason and that combined, these deaths total 142 million deaths attributable to brutal Communism, which was invented and advanced by the world's Jewish-Freemason elite sociopaths to achieve world domination?

9. This 20th century death toll exceeds all the deaths in all the wars of recorded human history and is the true holocaust that ought to be evoking intense moral outrage at the perpetrators of these crimes?

10. 800,000 Palestinians were driven from their homes and villages in 1947 and 1948 in a campaign of genocide and ethnic cleansing by Zionist terrorists and the Israeli army directed by the founder of modern day Israel, David Ben Gurion in order to ensure that the resulting population mix in the new Jewish state of Israel would be 80% Jewish Rothschild-Zionists?

193

11. Jewish-Freemason globalists own and control the top 5 or 6 mainstream media conglomerates which control the vast majority of the propaganda and brain washing indoctrination we have been fed all our lives to keep us in the dark and deceived?

12. Almost everything we have ever been taught by these tools of sociopaths is a lie and a fraud?

13. The devil, the father of lies, is very real and rules our world, using human sociopaths, controlled by the devil's demons, as his agents of destruction?

14. The Bible reveals that all of this had to happen to set up the conditions for the fulfillment of end times Bible prophesy, which is now occurring?

The likely answer to most of the questions I pose here is that you do not know many of these things. In fact, it is quite likely that some of these truth claims I write here make you angry with me for writing them. If that's so, it's because you have been brain washed and programmed by the global elites and the media and education systems which they own and control to advance their lies. So when you read or hear the truth, you have been programmed to respond with strong negative emotions toward the person revealing such truths. All this has been calculated and planned quite deliberately, by the world's rich and powerful elites. Moreover, your brain goes into cognitive dissonance when you encounter truth claims which refute what you have believed to be true all your lives. It hurts your pride to realize that you may have been hideously deceived, betrayed and duped. I know; I've been there too. But I'm now way past that. So why do I bother sharing this with you?

The answer is quite simple: unless you know the truth, you have no way of solving your problems caused by your false beliefs. Moreover, as long as you

194

continue to trust sources of information and people who claim to be God's chosen people, and really are not, you are being deceived, lied to and harmed. You are trusting wicked people who secretly hate you and intend to harm you and your families. In case you haven't figured it out yet, we live in a world at war. That war, at its essence, is a war between forces of good vs. evil, between the truth and lies, between God, Jesus and His people vs. the devil, demonic spirits and those who serve the devil, wittingly, or unwittingly. It is the story of the entire Bible, probably no more clearly spelled out than in the book of wisdom, the Book of Proverbs, which teaches us how to discern between truth and error, the righteous and the wicked, the wise and the foolish – if we would merely read it!

Everything you hear and see in the MSM is nothing but lies and distractions to take your eyes off of the greatest theft being perpetrated upon humanity by the thieving global elites whose worldview and belief system is shaped by the hateful, bigoted and racist teachings of the Jewish rabbis from the Jewish Talmud and Kabbalah. These teachings hideously distort the teachings of the Bible and advance the causes of eastern mysticism, magic and the occult. In other words, they serve the devil, even though they claim otherwise.

Every world and institutional leader today and virtually every institutional church pastor is part of this wicked system. The way you can tell is that they rule by power, force, intimidation and lies and not by love, compassion, humility and the truth. Wisdom tells us not to trust anyone who exhibits the behaviors of the former. At some level, we all know this. But we tolerate and compromise with it: that which is evil. When we do, we are complete fools. The Book of Proverbs says so.

So what can we possibly do about all this? A great deal actually.

First, we can get ourselves educated as to the truth. I know, I know, I'm asking you to read some books and educate yourselves. Yes, that takes time and effort. Get over it and just do it. Turn off the TV that is the biggest mind control machine in most homes, and pick up some books and start reading as I did about a dozen year ago. You will be amazed at how informed you will become; and how much more an interesting conversationalist you will become too!

Second, we can inform those with whom we have trusting relationships and urge them to look at the evidence we have uncovered concerning the truth. All truth is discernable through three ways: 1) hard objective evidence (the facts), 2) logical coherence (does a claim line up with other facts and conditions we know to be true?) and 3) trusted authority. Most of us lean heavily on what our parents, schools and media have taught us, as allegedly trusted authorities. The problem is: they seldom are what we assumed them to be. Any lie repeated often enough becomes accepted as the truth and this is how you and I have been duped and deceived by those whom we falsely believed to be trusted authorities. Now we must go back and correct our broken paradigms.

It is true that the Bible claims to be the flawless words of God and the truth. I am convinced that it is everything it claims to be. But it is not everything. God gave us critical thinking minds and He expects us to use them to look at the evidence in our world and reason logically from that to the truth, using all three sources to arrive at a solid footing and true wisdom.

Third, we need to develop the skills to detect false teachers quickly and promptly disengage from having anything to do with them. Proverbs teaches us that those who listen to liars will be destroyed. So we must stop listening to liars and surround ourselves with safe, trustworthy people instead. The only way I know how to do this is to soak in the Book of Proverbs deeply and master its life lessons.

I am on a journey to read one chapter a night in the Book of Proverbs for a decade so that I might become wise. Now I'm challenging you to join me on that journey. I am about 4 ½ years into my own journey and I can assure you that while I have not arrived, I am much more discerning than I was when I embarked on this journey. I just read the chapter whose number corresponds to the date of the month every night. So tonight I will be reading Chapter 19 of the Book of Proverbs. And I always do what it says now.

The world encourages us to be tolerant of everybody, to compromise with everyone and to celebrate diversity. But Proverbs teaches us that this is sheer madness and foolishness! Which is right? The answer ought to be obvious. There are wicked, prideful, greedy, materialistic, self-absorbed, foolish people and there are righteous, humble, giving, content, caring and wise people. Each of our jobs in life is to learn how to differentiate between the two and shun the former and invest our time with the latter type of person. Not everyone is wise, kind or safe for us and we simply have to come to terms with this reality.

Fourth, the truth is the most powerful weapon in the world; we need to use it to advance the kingdom of God and oppose the kingdom of darkness. Jesus is the truth. He told us this in John 14:6 when He told his disciples, *"I am the way, **the truth,** and the life: no man comes to the Father (God), but by me."* He told Pilate the same thing in John 18:37: *". . . for this cause I came into the world, that I should bear witness to **the truth**. Every one that is of **the truth** hears my voice."*

The Bible reveals to us that God does not and cannot lie, change or fail. His opponent, the devil, lies continuously and seeks to steal, kill and destroy (see John 10:10). He seeks to destroy all of mankind through trickery and deception. How much more evidence do we need of the infallibility of the Bible in this regard than this, in light of today's reality in our broken world? It's pretty obvious for those of us who have spiritual sight. Those who are not of God, lack this spiritual sight and will never get it unless God takes the initiative to save them and reveal these things to them. This is a hard reality to come to terms with, but it is the truth.

Those of us who truly number among God's born-again elect are called to speak the truth in love to advance God's kingdom. Sometimes love does not "feel" nice, warm and affirming. Sometimes it convicts wicked hearts of sin. But that is a good thing, if it leads a person to confess and repent of their sins and turn their lives over to Jesus as their Lord over every aspect of their lives, and so be saved from an eternity of torment in hell, which is where they are likely headed today. How can we claim we genuinely love someone, if we knowingly stay silent and permit them to jump off the cliff into the fires of hell for all eternity? The short answer is, that we can't. We are cowardly, selfish and unloving if we say nothing; God will call us to account one day for that cowardice and unloving spirit too.

Political Correctness is cowardice and is of the devil and a tool of demonic Marxism/Communism. It's time we woke up to this reality and refuse to play by such foolish rules any longer. Expose the lies and the liars and they will flee, teaches the Bible. Why aren't we doing it? I would submit that fear and cowardice are near the top of the list in explaining such hypocritical behavior on our part. We fear scorn, mockery, persecution and people's hatred for speaking the truth in love. Instead, we prefer wicked mankind's approval, and risk spending our eternities in torment in hell for it. This is a very dumb choice. But most people are making just that choice today. At least the foolish and the wicked can console themselves that they will have lots of company. How comforting will that be when each is living his own private hell for all eternity? It will mean nothing.

For those of you interested in learning more concerning the truths I laid out at the start of this thought piece, I encourage you to drop me a note and I will be more than happy to furnish you with suggested sources and readings (books) to inform yourself on the real facts and to corroborate those truth claims with other sources which add credibility and credence to those controversial truths.

The key thing you need to concentrate on is this: if there is substantial evidence that any truth claim is being concealed, suppressed or silenced, what does that probably tell you? It tells you that it is probably the truth and that someone wicked is trying to keep it from you to deceive and harm you. That should motivate you all the more to examine the evidence, logic and trustworthiness of the authority claiming it and the claim itself.

We really need to wise up and start doubting just about everything until we have examined the hard evidence, the logical coherence for a claim and the real source of the facts and the claims (is it really a trustworthy authority?). Even then, we should always remain open to new evidence or new logic that might suggest that our existing paradigm is still not quite right. This requires a humble and teachable spirit that is subject to correction from others.

We live in a time in history in which deception and fraud are rampant. The Bible teaches us to expect this and to be hyper-vigilant so as to avoid being deceived. If we are genuinely born-again and are truly submitting and surrendering our wills and our lives to Jesus as our Lord over every aspect of our lives, His Holy Spirit will lead us to the truth (the objective truth as God perceives it). If we try to do this on our own, forget it. We will fail and will be deeply deceived and destroyed in the process. Jesus is our only truly trustworthy authority. He will lead us to the authentic facts and the coherent logic and critical reasoning necessary to avoid being deceived. That has been my experience. But only after I fully submitted and surrendered my will and my life to Jesus in all things. I urge you to do the same. You will be amazed by what God reveals to you, if and when you do. But be prepared for Him to rock your world and your comfort when He does. It can be a wild ride.

Warm regards,

Watchman on the Wall

Clearly that wife of the church elder could not process or hear much of anything I wrote in the above thought piece. She is spiritually blind and has no clue that she is. She is a complete fraud. This same woman had also made it very clear that she did not believe in the doctrine of election, which Ralph had previously taught accurately in his church during my time there (an obvious inconsistency, I know, with his distortion of what election means in the context of his pre-trib rapture false teaching).

So this wife of an elder in Ralph's church was demonstrating that her husband did not fit the Biblical requirements for any overseer or deacon in any church, inasmuch as his wife was openly contradicting what the Bible says and teaches, and thus, her husband, the elder, was not running an orderly household. Even more, her threat to send a curse on my computer and her final mean-spirited remark to me to "get a job" in her email demonstrated that she was not a genuine follower of Christ in the least, and perhaps even a demon-infested witch besides!

Needless, to say, I chose to have nothing further to do with the Bible study group in their home from that point forward.

By mid-October 2012, I was settled into the home I had leased through the winter and, in light of the fact that my non-believing wife had left me relationally, the Bible teaches that I was free to date and remarry. The world today imposes an elaborate set of legal hurdles which one must jump over to be declared legally divorced, but according to the teachings of the Bible, I was already divorced in God's eyes, and so I decided to try my hand at online dating, knowing that the online dating scene is often frequented by various forms of predators, but trusting that YHWH would protect me from harm.

I posted a profile on match.com in which I made it clear that I was a Biblical Christian and that my faith defined me, knowing full well that such a profile would be of little interest to the majority of single women in our godless culture, but that failing to reveal my core nature up front would merely mislead and irritate others and lead to my meeting women with whom I would have no real rapport or common values and interests. I prayed that YHWH would bring a godly Proverbs 31 woman into my life.

About a month later, a woman named Marsha from match.com sent me a brief note revealing that she lived in Idaho Falls (about 70 miles away), but frequently visited my town and the organic food store I frequented. She told me if I saw a red Jeep on the road to pull her over and introduce myself. I happened to have an appointment in Idaho Falls a few days later and suggested that we meet over coffee and a sandwich there. Marsha and I shared an interest in camping, fishing and hiking.

In our first meeting, she shared with me her story that about a year earlier, her 56 year old husband of 26 years had informed her he wanted a divorce and was shacking up with an 18 year old girl who worked at his place of employment with him. Marsha was devastated by his announcement. They were divorced in May 2012. She shared with me how she had recently completed a course at her church in Idaho Falls, called

"Healed and Set Free," and she described to me how cathartic that course had been for her in letting go and forgiving her ex-husband for betraying her and for turning her life upside down. She described how she had grown up in a Mormon family, but had largely walked away from the LDS church at 18 and had only recently been attending Calvary Chapel and had been baptized in the Snake River a few months before we met. We went down to a small park along the Snake River where Marsha had done a project as a master gardener, and while there, we discovered that our birthdays were only five days apart from one another.

Over the next couple of months, I drove to Idaho Falls and took Marsha to church, which was an indescribable pleasure for both of us. Both of us had gone to church by ourselves for years, in my case for about eight years, and for Marsha, for at least a year, both of us having been married to fairly rabid non-believers, who had no interest in the Bible or the ways and thoughts of God. We both had witnessed numerous other couples at church who seemed to be so much more of one mind and committed to doing life God's way vs. selfishly and at odds with one another that we both delighted in being able to hold hands or sit with my arm around her and participate in the church service together. Afterwards, we grabbed a bite to eat for lunch before I returned home.

We began to text and call one another on the phone, most of it being light banter. Marsha was a geriatric and rehabilitation nurse at a skilled nursing facility located a block away from where she was living in Idaho Falls. She worked twelve and a half hour shifts three or four days a week and would tell me about her residents and the issues she was having to contend with at work and I developed a real admiration for her obvious technical competence as a nurse, but even more importantly, I saw in her a loving, kind heart for others with a sunny disposition that made others feel better just by being in her presence. Her days off were frequently filled with crafts and gardening projects and I quickly figured out that she and I shared similar Type A driven personalities, although I had perhaps learned to temper mine a bit more than Marsha had yet learned how to do.

By January 2013, I had fallen in love with Marsha. I was a bit ahead of how she felt towards me, but I chose to take the chance and reveal how I felt to her. Thankfully, my disclosure to her didn't frighten or chase her away. I had shared with her how I read a chapter every night in the Book of Proverbs and had been doing so for four and a half years, and when she came to visit me or I went to visit her, we started reading a chapter together. Before long, I was calling her at 8:00 p.m. every night when we were apart, and reading Proverbs and a daily devotional I use and had given her a copy of, and we began to pray together.

By around March or April of 2013, I met two of Marsha's three young adult children. Both were clearly products of our broken American culture, seriously lacking in wisdom and good judgment, and completely clueless about how completely clueless they were. Her 35 year old son, Jason, from Marsha's first marriage, was a VA hospital administrator who clearly knew his craft, but whose primary motivation in life was to become famous. Jason's pride, arrogance and ambition was over the top, and his personal life was largely a mess, as a result. His 28-year old sister Julia, proved to be highly opinionated about everything, was incapable of benefitting from any coaching or correction from anyone and was quite self-absorbed, self-centered and narcissistic. Marsha and I took her and her boyfriend, Tom, out to dinner for them to meet me and vice versa and during our conversation, I mentioned to them that all three of my young adult children were demon infested and wished to have nothing to do with me.

I later learned that my comment had branded me in Julia's eyes as some kind of "Jesus freak," and that she was determined to have nothing further to do with me. Marsha told me that Julia had always been rather prickly, ever since she was a child. It was clear to me that her emotional maturity and judgment had been arrested at a fairly early age.

Marsha and I were invited to celebrate Easter at the home of a couple, whose wife was a friend of and fellow nurse with Marsha. The couple were in their late 30's or early 40's. Of the ten to twelve adults who were at their party, every last one of us were divorced or were going through a divorce. It was quite clear to me that divorce in America was a much more prevalent problem than has been reported as 52% of all marriages ending in divorce. It certainly appeared to me that the truth was much higher than that, and from all of my research and study on the agenda of the global elites, I knew it was entirely deliberate and intentional, designed to destroy the American family and traditional marriage and to emasculate and impoverish American men, especially white, Biblical Christian men.

Meanwhile, I had attempted to mediate my divorce from Barbara in December 2012 with no success. Barbara had hired an aggressive woman divorce lawyer who was a psychological terrorist and pathological liar, who deliberately did everything possible to make false allegations against me and show gross disrespect towards me, which negated any possibility of our finding common ground to negotiate over. It was clear from my attempt at mediation that the other side's sole motivation with mediation was to frustrate me and deplete my financial resources and that they had no intention of dealing in good faith with me, based on the hard facts.

So in late January 2013, I hired my third divorce attorney to represent me and buffer me from having to deal directly with Barbara's lawyer, who by this time I had come to loathe. I had had to terminate the first two divorce lawyers I hired because they failed to take direction from me, and the second one even insisted that unless I accepted the Marin DA's plea bargain and agreed to accept a five year restraining order against me that he would not represent me. I was going to be damned if I would tolerate such a blatant abuse of a healthy client-attorney relationship and so terminated his services immediately.

California is a community property state in which the shared assets of spouses in a divorce are to be divided 50% to each spouse, after accounting for any separate property which either spouse brought into the marriage or inherited separately during the marriage. Barbara's and my biggest asset by far was the equity in the home we had lived in and improved three times since 1982, which she now held hostage by virtue of the restraining order she had secured against me under false pretenses. I had inherited a rather substantial sum from my grandparents which I had invested in financing a major addition to our home 20 years earlier, which I was claiming was my separate property which, if the courts had any integrity to them and would have applied the divorce statutes objectively, would have awarded me close to two thirds of the net assets shared between Barbara and me. Yet through a lengthy series of court motions, it became clear to me that the court system was rigged to deny me anything close to justice or a fair application of the legal system's own rules.

As part of the process, the divorce courts often arrange for a panel of retired and current divorce attorneys to hear the arguments on both sides and seek to facilitate a negotiated settlement agreement to try to avoid a lengthy and expensive court trial, which merely depletes the assets of both parties and whose outcomes are designed to be highly uncertain and often rigged. In early September 2012, I drove to California from Idaho to spend an entire day with my lawyer negotiating the terms of a divorce settlement. We arrived at an outcome that was "good enough." It was clear to me that God willed for me to conclude the battle and move on with the rest of my life. At the end of the day, after we had arrived at a marital settlement agreement, we met with the judge who had facilitated our negotiations, who declared us divorced effective immediately. I was finally free of the talons of my my sociopathic ex-wife and felt immense relief!

Before she declared our marriage dissolved, the judge asked either of us if we cared to say anything. Surprisingly, Barbara did. She turned to me after spending most of the day crying in order to prey on others' sympathy and pity (a common tactic of sociopaths) and told me that she regretted how things ended and that she would always love me. As she left the court ahead of me she approached me and sought to embrace me a final time.

I was dumb-founded, but chose to be gracious and permit it and she repeated that she would always love me. It was the most bizarre and incredible thing I could have ever imagined. This woman had engaged in every act imaginable to assassinate my good character and public reputation, she and our daughter had lied and made false allegations about me in court, she had slapped a restraining order on me, barring me from even communicating with my adult children for five years, accused me of being violent, and crazy because I believe God and believe what the Bible says. I felt as though I was witnessing an insane asylum run by lunatics and wicked fools.

As we left the courthouse that afternoon, my attorney told me he had never witnessed such a thing in his 40 plus years of practicing law. He also pointed out that I was now free to remarry, if I chose to. I explained to him that a marriage ceremony is not needed, according to the Bible, for a husband and wife to be married in God's eyes. I was quite surprised, but my attorney knew precisely what I was referring to, even though I knew him to be a willing agent of the Jewish global elites and made a living preying off of the legal money battles of divorcing couples, none of which would be needed if men and women merely conformed themselves to the teachings of the Bible concerning the covenant and commitments of holy marriage.

Upon my return to Idaho, Marsha and I took a couple of days to visit the Grand Tetons and over dinner the first night, I asked Marsha to marry me and she accepted. Two months later, we combined our households, moved to Teton Valley, and were married before a local judge in a private ceremony. Marsha's adult children had made it abundantly clear that they wanted nothing to do with me and chose to punish their mother over it, and so a quiet, private ceremony seemed the wise thing to do. Today, Marsha and I are so very blessed and grateful that God has led us to each other and we are thriving as husband and wife with YHWH and Yahushua at the center of our marriage, submitted and surrendered to YHWH's will in all things. In return, YHWH is redeeming the many years the locusts have eaten in both of our lives, just as He promises us He will in Joel 2:25:

> *"And I will restore to you the years that the locust hath eaten, the cankerworm, and the caterpillar, and the palmerworm, my great army which I sent among you."*

In January 2014, we both celebrated our 60th birthdays, experiencing a joy and a peace neither of us have ever known before.

We deliberately moved to the country to avoid the ever-growing insanity and demonic behaviors we have been observing all around us. I can teach through my writing from nearly anywhere, as we watch for and await the end of the great tribulation and the second coming of Yahushua, the climax of YHWH's story. Meanwhile, it has become quite obvious to me that God (YHWH) has allowed many trials, many of them very painful, to come into my life, for a way bigger purpose: to serve Him as one of His true prophets in these final days of the great tribulation and as one of His watchmen on the wall in the tradition of Ezekiel 3:17-21 and 33:1-11:

> *"Son of man, I have made thee a watchman unto the house of Israel: therefore hear the word at my mouth, and give them warning from me. When I say unto the wicked, Thou shalt surely die; and thou givest him not warning, nor speakest to warn the wicked from his wicked way, to save his life; the same wicked man shall die in his iniquity; but his blood will I require at thine hand. Yet if thou warn the wicked, and he turn not from his wickedness, nor from his wicked way, he shall die in his iniquity; but thou hast delivered thy soul. Again, when a righteous man doth turn from his righteousness, and commit iniquity, and I lay a stumblingblock before him, he shall die: because thou hast not given him warning, he shall die in his sin, and his righteousness which he hath done shall not be remembered; but his blood will I require at thine hand. Nevertheless if thou warn the righteous man, that the righteous*

sin not, and he doth not sin, he shall surely live, because he is warned; also thou hast delivered thy soul." Ezekiel 3:17-21

"Again the word of the LORD (YHWH) came unto me saying, Son of man, speak to the children of thy people, and say unto them, When I bring the sword upon a land, if the people of the land take a man of their coasts, and set him for their watchman: If when he seeth the sword come upon the land, he blow the trumpet, and warn the people; Then whosoever heareth the sound of the trumpet, and taketh not warning; if the sword come, and take him away, his blood shall be upon his own head. He heard the sound of the trumpet, and took not warning; his blood shall be upon him. But he that taketh warning shall deliver his soul. But if the watchman see the sword come, and blow not the trumpet, and the people be not warned; if the sword come, and take any person from among them, he is taken away in his iniquity; but his blood will I require at the watchman's hand. So thou, O son of man, I have set thee a watchman unto the house of Israel; therefore thou shalt hear the word at my mouth, and warn them from me. When I say unto the wicked, O wicked man, thou shalt surely die; if thou dost not speak to warn the wicked from his way, that wicked man shall die in his iniquity; but his blood will I require at thine hand. Nevertheless, if thou warn the wicked of his way to turn from it; if he do not turn from his way, he shall die in his iniquity; but thou hast delivered thy soul. Therefore, O thou son of man, speak unto the house if Israel; Thus ye speak, saying, If our transgressions and our sins be upon us, and we pine away in them, how should we then live? Say unto them, As I live, saith the Lord God (Adonai YHWH), I have no pleasure in the death of the wicked; but that the wicked turn from his way and live: turn ye, turn ye from your evil ways; for why will ye die, O house of Israel?" Ezekiel 33:1-11

This clearly reveals why God (YHWH) chose to put me through the ringer for many years: so that I might blow the trumpet and sound the alarm and warn of the coming cataclysm of the second coming of Yahushua (Christ) which is now less than a year away. No one in his right mind would seek out such a role and I have never sought it, nor asked for it. Yet clearly God (YHWH) had different plans for my life from the outset and has orchestrated every event and thought and circumstance throughout my life to lead me to this point, and my understanding of why I am here. I am humbled by it. And I choose to submit and obey. For this reason was I born and for this reason was I created: to testify to the truth of the prophecies of the end times in the Bible.

8. Exposing the Greatest Lies and Frauds of the Last Hundred Years

Our world is, and always has been, ruled by lies, treachery and deceit perpetrated upon the majority of mankind by a small number of very wealthy and powerful elites. Yet very few of us are even aware of this objective reality, even today. Instead, most of humanity lives the majority of their lives disconnected from objective reality and truth. This is by design: YHWH's (God's) design. We get a glimpse of this in the following:

"It is the glory of God (Elohim) to conceal a thing: but the honour of kings is to search out a matter." Proverbs 25:2

Four years ago, YHWH led me to discover that virtually everything I had ever been told or taught was a lie of hideous proportions. In the decade before 2011, my world had been turned upside down by a number of challenging and painful events in my life, which peaked when I was ambushed one night by a group of leaders from a church I was a member of at the time. Such a bizarre and outrageous event should have never occurred under normal circumstances. I knew that it was very significant and I resolved to myself to figure out what was going on that I clearly did not understand. My lack of understanding of what was going on was resulting in my getting seriously blindsided and whacked multiple times, for reasons that I could not comprehend.

The DVD, *Agenda: Grinding America Down*, revealed to me a big picture perspective on America in the 21st century that explained to me that what I had been experiencing in my life was no accident or set of random events. It was way bigger than that. I bought a number of the books referenced in that documentary film, and several others, whose titles were recommended to me by Amazon.com when I placed my order for my first set of books, and began devouring them in early 2011. The first set of book titles included the following:

1. *None Dare Call it Conspiracy*, by Gary Allen

2. *The Unseen Hand: An Introduction to the Conspiratorial View of History*, by Ralph Epperson

3. *The Naked Communist*, by W. Cleon Skousen

4. *The Naked Capitalist.* by W. Cleon Skousen

5. *Illuminati: The Cult that Hijacked the World*, by Henry Makow

6. *He Came to Set the Captives Free*, by Rebecca M. Brown, M.D.

These books referenced other books which I bought and read and that second set of books led me to a third round of books, all of which I devoured as though I was drinking water from a fire hose. All of those books are listed in the bibliography at the end of this book. Each book corroborated and amplified upon the previous ones I had read, and by the end of 2011, my entire outlook on what was true and what was not had been turned on its head. Keep in mind, I was blessed to have accumulated an extensive and accomplished knowledge base from my broad study of economics, political science, world history, psychology, philosophy, finance, business strategy, organizational behavior, American sociology and Biblical theology from my college and business school education and my extensive reading over the last four decades. Yet even in my major field of study, economics, I discovered that I had been left largely clueless as to how America's economy and monetary system really worked.

Here's what I discovered, quite to my shock and dismay:

1. America is ruled and controlled by a relatively small global conspiracy of extremely wealthy and powerful elites. This conspiracy is largely Jewish in beliefs, strategies, tactics and aims, and has been in a position of power and control since at least the Presidency of Teddy Roosevelt. In short, the Jews rule the world today with an unseen, but iron fist.[7][8][9]

2. The Jews of today are not really Jews at all. Greater than 95% of all those professing to be Jews worldwide today are Ashkenazi Jews, who are descendants of the Turko-Mongolian Khazars, whose ancestors converted from pagan phallic worship (which many still secretly practice) to Talmudic Judaism for reasons of political expediency in 740 A.D.[10]

    a. The implications of this discovery alone are huge. Those professing to be Jews have claimed for centuries that they are the true descendants of the 12 Hebrew tribes of Abraham, Isaac and Jacob of the Book of Genesis of the Bible, thus making them Semites, or descendants of Shem, one of the three sons of Noah, and Israelites and Judahites (Jew is a shortened form of Judahite, a person of the tribe of Judah or of the southern kingdom of Judah or Judea after the reign of King Solomon around 1000 B.C.). Now that we know that those who claim to be Jews are not Jews at all, but rather are Khazars who converted to Talmudic Judaism, we know that the claim of those professing to be Jews to be the true heirs of the promises of God made to Abraham, Isaac and Jacob are a complete hoax, fraud and lie. Here are the promises made by God to Abraham which the Jews and modern day Israelis invoke to elicit support

---

[7] *Protocols of the Meetings of the Learned Elders of Zion.* 1934.
[8] Allen, Gary. *None Dare Call It Conspiracy.* 1971.
[9] Makow, Henry. *Illuminati: The Cult that Hijacked the World.* 2001.
[10] Koestler, Arthur. *The Thirteenth Tribe.* 1976.

from non-Jews, especially from Christian Zionists
who are deeply deceived:

> *"And I will make of thee a great nation, and I will
> bless thee, and make thy name great; and thou shalt
> be a blessing: And I will bless them that bless thee,
> and curse him that curseth thee: and in thee shall all
> families of the earth be blessed."* Genesis 12:2-3

b. So from this, we can deduce that the impostors posing
as Jews and modern day Israelis are not the chosen
people of God which they lie and falsely claim to be.
Moreover, we have evidence from one of their own,
that indeed those professing to be Jews are not who
they claim to be:

> *"We Jews do not like to admit it, but our God is
> Lucifer . . . We are his chosen people. Lucifer is very
> much alive."*—Harold Rosenthal from *The
> Hidden Tyranny*, (1976)[11]

Furthermore, Jesus confirms this same thing:

> *". . . I know the blasphemy of them which say they
> are Jews, and are not, but are the synagogue of
> Satan."* Revelation 2:9

> *"Behold, I will make them of the synagogue of
> Satan, which say they are Jews, and are not, but
> do lie; behold, I will make them to come and
> worship before thy feet, and to know that I have
> loved thee."* Revelation 3:9

3. Impostors posing as Jews of today lie and claim falsely that
they follow and obey the teachings of the Old Testament
of the Bible, when in fact they do not at all. Instead, Jewish
rabbis teach impostors posing as Jews from the Babylonian
Talmud, a set of books of 64 volumes and from the
teachings of the Zohar Kabbalah of the occult. These two
core teachings of Judaism contain a set of the most vile,

---

[11] Marrs, Texe. *Conspiracy of the Six-Pointed Star.* 2001. p. 31.

hate-filled, racist, bigoted, deceptive, anti-Christ and anti-Christian teachings the world has ever known. Some of the most disturbing teachings contained in these volumes are the following:

a. Yahushua (Jesus) was the bastard son of a whore (Mary), who sits in a boiling vat of human excrement and semen in hell.[12]

b. The Jews are the "master race" who are pure and morally good, while all the rest of humanity are subhuman, less than animals and pure evil.[13]

c. The Jewish people are the Messiah, the chosen people of their god (in reality Lucifer), born to take dominion over the entire earth and rule it with an iron fist, in what has become known more recently as their New World Order police state, with the Jews running everything behind the scenes with the rest of humanity bound in slavery to them.[14]

d. It is perfectly moral and acceptable to deceive, steal from and even murder a non-Jew, who is merely pure evil anyway, and bound for hell.[15] Included in this set of teachings, once a year at Yom Kippur, the Day of Atonement, all Jews are taught to pray the prayer of

---

[12] Hoffman, Michael. *Judaism's Strange Gods.* 2011. p. 240 and 244, Hendrie, Edward. *Solving the Mystery of Babylon the Great: Tracking the Beast from the Synagogue to the Vatican.* 2010. p. 119 and Clèraubat, Brian Alois. *A Greater "Miracle" Than the Lost Ten Tribes Discovered . . . – The Dead "SIX MILLION" Uncovered . . . !* 2007. p. 283.

[13] Hoffman, Michael. *Judaism's Strange Gods.* p. 39 and Hendrie, Edward. *Bloody Zion.* 2012. p. 224.

[14] Hendrie, Edward. *Bloody Zion.* 2010. pp. 221-222 and Weiland, Ted R. *God's Covenant People: Yesterday, Today and Forever.* 1994. pp. 228, 230.

[15] Pranaitis, Rev. I.B. *The Talmud Unmasked: The Secret Rabbinical Teachings Concerning Christians.* 2010. pp. 68-85.

Kol Nidrei, which exonerates them in advance from having to honor any promises, commitments or contractual obligations they may make with non-Jews in the coming year. In short, the words and commitments of all Jews means nothing and should never be trusted by all non-Jews.[16]

e. It is acceptable for a woman to have sex with a boy up to the age of nine and for a man to have sex with a girl up to the age of three.[17] Any such sexual immorality of incest, pedophilia or homosexuality inevitably results in the transference of demon spirits from the adults to the children, thereby enslaving the children to the occult practices of witchcraft which are at the core of the fanatical religious satanic cult of Judaism. Similarly, within orthodox Judaism it is quite common for the mohels, or rabbis who perform the circumcisions on baby boys at eight days old, to suck the blood from the penises of the baby boys, thereby infesting them with a number of vicious demon spirits with which the mohels are infested or possessed through such immoral pedophile and homosexual practices.[18]

4. The true genetic descendants of the 12 Hebrew tribes of Abraham, Isaac and Jacob, true Semites (descendants of Shem, son of Noah), true Israelites and true Judahites (or Jews) are not those who claim to be Jews today, who are complete impostors, but rather are the descendants of white Europeans, or the white race. Around 500 B.C., the former exiles of the northern kingdom of Israel (after the reign of King Solomon) who had been defeated and exiled by the Assyrians, and the exiles of the southern kingdom of Judah (after the reign of Solomon also) who had been defeated and exiled by the Babylonians migrated in three massive human waves of migration through the Caucasus

---

[16] Hoffman, Michael. *Judaism's Strange Gods.* 2011. p. 339.
[17] Ibid. pp. 358, 362.
[18] Ibid. pp. 361.

mountain range between the Black and Caspian Seas, and northwest into Europe, where they reappeared as the Danes (tribe of Dan), Jutes (tribe of Judah), Angles and Saxons (sons of Isaac), Franks, Celts, Scandinavians and other kindred peoples. These people groups all had white skin in common and were collectively known as Caucasians ever since, by virtue of the mountain range they passed through on their way into Europe.[19]

a. The implications of this discovery are huge! In particular, the Bible makes reference to the nation of Israel in both the Old and New Testaments. With this key piece of the puzzle now known, we can deduce quite simply that those references to the Jews and Israelites in both Testaments of the Bible usually refer to those of the white race and do not pertain to the impostors of today who claim to be Jews and are not (because they are Talmud-believing Khazars).

b. When it comes to the promises of YHWH (God) to the nation of Israel through Abraham, Isaac and Jacob, the teachings of the New Testament reveal that the true heirs of those promises have virtually nothing to do with one's genetic lineage, but instead are secured by one's faith in Yahushua (Jesus Christ) alone:

> *"Even as Abraham believed God (Eloah), and it was accounted to him for righteousness. Know ye therefore that they which are of the faith, the same are the children of Abraham. And the Scripture, foreseeing that God (Eloah) would justify the heathen through faith, preached before the gospel unto*

---

[19] Balacius, Robert Alan. *Uncovering the Mysteries of Your Hidden Inheritance.* 2001, pp. 17-21, Clèraubat, Brian Alois. *A Greater Miracle Than the Ten Lost Tribes Discovered . . . – The Dead "SIX MILLION" Uncovered . . . !* 2007. p. 271 and Weiland, Ted R. *God's Covenant People: Yesterday, Today and Forever.* 1994. pp. 148-149.

Abraham, saying, In thee shall all nations be blessed. So then they which be of faith are blessed with faithful Abraham." Galatians 3:6-9

"Now to Abraham and his seed were the promises made. He saith not, And to seeds, as of many; but as of one, And to thy seed, which is Christ (the Messiah)." Galatians 3:16

"For ye are all children of God (Eloah) by faith in Christ Jesus (Yahushua the Messiah). For as many of you as have been baptized into Christ (Yahushua the Messiah) have put on Christ (the Messiah). There is neither Jew nor Greek, there is neither bond nor free, there is neither male nor female: for ye are all one in Christ Jesus (Yahushua the Messiah). And if ye be Christ's (the Messiah's), then are ye Abraham's seed, and heirs according to the promise." Galatians 3:26-29

These promises are made not to the genetic descendants of Abraham, but rather to his spiritual heirs: all those of all races, peoples, nations, tribes and tongues who number among God's elect, as evidenced by their being born again in God's Holy Spirit and fully submitted and surrendered to Yahushua (Jesus) as Lord over all things.

5. The alleged death by gassing of 6 million Jews by the Germans in the concentration camps and mobile gassing vans during World War II, widely referred to as the "holocaust," never happened. The claim of the Jews that it did happen is the most colossal fraud, lie and con job of all time. Author Brian Alois Clèraubat, in his book, *A Greater "Mystery" Than the Ten Lost Tribes Discovered . . . − the Dead "SIX MILLION" Uncovered . . . !*, provides all the

compelling evidence one will ever need that such an atrocity could never have occurred as claimed.[20]

a. The most compelling argument which proves the alleged holocaust to be a colossal fraud and hoax (the holohoax) is provided by worldwide Jewish population statistics from the *World Almanac and Book of Facts* for 1934 and 1945, which report that there were 15.6 million and 15.2 million Jews worldwide in each of those years. The alleged gassings are alleged to have occurred from 1942 – 1945.[21] So where did those 6 million Jews who were allegedly gassed to death by the Germans disappear to?!? Anyone of any common sense and integrity can clearly see that the holohoax lie withers and collapses under the most simple examination and application of logical reasoning: it simply never happened!

b. Clèraubat and others have made extensive calculations of the amount of fuel, time and resulting ashes from the alleged cremations that would have been required to exterminate and then cremate 6 million bodies during the timeframe in which the gassings are alleged to have occurred. The numbers are so massive that it defies all reason, logic and common sense as well. There is simply no credible evidence that such fuel sources as would have been required would have been available for such a volume of alleged cremations. There is no evidence of smoke and ash pollution that Allied aviators would have most assuredly observed and reported (they did not). Moreover, no massive burial of the volume of cremation ashes that would have had to have been produced from such an alleged

---

[20] Clèraubat, Brian Alois, *A Greater "Miracle" Than the Ten Lost Tribes Discovered . . . – The Dead "SIX MILLION" Uncovered . . . !* 2007.
[21] Ibid. pp. 196-197.

extermination program have ever been unearthed or discovered.[22]

c.   One German researcher, Ernst Zündel, retained a team of materials scientists to take samples from the interior walls of the showers in which the alleged victims were allegedly asphyxiated using Zyklon-B gas generated from pellets manufactured by German chemical company I.G. Farben. Such gas is known to leave traceable residues years after their use. Zündel's materials scientists detected no such residues from the walls of the showers alleged to be homicidal gas chambers in disguise.[23] Zündel widely published his findings and conclusions in Germany and Canada and has been viciously defamed and persecuted by the ADL (Anti-Defamation League, more accurately described as the Jewish Defamation League) and other Jewish propaganda and social control organizations designed to suppress the truth and advance the lies of Jewish racial and moral superiority.[24]

d.   Clèraubat documents extensively, in nearly 200 pages of exhibits, the deplorable tales of Jewish slander, defamation and persecution of those researchers and whistleblowers who were brave enough to risk their reputations, fortunes and lives to reveal publicly their discoveries of the facts concerning the holohoax.[25] Such vicious tactics of intimidation were clearly intended to punish those who dared to challenge the false narrative that the Zionist leaders had concocted to conceal the hideous crimes of the Communist Jews in the 20th century in which 142 million non-Jewish Russians, Chinese, Vietnamese and Cambodians were

---

[22] Ibid. pp. 217-230.
[23] Ibid. pp. 210-211 and 375-377.
[24] Ibid. pp. 443-449.
[25] Ibid. pp. 323-512.

brutally murdered by their Jewish-inspired, satanic Communist governments in the 20th century to consolidate their political power and eliminate all potential enemies.[26] *This* is the real holocaust that no one ever dares to speak of. These deaths are greater than all the deaths in all the wars of recorded human history, according to the film documentary, *Agenda: Grinding America Down.*

e. In addition, the holohoax served, and continues to serve, as a very effective tool to prey upon the pity and sympathy of the non-Jewish world for the alleged plight of the allegedly unjust treatment of the Jewish people by the Germans during World War II. The common ploy of all sociopaths and psychopaths, according to Martha Stout, Ph.D., in her book, *The Sociopath Next Door*, is to prey upon the sympathy and pity of their victims and others so as to avoid detection and accountability for their moral and legal crimes.[27] This is precisely the dynamic at work with the psychopath Jewish Zionist global elites who have hijacked and rule our world today. The Zionists knew that in order to garner world public opinion in their favor at the end of World War II in order to grant the Jews the land of Palestine to create a Jewish state, they would need a ruse to grant them moral immunity from careful scrutiny and any potential challenges to their secret aims to dominate the world via their hideous vision for a New World Order Communist global police state which they intend to run behind the scenes with all non-Jews as their slaves. The lie of the

---

[26] See Appendix E. The number of deaths assumed here is 66 million non-Jewish Russians, 70 million Chinese, 4 million Vietnamese and 2 million Cambodians. The total number may exceed 259 million deaths from all Communist countries for the first 87 years of the 20th century.

[27] Stout, Martha, PhD. *The Sociopath Next Door.* 2005. pp. 107-109.

holohoax was their key tool for accomplishing just this. And until now, it has worked nearly flawlessly.

f. Clèraubat further documents in his book 200 instances in which kingdoms and nations have expelled Jews from their borders for reasons of sedition and immorality that were undermining the moral cultures of their host countries over the past 2,000 years. Clèraubat's list in reformatted form appears as Appendix D. Now that we understand the secret beliefs of the Jews, shaped by the vile, hate-filled, racist, bigoted, anti-Christ and anti-Christian teachings of the Jewish rabbis from the Babylonian Talmud and Zohar Kabbalah, the under-handed, deceitful actions and endless betrayals of the impostors posing as Jews for the past 2,600 years of world history becomes quite understandable and predictable. What you believe affects your actions, no matter whether they are truthful, or hideous lies. In the case of the impostors posing as Jews, they have been taught hideous lies by their Pharisee rulers and rabbis ever since the Babylonian exile, which started in 586 B.C., that have led the impostor Jews to be the most destructive force the world has ever known.

6. Not only did the holohoax never happen, but America and the Allied forces under the command of General Dwight D. Eisenhower who occupied post World War II Germany were responsible for the deaths of roughly 1 million German POWs held inside barbed wire fenced open fields and left to die by starvation, exposure and disease during the winter of 1945. Eisenhower issued written orders that any guards or civilians caught giving food to the German POWs were to be shot on sight. In addition, 10 – 11 million German civilians starved to death under Allied occupation from 1945 – 1948. Both actions were deliberate and intentional on the part of the Allied forces, led by the Americans, as part of the Morgenthau Plan developed by Jewish globalist and Secretary of the Treasury

Henry Morgenthau, which was authorized by 32nd Degree Mason and President Harry Truman and executed by half-Jew Dwight D. Eisenhower.[28]

7. In addition to the real holocaust caused by the Jews, in which 142 million innocent non-Jewish Russians, Chinese, Vietnamese and Cambodians were brutally murdered at the hands of their Jewish-inspired, satanic Communist governments in the 20th century, the founders of the modern day Jewish state of Israel waged a brutal campaign of ethnic cleansing and genocide that resulted in 800,000 Palestinians being murdered or driven from their homes and villages in Palestine in 1947 and 1948, so as to reduce the percentage of non-Jews inside the new borders of the Jewish state of Israel to less than 20%. Non-Jewish residents of the rogue terrorist state of Israel are subjected to permanent second class citizen treatment and status in the Jewish state, akin to apartheid in the former South Africa.

    Israeli historian Ilan Pappe has thoroughly documented the brutal campaign of genocide, ethnic cleansing, terror and murder of Palestinians at the hands of Jewish terrorist organizations and the Israeli army in 1947 and 1948 under the leadership of David Ben Gurion, founder of the of the modern day state of Israel, compiled from the author's examination of Israeli military records, in his book, *The Ethnic Cleansing of Palestine*. At no time were the Jews threatened with being driven from the land of Palestine in 1948 by surrounding Arab nations, as the impostor Jews still falsely claim today, in order to once again appeal to the non-Jewish world's naive and gullible sympathy and pity, behind which the impostor Jewish psychopaths and murderers hide and conceal their repeated history of savagery and brutality against all non-Jews.

---

[28] Bacque, James. *Other Losses: An Investigation into the Mass Deaths of German Prisoners at the Hands of the French and Americans after World War II.* 2011. pp. xv-xvi and lxvii.

8. Exposing the Greatest Lies and Frauds of the Last Hundred Years

8. The Federal Reserve Act of 1913 was passed with trickery and chicanery by Jewish New York investment bankers, which granted a cartel of private banks, led and controlled by the Rothschild investment banking family, a legal monopoly to print dollars (United States Federal Reserve notes) out of thin air and loan them to the federal government in exchange for the right to collect interest on all debt incurred by the federal government.[29] There is nothing governmental about the Federal Reserve Bank. It is a privately owned bank controlled by Jewish banking interests who share a New World Order agenda to enslave the world in a one world government Communist police state, owned and controlled behind the scenes by a cabal of very wealthy and powerful Jewish and Masonic banking interests and families, who believe they are the master race, entitled to rule over the non-Jewish world with a brutal and intolerant iron fist.

    a. Once the Jewish banksters had a tight control on America's money supply through the Federal Reserve Bank and System, they proceeded to coerce American Presidents to incur government debt (to be owed to them) by waging costly wars through bribes, threats and intimidation.[30]

    b. Additionally, through coordinated and secret agreements between private Jewish investment banks, the Federal Reserve Bank and all major media channels, which they owned and controlled, Jewish banksters have repeatedly caused planned boom and bust cycles in the American and world economies which have driven private business interests out of business through lack of credit, forcing sales of valuable assets at liquidation sale prices to the banksters and their collaborating allies who were given advance notice of what was coming in time for them to sell their assets at inflated prices and buy them back

---

[29] Mullins, Eustace. *The Secrets of the Federal Reserve*. 1991.
[30] Ibid. pp. 69-113.

after the crashes for cents on the dollar. This is the essence of what caused the crash of 1929 and the Great Depression which followed, bringing misery and suffering to millions of people around the world.[31]

9. The attack on the World Trade Center towers in Manhattan on 9-11-01 was an inside job and false flag attack perpetrated upon Americans by the Israeli Mossad, our own CIA, the 4,000 members of the Council on Foreign Relations (75% of whom are Jewish) and the highest levels of our federal government officials, which served as justification for launching an unending and fraudulent war on terror and serving as the pretext to create a massive government surveillance bureaucracy under the newly formed Department of Homeland Security, the Patriot Act and the National Defense Authorization Act of 2012.

   a. The most compelling evidence for this reprehensible fraud that I have seen is an interview with film producer Alan Russo in 2007, roughly a year before he died of cancer, in which he related how as an independent film producer in Hollywood who had produced a documentary film exposing the global conspiracy and its tactics entitled, *Mad as Hell and Not Going to Take It Anymore*, and had made an unsuccessful run for Governor of the state of Nevada where he garnered over 30% of the vote, he was approached by Nathan Rockefeller, a member of the CFR (Council on Foreign Relations, the most visible and powerful arm of the Illuminati in America) to recruit Russo to join them and cease making trouble for them. Russo declined their offers. However, in the course of over a year, he and Rockefeller and their wives had several lengthy conversations and developed a relationship over dinners they shared together.

---

[31] Ibid. pp. 114-130 and 143-150.

8. Exposing the Greatest Lies and Frauds of the Last Hundred Years

Russo reports that Rockefeller told him 11 months before 9-11 happened that within a year an event would occur which would result in an unending war on terror, America going to war against Iraq and Afghanistan, and the creation of a surveillance police state in America, all of which have subsequently happened as a result of the 9-11 false flag attack. At first, after the event of 9-11, Russo didn't recognize the attack as the same event Rockefeller had predicted to him 11 months prior to it; but as he witnessed the subsequent events unfold, Russo made the obvious connections.[32]

The CFR is composed of wealthy, powerful and influential leaders from government, the military, intelligence agencies, corporate titans, leading academics from universities and think tanks, heads of major non-profit organizations, pastors, media heads, top television news anchors, and leading commercial and investment bankers in America. It was founded in the early 1920s and first led by Col. Edward Mandel House, President Woodrow Wilson's globalist handler, alter ego, confidant and perhaps even spiritual channeler, who was instrumental in passing the Federal Reserve Act of 1913 and dragging America into World War I.

House was an agent of the Rothschild banking family who had financed the creation of the Illuminati under Adam Weishaupt in 1776. The CFR is the equivalent of the Round Table Group in the U.K. and other European nations and is the most public and visible arm of the Illuminati and banking establishment in America. In short, the CFR is the vehicle through which America's shadow government exists and is

---

[32] *Reflections and Warnings: An Interview with Aaron Russo.* DVD. 2009.

run.[33] Many of its members are high level Freemasons, which has been acknowledged by one of its leaders, Albert Pike in the late 1800s, to be Jewish to its core and rooted in the worship of Lucifer, or Satan.[34]

b. The twin towers collapsed in a remarkable fashion, as though they fell as part of a planned demolition, imploding in on themselves. Moreover, a third building, Building 7, owned by the same owner of the World Trade Center towers, Jewish real estate tycoon Larry Silverstein, which was not alleged to have been hit by any plane on 9-11, miraculously collapsed in a vertical implosion in the same way on 9-11.[35] Not coincidentally, Silverstein has been reported to have reworked his insurance policy on these three real estate properties just weeks before the event of 9-11.[36] How fortuitous was that!?!? Could he have had inside information as to what was coming? Of course he did, and to suggest otherwise is beyond foolhardy and naive.

c. There was no debris found in a field in Pennsylvania as has been falsely reported by our Jewish-owned and controlled mainstream media (whose key owners are members of the CFR). It appears that such a plane, if it ever existed, was destroyed with a missile to destroy any evidence of it.[37] Similarly, there were no wings or

[33] Epperson, Ralph A. *The Unseen Hand: An Introduction to the Conspiratorial View of History.* 1985.

[34] Marrs, Texe, *Conspiracy of the Six Pointed Star*, 2011. pp. 269-270.

[35] Hendrie, Edward. *9/11 Enemies Foreign and Domestic: Secret Evidence Censored from the Official Record Proves Traitors Aided Israel in Attacking the USA.* 2011.

[36] Thorn, Victor. *Made in Israel: 9-11 and the Jewish Plot Against America.* 2011. p. 7.

[37] Hendrie, Edward. *9/11 Enemies Foreign and Domestic.* pp. 34-48.

jet engines found in the crash site of the alleged plane which hit the Pentagon that day. The hole that was created by whatever impacted it, appears far more likely to have been a cruise missile or bomb explosion from within.[38]

d. From this evidence alone, and there is countless more supporting the thesis and claim that 9-11 was an inside job and false flag attack, what has to be evident to any clear thinking person, is that America has been hideously lied to by our government and media, both of which are firmly controlled by the Jewish and Masonic global elites of the CFR and other globalist organizations. What other conclusion can we possibly arrive at other than that America, and by extension, the world, has been hijacked and is being run by a set of dangerous, deceitful psychopaths and mass murderers who seek to enslave the world in a hideous New World Order global government police state under their iron-fisted tyranny and control?!? To hold any other belief is nothing short of delusional, in denial of the obvious and insane!

10. If those who profess to be Jews are liars and impostors who falsely claim to be the Messiah (which is impossible because Yahushua clearly is the Messiah, the Christ), and in truth they have always served and worshiped Lucifer, a.k.a. Satan, then does it not follow quite simply and logically that the Jewish people of today are, in fact, the Antichrist and first beast of end times prophecy? It most certainly does!!

11. The false religion of pseudo-science falsely teaches us that the earth spins on an imaginary axis a full rotation in 24 hours and revolves around the sun in one year. This lie is known as Copernican heliocentrism, or a sun-centered solar system, in which the sun is revered and worshipped by pagan sun worshippers, in which the sun god is Lucifer,

---

[38] Ibid. pp. 14-33.

the bearer of light, a.k.a. Satan, a.k.a. the devil. The Bible, in 67 separate verses, clearly states that the earth does not move. Marshall Hall, in his book, *The Earth is not Moving*, and on his website, *www.fixedearth.com* provides extensive evidence and compelling logical reasons that debunk the Copernican view and confirms that the Bible's teachings of the earth not moving and being at the center of the universe with the sun circling above the earth every 24 hours *has* to be true.

a. Simple logic based on known, irrefutable facts, reveals that the Copernican heliocentric view of the world cannot possibly be true. Yet this is what has been taught as proven fact for the last 450 years by those who control our world for one reason and one reason only: to discredit the teachings of the Bible, the flawless and inspired words of God to mankind, that have never been successfully proven in any respect to be false.[39]

b. No bombardiers in military airplanes, those planning missile launches targeted at a destination on earth, or navigators of aircraft flying from one point to another ever factor into their calculations a spinning earth or the latitudes of the points of origin and destination, that would be necessary, if the Copernican model of the earth were true. These facts alone provide conclusive evidence that the earth does not spin on an imaginary axis that would require the earth to spin at roughly 1,040 miles at the equator and at a somewhat lesser speed at latitudes north or south of the equator.[40]

c. We are told tht the sun is located approximately 93 million miles from the earth. If the Copernican model were true, earth would orbit around an 585 million mile circumference (93 million miles x 2 x 3.1416, or

---

[39] Hall, Marshall. *The Earth is Not Moving*. 1991. pp. 101-102.
[40] Ibid. pp. 228-232.

pi times the diameter) around the sun in 365 days or 8,760 (365 days x 24 hours per day) hours, at a required speed of 66,705 miles per hour (585 million miles divided by 8,760 hours). If the earth were hurtling through space at roughly 67 times the speed of sound, we should expect two things to occur: 1) the earth's atmosphere should be ripped off its surface, and 2) the stars should appear as mere streaks and blurs in the sky. Yet neither of those two things happen! Thus, we can safely conclude that the earth *does not* revolve around the sun, as we all have been falsely taught![41]

d. The long distances from earth to stars, measured in light years, have been calculated by scientists using trigonometry and an assumed rotation about the sun that places the earth 186 million miles apart from its starting location six months later. Since we now know that this assumption is an invalid one, all the massive distances between stars and galaxies, shrinks astronomically. According to Marshall Hall, the stellatum, the perimeter of the universe in which the stars are located, is contained within a space of roughly one trillion miles, which is less than one twenty-fifth of the distance space scientists tell all of us the universe occupies and is further expanding every day. [42] These radically reduced distances seriously undermines the Big Bang theory that claims, with no proof for it, that the universe is 15 – 20 billion years old and that the earth is 4.6 billion years old: claims that the lie of Darwinism and macro-evolution, which we will address next, depends upon to support its false claims.

12. We are further told that the earth is a sphere, rather than flat, as it appears to be to all of us without the distortions of camera optics. Countless scientific experiments have

---

[41] Ibid. pp. 234-235.
[42] Ibid. pp. 282-288.

been conducted over the last couple of centuries which prove beyond a shadow of a doubt that, in truth, the earth is flat, and not a sphere at all! Many of these experiments have measured the distance between a ship at sea and lighthouses with a known height and employed spherical trigonometry to deduce that if the earth where a sphere, having a circumference of 25,000 miles, as the pseudo-scientists claim, that such lighthouses ought to be well below the horizon from the viewing location and yet they remain clearly visible, thus proving that the earth is not spherical, as falsely claimed, but is instead flat.

Furthermore, the natural physics of water and other fluids always result in their finding their level and remaining flat. Said differently, "The upper surface of a fluid at rest is a horizontal plane."[43] Gravity upon a spherical earth in no way alters this natural law of physics. Therefore, a spherical earth cannot possibly be true.[44]

13. The Pharisees of pseudo-science falsely claim that man evolved from single cell organisms from the primordial goo over billions of years through a process of natural selection and that life spontaneously emerged from non-life by pure accident. Much of this lie is based on the work of Charles Darwin and the publishing of his book, *Origin of the Species*, in 1859. Once again, this false science has been promoted and advanced by the Pharisees of the Babylonian Talmud and Zohar Kabbalah in order to discredit the creation story of the Bible, so as to undermine all of its other teachings concerning God's morality, Yahushua (Jesus), heaven, hell and eternal life.

    a. Greg Koukl, Christian apologist, author and president of Stand to Reason, a Christian apologist ministry, has

---

[43] Dubay, Eric, *The Flat Earth Conspiracy*. 2014. p.25.
[44] https://www.youtube.com/watch?v=R77j9rUuky4#t=17.

recorded a talk on CD entitled, *Why I'm Not an Evolutionist,* in which he explains that macro-evolution (changes across species through breeding over long periods of time) cannot possibly be true for two primary reasons: 1) abiogenesis, the notion that life can possibly spring from non-living matter, has never been successfully demonstrated or even credibly explained, and 2) the evidence of transitional life forms in the fossil record, which should be everywhere if macro-evolution were true, simply do not exist. According to Koukl, Darwin himself admitted that his whole theory of macro-evolution crucially depends upon these two pillars or assumptions being true. If one or both of them were later proven to be false, his whole theory would be false, Darwin himself admitted.

Koukl explains that over an illusory period of billions of years, if Darwin's theory were true, the fossil record should be strewn with evidence of transitional life forms. Yet they don't exist. How do we know they don't exist? Because a creature in transition between a water dwelling fish and a land dwelling amphibian or mammal with no fins and no legs would become the nearest lunch for the next carnivore that happened to pass by and so such creatures would never reach the age to reproduce! And without reproduction, the gene pool doesn't get carried on and the theory withers under simple logical reasoning from known facts.[45]

b. Moreover, macro-evolution brazenly requires that two key known laws of biology and physics would have had to be suspended for billions of years and then the laws miraculously came into being, which simply is a preposterous notion. In high school biology, we all were taught that animals of the same species can mate and reproduce, but that creatures of two different

---

[45] *Ambassador Basic Curriculum, Course 3, Why I'm Not an Evolutionist.* Gregory Koukl. CD. 2003.

species, even if they engage in the act of sexual intercourse, cannot reproduce and create the next generation with genes from parents from two separate and distinct species. Evolutionists side-step this inconvenient fact and known law of biology and stubbornly stick to their conviction that macro-evolution HAS to be true. Likewise, the second law of thermodynamics in physics, also known as the law of entropy, states that all matter, living and inanimate, goes from a state of order to disorder, and devolves from complex states to simple states, not the other way around. Yet for macro-evolution to be true, this law had to have been suspended for billions of years to go from a state of disorder to order; from the simple to the complex, and then somehow the second law of thermodynamics was miraculously introduced, with no explanation from the priests and Pharisees of pseudo-science as to how this could possibly have occurred. "Just trust us," they tell us.

c. Finally, and perhaps the most damning evidence of all for the fraud of macro-evolution, the Pharisees of Zionism, in the *Protocols of the Learned Elders of Zion*, brazenly boast how easily they invented and promoted Darwinism, Communism and the godless philosophies of Fredrich Nietzsche:

> *"The intellectuals of the goyim will puff themselves up with their knowledges and without any logical virification (sic) of them will put into effect all the information available from science, which our agentur specialists have cunningly pieced together for the purpose of educating their minds in the directions we want.*
>
> *Do not suppose for a moment that these statements are empty words:* **think carefully of the successes we arranged for Darwinism, Marxism, Nietzsche-ism.** *To us Jews, at any rate, it should be plain to see*

232

8. Exposing the Greatest Lies and Frauds of the Last Hundred Years

what a disintegrating importance these directives have had upon the mind of the goyim." [46] (emphasis added)

Actor and film producer Ben Stein in his film, *Expelled: No Intelligence Allowed,* documents that the teaching profession, monopolized by the politically powerful National Educators' Association (NEA), ensures that no one is permitted to teach anything but the false religion of evolution in America's government-owned schools. To suggest that an active and vicious conspiracy to suppress and silence the truth that evolution is a hideous lie, whose ultimate aim is to deceive people into believing that there is no God, is a gross understatement and a complete no-brainer.

I can personally attest to the harmful effect of the teaching of evolution in my own life. I was taught evolution as scientific fact in high school and at age 18 I walked away from the church and God and for the next 28 years, lived my life apart from God as an agnostic. Thankfully, God brought me back into His fold much later in life. When I first learned of the reasons why evolution was a lie from Greg Koukl, I was enraged at the brazen treachery and betrayal of my high school biology teacher and a government-owned school system and culture that had so viciously and cruelly betrayed my trust in them. That was to be the first in a long line of such discoveries of betrayal, which today I regard as commonplace and quite the norm. The bottom line is, the world is a wicked and deceitful place and no one but YHWH, Yahushua and the Bible can be fully trusted for anything without proving themselves to be of honesty and integrity – attributes that are more rare today than gold. The betrayal and lie of Darwinian evolution which is

---

[46] *Protocols of the Meetings of the Learned Elders of Zion.* 1934. Protocol 2 paragraphs 3 & 4, p. 13.

promoted endlessly in our culture everywhere, proves this beyond a shadow of a doubt.

14. America never put a man on the moon. The whole thing from top to bottom is part of a colossal fraud perpetrated on mankind through the deception of advanced film technologies. NASA hired Hollywood film director Stanley Kubrick to film the scenes of the moon landings at night in the Nevada desert, which were then broadcast via television to a naive, gullible and overly trusting American public, of which I was a part. Pat Shannon, in Section 3 of his book, *Everything They* Ever Told Me Was a Lie*, thoroughly documents these facts which were also presented at the 2012 Conspiracy Conference in Santa Clara, California in May of 2012 that I attended, by a presenter who was intimately familiar with the work of Stanley Kubrick and the nuances of the advanced film technology and techniques he used to create his and NASA's deception.

 a. The moon landings could never have taken place. The nuclear radiation from the sun is so powerful that to properly protect astronauts from the dangerous cancer-causing radiation outside of the protective magnetic Van Allen belts, which we are told encircle and protect the earth, would have required a space vehicle with walls made of lead one foot thick.[47]

 b. NASA is nothing more than an expensive fraud to advance the lie of evolution through its mission to seek out evidence for extraterrestrial life on other planets or in other galaxies, far, far away, which we now know to be a complete hoax as well. But it all feeds the elaborate matrix of lies and deceptions which all of humanity has been fed by Satan and his army of Satan-worshipping Pharisees of the

[47] Shannan, Pat. *Everything They* Ever Told Me Was a Lie*. 2010. p. 84.

Babylonian Talmud and Zohar Kabbalah, who have hijacked and rule our world today.

15. Since the 1990s, Americans have been subjected to an unending stream of propaganda and lies that the earth is on the brink of extinction due to the greenhouse gas effect of man-made emissions of carbon dioxide (CO_2). Charlatan, snake oil salesman and former Vice President Al Gore has handsomely profited by shamelessly promoting this lie and spreading fear with claims of the polar ice caps melting and sea levels rising by 20 feet or more by the year 2000. Well, 2000 came and went and Al Gore has been proven to be a liar and a false prophet. No sea level rising occurred. In fact, over the past fifteen years, average temperatures around the globe have declined, thereby revealing the absurdity of the lie of alleged global warming. As a result, the Pharisee sorcerers of our world have tried to pull a sleight of hand and rename their fraud "global climate change," still blaming man-made CO_2 emissions as the cause. Nothing could be further from the truth.

   a. Meteorologist and author Brian Sussman, in his book, *Climategate*, exposes the fraud and hoax of "global warming" for what it is and what the real agenda of those promoting this scam really is. In his book, Sussman reveals that only .116% of the earth's atmosphere is composed of man-made CO_2 emissions.[48] In other words, man's contribution to an unproven problem is barely measurable. It amounts to insignificant fly manure and nothing more. Of course the mainstream media that is owned and controlled by the oligarchs of the global elite conspiracy are unfazed by any of this. They just keep endlessly repeating the same old lies and tired tripe, knowing that if you repeat any lie often enough unchallenged, that the majority of a population will be brain washed and mind control programmed into believing it to be true. In the case of

---

[48] Sussman, Brian, *Climategate*. 2010. p. 70.

this particular lie and deception, numerous reputable scientists of honesty and integrity have added their voices to expose this fraud for what it is, collectively declaring that there is no credible scientific evidence to support the fear mongering and lies of global warming or global climate change.[49]

16. Perhaps you have noticed the unending traces of chemtrails criss-crossing our skies from horizon to horizon, eventually turning the sky into a murky haze. Most of us have very little knowledge of what our lying and deceitful government is up to in this regard, but a number of us are beginning to ask the hard questions and to learn something of what this massive program is all about which is international in scope. The scientific community, which is in on this scam, refers to the program as "geo-engineering," and justifies it as a man-made solution to the non-existent "global warming" hoax to conceal its real intent from the general public. In 2010, independent researchers around remote Mt. Shasta in northern California discovered alarmingly high levels of the heavy metals aluminum, barium and strontium in private ponds which have been turned cloudy and milky by whatever is being sprayed above us.[50] Various possible explanations for this range from 1) weather modification (in tandem with the HAARP system in Alaska perhaps), 2) poisoning conventional crops by inhibiting the ability of plants to absorb nutrients from the soil through their roots, which GMO or Genetically Modified Organism crops are resistant to, 3) poisoning humans with non-lethal doses of poisons or chemicals known to cause autism, Alzheimer's

---

[49]http://www.forbes.com/sites/jamestaylor/2013/11/20/the-latest-meteorologist-survey-destroys-the-global-warming-climate-consensus/.

[50] *What in the World are they Spraying?: The Chemtrail/Geo-Engineering Cover-up.* G. Edward Griffin, Michael Murphy and Paul Wittenberger. Truth Media Productions. DVD. 2010.

Disease and other neurological disorders in furtherance of globalist plans to reduce the global population 4) high-frequency electro-magnetic pulse weaponry, to 5) mind control reflective technology in concert with the HAARP system.[51] Recently, a new theory has surfaced among the community that is seeking to make sense out of what chemtrails are all about over the internet. Community members are reporting the appearance of a reddish celestial body appearing in the southwestern sky from areas such as Arizona and speculating whether this might be the brown dwarf star Nibiru, otherwise known as Planet-X or Wormwood, foretold in Bible prophecy at Revelation 8:10-11. Chances are that the chemtrails serve multiple purposes, all of them injurious to human health, but if recent speculations and celestial body sightings are indeed true, they have the potential to blow the roof off of the globalists' numerous con jobs to defraud and deceive us.

17. The American political system is a horrendous fraud from top to bottom. The Jewish Illuminati Freemason Zionist global elite conspiracy that is extensively documented and revealed in a number of books written since the 1950s, is very real. The *Protocols of the Learned Elders of Zion*, documents their blueprint for taking over the world and enslaving it in a New World Order Communist police state which the globalists seek to own and control behind the scenes.

There is no aspect of American society that is exempt from the influence of this group of rich and powerful elites who have hijacked the world in their sick, satanic cult. America is ruled by a shadow government, comprised of corporate titans, government and military leaders, media moguls, academics, heads of non-profit foundations, pastors and other opinion leaders who make up the 4,000 members of the Illuminati's public arm in America, the Council on Foreign Relations, roughly 75% of whose membership is

---

[51] Smith, Jerry E. *HAARP: The Ultimate Weapon of the Conspiracy.* 1998. p. 126-154.

Jewish and most of the remainder of whom are high level Freemasons. Both Judaism and Freemasonry is directed by the satanic and vile teachings of the Babylonian Talmud and Zohar Kabbalah of Judaism.

a. While the *Protocols of the Learned Elders of Zion* reveal the actions, tactics and aims of the Illuminati-led global conspiracy, the essence of it is that a group of very dangerous psychopaths rule our world today through deceit, treachery and force. Nothing is what it appears to be. Almost everything we witness in the public sphere is little more than fraud and make believe.

b. Our politicians are selected from among people who possess two essential attributes: 1) they lie well and get away with it (easy to do when a person is a psychopath: someone without a conscience), and 2) they have one or more indiscretions in their pasts which make them easy to compromise and blackmail into doing the bidding of their globalist masters.

   i. The Republican and Democratic parties are nothing more than two branches of a one party system, both of which are owned and controlled by the same paymasters: the global elites of the Illuminati-controlled CFR.

   ii. Voting is a sham of monumental proportions, and exists solely to deceive the American public into believing that we live in a free and democratic country, when in reality, we do not at all. We are presented with two psychopath candidates to choose between, from which the global elites select one of them, and inform us of their choice hours after the voting polls close. It matters not one whit how many votes each candidate receives. All that matters is who gets to declare the winner which the globalists have chosen for us. Such results are entirely manufactured and supported by polling organizations and the mainstream media (which is owned and controlled by the

global elites for just this purpose), which pump
out propaganda and manufactured polling results
to deceive us into believing that our political
processes are legitimate and on the up and up.
They most assuredly are nothing of the kind!

iii. Anyone who dares expose this colossal fraud is
endlessly slandered, defamed and dismissed by the
media thought police and internet trolls, paid by
the globalists to suppress and silence any
semblance of the truth. In short, anyone of the
truth, who dares to expose this colossal fraud is
subjected to an endless tirade of psychological
warfare techniques designed to intimidate and
silence the few who catch on to what is really
going on in our nation.

iv. Every leader in every sphere of human endeavor
today was selected for their roles by the Illuminati
or their agents because of their deficient
characters and their penchant to lie and deceive
others. The public trappings of success in our
world today require a person to sell out to the
conspiracy and its lies and to go along to get along
with that which is harmful and evil. This set of
behaviors is commonly referred to as "being a
team player." Observing a person to be "a team
player" is a tell-tale sign that such a person has
sold his soul to the devil for 30 pieces of silver,
just as Judas Iscariot did when he betrayed Jesus
to the Pharisees.

c. The Sixteenth Amendment authorizing the imposition
of the income tax and the creation of the Internal
Revenue Service was never properly and lawfully
legislated and ratified by a single one of the 48 states
which made up the United States immediately prior to
the Sixteenth Amendment being declared properly
ratified by the U.S. Secretary of State. One of the
central planks of the Communist Manifesto authored

by Karl Marx and Fredrich Engels was the imposition of a regressive income tax whose aim would be to deplete the financial assets of the middle class. The sordid history and rampant fraud perpetrated by state and federal politicians and judges that led to this form of extortion of the American people is thoroughly documented in *The Law That Never Was: The Fraud of the 16th Amendment and Personal Income Tax* by Bill Benson and M.J. "Red" Beckman.

18. Television programmers are able to hypnotize television viewers through the flickering screens intrinsic to television technology. This allows television programmers to employ mind control programming techniques to subliminally plant thoughts into the subconscious minds of viewers without their even being aware of them, only to be evoked with the use of common trigger words such as "hater," "bigot," "racist," "anti-Semite, "Nazi," "skinhead," "conspiracy theorist," "truther," among others.

   a. Television content has been deliberately altered gradually, over a long period of time, by the Illuminati and their agents, to sexualize society, to normalize the violent and the profane and to undermine normal, healthy functioning and healthy gender differences between men and women. The overall goal in all of this has been to defile and corrupt the mores of American society and to destroy the traditional family, the social institution designed by God for the transmission of knowledge, morals and wisdom from one generation to the next.

19. Modern allopathic medicine is deliberately designed and used by the Illuminati to treat symptoms, rather than root causes of diseases, in order to perpetuate dependence of its patients upon the American healthcare system, to generate massive recurring revenues to Illuminati-controlled healthcare industries and to bring unnecessary pain and suffering to millions of Americans.

8. Exposing the Greatest Lies and Frauds of the Last Hundred Years

a. The evidence indicates quite conclusively that the causes of cancer are known, and actively suppressed and silenced by the healthcare industry, in collusion with a complicit Illuminati-owned and controlled media. Researchers and cancer specialists report that cancer cannot survive in a body with an alkaline body pH of 7.5 or greater. And yet, the typical American diet is deliberately and intentionally heavily laden with acid-forming foods and beverages designed to make us sick with cancer, heart disease and diabetes. In California, a physician may lose his license to practice medicine and be jailed if he discusses any form of cancer treatment other than the "big three" treatment therapies: to cut, poison and irradiate the cancer patient's body, all of which treat the symptoms of cancer tumors, without eliminating the root causes of it so cancer does not reoccur. This is why, in the vast majority of instances, cancer returns and usually kills cancer patients. Such was the fate of both of my parents: my father to recurrent lung cancer and my mother to recurrent breast cancer.

   i. Cancer treatment is big business in America. An average cancer patient is worth $50,000 per year in revenues to the oncology industry, representing a $50 billion a year industry in America alone. This is why physicians in states like California are legally punished if they dare to reveal alternative approaches to cancer treatment with their patients.

   ii. The pain and suffering brought upon cancer victims and their families by the suppression of this truth alone is vile, wicked, evil and reprehensible beyond description!

   iii. Changing one's diet to consuming strictly alkaline-forming foods and beverages is quite simple, straight-forward and easy to do. I have used my own body as a guinea pig multiple times to test

241

what it takes to achieve an alkaline 7.5 or 8.0 pH body chemistry, simply through altering my diet. Furthermore, for certain types of soft-tissue cancers, consuming a cup of lukewarm water with 2 teaspoons of common baking soda (an alkaline substance) and organic molasses or maple syrup has been reported on the internet to be effective in eliminating such cancers.[52] Finally Dr. Hulda Clark's research into the interactions of intestinal flukes (a common food-borne parasite) with chemicals in the body in the liver and other organs reveals that a simple combination of three herbal substances: wormwood, black walnut hulls and cloves, can eliminate the root cause of cancer formation and growth from such a source.

iv. Much of the dietary changes that can cure most cancers have similar beneficial effects upon other chronic diseases common among middle-aged Americans, including heart disease and diabetes.

20. The sexual revolution and no-fault divorce of the 1960s, feminism of the 1970s, the promotion of homosexuality and other forms of sexual immorality and perversions in the 1990s, and the current public sanctioning of same-sex marriage are all part of a 75 year old plan to destroy the traditional family and marriage, the two foundations for any healthy and moral society.

a. All forms of sex, outside of the covenant of marriage between one man and one woman for life, inevitably lead to demon spirit infestation or possession of those engaging in such activities. This is why all forms of witchcraft, the occult and Satanism engage in incest, sexual orgies, homosexuality, pederasty and other

---

[52] Johnston, Vernon,
https://www.youtube.com/watch?v=Yl8Y8I_TsjI and
www.phkillscancer.com.

forms of sexual deviancy to infest and control its
members.

b. The sexual revolution did not liberate women, as was
widely claimed. It liberated men from responsibility
and commitment to care for the women entrusted by
God to their care and protection.[53] As a result, the
promiscuity of the sexual revolution turned women
into unrestrained harlots and men into irresponsible
boys, and all of society lost.

c. Feminism, actively promoted by the Illuminati
through the CIA and the American Communist Party,
reversed the Biblical roles of men and women and has
intentionally created social chaos and mayhem for
men, women, marriages, family and society at large.
Men are naturally wired to provide, protect, lead and
teach their wives and children, and women are
naturally wired to support, encourage and respect their
husbands. When women seek to usurp the role of
men, men don't compete with women. They become
passive, wimpy and feminized, which women find
unattractive, so they become lesbians. Today, America
is filled with women who have no clue what it means
to be a real feminine woman, and is filled with men
who are soft, wimpy, passive, who take no initiative
and have no clue what it means to be an authentic,
masculine male.[54] No wonder marriages are failing at
a higher rate than ever before: men, women and their
children are confused, frustrated, angry and miserable
much of the time. Meanwhile the devil is laughing his
head off in glee over the carnage he has wreaked on
the traditional American family and the misery and
pain he has brought upon millions of unsuspecting

---

[53] Lewis, Robert. *The New Eve: Choosing God's Best for Your Life.*
2008. p. 160.
[54] Makow, Henry. *Cruel Hoax: Feminism and the New World Order.*
2010. p. 117-121.

Americans, who still don't understand the root cause of why they are so miserable.

d. Homosexuality is one of the most pernicious forms of sexual sin and results in the most angry and violent forms of demon spirit possession for those engaged in it. This is why homosexuality is being so heavily promoted throughout American society today by Illuminati-owned and controlled Hollywood, the media and government-owned schools. Communism is an invention of Jewish Illuminati Freemasonry. In 1958, W. Cleon Skousen published *The Naked Communist*, in which he revealed the top 45 goals of international Communism at the time. Included was the following aim:

> *"26. Present homo-sexuality, degeneracy and promiscuity as 'normal, natural, and healthy."*[55]

21. The Illuminati, through the United States government, has actively promoted the use of hallucinogenic drugs, while encouraging the illegal and often violent drug trade in order to dumb-down American society and make it easier to manipulate and control the American people.

   a. All hallucinogenic drugs open a direct pathway for a drug user to see and communicate with the spirit world of demon spirits, leading many to demon spirit infestation and possession that often leads to insanity and premature deaths caused by drug overdoses.[56]

   b. Illegal drug use is big business and very profitable for those who are allied with Illuminati insiders. The United States Coast Guard is used to intercept illegal drugs coming from Central and South America before it reaches the United States. When a boat or ship is stopped, the Coast Guard cutter captains frequently

---

[55] Skousen, W. Cleon. *The Naked Communist*. 1958. p. 261.
[56] *Spiritual Warfare*. Rebecca Brown, M.D., D.D. CDs. 2004.

communicate directly with the White House to receive instructions on how to proceed. Why? This can only be because the White House (which is Illuminati-controlled) is deciding whose drug traffic gets through and whose does not (who profits and who loses).

    c. One of the primary reasons for the United States war in Afghanistan since late 2001 was to reopen the trade of opium poppies and heroin owned and controlled by the British royal family and the CIA, among other beneficiaries.

22. Rock and roll music was developed and has been promoted by the Illuminati Freemasons to enslave several generations of youth into music that is demonic and of the occult. The music's rhythmic, pulsating and repetitive beat and decadent lyrics once again open pathways to demon spirit infestation and possession.[57] [58]

    a. My younger son was attracted to heavy metal rock music. At the time, I didn't know any better and drove him to and from many such concerts. In hindsight, it opened him to demon spirit infestation and destroyed whatever relationship we might otherwise have had.

23. Tattoos and body piercings are common among young and even older Americans today, and much of this comes from those who practice the occult. Earrings in men started when cabin boys on ships were used to signify whom different cabin boys were owned by to serve their homosexual gratification, with one ear signifying that a cabin boy belonged to the ship's officers and the other ear signifying that they belonged to and serviced the ship's crew. Jewish satanic Hollywood adopted and promoted

---

[57] Hendrie, Edward. *The Anti-Gospel: The Perversion of Christ's Gospel.* 2005. p. 333.

[58] *They Sold Their Souls For Rock N Roll.* Joe Schimmel. Good Fight Ministries. DVD. www.goodfight.org.

this practice in more recent times.[59] Tattoos have had a long association with those who engage in the occult. My wife informs me that when she was a nurse at a state prison that her lieutenant informed her that it was a proven fact that the greater number of tattoos that an inmate had, the harder he was to rehabilitate. The likely reason? The more tattoos, the more severe the inmate's demon spirit infestation or possession.

24. The New Age movement is nothing more than the pagan occult religion of ancient Babylon and eastern mysticism. It is anti-Christian to its core and pervades American culture today.[60]

For readers seeking to learn more about any one of these lies, I provide references to other books and resources in the bibliography. My purpose in sharing this list of lies is to expose you to how deeply deceived our world is. The bottom line is that we all live in a world of make believe, treachery and lies so pervasive that it boggles the mind and leaves anyone of the truth, when they first discover it, dazed and confused, as they come to terms with how misled and betrayed they have been. It is normal to experience disorientation for several months while processing out in their own minds what the implications of all of this is. The technical term for this phenomenon is cognitive dissonance: it is as if one has experienced a blow to the head, leaving one disoriented, confused and often quite angry. Nevertheless, it is a very healthy process for anyone who has the moral character to go through it.

Many more people will never be able to integrate this new information and these insights into their mental maps and the reasons for it are rooted in the spiritual dimension and where we are in God's Biblical timeline of world history. Those who are of God's elect, His spiritual sheep, are of the truth and can hear the voice of Jesus and will be able to read and hear this

---

[59] *Spiritual Warfare: Personal Deliverance CD #1.* Rebecca Brown, M.D., D.D. CDs. 2006.
[60] Marrs, Texe. *Dark Secrets of the New Age.* 1999, pp. 15-19.

new information, integrate it into their cognitive maps and
become considerably wiser and more well-informed of how
the world really works, and their relationship with God and His
perfect nature will become closer and more tangible. Those far
more numerous people who number among God's non-elect,
His spiritual goats, those who are of the lie, cannot hear the
voice of Jesus, and knowingly or unknowingly serve the father
of lies, the devil. To every last one of these people, YHWH
(God) has sent a strong delusion so that they will believe a lie,
and so be condemned (to hell) for rejecting the truth and
delighting in unrighteousness, in fulfillment of the prophecy of
2 Thessalonians 2:10-12 with hair-splitting accuracy:

> *"And with all deceivableness of unrighteousness in them that
> perish; because they received not the love of the truth, that they
> might be saved. And for this cause God (Eloah) shall send
> them strong delusion, that they should believe a lie: That they
> all might be damned who believed not the truth, but had
> pleasure in unrighteousness."* 2 Thessalonians 2:10-12

For such people, and I have witnessed this many times, I can
provide overwhelming and irrefutable evidence and simple
logical reasoning to them from the most trustworthy of
authorities that reveal the truth, and it will make no difference.
They remain unable to see the truth that to God's born again
elect, seems so obvious and apparent. And it is to us, but not
to them.

Instead, such people will reveal themselves by their actions and
their words to be wicked and quite foolish. The Book of
Proverbs provides numerous examples comparing and
contrasting the behaviors of the wicked versus the righteous
and the foolish versus the wise. The spiritually blinded will
abuse, mock, scorn, ridicule, dismiss, demean, slander, libel,
hate and persecute those of us who are of the truth, of
Yahushua and who can see these things. It is not a pleasant
experience, I can assure you. I have been subjected to countless
demonic attacks by people afflicted with demon spirits and I
have come to recognize the reality that I am communicating

with the demon spirits which have taken over control of such people, just as the Apostle Paul tells us:

"For we wrestle not against flesh and blood, but against principalities, against powers, against the rulers of the darkness of this world, against spiritual wickedness in high places."
Ephesians 6:12

In other words, those who are spiritually perishing, those who number among God's non-elect, have been taken over by demon spirits, and when I am subjected to a demonic attack by them, it is not that person in the flesh who is attacking me, it is the demon spirit which controls them with whom I am having to contend.

The take away from this chapter is this: the world is not what it seems at all. We live in a world of make believe, lies, treachery and deceit so pervasive that it boggles the mind. When we first encounter this, our first reaction is quite appropriately anger at being betrayed so viciously by our teachers, our parents, churches, institutions and the world in which we live. But like stages of grief, we must move on. Many of those who deceived us were equally deceived and unknowingly passed onto us what they too believed to be true. Some knew, and intentionally lied to us. But God allowed it all to happen as it did in order to fulfill His perfect plan – not ours. So we must learn to get over it.

The implications of this discovery are astounding and profound. First of all, it means that the Bible is, and always has been, 100% true and trustworthy down to the very last jot and tittle. That means everything that conflicts with it in any way is a lie and should be disregarded. Second, it proves that we are now living in the end times prophesied in the Bible for thousands of years. I will have much more to say about this in the following chapter. Nevertheless, much of what I have revealed here in this chapter has been concealed for thousands of years. It is no accident that it is coming to light right now. The fact that God has revealed this to me, and I am now revealing it to you, is a clear and compelling sign that we are

living in the final days of the end times. Here is what Yahushua
told His disciples:

> *"Fear them not therefore: for there is nothing covered, that
> shall not be revealed; and hid that shall not be known. What
> I tell you in darkness, that speak ye in light: and what ye
> hear in the ear, that preach ye upon the housetops. And fear
> not them which kill the body, but are not able to kill the soul:
> but rather fear him which is able to destroy both soul and
> body in hell."* Matthew 10:26-28

Until quite near the bitter end, God had every reason to
conceal many of the things I have just revealed in this chapter
from all of mankind, in order set conditions up for quite a
startling surprise to unfold at the climax to His story of
mankind for the last 6,000 years. Now, right before the end,
Yahushua has blessed me with many of these startling discoveries. Why? The only possible reason can be so that I would
obey this commandment and share it with you, my readers.

9. Evidence That We Are Living Through the Great Tribulation

End times Bible prophecy is probably one of the least understood and most confused subjects of the Bible and of all time. My objective here is not to contribute to that confusion, but to simplify it so that the common man can understand the basics by going right to the source. Once again, that source is what the Bible itself *says,* unfiltered by the words and interpretations of man for which the words of Scripture provide no support.

Almost everyone who professes to be a follower of Yahushua, or a Christian, has their own pet idea of what end times Bible prophecy says, where to start and what's most important and what is not. My primary concern and point of reference is going to be that of God's elect. My reason for this is simple: I am one of God's elect, my target audience is my fellow members of God's elect, and those who are not of God's elect cannot understand and will not believe any truth I have to share with them anyway. I will try to correct a number of false notions concerning the end times, but it is virtually impossible to anticipate and correct all such false notions. In the end, every reader must do his or her own study of Scripture to test me and determine if what I am sharing here conforms to what Scripture *says*. I believe it does, but I am by no means infallible and I remain eager to receive correction wherever Scripture indicates it is warranted.

Chapter 12 of the Book of Daniel and Matthew 24 are my starting points. Both passages are so vitally important that I must take the time to quote both of them rather extensively and then we can discuss what they mean.

9. Evidence That We Are Living Through the Great Tribulation

Here's how the final chapter, Chapter 12 of the Book of Daniel describes what is known as the "great tribulation:"

"*1 And at that time shall Michael stand up, the great prince which standeth for the children of thy people: and there shall be a time of trouble, such as never was since there was a nation even to that same time: and at that time thy people shall be delivered, every one that shall be found written in the book.*

2 And many of them that sleep in the dust of the earth shall awake, some to everlasting life, and some to shame and everlasting contempt.

3 And they that shall be wise shall shine as the brightness of the firmament; and they that turn many to righteousness as the stars for ever and ever.

4 But thou, O Daniel, shut up the words, and seal the book, even to the time of the end: many shall run to and fro, and knowledge shall be increased.

5 Then I Daniel looked, and behold, there stood other two, the one on this side of the bank of the river, and the other on that side of the bank of the river.

6 And one said to the man clothed in linen, which was upon the waters of the river, How long shall it be to the end of these wonders?

7 And I heard the man clothed in linen, which was upon the waters of the river, when he held up his right hand and his left hand unto heaven, and sware by him that liveth for ever that it shall be for a time, times, and an half; and when he shall have accomplished to scatter the power of the holy people, all these things shall be finished.

8 And I heard, but I understood not: then said I, O my Lord (Adon), what shall be the end of these things?

9 And he said, Go thy way, Daniel: for the words are closed up and sealed till the time of the end.

10 Many shall be purified, and made white, and tried; but the wicked shall do wickedly: and none of the wicked shall understand; but the wise shall understand.

11 And from the time that the daily sacrifice shall be taken away, and the abomination that maketh desolate set up, there shall be a thousand two hundred and ninety days.

12 Blessed is he that waiteth, and cometh to the thousand three hundred and five and thirty days.

12 But go thy way till the end be: for thou shalt rest, and stand in thy lot at the end of days."

In Matthew 24:3 the disciples of Yahushua (Jesus) asked him:

". . . and what shall be the sign of thy coming, and of the end of the world?"

Jesus replied to this part of their question starting at verse 15 and following, as follows:

"15 When ye therefore shall see the abomination of desolation, spoken of by Daniel the prophet, stand in the holy place (whoso readeth, let him understand:)

16 Then let them which be in Judaea flee into the mountains:

17 Let him which is on the housetop not come down to take any thing out of his house:

18 Neither let him which is in the field return back to take his clothes.

19 And woe unto them that are with child, and to them that give suck in those days!

20 But pray ye that your flight be not in the winter, neither the sabbath day:

21 For then shall be great tribulation, such as was not since the beginning of the world to this time, no, nor ever shall be.

9. Evidence That We Are Living Through the Great Tribulation

22 *And except those days should be shortened, there should no flesh be saved: but for the elect's sake those days shall be shortened.*

23 *Then if any man shall say unto you, Lo here is Christ (the Messiah), or there, believe it not.*

24 *For there shall arise false Christs (false Messiahs) and false prophets, and shall shew great signs and wonders; insomuch that, if it were possible, they shall deceive the very elect.*

25 *Behold, I have told you before.*

26 *Wherefore if they shall say unto you, Behold he is in the desert; go not forth: behold, he is in the secret chambers; believe it not.*

27 *For as the lightning cometh out of the east, and shineth even unto the west, so shall also the coming of the Son of man be.*

28 *For wheresoever the carcase is, there will the eagles be gathered together.*

29 *Immediately after the tribulation of those days shall the sun be darkened, and the moon shall not give her light, and the stars shall fall from heaven, and the powers of the heavens shall be shaken:*

30 *And then shall appear the sign of the Son of man in heaven: and then shall all the tribes of the earth mourn, and they shall see the Son of man coming in the clouds of heaven with power and great glory.*

31 *And he shall send his angels with a great sound of a trumpet, and they shall gather together his elect from the four winds, from one end of heaven to the other.*

32 *Now learn a parable of the fig tree; When his branch is yet tender, and putteth forth leaves, ye know that summer is nigh:*

33 *So likewise ye, when ye shall see all these things, know that it is near, even at the doors.*

34 Verily I say unto you, this generation shall not pass, till all these things be fulfilled.

35 Heaven and earth shall pass away, but my words shall not pass away.

36 But of that day and hour knoweth no man, no, not the angels of heaven, but my Father only.

37 But as the days of Noe (Noah) were, so shall also the coming of the Son of man be.

38 For as in the days that were before the flood they were eating and drinking, marrying and giving in marriage, until the day that Noe (Noah) entered into the ark,

39 And knew not until the flood came, and took them all away; so shall also the coming of the Son of man be.

40 Then shall two be in the field; the one shall be taken, the other left.

41 Two women shall be grinding at the mill; the one shall be taken and the other left.

42 Watch therefore: for ye know not what hour your Lord (Adon) doth come."

Unless one is familiar with a large portion of the Bible, these passages on the great tribulation can be very confusing and are frequently misunderstood and distorted by the endless number of false teachers inside all forms of organized religion. Consequently, I need to take the time to unpack what these two passages concerning the great tribulation are telling us, referencing other passages in the Bible, where needed, so that you, my readers, can go back and verify these things for yourselves. You must not take my word for it. It is way too important for you to entrust your eternity to any man, no matter how much I may have earned your trust and confidence so far, and hopefully I have by now.

God reveals to mankind through the inspired and flawless words of His Bible, that the world will not last forever. God has a specific plan that He is orchestrating and unfolding through the thoughts and circumstances which He brings into each of our lives, knowing with absolute precision how we will react beforehand. Overall, God is seeking to grow and mature those of us who number among His elect, His spiritual sheep, those whom He chose since before the world began to become His born again adopted sons and daughters at a time and in a manner of His choosing and at His initiative, whose names are written in the Lamb's book of life, into the likeness and character of His son Jesus, knowing good from evil, choosing that which is good and opposing that which is evil, so that God might enjoy an eternity of genuine relationships with us in a new heaven and a new earth.

The way God has designed life is to subject His elect to trials, affliction, opposition and suffering to test and refine us, and He does so by surrounding us with others, who number among His non-elect, His spiritual goats, destined for their day of destruction, who reject the truth and behave selfishly and wickedly throughout their lives, targeting especially, those of us who number among God's elect. The members of God's non-elect who oppose and afflict God's elect the most, are those closest to us; frequently they are members of our own families:

> *"Think not that I am come to send peace on earth: I came not to send peace, but a sword. For I am come to set a man at variance against his father, and the daughter against her mother, and the daughter in law against her mother in law.* ***And a man's foes shall be they of his own household.*** *He that loveth father or mother more than me is not worthy of me: and he that loveth son or daughter more than me is not worthy of me. And he that taketh not his cross, and followeth after me, is not worthy of me. He that findeth his life shall lose it, and he that loseth his life for my sake shall find it."* Matthew 10:34-39 (emphasis added)

Thus, God subjects each one of His elect to many trials and much pain and suffering which require that we make choices which test and prove the wisdom of putting our faith (trust) in God to provide for our every need and to guide us in life. All around us, He surrounds us with earth dwellers: those who number among His non-elect, who choose the lures and enticements of the world, the flesh and the devil, at the expense of a personal and intimate relationship of truth and wisdom with the creator of the universe. He surrounds us with lies and treacherous liars who secretly seek to harm us to throw us off balance and lead us away from submitting and surrendering our lives and our wills to Yahushua as Lord over our lives and our wills in all things.

Meanwhile, the earth dwellers all around us mock, scorn, ridicule and demean God and the trust we place in Him, which we have considerable evidence to believe is warranted, but which they cannot see, because God has not revealed Himself to them, as He has to us. The attributes God is seeking to develop in each of His elect are discernment (between right and wrong, good and evil, the wise and the foolish), a steadfast dedication to objective truth, a heartfelt love and compassion for our fellow man, virtue, nobility, courage, wisdom, submission and surrender, and an intimate and personal relationship that is unique between Him and each one of us.

All of mankind is born depraved, sinful, selfish, and separated from God at birth and heading to an eternity of torment and agony in hell as punishment for the inevitable sins we will commit during our lifetimes. Just as when we break a legal law, we are fined, jailed or otherwise punished to deter bad behavior, so too when we break God's moral laws, we deserve to be punished for them. Moreover we are all guilty for no one is without sin; all of us fall short of the glory of God, as Romans 3:23 puts it. So we all deserve to be punished for our sins and go to hell when we die. This is very bad news that applies to all of us.

Only God can rescue us from our predicament. Moreover, He only chooses to rescue those of us who number among His elect and everyone He rescues, He rescues differently. God doesn't have to do such a thing. He would be perfectly fair and just to send us all to hell for our sins. But in His grace and mercy, He chooses to offer a pardon to some of us: those whom He chose since before the world began to become His adopted sons and daughters, as, when and how He chooses.

False teaching forms of organized religion lie and teach that God's grace and mercy is free and available to all and that all we have to do is believe in Jesus and we will be saved. But the Bible explains that such is simply not the case at all. The Bible explains that God chooses us first (see Ephesians 1:4-5) and that He must do it all (see Ephesians 2:1-11) The Bible further explains that God simply does not love everybody and that He chooses favorites (see Romans 9:11-24) in the form of His elect.

Once we are saved, the real work begins, as God remakes each of us into the image and character of His son, Yahushua. This is usually very painful and takes years of hard work on our part to grow up, mature, become wise and loving in a world ruled by the devil, who seeks to oppose us at every turn and turn us away from submitting our lives and our wills to Yahushua in all things.

Most of the time, the devil opposes us through the actions of those who serve him: God's non-elect who are usually infested or possessed by one or more destructive and contentious demon spirits which they invited into their lives through sins they committed. To make things even more challenging, this spirit world, which is very real and controls what happens in the physical and material world in which we live, is something that most of us cannot see most of the time. We can certainly see its effects, and that is how we can be sure it exists, but because we cannot see it, we are forced to walk by faith and trust God in what He reveals to us through His Word, the Bible, and other sources of truth He orchestrates and brings into our lives to teach us what He chooses to reveal to us.

As we shall see from examining Scripture, the great tribulation immediately precedes (comes before) the gathering of God's elect, which is commonly referred to as the rapture. After God's elect have been resurrected in bodies like that of Jesus when He rose from the dead, the Bible tells us that God plans to pour his wrath out upon the wicked (His non-elect, His spiritual goats) who remain, in order to cleanse the world of evil once and for all.

At this point I must expose a lie and false teaching concerning the timing of the rapture relative to the timing of the great tribulation. For well over the last 150 years, seminaries have been infiltrated and corrupted with the false doctrine of the pre-trib or pre-tribulation rapture, which falsely claims that the Bible teaches that all Christians will be gathered up or raptured from the earth *before* the great tribulation begins. As a result of this fraudulent teaching permeating seminaries for well over a century and a half, few seminary-trained pastors have taught the truth or even know what it is for that period of time, misleading billions of followers in the process.

The lie of the pre-trib rapture has grave and serious implications. If those who are members of various forms of organized religion were taught that they would have to experience troubles and suffer serious persecution during the great tribulation, most people would have nothing to do with any form of Christian organized religion. Churches would empty, and so too would the offering plates, and because organized religion today is big business, such an outcome could not be permitted to occur by worldly pastors, ministers and priests.

So Satan and his army infected organized religion with the fraud of a pre-trib rapture teaching to lure God's non-elect, His spiritual goats, into organized religion and deceive them into believing they were saved when, in fact, they are not, and never can be. Such deception and trickery cannot possibly be of God, who is the source of all truth and love. It can only be of the enemy, the father of lies, the devil. As we will see in the next to last chapter, this is precisely who rules all forms of organized Christian religion today: the devil and his demon spirits, and I will show why this has to be the case, and illustrate it with numerous examples of what false organized religion teaches today, which contradict what the Bible says, and therefore have to be false and lies.

9. Evidence That We Are Living Through the Great Tribulation

Returning to Daniel 12, let's dissect what it is actually revealing to us concerning the great tribulation.

> *"1 And at that time shall Michael stand up, the great prince which standeth for the children of thy people: and there shall be a time of trouble, such as never was since there was a nation even to that same time: and at that time thy people shall be delivered, everyone that shall be found written in the book."*

Michael is the archangel Michael who is referred to in Revelation 12:7 who led two thirds of the angels in heaven in a war against the dragon (otherwise known as Lucifer or Satan) and one third of the angels who sided with Satan who lost the war and were thrown out of heaven to earth to persecute the people of God. Ephesians 6:12 teaches us:

> *"For we wrestle not against flesh and blood, but against principalities, against powers, against the rulers of darkness of this world, against spiritual wickedness in high places."*

So Michael, the good spiritual prince, opposes spiritual princes of evil and stands for (protects) the people of Daniel, namely, God's people who are His elect.

The verse goes on to describe a time of trouble more severe than any such period of time in all of world history up to that point which is the same description Yahushua uses in Matthew 24:21 to describe a time of great tribulation. According to *Noah Webster's 1828 America Dictionary of the English Language*, tribulation in Scripture often denotes the troubles and distresses which proceed from persecution, as in John 16:33 when Yahushua promises His disciples,

> *"In the world ye shall have tribulation . . . "*

So tribulation is something common to all of God's elect. It is *not* at all the same thing as experiencing God's outpouring of wrath upon the wicked, as is often falsely taught by many forms of organized religion. The verse concludes by explaining that all of God's people, meaning His elect, those whose names are written in the Lamb's book of life, will be delivered through

259

this time of trouble, not delivered from it, as is so often falsely taught.

> *"2   And many of them that sleep in the dust of the earth shall awake, some to everlasting life, and some to shame and everlasting contempt."*

Those who sleep in the dust of the earth is a metaphor for those who have died, who will be resurrected just as Yahushua was resurrected in a new physical body, some of whom will go to everlasting life (those who number among God's elect, whose names are written in the Lamb's book of life), and others of whom will be resurrected to everlasting shame and contempt (those who were God's non-elect, His spiritual goats, whose names were not written in the Lamb's book of life).

> *"3   And they that be wise shall shine as the brightness of the firmament, and they that turn many to righteousness as the stars for ever and ever."*

Those who fear God are those who acquire true knowledge and become wise the Book of Proverbs tells us. Only God's elect properly respect, revere and fear God for His awesome power and might. These resurrected saints or believers will shine like the stars of heaven and those who lead others to find the truth of God and a right relationship with Him (which is what righteousness is: right relationship with God) will shine like the stars for all eternity, is what this verse is telling us.

> *"4   But thou, O Daniel, shut up the words and seal the book, even to the time of the end: many shall run to and fro, and knowledge shall be increased."*

This verse reveals that the time of trouble referred to in verse 1 will come at the end of times. In the meantime, many shall scurry about and knowledge (such as scientific knowledge) will be increased, but this does not necessarily imply that wisdom will increase. It is instructive that Proverbs 1:7 teaches us:

> *"The fear of the LORD (YHWH) is the beginning of knowledge: but fools despise wisdom and instruction."*

Wisdom is the application of knowledge. Verse 4 merely refers to knowledge itself, which can often puff men up with pride, thinking they know it all when, in reality, they do not.

> *"5 Then I Daniel looked, and behold, there stood other two, the one on this side of the bank of the river, and the other on that side of the bank of the river."*

The other two are likely to be angels of some sort, on opposing sides of a river which appears to be the very same river described in the vision the Apostle John describes in Revelation 22:1-2 concerning a pure river of the water of life in a new heaven and earth.

> *"6 And one said to the man clothed in linen, which was upon the waters of the river, How long shall it be to the end of these wonders?"*

The man clothed in linen standing upon the waters of the river is likely the pre-incarnate Christ, or Yahushua, who is frequently described in the Book of Revelation in similar terms. One of the angels is asking Him, "How long will this period of troubles last?"

> *"7 And I heard the man clothed in linen, which was upon the waters of the river, when he held up his right hand and his left hand unto heaven, and sware by him that liveth for ever that it shall be for a time, times and an half; and when he shall have accomplished to scatter the power of the holy people, all these things shall be finished."*

Here the pre-incarnate Yahushua raises His arms to heaven and swears by YHWH (God) that the time of troubles, the great tribulation, will last for three and a half years (times), or 42 months. We will see this period of time referenced in Chapter 11 of the Book of Revelation, pertaining to this same sequence of events. Jesus goes on to explain that the tribulation will end only after God has scattered the power of His people, His born again elect, where we will have no effective influence in a world and culture given over to sin, wickedness and immorality.

> *"8   And I heard, but I understood not: then said I, O my Lord (Adon), what shall be the end of these things?"*

Here Daniel is not understanding the word of Yahushua (Jesus) and seeks to know precisely when these things will occur.

> *"9   And he said, Go thy way, Daniel: for the words are closed up and sealed until the time of the end."*

Yahushua responds to Daniel by telling him that the answer to his question is not for Daniel to know, only at the time of the end, when the great tribulation occurs.

> *"10 Many shall be purified, and made white, and tried; but the wicked shall do wickedly: and none of the wicked shall understand; but the wise shall understand."*

Those who are purified, made white and tried are God's born elect, His people who will experience trouble, opposition, affliction and persecution during the great tribulation, which will refine and strengthen the faith and characters of God's elect. The wicked are God's non-elect, His spiritual goats, who will behave wickedly and will not understand what is going on during the time of the great tribulation, but God's people, who fear and revere God, will understand because God will reveal the truth to His elect. 2 Thessalonians 2:10-12 reveals that in the end times:

> *"And with all deceivableness of unrighteousness in them that perish; because they received not the love of the truth, that they might be saved. And for this cause God (Eloah) shall send them strong delusion, that they should believe a lie: That they all might be damned who believed not the truth, but had pleasure in unrighteousness."*

Thus, God reveals that He planned to send, and has now already sent, a strong delusion on God's non-elect (the wicked), so that they are unable to accurately comprehend the signs that are revealed to God's elect during the great tribulation, which will alert us to be prepared for the second coming of Yahushua shortly after the end of the great

tribulation. This is why the wise shall understand, but the
wicked shall not understand any of this, for they have been
spiritually blinded to the truth by God Himself and no efforts
of man can reverse what God has put in place.

> *"11 And from the time that the daily sacrifice shall be taken
> away, and the abomination that maketh desolate set up,
> there shall be a thousand two hundred and ninety days."*

The daily animal sacrifices in the Temple were no longer
necessary once Christ, the perfect sacrifice of the Lamb of
God, died on the cross. Then in the prophecy of Matthew
24:15, Jesus reveals that when we see the abomination that
causes desolation standing in the holy place, that event signals
the start of the great tribulation. But this verse tells us that the
abomination that causes desolation must be fully set up or
established, not just first revealed and that such an event will
not occur until after Christ has died on the cross, which was
an event which occurred roughly 568 years after Daniel's
ministry ended in 535 B.C. This verse is revealing to us (with
the benefit of the prophecy of Matthew 24:15, which was
spoken much later than Daniel's prophecy here) that from the
start of the great tribulation to its end, when the abomination
that causes desolation is fully set up, will be 1,290 days. This
estimate of the duration of the great tribulation in days
coincides quite closely with the first estimate which Yahushua
provides in verse 7 as three and a half years, which comes to
1,260 days, assuming a 360 day year. Not coincidentally, three
and a half years matches half of the final week of years referred
to in chapter 9 of the Book of Daniel, particularly Daniel 9:27,
which we will return to examine later, because this passage has
frequently been misunderstood and falsely taught to mean
something other than what it actually means.

> *"12 Blessed is he that waiteth, and cometh to the thousand
> three hundred and five and thirty days."*

From the context of the prior verse, we know that the great
tribulation will last 1,290 days. From this verse, we learn that
1,335 days after the start date of the great tribulation, and thus
45 days after its end, a day of blessing will arrive for those that

wait and come to this blessing date. What might this day of blessing refer to? From the context of verse 10, we can safely deduce that those blessed will be the wise, namely God's elect, His spiritual sheep, whom God seeks to bless for our obedience and submission to Him. Matthew 24:29-31 give us some essential clues as to what God has in store for His elect, shortly after the end of the great tribulation. I will develop this more as we examine the passage in Matthew 24, but for now let me lay out what I believe the blessing consists of: 1) the gathering of God's elect into the clouds with Yahushua (described in Matthew 24:30-31) and 2) the marriage supper of the Lamb between Christ and His bride, the resurrected body of believers, described in Revelation 19:7-9. Thus, if we know when the great tribulation began, then from the clues from Daniel 12:11-12, we can predict with considerable accuracy when it will end and when God's elect shall be gathered or raptured to be with Christ in heaven in resurrected bodies, much like His and to be invited to the marriage supper of the Lamb (see Revelation 19:9, in particular). As we will soon see, we do now know when the great tribulation started. But let's not get ahead of ourselves.

"13 But go thou thy way till the end be: for thou shalt rest, and stand in thy lot at the end of days."

Yahushua concludes the Book of Daniel by directing the favored prophet of God to wait until the end times, for he will die, be buried and rest until the end times, when Daniel will be among God's resurrected people as part of the gathering or rapture, briefly described in verse 2 here, and further described in several passages in the New Testament which was not written for over 500 years after the ministry of Daniel had ended.

Let us now turn to Matthew 24, in which Yahushua responds to the questions of His disciples who ask when shall His second coming and the end of the world be, and what will be the sign or signs of His second coming.

9. Evidence That We Are Living Through the Great Tribulation

"15 When ye therefore shall see the abomination of desolation, spoken of by Daniel the prophet, stand in the holy place, (whoso readeth, let him understand:)"

Here Yahushua is alerting us that when we see the abomination that causes desolation standing in the holy place, we know that the great tribulation has begun, as He goes on to reveal to us in verse 21. Abomination means an object of extreme hatred, according to *Noah Webster's 1828 American Dictionary of the English Language*. Desolation means destruction, ruin or waste.

Prior to the first coming of Yahushua, in 166 B.C. the first abomination that caused desolation standing in the holy place, prophesied in Daniel 11:31, occurred when the Greek ruler Antiochus Epiphanies IV had a pig (an unclean animal) sacrificed on an altar in the Temple (the holy place) in Jerusalem, thus defiling it, and putting an end to the daily animal sacrifices for the next two years, at the end of which, Judas Maccabeus and his followers drove out the Greeks from Jerusalem, cleaned up the Temple and rededicated it in December of 164 B.C., which is commemorated today as the Jewish holiday of Hanukkah. However, the spiritual redemption of the defilement of the Temple, the holy place, occurred with the sacrifice of the perfect Lamb of God, Yahushua, on the cross roughly 200 years later in 33 A.D., which put an end to the need for the daily animal sacrifices in the Temple for all time.

Notice that it took an act of Yahushua to redeem the first defilement or abomination that causes desolation standing in the holy place and we will see that in a similar fashion, God plans for Yahushua to redeem the second abomination that causes desolation standing in the holy place in His end times prophesies too. This is a very common way that God operates: He foreshadows events in the New Testament with events or prophecies in the Old Testament period which foreshadow, or point to, the more complete spiritual fulfillment of prophesies in the New Testament.

Many have falsely concluded that the "abomination that causes desolation" was the destruction of the Temple in Jerusalem by the Roman army under the Roman general Titus in 70 A.D. Yet a closer reading of Matthew 24:15-31, combined with a proper understanding of the length of the great tribulation from Daniel 12 of three and a half years, reveals that this cannot possibly be the case. Yet that certainly does not deter many false teachers from clinging to a sloppy analysis of what this passage refers to, in order to deceive many.

> *"16 Then let them which be in Judaea flee into the mountains:*
>
> *17 Let him which is on the housetop not come down to take any thing out of his house:*
>
> *18 Neither let him which is in the field return back to take his clothes.*
>
> *19 And woe unto them that are with child, and to them that give suck in those days!*
>
> *20 But pray ye that your flight not be in the winter, neither on the sabbath day:"*

Judaea was the Roman province and land of the Jews in the days of Yahushua, signifying the more populated areas of the region, whereas the mountains were the less populous wilderness areas of this Roman province. Metaphorically, Judaea signified organized religion, whereas the mountains symbolized YHWH (God) himself. Thus, it is quite possible that Yahushua is signaling to God's elect that when we see the abomination that causes desolation standing in the holy place, we ought to flee all forms organized religion and seek God directly in His Word, the Bible, as our only trustworthy source of truth. I believe there is considerable evidence in our world today and in other end times Bible prophesies which we will examine in the next chapter that support this likely understanding of verse 16 here.

Recall in my own story how I fled both organized religion and the satanic culture of Marin County, California for the mountains of southeastern Idaho in the late summer of 2012, and part of my motivation for doing so was God giving me the insight that I was no longer safe inside organized religion or

the more populous and demon-infested state of California. I
was knowingly being obedient to this passage when I did so,
even though the event prophesied in Matthew 24:15 had not
yet occurred.

Verses 17-20 reflect Yahushua's method of teaching in which
He frequently spoke in parables, and these four verses should
be understood metaphorically, not literally. Yahushua is telling
us not to hesitate in fleeing from organized and false religion
and not to hesitate from physically moving from more
populous areas to more mountainous and unpopulated ones
during the time of the great tribulation. In times of danger,
mothers-to-be who are pregnant and nursing mothers, those
traveling in winter and those needing to travel on the sabbath
day, will clearly find themselves struggling more and being at
greater risk than those who are not afflicted with such greater
challenges.

> *"21 For then shall be great tribulation, such as was not since
> the beginning of the world to this time, no, nor ever shall
> be."*

Yahushua clearly is revealing here in verse 21 that when we see
the abomination that causes desolation standing in the holy
place, it signals the start date of the great tribulation. Moreover,
He uses language to describe this time of troubles and
persecution that parallels the description of the days of
troubles described in Daniel 12:1 as a period unlike any other
in all of world history up to that point, and greater than in any
period that will follow. This is how we can be quite confident
that Daniel 12 and Matthew 24:15-31 are referring to the very
same timeframe in Biblical prophecy. This linkage between the
two passages is very important, because to properly understand
end times Bible prophecy in this regard, the two passages play
off against, and can only properly be understood in
conjunction with, one another.

Additionally, Yahushua is telling us here just how troubling and
trying the 1,290 days of the great tribulation will be for God's
elect. Never before in all of world history will God's people
experience the sort of bizarre, irrational, demonic and insane

behaviors and incompetence which will become commonplace during the great tribulation.

> *"22 And except those days should be shortened, there should no flesh be saved: but for the elect's sake those days shall be shortened."*

God does not reveal to us here what the days of the great tribulation will be shortened from. God always fulfills Bible prophecy with hair-splitting accuracy and He has prophesied in Daniel 12:11 that it will last 1,290 days. Thus there is no valid reason for us to conclude that the great tribulation will last any less than 1,290 days, but perhaps God is making these days seem to pass by more swiftly for His elect, than might otherwise seem to be the case. But what is clear is that however He intends to shorten the days of the great tribulation, He will do such a thing strictly for the benefit of His elect.

Now if the doctrine of devils of the pre-tribulation rapture were true (it's not), this verse poses serious problems for those promoting this false doctrine, since this verse as much as tells us that the elect shall have to suffer and endure **through** the great tribulation period, not be rescued **from** it. Moreover, this understanding finds support in the story of Noah's flood, in which Noah and his family were brought through the flood in the ark with all the animals, and were not rescued from it. Here, Noah's flood and how God handled Noah and his family foreshadows how God intends to shepherd His elect through the days of the great tribulation in a similar fashion.

The way the false teachers of the pre-trib rapture get around this inconvenient piece of Scripture is to suggest that the Bible prophesies two distinct gatherings or raptures and that the elect being referred to here are those not yet born again in God's Holy Spirit. But such an explanation creates its own set of problems for these false teachers, because Scripture refers to God's elect (not God's not-yet-born-again people) and this term means those whom God chose since before the world began, whose names are written in the Lamb's book of life, and who will one day, have God place His Holy Spirit in them, orchestrate events for them to hear the gospel preached and believe it and become one of His born again adopted sons or daughters. So the false notion of two raptures or resurrections simply does not pass the test of reasonableness when properly dividing God's Word of truth.

> *"23 Then if any man shall say unto you, Lo, here is Christ (the Messiah), or there, believe it not.*
>
> *24 For there shall arise false Christs (false Messiahs), and false prophets, and shall shew great signs and wonders; insomuch that, if it were possible, they shall deceive the very elect."*

Yahushua begins to reveal to us that His second coming will not be subtle or hidden: it will be out in the open and visible to all. Further, just as we have witnessed in the latter part of the 20th century and early in the 21st century, we have seen a number of false prophets (Harold Camping of Family Radio and his prediction of the rapture and end of the world on May 21, 2011 is the latest which comes to mind) warn that the end is near and time has proven them to be false.

Similarly, in many forms of false organized religions today, we have seen different Christs and different Jesuses than we see revealed to us in God's Word, the Bible. Yahushua tells us that these claims and these times of the great tribulation will be so deceptive and misleading, that if it were possible to deceive God's elect, we would be deceived. However, it is equally clear from the wording of this verse that it will not be possible for God's elect to be deceived by false Christs, false prophets and their great signs and wonders. This is because God will protect His elect and reveal the truth to us somehow.

The corollary to this is that all those who do not number among God's elect will most assuredly be deceived during the days of the great tribulation. Why this is so is revealed in the fulfillment of the prophecy of 2 Thessalonians 2:10-12 which we have already examined in connection with our analysis of Daniel 12:10, namely, God will send, and in fact, has now already sent a strong delusion on many, so they will believe a lie and so be damned for delighting in unrighteousness and rejecting the truth.

> *"25 Behold, I have told you before.*
>
> *26 Wherefore if they shall say unto you, Behold he is in the desert; go not forth: behold he is in the secret chambers; believe it not.*
>
> *27 For as the lightning cometh out of the east, and shineth even unto the west; so shall also the coming of the Son of man be.*
>
> *28 For wheresoever the carcase is, there will the eagles be gathered together."*

Here Yahushua continues to explain that His second coming will not be a secret. It will be as visible and apparent as a bolt of lightening flashing from the east to the west. His remark about the eagles gathered together around the carcass is a metaphor telling us that where we see the signs of His second coming clustered (symbolizing multiple fulfilled end times Bible prophecies), His second coming cannot be far behind, just as when we see birds of prey gathered together, we can be reasonably certain that a dead or dying animal is likely to be nearby.

> *"29 **Immediately after** the tribulation of those days shall the sun be darkened, and the moon shall not give her light, and the stars shall fall from heaven, and the powers of the heavens shall be shaken:"*

Here we see that four dramatic celestial events will occur immediately *after* the 1,290 days of the great tribulation are concluded. The sun being darkened and the moon not giving off her light may refer to solar and lunar eclipses, respectively, followed by a meteor shower of some intensity, followed by a global earthquake perhaps. I believe it is likely to be far more dramatic than that. I believe those four celestial events are more likely to be the result of a near fly-by of the brown dwarf star known by various names, Planet-X, Nibiru and Wormwood, being among them. It certainly appears to me that these four celestial events are also described in terms of the opening of the sixth seal in Revelation 6:12-17 as follows:

> *"And I beheld when he had opened the sixth seal, and lo, there was a great earthquake; and the sun became as black as sackcloth of hair, and the moon became as blood; And the stars of heaven fell unto the earth, even as a fig tree casteth her untimely figs, when she is shaken of a mighty wind. And the heaven departed as a scroll when it is rolled together; and every mountain and island were moved out of their places. And the kings of the earth, and the great men, and the rich men, and the chief captains, and the mighty men, and every bondman, and every free man, hid themselves in the dens and in the rocks of the mountains. And said to the mountains and rocks, Fall on us, and hide us from the face of him that sitteth on the throne, and from the wrath of the Lamb: For the great day of his wrath is come; and who shall be able to stand?"*

This passage describes a set of celestial events almost identical in description to the one in Matthew 24:29 which are of unprecedented magnitude, force and power. It is widely known that the U.S. military has built 150 − 200 underground cities, known as Deep Underground Military Bases (or DUMBs), which they have been constructing since the early 1980s, ostensibly in the event of a nuclear war, but a far more likely reason is that our government leaders know about and are monitoring the incoming fly-by of a large brown dwarf star generally reported to be four and a half times the mass of earth. In such an instance, a near fly-by of earth could produce massive electro-mechanical discharges from the brown dwarf star to earth and could result in equally massive gravitational effects that could induce a pole shift in which the outer crust of the earth could slip over its inner molten mantle, resulting in a global earthquake the likes of which we can barely imagine and have never before witnessed.

Similarly, the Roman Catholic Church has invested in three observatories around the world. What could possibly account for the largest institutional church in the world making such significant investments in astronomy observatories unless it

271

was something related to end times prophecy, such as what I have just alluded to?

> "As an interesting side note, the Vatican recently built several 'state-of-the-art' solar observatories around the world. Suspiciously, all the doors of these expensive/high-tech observatories are sealed to the public. And further, the Vatican subsequently refuses to discuss the real purpose of those observatories or what their telescopes are currently searching for. Now why would the Vatican, a religious institution, be so interested in what's going on in outer space? And why would they need several exotic observatories strategically located at key points around the planet?

> Could these observatories all be busy gazing at the same incredible incoming celestial object − a brown dwarf start called 'Wormwood' as found in the New Testament's Book of Revelation?

> And will the appearance of this massive and terrifying celestial visitor trigger a pole shift that will bring down the Vatican in a swift and sudden event long-predicted − but never publicly admitted to − by past Popes and the Catholic Church hierarchy currently running the Vatican?"[61]

This would explain the real reason behind the U.S. government creating the Department of Homeland Security and making massive investments in preparation for what appears to be martial law and for widespread deaths from an unidentified source. Perhaps this is it. I believe it is.

> *"30 **And then** shall appear the sign of the Son of man in heaven: and then shall all the tribes of the earth mourn, and they shall see the Son of man coming in the clouds of heaven with power and great glory.*

---

[61] Rand, Jaysen Q., Ph.D. *The Return of Planet-X and Its Effects on Mother Earth.* 2007. p. 193.

9. Evidence That We Are Living Through the Great Tribulation

31   And he shall send his angels with a great sound of a trumpet, and they shall gather together his elect from the four winds, from one end of heaven to the other."

These two verses refer to the gathering, commonly referred to as the rapture of God's elect. This whole event in God's prophetic timeline warrants a bit more explanation, which the Apostle Paul provides to us in the following two passages from his epistles:

"But I would not have you to be ignorant, brethren, concerning them which are asleep, that ye sorrow not, even as others which have no hope. For if we believe that Jesus (Yahushua) died and rose again, even so them also which sleep in Jesus (Yahushua) will God (Eloah) bring with him. For this we say unto you by the word of the Lord (Adon), that we which are alive and remain unto the coming of the Lord (Adon) shall not prevent them which are asleep. For the Lord (Adon) himself shall descend from heaven with a shout, and with the voice of the archangel, and with the trump of God (Eloah): and the dead in Christ (the Messiah) shall rise first: Then we which are alive and remain shall be caught up together with them in the clouds, to meet the Lord (our Adon) in the air: and so shall we ever be with the Lord (our Adon)." 1 Thessalonians 4:13-17

"Behold, I shew you a mystery; We shall not all sleep, but we shall all be changed. In a moment, in the twinkling of an eye, at the last trump: for the trumpet shall sound, and the dead shall be raised incorruptible, and we shall be changed. For this corruptible must put on incorruption, and this mortal must put on immortality. So when this corruptible shall have put on incorruption, and this mortal shall have put on immortality, then shall be brought to pass the saying that is written, Death is swallowed up in victory. O death, where is thy sting? O grave, where is thy victory? The sting of death is sin; and the strength of sin is the law. But thanks be to God (Eloah), which giveth us the victory through our Lord Jesus Christ (our Adon Yahushua the Messiah)." 1 Corinthians 15:51-57

Paul tells us that those who are dead in Christ, meaning that they were born again followers of YHWH or of Christ before

273

they died, who thus evidenced their election by God through their baptism in the Holy Spirit of God, will be raised in resurrected bodies, just like Jesus' when He rose from the dead. Then those of us who number among God's born again followers of Yahushua, who thus evidence our election by God, will be converted, in the twinkling of an eye, from mortal bodies to immortal ones, just like Yahushua's, and we will rise into the clouds to be with Him forever after. This is referred to in Revelation 20:5 as the first resurrection (of the saints or God's true elect).

In Revelation 7:9-14 we see where those who are gathered as part of the gathering of Matthew 24:30-31 appear in heaven:

> *"After this I beheld, and lo, a great multitude, which no man could number, of all nations, and kindreds, and people, and tongues, stood before the throne, and before the Lamb, clothed with white robes, and palms in their hands; And cried with a loud voice, saying, Salvation to our God (Eloah) which sitteth upon the throne, and unto the Lamb. And all the angels stood round about the throne, and the elders and the four beasts, and fell before the throne on their faces, and worshipped God, Saying, Amen: Blessing and glory, and wisdom, and thanksgiving, and honour, and power, and might, be unto our God (Eloah) for ever and ever. Amen. And one of the elders answered, saying unto me, What are these which are arrayed in white robes? and whence came they? And I said unto him, Sir, thou knowest, And he said to me, These are they* **which came out of the great tribulation,** *and have washed their robes, and made them white in the blood of the Lamb."*
> Revelation 7:9-14

The Book of Revelation, which reveals the majority of end times prophecy, describes seven seal, seven trumpet and seven vial judgments. God's elect must endure the first six seal judgments, the last one being the four celestial events which we have discussed earlier. Later, after God's elect have been gathered up from the earth to be with Yahushua in the clouds and in heaven, God plans to pour out the seventh seal judgment, the seven trumpet judgments, followed by the seven vial judgments upon the wicked, who remain on earth. Anyone who is not one of God's born again elect, is deemed wicked and one of God's non-elect.

> *"32 Now learn a parable of the fig tree: When the branch is
> yet tender, and putteth forth leaves, ye know that summer
> is nigh:*
>
> *33 So likewise ye, when ye shall see all these things, know that
> it is near, even at the doors."*

Yahushua is repeating His teaching concerning remaining watchful for the signs of the great tribulation as evidence that His second coming is just around the corner. What are these signs? Well, a key part is seeing the fulfillment of a number of other end times prophecies in Scripture.

The Bible reveals in several places that God's people, the righteous, His elect, will be led to the truth and given the spiritual discernment to see these things, while those who are not His people, the wicked and the foolish, His non-elect, His spiritual goats, will be sent a strong delusion by God that will blind them to the truth of end times events that are spiritually discerned. Here, it is important to digress for a moment and study and unpack three Bible passages that reveal this reality, because it is very important for all of God's elect to comprehend what's going on today.

2 Thessalonians, chapter 2 reveals some essential things which must come to pass before the second coming of Yahushua (Jesus) can occur. At verse 3 it reveals that the "falling away" must occur and that the man of sin, the son of perdition, a.k.a. the Antichrist, must be revealed before Christ's second coming can occur. Both of those events and prophecies have now been fulfilled with hair-splitting accuracy and very few people can see it. Here's how verse 3 reads with my parenthetical explanations added:

> *"Let no man deceive you by any means: for that day (meaning
> the second coming of the Lord Jesus Christ, as revealed from
> verse 1 of this same chapter) shall not come, except there come
> a falling away first (meaning a falling away, apostasy or*

departure from the teachings of YHWH and Yahushua of the Bible in its entirety — which all forms of organized religion are now guilty of), and that man of sin be revealed, the son of perdition (meaning the Antichrist, who we now know are impostors posing as Jews, who falsely claim to be the Messiah, and are secretly following the anti-Christ teachings of the Babylonian Talmud and Zohar Kabbalah of the occult, who have hijacked and rule our world today as the Jewish Illuminati Freemason Zionist global elite conspiracy);"

Then in verses 10-12 of chapter 2 of 2 Thessalonians, Paul reveals that once these two events and prophesies of verse 3 have been fulfilled, God will send a strong delusion upon the wicked (God's non-elect, His spiritual goats) so that they will believe a lie and so be condemned to hell for delighting in unrighteousness and repeatedly rejecting the truth. Here's how it reads:

*"And with all deceivableness of unrighteousness in them that perish; because they received not a love of the truth, that they might be saved. And for this cause God (Eloah) shall send them **strong delusion**, that they should believe a lie: That they all might be damned (condemned to hell) who believed not the truth, but had pleasure in unrighteousness."* (emphasis and parentheticals added)

This prophecy too has now been fulfilled with hair-splitting accuracy. My dear bride and I have witnessed this phenomenon extensively in my own blogging on numerous political and religious websites over the past two years, and many bloggers who profess to be Christians become downright angry, mocking, ridiculing, scorning and verbally abusive to me when I dare to reveal these truths to them and to others.

These are not behaviors evidencing the fruit of the Spirit of Galatians 5:22-23 which all true followers of Yahushua will increasingly manifest in their lives and behaviors as they submit their lives and their wills more fully to Christ, those attributes of fruit being love, joy, peace, longsuffering (patience), gentleness, goodness, faith, meekness (humility), and temperance (self-control). These bloggers' behaviors are the works of the flesh described by Paul in Galatians 5:19-21 which are the opposite of the fruit of the Spirit, which allow us to discern and distinguish between true followers of Christ and the many more numerous frauds and self-deceived people, who claim to be Christians, but clearly are not. If they were, they would consistently exhibit the nine attributes of the fruit of the Spirit and two essential and core traits which Christ modeled to us and taught during His life: 1) a love for the objective truth, and 2) a love for the eternal well-being of mankind over their own selfish wants and comforts.

In these most deceptive of time periods in all of world history, if we are not constantly measuring people's actions and words against these standards of what a true Christian is, we will almost certainly be deceived. Moreover, our trying to convince anyone who has been sent the strong delusion by God of any of the truths I am teaching in this chapter, will never work. Instead, we will be subjected to verbal abuse, scorn, mockery and hatred from such people who, at some level, know they are perishing spiritually, but will refuse to and are unable to admit it because the eternal implications of such a conclusion are too horrible to contemplate. If they did, it would drive them insane.

Third, Daniel 12 speaks to the period of the great tribulation and in verse 10 the prophet Daniel reveals the dichotomy between the experience of God's elect, the righteous, and the wicked, God's non-elect, as follows:

> *"Many shall be purified, and made white, and tried (meaning God's elect during the days of the great tribulation, or time of troubles); but the wicked (all others) shall do wickedly: and none of the wicked shall understand; but the wise (meaning God's elect) shall understand."* (parentheticals added)

Now that we understand from 2 Thessalonians 2:10-12 how God has sent a strong delusion on the vast majority of mankind in the world, we can see how it is that the wicked of this world will remain clueless of the truth of what end times prophecies say and mean right up to the bitter end, when

Christ returns in the clouds with power and great glory to gather up His elect, as revealed to us in Matthew 24:30-31. Recall from our previous unpacking of this verse that "all the tribes of the earth shall mourn" when they witness this event that will be clearly visible to everyone on earth. Only then will the wicked of this world wake up to objective reality and the truth of God's Word concerning all things. So my purpose here is to alert and educate God's people, His elect, His spiritual sheep to these truths so that they will not be deceived during these deceptive days of the great tribulation. Those who are able to grasp and see these truths manifest the evidence that they number among God's elect.

Those who reveal that they are incapable of grasping these truths and verifying for themselves what Bible Scripture clearly teaches on these matters, are revealing to God's elect that they number among God's non-elect, for whom we can do nothing, because God has willed it that way.

I must confess that while I understand that God has designed some people to become His born again elect, (His spiritual sheep, His adopted sons and daughters) and many more people who are not so designed (His non-elect, His spiritual goats), I will be the first to admit that I do not fully comprehend God's thinking on this matter. Nevertheless, Isaiah 55:8-11 makes it clear,

> "For my thoughts are not your thoughts, neither are your ways my ways, saith the LORD (YHWH). For as the heavens are higher than the earth, so are my ways higher than your ways, and my thoughts than your thoughts. For as the rain cometh down, and the snow from heaven, and returneth not thither, but watereth the earth, and maketh it bring forth and bud, that it may give seed to the sower, and bread to the eater: So shall my word be that goeth forth out of my mouth: it shall not return unto me void, but it shall accomplish that which I please, and it shall prosper in the thing whereto I sent it."

Clearly, God's Word (the Bible) teaches the doctrine of election, which almost all forms of organized religion today vigorously dismiss and teach against (a clear error and false

278

teaching). In His infinite wisdom, God has determined that in
order to mature and refine certain people (His elect) to warrant
His desiring to have a personal and intimate relationship with
those of us of integrity, wisdom and character, that He must
test, chasten, refine and mature us and develop our trust in
Him through numerous challenges, trials, tribulations,
struggles and suffering. He has determined that the only
effective way that He can accomplish this goal is to subject us
to opposition and affliction at the hands of other people more
numerous than we are, who are wicked, deceitful, treacherous
thieves, murderers, adulterers and psychopaths who will
possess far more worldly power and influence than we will
have, and subject us to grave injustices. God has designed our
characters uniquely from the beginning and thus He knows
precisely how each of us will respond to each and every
circumstance and thought He planned in advance that He
would bring into our lives, from the moment we were born to
the moment we die, to mold our characters into the likeness of
His son, Yahushua (Christ).

The problem most people have is coming to terms with the
ramifications and implications of this divine plan upon God's
non-elect, His spiritual goats, whom He has designed for their
day of destruction as Proverbs 16:4 clearly teaches:

> *"The LORD (YHWH) hath made all things for himself: yea,
> even the wicked (God's non-elect) for the day of evil."*
> (parenthetical added)

If indeed God has crafted some men and women for glory and
many more for eternal damnation and punishment for their
sins, "how is this fair or just?" one concerned about justice and
fairness might ask. False teaching theologians and pastors
inside fraudulent and apostate organized religion today will
teach the doctrine of devils that God is pure love, filled with
mercy and forgiveness and that in the end, all men will be saved
and spend eternity with God and the rest of humanity in
heaven. This certainly appeals to those whose lives are devoted
to pursuing the lures of the world, the flesh and the devil, but
is such a thing fair and just to God's elect and does it conform

with God's perfect will as revealed to us in Scripture? Moreover, does it reflect the full character and nature of an almighty and sovereign God who created all things for His good pleasure, not ours? No, it simply does not.

It is true that YHWH and Yahushua reveal to us through God's Word, the Bible, that God is loving, merciful, gentle and forgiving – to those who will confess and repent of (turn from) their sins and submit their lives and their wills fully to the commandments of Yahushua in all things. But that is only half of the story, and a half truth remains a lie. Moreover, all lies and liars are of the devil. It is equally true that God's nature is perfectly holy and just. YHWH has no tolerance for sin and rebellious, defiant, wicked, selfish fools. YHWH's word clearly tells us in Romans 6:23,

> "For the wages of sin is death; but the gift of God (Eloah) is eternal life through Jesus Christ our Lord (our Adon Yahushua the Messiah)."

Thus, God has created all things and all people in accordance with His perfect will. He has created all of mankind to be born separated from a right relationship with Him, with a bent to be selfish, deceitful and sinful. And since the wages of sin is death, we all deserve to die and be punished for our sins in hell or the burning lake of fire and brimstone for all eternity. This is the fate of all of mankind at birth, whether we choose to admit it or not. Most of humanity lives in denial of this God-revealed reality, but their denial makes it no less true. So we're all bound for hell at birth. This is what God's Word reveals to mankind, regardless of the "feel-good" false doctrines that the frauds of organized religion of all forms try to convince us of. Then God chooses to offer the chance for a pardon to a few of us (His elect, His spiritual sheep) at a time and in a manner of His choosing, and at His initiative, not ours.

God never lies, changes or fails in anything. What He wills, happens 100% of the time. So if we are chosen by God to become one of His born again adopted sons or daughters at some point in our lives, nothing, not even the gates of hell, can prevent this from happening as and when God chooses. Now there is a catch to this pardon. We must believe and trust God and Jesus in all things and obey them completely. We don't get to claim that we have been born again and are Christians and then continue to lie, cheat and steal from others. Yet this is precisely the con job and fraud which 99 out of every 100 people who profess to be Christians try to pull over on God and on the rest of us. Don't buy it. They're liars, frauds and con artists and when the hammer of God's wrath and fury falls in a few short years, they will be on the receiving end of it. God's Word **says** so at Matthew 7:23 thusly:

> *"And then will I profess unto them, I never knew you: depart from me, ye that work iniquity."*

God has intentionally created hell to be a horrific place that ought to drive every sane human being to confess and repent of his sins and submit his life and his will to Yahushua in all things without hesitation. Yet few men or women do so, in spite of it being in their obvious best interests for all eternity. It is a complete no-brainer to those of us who can see it.

And this reveals the heart of the problem: all of humanity is blind to objective reality until and unless God chooses to reveal it to us. In the meantime, the vast majority of the world lives in denial of and disconnected from objective reality, precisely as God has orchestrated and intended it. We have a word for this condition: we call it insanity, and that is precisely what it is. Insanity, lies and deceit are directly related to one another. You cannot have one without the others. Thus, the cure for insanity is a vigorous love for and pursuit of the objective truth, no matter how unpleasant it may seem at first. That is what this book is intended to teach and model to God's elect: the only people capable of grasping the truths contained here.

So, returning to Matthew 24:34-44, let's unpack the rest of it:

> *"34 Verily I say unto you, this generation shall not pass, till all these things be fulfilled.*
>
> *35 Heaven and earth shall pass away, but my words shall not pass away.*

> *36 But of that day and hour knoweth no man, no not the angels of heaven, but my Father only.*"

Verse 34 here is often misapplied to conclude that the prophecies Yahushua reveals in Matthew 24:4-31 would all occur within the lifetimes (the same generation) of his disciples to whom he was speaking. Consequently, a common false teaching concerning this entire passage is that all of these things were fulfilled with the destruction of the Temple and the city of Jerusalem by the Roman army under the Roman general Titus in 70 A.D. and thus no longer apply to us today. Nothing could be further from the truth!

The Greek word genea (Strong's 1074), that is translated from the original Greek manuscripts by the KJV into the English word "generation" at verse 34 means one of several things: age, generation, nation or time. Context allows us to discern which one these definitions applies in the case of this verse. Clearly, the events of Matthew 24:29-31 have never occurred in all of world history, therefore it cannot possibly limit Yahushua to the generation of those living at the time of His ministry, but more rightfully ought to be viewed as an age or period of time, such as the time in which we are now living often referred to as the "church age" following the life of Yahushua.

A little simple logical reasoning usually resolves the meaning of the text in Scripture, if done in a Spirit of intellectual integrity and humility, traits that are often lacking in alleged Christians debating competing interpretations of what a passage in Scripture says (due to different translations) and means and how it applies to our lives today. The simple fact of the matter is that every passage in Scripture has one meaning intended by its divine author (YHWH) and revealed to YHWH's elect, by His Holy Spirit working in and through us. All other interpretations therefore, have to be false. It's really that simple. Yet arrogance, power plays, deceit and many false teachings abound when it concerns almost everything, especially concerning Biblical and spiritual matters, in these days of the end times.

9. Evidence That We Are Living Through the Great Tribulation

In verse 35, Yahushua is teaching that not only will all these things He has prophesied be fulfilled before the present age passes away, but that His Words, meaning those captured in the writings of the New Testament of the Bible, will never pass away, even though heaven and earth shall pass away, as is revealed to us in Revelation 21:1:

> *"And I saw a new heaven and a new earth: for the first heaven and the first earth were passed away; and there was no more sea."*

Verse 36, whose message is repeated in verse 42, is telling us that no man knows the day or the hour of Yahushua's second coming; only God the Father does. But it is very important not to misconstrue what this verse is telling us and wrongly conclude that we cannot discern approximately when He will return from faithfully watching for the signs which He and the Apostle Paul give us to watch for which foretell of His imminent return; not down to the day and the hour, but perhaps to within a 45 day window of time, once we have seen the prophecy of Matthew 24:15 fulfilled, as we now have. Anyone who dismisses any attempts to show them these signs, is being disobedient to Yahushua when He commands us to remain watchful and to avoid the error of the five virgins of Matthew 25 who were not prepared when the bridegroom arrived and so were denied entry to the marriage supper of the Lamb. Yahushua continues,

> *"37 But as the days of Noe (Noah) were, so also shall the coming of the Son of man be.*
>
> *38 For as in the days that were before the flood they were eating and drinking, marrying and giving in marriage, until the day that Noe entered into the ark,*
>
> *39 And knew not until the flood came, and took them all away; so shall also the coming of the Son of man be.*
>
> *40 Then shall two be in the field; the one shall be taken, and the other left.*

41 Two women shall be grinding at the mill; the one shall be taken, and the other left.

42 Watch therefore: for ye know not what hour your Lord (Adon) doth come."

Here Yahushua reveals the parallels between the days right before Noah's flood and the days right before His (the Son of man's) second coming. Just as people were eating drinking and marrying right before the flood, oblivious to what was coming, so too the vast majority of the world, including most professed Christians who are not really born again, will be clueless until the bitter end. He explains that when the gathering prophesied at verse 31 occurs, two people may be working side by side and one (the elect) will be gathered to be with Yahushua in the clouds and the other (the non-elect) will be left behind. Finally, Yahushua tells us that we all must watch carefully for the signs of His imminent second coming, for it is impossible for anyone to know the precise hour of His coming.

Just to be clear here, I don't know the hour of His coming any more than anyone else, and I am in no way contradicting what Yahushua tells us. But I will be revealing shortly how we can now know the 45 day window of time within which His second coming will almost certainly be fulfilled. That alone ought to be good enough for anyone. It certainly is for me and I am living my life accordingly, because it changes *everything!*

The Fulfillment of the Prophecy of Matthew 24:15

On March 22, 2013, the fulfillment of the prophecy of Yahushua in Matthew 24:15 occurred; thus signaling the start date of the great tribulation. Given this key piece of information, combined with the prophecies of Daniel 12:11-12, we are now able to deduce when the great tribulation will end and how soon thereafter the prophecies of Matthew 24:29-31 and Revelation 19:7-9 are likely to be fulfilled.

For those of us who number among God's elect, this new information is vitally important and ought to change our entire outlook on life from this point forward. For God's non-elect,

284

this information will almost certainly cause them to become quite angry and abusive to those of us who number among God's elect. This reaction is something we must expect; there's no avoiding it. For God's elect, this is very good news; but for God's non-elect it is very bad news. It signals that the jig is up and the end of this era of deceit, deception, wickedness, sin, selfishness and injustice is just about over. Moreover, what comes next for God's non-elect, according to end times Bible prophecy, is rather horrific and terrifying for them and there is no stopping what's coming. It proves that God's Word, the Bible is, and always has been, 100% true and trustworthy.

On March 22, 2013, President Barack Obama stood in the grotto underneath the Church of Nativity in Bethlehem, purported to be the birthplace of Christ, thus fulfilling the prophecy of Matthew 24:15 both literally and, more importantly, metaphorically. In this passage, Yahushua tells us that when we see the abomination that causes desolation standing in the holy place, those who are in Judea ought to flee to the mountains and that it signals the start of the great tribulation, which Daniel 12:11 reveals to us will last 1,290 days.

Barack Obama is a symbol. He is a known homosexual since his teenage years in Honolulu Hawaii, at Occidental College in southern California, and later as a frequenter of gay bath houses in Chicago, Illinois where he was a State Senator before becoming a U.S. Senator and then President of the United States. Furthermore, he is a puppet of the Jewish Illuminati Freemason Zionist global elites who have hijacked and rule our world today. He has consistently revealed himself to be a pathological liar, exhibiting the classic behaviors of a psychopath, especially revealed by the common trait of all character-disordered psychopaths in which they routinely accuse their enemies of the very crimes they are most guilty of, in order to put their enemies on the defensive and deflect public scrutiny and attention away from themselves. Regrettably, this character disorder is the norm, rather than the exception, among the world's and our nation's global elites today. The nasty truth is that all of the world's global elites have

285

sold their souls to the devil, referred to in the Bible as the father of lies and the prince of this world. The global elites are essentially Jewish in worldview and lead the community of Jewish people around the world, who are the Antichrist of end times Bible prophecy. This deceit has been cleverly disguised for centuries, but has now been revealed to a number of God's elect through the writings of a number of experts on the global conspiracy, the New Age movement and the occult, all of which I am quite well versed in.

Obama's promoters and handlers refer to America today as the "Obama-nation," which is a deliberate and intentional play on the word "abomination." The symbol of that "Obama-nation," Obama himself, stood in the place purported to be the holy place of the birthplace of Yahushua, thereby defiling it with his presence, given his apparent involvement in Freemasonry, the Illuminati and the occult of Judaism. It was no coincidence that Obama's itinerary was orchestrated by his handlers in the White House to have him be there on that day. We can be sure that it was coordinated by the highest levels of the Satan-worshipping Illuminati, who are deeply steeped in the practices of witchcraft, magic and the occult, and who direct Barack Obama's every move as their servile and obedient puppet.

Three other clues all point to this same date of March 22, 2013:

1. The Order of Skull and Bones at Yale University of which Prescott, George H.W. and George W. Bush and John Kerry were or are all members, the premier recruiting tool of the Illuminati in America since 1832, bears the Chapter number 322, likely signifying the date March 22 (3/22).[62] Why else would an early chapter of the occult Illuminati carry such an odd numbered chapter number when it is widely known that those who engage in the occult are deeply steeped in numerology?

---

[62] Marrs, Texe. *Dark Majesty: The Secret Brotherhood and the Magic of a Thousand Points of Light.* 2004. p. 153.

2. Exactly 33 years prior to this date, on March 22, 1980,
    the Georgia Guidestones were erected and dedicated
    outside of Atlanta Georgia. This five granite monolith
    structure, carrying the ancient scripts of four Middle
    Eastern cultures and four other modern languages,
    documents a ten point agenda for the world's Satan-
    worshipping global elites, starting with their target for
    the world's population at half a billion people.[63] In
    light of the world's current population standing at 7.0
    billion people, this translates into the elimination of 13
    out of every 14 people alive on the planet and is truly
    horrific and rooted in the satanic. The Guidestones
    frequently serve as the venue for occult rituals at night
    that are of a satanic nature. 33 is a number of deep
    significance to those practicing the occult. The highest
    degree in the Scottish rite of Freemasonry, a secret
    society which houses the even more secret society of
    the Illuminati within it, is the 33rd degree. I'm making
    an educated guess here, but I believe the number 33
    has such deep significance to the practitioners of the
    occult because Christ was crucified in 33 A.D.

3. If you go to:

    https://www.youtube.com/watch?v=wWC-80ogIuc

    and view the two hour long movie entitled *Daniel's
    Timeline*, you will see that the film producer, Dewey
    Bruton, through a long and convoluted sequence of
    steps, purported to be derived from end times Bible
    prophecy (with which I do not wholly concur), not
    coincidentally arrives at this same date of March 22,
    2013 as the start date of the great tribulation.

If just one of these four clues pointed to March 22, 2013, it
might be interesting, but not compelling or conclusive that this
date signals the start of the great tribulation. However, when
all four of these clues point to this same date, it ought to cause

---

[63] http://www.radioliberty.com/stones.htm.

all of us but the most die-hard cynics and skeptics, to sit up and take notice.

There is no such thing as mere coincidence. What appears often to be random and disconnected events never are. They are events being orchestrated by God, designed by Him to teach us something, if we would only pay attention and put together the clues He leaves us. Can God communicate insights to us through the actions of those who engage in the occult? Of course He can, and I believe this is precisely what He has done in this instance.

What's all the more intriguing is that Obama arrived in Jerusalem exactly five days prior to Passover in 2013, the 14th of the first Hebrew month of Nissan, thus parodying and making a mockery out of the triumphal entry of Yahushua into Jerusalem on Palm Sunday in 33 A.D., five days before Passover in that year. Additionally, during Obama's trip to Jerusalem, an ice carving festival was held in which an ice carving of Obama's head was carved and displayed, subtly promoting Obama's public relations contrived image as a Messiah-like figure (which he most assuredly is not). Clearly, Obama is a servile and obedient puppet and dupe of the Jewish Illuminati Freemason Zionist global elites whom he serves, and his being in Jerusalem at that time in 2013 was no accident. Of that much, we can be absolutely certain.

In addition to the literal fulfillment of the prophecy of Yahushua of Matthew 24:15, Obama's standing in the grotto in Bethlehem on March 22, 2013 represents the symbolic and spiritual fulfillment of the prophecy as well. Obama is a symbol for a number of things. He is a known homosexual by those who have closely studied his background and past and this information is easily accessible via the internet by Googling for it. The metaphorical manifestation of the "abomination of desolation" of Matthew 24:15 is the public sanctioning of same sex marriage, which the UK, France, Australia and the United States all did in the first half of 2013. Same sex marriage, if taken to the extreme, would have the effect of desolating and depopulating the human race, in defiance against the commandment of God in Genesis 1:28 to *"be fruitful and multiply, and replenish the earth, and subdue it."* Moreover, same sex marriage stands in the place of holy matrimony, designed by God between one man and one woman for life. Homosexuality is described in God's Word, the Bible, as an abomination:

> *"Thou shalt not lie with mankind, as with womankind: it is* **abomination.***"* Leviticus 18:22

> *"If a man also lie with mankind, as he lieth with a woman, both of them have committed an* **abomination:** *they shall surely be put to death; their blood shall be upon them."* Leviticus 20:13

Furthermore, in Romans 1:24-28, the Apostle Paul continues to reveal the special hideousness with which God regards homosexuality:

> *"Wherefore God (Eloah) also gave them up to uncleanness through the lusts of their own hearts,* **to dishonour their own bodies between themselves:** *Who changed the truth of God (Eloah) into a lie, and worshipped and served the creature (the devil) more than the Creator, who is blessed for ever. Amen. For this cause God (Eloah)* **gave them up unto vile affections:** *for even their women did change the natural use into that which is against nature: And likewise also the men, leaving the natural use of the woman,* **burned in their lust one toward another; men with men working that which is unseemly,** *and receiving in themselves that recompence of their error which was meet (suitable). And even as they did not like to retain God (Eloah) in their knowledge,* **God (Eloah) gave them over to a reprobate mind,** *to do those things which are not convenient."* (emphasis and parentheticals added)

Anyone with any honesty and integrity cannot help but see that YHWH (God) looks upon homosexuality with complete abhorrence and that those practicing such sinful and sexually immoral behaviors will be severely punished for them. This is the hard truth that few dare even speak against out of intimidation and fear that they will be branded and ostracized by others as "hateful, unloving, a homophobe and a social deviant" for doing so. This cultural phenomenon of recent years is patently absurd relative to the teachings of God's Word of the Bible. Nevertheless, such absurdity in which that which is good has been redefined as evil and that which is evil has been redefined as good is all we can expect to witness during the period of the great tribulation in which we are now living. The world and America are in abject disobedience to and defiance of the teaching of the Apostle Paul to the Romans:

> *"I beseech you therefore, brethren, by the mercies of God (Eloah) that ye* **present your bodies a living sacrifice, holy, acceptable unto God (Eloah)**, *which is your reasonable service.* **And be not conformed to this world** *(the popular culture): but be ye transformed by the renewing of your mind (by the reading and obedience to all Scripture), that ye may prove what is that good, and acceptable, and perfect, will of God (Eloah)."* Romans 12:1-2 (emphasis and parentheticals added)

Both this abomination of desolation and the one that occurred in 166 B.C. (as prophesied by Daniel at Daniel 11:31) were or will be redeemed by the cleansing work of Yahushua, once again illustrating how events of the Old Testament point to and foreshadow events of the New Testament period. In 166 B.C., the Greek ruler Antiochus Epiphanies IV defiled and desecrated the Temple in Jerusalem by sacrificing a pig (an unclean animal) there to demoralize the Hebrew people. Two years later, Judas Maccabeus and his followers drove out the Greeks from Jerusalem, cleansed the Temple and rededicated it in what is today commemorated as the Jewish festival of Hanukkah. But the spiritual cleansing from that event did not occur until roughly 200 years later when Yahushua, the perfect Lamb of God, sacrificed Himself on the cross, thus doing away with the animal sacrifices forever. In a similar fashion, immediately following the gathering prophesied in Matthew 24:30-31, 1 Thessalonians 4:13-17 and 1 Corinthians 15:51-55, Yahushua will redeem the covenant of holy matrimony between one man and one woman for life from the defilement of same sex marriage by marrying His bride, the gathered church of believers from all time (the last 6,000 years), as the bridegroom, as evidenced by the marriage supper of the Lamb described in Revelation 19:7-9:

> *"Let us be glad and rejoice, and give honour to him: for the marriage of the Lamb is come, and his wife hath made herself ready. And to her was granted that she should be arrayed in fine linen, clean and white: for the fine linen is (or reveals) the righteousness of saints (God's elect and true born again followers of Yahushua). And he saith unto me,* **Write, Blessed are they which are called unto the marriage supper of the Lamb.** *And he saith unto me, these are the true sayings of God (Eloah)."* (emphasis and parentheticals added)

Notice that the angel of God who speaks to the Apostle John in this passage, tells him to write that the gathered church (body) of true believers is **Blessed.** This is a vitally important clue that connects back to Daniel 12:12 which reads as follows:

> *"**Blessed** is he that waiteth, and cometh to the thousand three hundred and five and thirty days."*

This 1,335 days refers to a period of time beginning with the start date of the great tribulation, which Daniel 12:11 informs us will last 1,290 days. Therefore, we can safely conclude that 45 (1,335 - 1,290 = 45) days **after** the tribulation is over, the events described in Matthew 24:29-31 **and** Revelation 19:7-9 will be fulfilled. Recall from what I revealed earlier that I am not able to predict the timing of these prophesied events with precision down to the day or the hour, but am only able to deduce a 45 day window of time in which they will occur, and this is that 45 day window of time I was referring to.

So let's put all the clues concerning the end times prophesies we now have together to reveal the timeline relevant to God's elect. Knowing the start date of the great tribulation prophesied in Matthew 24:15 was March 22, 2013, based on all the evidence and reasoning revealed earlier, and knowing that the great tribulation is prophesied in Daniel 12:11 to last 1,290 days, we can now calculate that the great tribulation, which we are now in, will end on October 2, 2016 (March 22, 2013 + 1,290 days = October 2, 2016). Additionally, we can calculate the date of blessing by which time the prophecies of Matthew 24:29-31 and Revelation 19:7-9 will be fulfilled will be November 16, 2016, calculated as March 22, 2013 + 1,335 days (from Daniel 12:12).

I have reflected these calculations in a simple chart which I use to keep track of where we are in YHWH's prophetic Biblical timeline relative to the end of the great tribulation and the blessing date shown in Figure 1 below.

Countdown to Blessing Date

		% Remaining	Years Remaining	Months Remaining	Weeks Remaining
Start Date of Tribulation	Mar 22, 2013				
# Days of Tribulation	1,290				
End of Tribulation Date	Oct 2, 2016				
Extra Days Until Blessing	45				
Blessing Date	Nov 16, 2016				
Today's Date	Oct 14, 2015				
# Days Until the Blessing	399	29.9%	1.1	13.1	57.0
# Days Until End of Tribulation	354	27.4%	1.0	11.6	50.6

Figure 1

Notice that thus far, I have only described the near term events foretold in Daniel 12 and Matthew 24 from the perspective of God's elect. However, to fully grasp the significance of what is soon to come and all of its implications and ramifications, we need to finish the story of YHWH's prophetic timeline clear to the end of the Bible. That is my aim in the next chapter. God's plan all along has been to bring His story (history) to its climax here in the last days which will bring glory and honor to Him and His son, Yahushua, precisely as end times Bible prophecies reveal. These prophecies have been intentionally spread throughout the Bible so that God's elect would diligently seek to discover all they possibly can about the ways, thoughts and nature of God. Nevertheless, the vast majority of end times prophecies are revealed to us in the Book of Revelation, the last book of the Bible, written by the Apostle John around 95

A.D. from the island of Patmos, where he was exiled, toward the end of his life.

Entire books have been written seeking to explain what the Book of Revelation says and means and it would be presumptuous of me to suggest that I can fully do this subject service, but I am going to try nevertheless, because many of those prior explanations have been false and quite misleading. Having said this, I challenge all readers to conduct their own thorough examination of what the Book of Revelation says and challenge any of my insights and understandings here which may be off the mark or in error. I am not infallible. I am only a man with clay feet like any other man. I pray to God that He will enable me to guide you, my readers properly, but that you will in turn share your added insights and corrections with me, if that seems warranted. My goal is to equip God's elect with a common understanding of what's coming quite soon so that you in turn might guide and teach others who might number among God's elect who may have been deceived on many of these points.

10. The Rest of God's End Times Story

John was the Apostle for whom Yahushua had a particular fondness and who authored the gospel of John and the three epistles of John which, while quite short, contain some deep spiritual teachings well worth the time to study and think about deeply. So it is fitting that Yahushua appeared to John rather late in his life and revealed what was to come to John so that he might write it down, for our benefit over 1,900 years later, as the Book of Revelation. Remember that the prophecies of the Bible which have already been fulfilled have always been fulfilled with hair-splitting accuracy. Thus, we have no reason to believe that such will not be also true for those prophecies which are coming true in our lifetimes, which I fully confess is all rather bizarre, but unavoidably true, at the same time.

The first three chapters of the Book of Revelation begin with John revealing that he is authoring the book to seven churches in Asia, in what is today modern day Turkey, revealing to them what Yahushua (Jesus) revealed to him concerning what the Bible refers to as the end times. Don't misunderstand: God is not saying that everything will end when we employ the term "end times." What He is revealing to us is that He plans to bring His story to a dramatic climax which will end one age of history and of man and usher in eternity for all: some to eternity with God and other believers (God's elect), and many more (God's non-elect) into eternal punishment in a burning lake of fire and brimstone for the sins they have committed during their lifetimes. John's revelations to us cannot be fully understood by a literal reading of many of the passages in the book. It is a book of complex symbols, metaphors and allegories which tell a story which is intentionally challenging to comprehend, so that God is revealing these things only to His elect, while leaving His non-elect largely in the dark, confused and clueless. This is analogous to why Yahushua primarily spoke in parables during His earthly ministry told in the four books of the gospel: Matthew, Mark, Luke and John. Here's how Matthew 13:13-15 explains Yahushua's intent in speaking in parables:

> *"Therefore speak I to them in parables: because they seeing see not; and hearing they hear not, neither do they understand. And in them is fulfilled the prophecy of Esias (Isaiah), which saith, By hearing ye shall hear, and shall not understand; and seeing ye shall see, and not perceive: For this people's heart is waxed gross, and their ears are dull of hearing, and their eyes they have closed; lest at any time they should see with their eyes, and hear with their ears, and should understand with their heart, and should be converted, and I should heal them."*

Proverbs 25:2 reveals that God delights in concealing truths from mankind and permitting His chosen ones to search out and discover those truths, while keeping them concealed from all others:

> *"It is the glory of God (Elohim) to conceal a thing: but the honour of **kings** is to search out a matter."*

In Revelation 1:6, John explains in his introduction to the seven churches of Asia (Minor):

> *"And hath made us **kings** and priests unto God (Eloah) and his (Yahushua's) Father; to him be glory and dominion for ever and ever. Amen."*

In other words, all those who number among God's born again elect are spiritual kings in YHWH's and Yahushua's eyes.

In Chapters 2 and 3 of the Book of Revelation, John writes down specific messages unique to each church, which Yahushua (Jesus) dictated to him to write. These seven churches were at Ephesus, Smyrna, Pergamos, Thyatira, Sardis, Philadelphia and Laodicea and represent seven different church ages over the past 2,000 years, as well as some specific issues unique to each of the seven churches which have found commonalities with many institutional churches throughout the church age up to the present day. Jesus both commends and affirms each church body and brings rebuke and correction to many of them, as well. I won't go into the specific messages Yahushua dictates to each church, but I do want to highlight two passages written to the churches at Smyrna and at Philadelphia which have long been ignored by most of Christendom, but which reveals, to those of us to whom God has led to the truth, that those claiming to be Jews (led by the Jewish Illuminati Freemason Zionist global conspiracy) are the Antichrist of end times Bible prophecy. Additionally, we will look more closely at Yahushua's message to the church at Laodicea, which finds its parallel and analog in all forms of organized religion today.

To the church at Smyrna, Yahushua says,

> *"I know thy works, and tribulation, and poverty, (but thou art rich) and* **I know the blasphemy of them which say they are Jews, and are not** *(because they are Talmud-believing Turko-Mongolian Khazars)***, but are the synagogue of Satan."** Revelation 2:9 (second parenthetical added for clarity)

And to the church of Philadelphia he says much the same thing for emphasis and to draw our attention to His message with repetition,

> *"Behold,* **I will make them of the synagogue of Satan, which say they are Jews, and are not, but do lie;** *behold, I will make them to come and worship before thy feet, and to know that I have loved thee."* Revelation 3:9

These two passages confirm and corroborate the admission by a prominent American Jew and former aide to Senator Jacob Javits, Harold Rosenthal, in his book, *A Hidden Tyranny* (1976):

10. The Rest of God's End Times Story

"We Jews do not like to admit it, but our God is Lucifer . . . We are his chosen people . . ."[64]

It doesn't get any clearer than this, folks! The impostors posing as Jews today, who have stolen the name "Jew" from its rightful owners (along with the names Hebrew, Israel and Semite), who lie and falsely claim that they are God's chosen people, are in reality the precise opposite of what they claim to be: they are the Antichrist of end times Bible prophecy! What is so incredible to comprehend is that this treachery and deceit could have been allowed to perpetuate itself for so many generations of mankind. Clearly a force of immense spiritual power has concealed this truth from the world for literally centuries. Moreover, Jesus hints at this very thing when He commands us in Matthew 10:26-28:

> *"Fear them not therefore: for there is nothing covered, that shall not be revealed; and hid that shall not be known. What I tell you in darkness, that speak ye in light: and what ye hear in the ear, that preach ye upon the housetops. And fear not them which kill the body, but are not able to kill the soul: but rather fear him which is able to destroy both soul and body in hell."*

It now becomes clear that Jesus was referring here quite specifically to the Jewish global conspiracy, a satanic cult, which has hijacked the world, as allowed by God, to fulfill His perfect plan for His elect, which is now coming to its climax and conclusion. It is equally clear to me that YHWH led me to these truths through books, leads from friends of mine and ideas from friends which have built upon my own insights and discoveries, to bring these truths to light, in obedience to Yahushua's command in this passage of Scripture. If this doesn't amaze and blow you away, I must confess that it certainly has that kind of impact on me.

To the church of Laodicea, Yahushua had these strong words:

---

[64] Marrs, Texe. *Conspiracy of the Six-Pointed Star.* 2001. p. 31.

"I know thy works, that thou are neither cold nor hot: I would thou wert cold or hot. So then because thou art lukewarm, and neither cold nor hot, I will spue (vomit) thee out of my mouth. Because thou sayest, I am rich, and increased with goods, and have need of nothing; and knowest not that thou art wretched, and miserable, and poor, and blind, and naked: I counsel thee to buy of me gold tried in the fire, that thou mayest be rich; and white raiment, that thou mayest be clothed, and that the shame of thy nakedness do not appear; and anoint thine eyes with eyesalve, that thou mayest see. As many as I love, I rebuke and chasten: be zealous therefore, and repent." Revelation 3:15-19

Yahushua is speaking to the churches of the current age, especially in America, all of which "play church," but manifest no real convictions and commitments about much of anything. In spite of America's vast material wealth and affluence, Yahushua is telling us that on the inside, in our hearts and in our spirits, America is wretched, unhappy, unable to see the truth of our spiritual bankruptcy, and filled with shame over our endless deceit, treachery, betrayal, theft and selfishness toward others. What is valuable and eternal (our relationships with others) has been rejected and replaced with meaningless stuff and pursuits that bring no lasting joy and peace. Hence Yahushua is bringing us correction, urging us to seek gold of Him, which is real integrity and character, refined by the fires of trials, suffering and tribulations, and white garments, symbolizing purity, holiness and virtue that might cover the shame brought upon us by our own depravity and wickedness.

In chapters 4, 5 and 6 of the Book of Revelation, John reveals the contents of his vision in which he was taken "in the spirit" to heaven where YHWH sits on the throne and where a scroll with seven seals upon it is brought forth and opened by Yahushua, the Lamb of God. This scroll is very likely the same book referred to in Daniel 12 in which it says:

"But thou, O Daniel, shut up the words, and seal the book, even to the time of the end: many shall run to and fro, and knowledge shall be increased." Daniel 12:4

10. The Rest of God's End Times Story

"And he said, Go thy way, Daniel: for the words are closed up and sealed till the time of the end." Daniel 12:9

These chapters refer to four mystical beasts and 24 elders who, it appears, correspond to the patriarchs of the 12 Hebrew tribes and the 12 Apostles, who are seated around the throne of God clothed in white garments, wearing crowns of gold and worshipping God.

In Chapter 6, the Lamb of God, Yahushua, opens the first six of seven seals on the scroll, and it seems to suggest that these seal openings all occur during the time of the great tribulation, the time period in which we are now living. After each of the first four seals are broken, John reports seeing horses of four different colors, commonly referred to as the four horses of the apocalypse.

The first horse, which is white, has a rider on it wearing a crown and having a bow who goes forth conquering. The second horse, which is red, bears a rider who has the power to take peace from the earth, such that people should kill one another and the rider is given a great sword. The third horse, which is black, carries a rider with a balance scale in his hands and John hears a voice in heaven stating that a measure of wheat and three measures of barely are worth a penny and commands that someone not hurt the oil and wine, which are food products that were deemed to be of value in the first century Middle East. The fourth and final horse, whose rider's name is Death, and some other entity whose name is Hell, followed with him and power was given to them over one fourth of the earth to kill with sword, hunger, death (disease perhaps?) and with beasts or wild animals of the earth.

Upon the opening of the fifth seal, John sees under an altar in heaven the souls of those who were slain or martyred for the the word of God and for their testimony and defense of it, who cry out to Yahushua asking how much longer before He will judge and avenge their deaths upon the wicked who dwell on the earth? White robes, signifying purity and holiness are given to these souls in heaven and they are told that they need to wait a little longer (the duration of time is not specified − for a little season, it says) until their fellow martyrs who have not yet been killed as they were, should occur.

Upon the opening of the sixth seal, John witnesses a great earthquake (global in scale, it appears), the sun becomes black as sackcloth of hair, the moon becomes red as blood, and the stars of heaven fall to the earth in what may be a meteor or asteroid shower, much like a fig tree which loses its figs when it is shaken by a mighty wind. Verse 14 of Revelation 6 describes heaven departing like a scroll when it is rolled together and that every mountain and island are moved out of their places. This last description appears to refer to a pole shift in which the earth's crust slips over the molten inner magma core, causing massive global earthquakes along the fault lines of the tectonic plates. These four descriptions very closely match the four celestial events described in the prophecy of Matthew 24:29 which, according to that verse, are to be fulfilled immediately after the great tribulation ends.

In a prior chapter, I revealed that NASA has been secretly monitoring the approach of a brown dwarf star, widely known as Plant-X, Nibiru or Wormwood, having an estimated mass of roughly 4.5 times the mass of earth. From numerous reports I have read, this brown dwarf star is likely to pass near the earth on a long elliptical orbit around the sun, which takes 3,600 to 4,000 years to complete a full orbit. In the event that such a celestial event happens, all of which would be permitted and orchestrated by YHWH (God), the electro-magnetic and gravitational forces passing between this apparent brown dwarf star and the earth could induce the sort of catastrophic and horrific global events described in Revelation 6:12-14.

In response to this calamity, it appears that the world's global elites have been preparing for this coming day in the form of their directing the construction of 150 – 200 Deep Underground Military Bases (DUMBs) in the United States, the majority of them located in the southwestern United States, and some 2,000 underground cities worldwide. Consider this possibility as we examine the words describing the response of the world's leaders to the events we are talking about here:

"And the kings of the earth, and the great men, and the rich men, and the chief captains, and the mighty men, and every bondman, and every free man, hid themselves in the dens and in the rocks of the mountains; And said to the mountains and rocks, Fall on us, and hide us from the face of him that sitteth on the throne (meaning YHWH), and from the wrath of the Lamb (Yahushua upon His second coming); For the great day of his wrath is come; and who shall be able to stand?" Revelation 6:15-17

Do these words not come very close to describing a situation in which the world's leaders, the rich and powerful, those in the military and anyone else who can gain access to those DUMBs that already exist, plan to hide in those underground cities and leave the rest of humanity on the surface of the earth to fend for ourselves? They most certainly do, and they go a long way toward explaining all the obvious preparations for the imposition of martial law in America which anyone on the alert has been witnessing by our government over the past several years.

The Bible does not give a clear explanation for precisely when the gathering of Matthew 24:30-31, 1 Thessalonians 4:13-17 and 1 Corinthians 15:51-55 will take place relative to these prophesied celestial events. However, Matthew 24:37-44 reveal to us that Yahushua's return will catch the world by surprise because, for the majority of people living on the planet today, life will amount to "business as usual," eating, drinking, marrying and giving in marriage right up to the time of Yahushua's second coming, just as it was in the days of Noah right before the Flood. All that it appears we can count on is that these celestial events will all occur between October 2 and November 16, 2016 and that YHWH remains firmly in control of all world events, just as He always has been, and as He always will be.

Based on God's revealed nature and promises in His Word to His elect, we have every reason to place our full trust in Him. Similarly, from the prophecies of the end times, God's non-elect appear to have no hope of escape from the wrath and fury of a just and holy God (YHWH) who seethes in rage and fury at the immorality and injustices perpetrated upon their fellow men by the wicked and the unjust of this world.

In Chapter 7 of the Book of Revelation, John hears a voice of an angel ascending from the east crying in a loud voice to four angels standing on the four corners of the earth holding the four winds of the earth so that the wind would not blow on the land, sea or on any tree, commanding them not to hurt the land, sea or trees until the angels have sealed (Strong's 4972 defines this word to mean stamping with a signet or private marks for security or preservation; by implication, to keep secret and to attest to something) the servants of God in (not on) their foreheads. Immediately thereafter, John hears that 144,000 people, 12,000 from each of the 12 Hebrew tribes are so sealed. Given what we now know about the fraud of the rogue terrorist state of modern day faux Israel and the impostors posing as Jews, we can know with certainty that the Bible is *not* referring here to the Jews of modern day Israel, but rather to born again followers of Yahushua who are also the genetic descendants of the 12 Hebrew tribes; namely, those who number among the white race. Later, we will see, that this sealed group of 144,000 born again Israelites will be accorded special honor in heaven. Then John tells us,

> *"After this I beheld, and lo, a great multitude, which no man could number, of all nations, and kindreds, and people, and tongues, stood before the throne, and before the Lamb, clothed with white robes, and palms in their hands; And cried with a loud voice, saying, Salvation to our God (Eloah) which sitteth upon the throne, and unto the Lamb. And all the angels stood round about the throne, and about the elders and the four beasts, and fell before the throne on their faces, and worshipped God (Eloah). Saying, Amen: Blessing and glory, and wisdom, and thanksgiving, and honour, and power, and might, be unto our God (Eloah) for ever and ever. Amen. And one of the elders answered, saying unto me, What are these which are arrayed in white robes? and whence came they? And I said unto him, Sir, thou knowest. And he said unto me,* **These are they which came out of the great tribulation**

and have washed their robes, and made them white in the blood of the Lamb." Revelation 7:9-14

Here is the clue we have been looking for. This multitude of people in heaven are those who have come out of the great tribulation, which Matthew 24:29-31 and Daniel 12:12 tell us will occur in the form of the gathering, within 45 days of the end of the great tribulation. In this process, first the dead will be raised in resurrected bodies (as 1 Thessalonians 4:13-17 explains) and then the living will be transformed, in the twinkling of an eye, 1 Corinthians 15:51-55 tells us, into resurrected bodies and gathered to be with Yahushua in the clouds of heaven.

The white robes in which the multitude is clothed in this passage, referred to in several other places in the Book of Revelation, signifies purity and holiness, brought about through the refining and testing fires of suffering, trials, and tribulations, which all true born again followers of Christ must endure in order to mature into the likeness of Christ during our lifetimes. Notice who is receiving all the glory here: it is YHWH (God) and the Lamb (Yahushua or Jesus).

The great tribulation plays a role here in that it draws our attention away from the foolish and meaningless pursuits of the world (sex, money and power), the flesh (our selfishness) and the devil, all of which are perishing anyway, and leads us to place all of our trust upon Almighty YHWH (God) and Yahushua. This is what the Bible has been telling us all along, but the tribulation period gives those of us who number among God's elect, all the more reason to heed, believe and trust in God's promises and not those of our perishing and wicked world.

Chapter 7 concludes with assurances for all of God's elect that once the gathering occurs, our sufferings and pain of this life shall be over:

"Therefore are they (the multitude which came out of the great tribulation) before the throne of God (Eloah), and serve him day and night in his temple: and he that sitteth on the throne

shall dwell among them. They shall hunger no more, neither thirst any more; neither shall the sun light on them, nor any heat. For the Lamb (Yahushua) which is in the midst of the throne shall feed them, and shall lead them unto living fountains of waters: and God shall wipe away all tears from their eyes." Revelation 7:15-17.

This passage tells us that God's resurrected elect will serve God day and night in His temple and that God will dwell with us. In Chapter 22 we will see this further described. Many people, throughout the ages, have jumped to the conclusion that this means that those who are saved will sit on clouds, wearing white robes, playing harps and singing hymns to God forever, and for most people, myself included, this seems incredibly boring and uninspiring. But it does not say this at all. Once again, this is the enemy, Satan, seeking to dissuade people from choosing a life serving God and doing His will and those who number among God's non-elect will always take the bait; while those who are of God's elect, will not.

Knowing the nature of God, as revealed to us by the wonders of his creation on earth, we have to know that God has many marvelous things and experiences in store for us when we are living with Him in a new heaven and a new earth described later in the Book of Revelation. What we do know is that the sun will no longer shine on us and we learn from Chapter 22 that God will be our light and there will be no more darkness (symbolizing evil and death). Yahushua will feed us and lead us to living fountains of waters, which is a metaphor for the good things mankind has always needed to thrive and experience joy and peace. Finally, God will wipe away all tears from our eyes, meaning we will no longer experience pain and sorrow. Here's how Isaiah 65:17-25 describes this time for all eternity:

"For behold, I (YHWH) create new heavens and a new earth: and the former shall not be remembered, nor come into mind. But be ye glad and rejoice for ever in that which I create: for behold, I create Jerusalem a rejoicing, and her people a joy. And I will rejoice in Jerusalem, and joy in my people (God's resurrected, born again, elect): and the voice of weeping shall be

no more heard in her, nor the voice of crying. There shall no more thence an infant of days, nor an old man that hath not filled his days: for the child shall die an hundred years old; but the sinner being an hundred years old shall be accursed. And they shall build houses, and inhabit them; and they shall plant vineyards, and eat the fruit of them. They shall not build, and another inhabit; they shall not plant, and another eat: for as the days of a tree are the days of my people, and mine **elect** *shall long enjoy the work of their hands. They shall not labor in vain, nor bring forth for trouble; for they are the seed of the blessed of the LORD (YHWH), and their offspring with them. And it shall come to pass, that before they call, I will answer; and while they are yet speaking, I will hear. The wolf and the lamb shall feed together, and the lion shall eat straw like the bullock: and dust shall be the serpent's meat. They shall not hurt nor destroy in all my holy mountain, saith the LORD (YHWH)."*

Notice here that YHWH reveals that He plans to create new heavens and a new earth, and that we won't even remember the former (existing) earth and heavens. Does this also mean that we won't remember the things which occurred to us during our lifetimes on this earth? Yes, probably. Revelation 21:1 reveals that this won't happen until after the great white throne judgment, which is described in Chapter 20.

God is revealing here that He intends to keep on creating and that He will abide in a new Jerusalem, a metaphor for where God's people, His elect, shall be. Once again, there will be no weeping, crying or sorrow in this new earth. The passage suggests that people will continue to exist in this new earth and will build houses and vineyards and will long enjoy the work of their hands without the threat of those things being taken from them and that God will reside with them.

How these people will live, grow old and die, is not clear relative to God's resurrected elect who come out of the tribulation, but it seems to suggest that these people described in Isaiah 65 will be the children of God's resurrected saints in some fashion. Finally, this passage indicates that animals will continue to exist and be with us, but that no animals will be predators and carnivores that will kill and devour other animals, but that they all shall eat plants instead, and live in harmony with one another and, by implication, with man.

In Chapter 8, Yahushua opens the seventh and final seal on the scroll and there is silence in heaven for about half an hour and John observes seven angels standing before YHWH (God) who are given seven trumpets. Yet another angel comes before a golden altar before the throne of God with a golden censer that he fills with much incense which, along with the prayers of all saints, he lays upon the golden altar where the smoke of the incense, combined with the prayers of the saints (all believers who number among God's elect) ascends up to God. After this, the angel takes the censer, fills it with fire from the altar and casts it to earth, and there are voices, thundering, lightening and an earthquake. I am speculating a bit here, but in reality, God may be planning to orchestrate a fly-by of the brown dwarf star Wormwood (otherwise known as Planet-X or Nibiru) which, as a result of electro-magnetic and gravitational effects could result in fire raining down on earth from heaven, or space.

After this event, the seven angels with their seven trumpets prepare themselves to sound, and with each angel blowing his respective trumpet, yet another judgment is poured out upon the earth and upon the wicked. When the first angel sounds his trumpet, hail and fire, mingled with blood is cast upon the earth and a third of the trees and all of the grass is burnt up. This could be the result of an electro-magnetic discharge from the brown dwarf star to earth, manifesting itself as fire, and the appearance of blood could very easily be the result of red iron oxide dust that has been gathered in the tail of the dwarf star as it passes through space, gathering the dust in its wake electro-magnetically, and then pours it upon the earth via the same electro-magnetic discharging mechanism.

When the second angel sounds his trumpet, John describes a great mountain burning with fire that is cast into the sea and a third of the sea becomes blood. As part of this, a third of the living creatures in the sea die and a third of the ships on the seas are destroyed by this calamitous event. What John is describing may be a burning meteor of some sort which might also be a result of a fly-by of the brown dwarf star Wormwood, but this is entirely speculation on my part; we just don't know for certain.

When the third angel sounds his trumpet, what John describes as a great star, burning as though it were a lamp, falls upon one third of the rivers of the earth and upon the fountains of waters, which seems to refer to the source of springs and rivers. Verse 11 tells us that the name of the star is called Wormwood and a third of the men of the earth will die from drinking the waters that will be made bitter by the effects of its passing by the earth. Is this one and the same Wormwood, Planet-X or Nibiru that is reported by some scientists to be four and a half times the mass of earth which seems to be heading our way? It would certainly seem so.

When the fourth angel sounds his trumpet, a third portion of the sun is smitten (by Wormwood?), a third part of the moon and one third of the stars, so that one third of the day is darkened, and likewise a third part of the night is darkened. Clearly, these are calamitous and horrifying events to the survivors who remain on the earth who are the subjects of God's almighty wrath and fury. Right after this event occurs, John witnesses an angel flying through the midst of heaven saying with a loud voice, "Woe, woe, woe to the inhabiters of the earth" because of the three trumpet judgments yet to be poured out upon the earth.

As Chapter 9 begins, the fifth angel sounds his trumpet and John sees a star fall from heaven but this is not a celestial star, but some sort of angelic being to whom has been given the key to the bottomless pit. This being opens the pit and smoke, as though from a great furnace, rises up and darkens the sun and the air, and out of the smoke come locusts to whom is given power upon the earth, as scorpions with their stinging tails have power. These locusts are given instructions not to hurt the grass of the earth, any green thing or any tree, but only those men who do not have the seal of God in their foreheads. Since by this time, all of God's elect, those who have the seal of God in their foreheads, have already been gathered during the events described or alluded to in Chapters 6 and 7, none of those who are left on earth will have the seal of God in their foreheads and so all will be tormented by the locusts.

For five months, these locusts do not kill, but they torment mankind with stings like that of scorpions. Men will wish to die, but will not find it. The locusts themselves are described by John as having the shapes of horses prepared for battle, wearing what appear to be crowns of gold, faces of men, hair like the hair of women (presumably long), teeth of lions, breastplates like iron, with wings which make the sounds of many chariots and horses running into battle, and tails like scorpions with the power to sting and hurt men for five months. These locusts have a king over them, the angel of the bottomless pit, whose name is "Destroyer" in both the Hebrew and the Greek languages. This is the first of the three woes called out by the angel in heaven in the last verse of Chapter 8 and there remain two more woes to be poured out upon the earth.

The sixth angel sounds his trumpet and a voice which emanates from the four horns (signifying power) of the golden altar before God in heaven gives instruction to the sixth angel with the trumpet to loosen four angels which are bound in the Euphrates River. The four angels which are loosed are prepared for a year, a month, a day and an hour to slay a third of mankind remaining on the earth (after many men will die from consuming the bitter water of Wormwood earlier). John reports that he saw in his vision 200 million horses and horsemen which had breastplates of fire, jacinth and brimstone and the heads of the horses were as heads of lions and out of their mouths issued fire, smoke and brimstone, which killed one third of mankind on earth. These horsemen have power in their mouth and in their tails which were like serpents with heads with which they bring pain and death.

In this passage, it is possible that John is describing modern day tanks with artillery and small arms fire. The only nation today capable of amassing a 200 million man army is China, having roughly 1.3 billion people located to the east of the Euphrates River, which is located in what is today the nation of Iraq. An alternative explanation may be that this is not a human army to which John is referring, but rather a spiritual one, led by the four angels which were formerly bound in the Euphrates River in some fashion.

In spite of the horrors of a third of mankind being destroyed over roughly a thirteen month period, the rest of mankind which is not killed by the judgments which have been poured out upon the wicked thus far, steadfastly refuse to repent of their wicked deeds in which they have worshipped devils (practiced the satanic arts, as in the secret societies of the Illuminati, Freemasonry, witchcraft and Satanism), idols of gold, silver, brass, stone and wood which cannot see, hear, nor walk. Nor do they repent of their murders, sorceries, fornications or thefts. In other words, the wicked who remain are headstrong, rebellious, defiant and reprobate beyond reason.

In Chapter 10, John sees another mighty angel come down from heaven who is clothed with a cloud, adorned with a rainbow upon his head, his face like the sun (radiant) and his feet as pillars of fire, who holds in his hand a little book that is open and he sets his right foot upon the sea and his left foot upon the the earth, signifying that he has authority over the entire earth. This angel cries with a loud voice, like when a lion roars, and then seven thunders utter their voices or speak. John is about to write down what the seven thunders have uttered, when a voice from heaven tells him to seal up those words and not write them down. Apparently, the seal is meant to hide what the seven thunders uttered. Then the angel which John saw lifts his arms to heaven and swears by God who created heaven, earth and sea that when the seventh trumpet is sounded, there will be no further delay before the fulfillment of God's perfect plan which he declared to His servants, the prophets.

John hears the voice from heaven instructing him to go take the little book from the hand of the angel who stands upon the sea and the earth. When John goes to the angel and asks him to give John the little book, the angel instructs him to take and eat the book, which will taste sweet as honey in his mouth, but will be bitter to his stomach or belly. Once John has done as he was instructed, the angel tells John that he must prophecy again before many peoples, nations, tongues and kings, presumably through the Book of Revelation which we are now seeking to understand.

In Chapter 11, the Book of Revelation switches gears and changes time periods, going back to the period of the great tribulation. John is given a reed like a rod to measure the temple of God, but the angel who gave him the little book to eat commands him not to measure the outer court outside the temple which is given to the Gentiles (meaning pagan, heathen, non-believing people and nations). The angel goes on to explain that the Gentiles will tread underfoot the holy city, meaning the saints or true believers, for 42 months. This 42 months coincides with the time, times and half a time (three and a half years) referred to in Daniel 12:7 and quite closely with the 1,290 days from Daniel 12:11. What other time period could God possibly be referring to here, **other than** the great tribulation? We know that the great tribulation has been planned by God to be a period of time of testing, trials and troubles for God's holy people, and in allegorical language, this is precisely what is being described here:

> *"But the court which is without the temple leave out, and measure it not; for it is given unto the Gentiles: and the holy city shall they tread under foot forty and two months."*
> Revelation 11:2

The chapter continues,

> *"And I will give power unto my two witnesses, and they shall prophesy a thousand two hundred and threescore (1,260) days,*

clothed in sackcloth. These are the two olive trees, and the two candlesticks standing before the God of the earth. And if any man will hurt them, fire proceedeth out of their mouth, and devoureth their enemies: and if any man will hurt them, he must in this manner be killed. These have power to shut heaven, that it not rain in the days of their prophecy: and have power over waters to turn them to blood, and to smite the earth with all plagues, as often as they will. And when they shall have finished their testimony, the beast that ascendeth out of the bottomless pit shall make war against them, and shall overcome them and kill them. And their dead bodies shall lie in the street of the great city, which spiritually is called Sodom and Egypt, where also our Lord (Adon) was crucified. And they of the people and kindreds and tongues and nations shall see their dead bodies three days and an half, and shall not suffer their dead bodies to be put in graves. And they that dwell upon the earth shall rejoice over them, and make merry, and shall send gifts one to another; because these two prophets tormented them that dwelt on the earth. And after three days and an half the Spirit of life from God (Eloah) entered into them, and they stood upon their feet; and great fear fell upon them which saw them. And they heard a great voice from heaven saying unto them, Come up hither. And they ascended up to heaven in a cloud; and their enemies beheld them. And the same hour there was a great earthquake, and the tenth part of the city fell, and in the earthquake were slain of men seven thousand: and the remnant were affrighted, and gave glory to the God (Eloah) of heaven."
Revelation 11:3-13

The Book of Revelation is filled with symbolism, allegory and metaphor that can only be understood by those who diligently seek the face of God by carefully dividing the word of truth, namely the words of the Bible. Here in Chapter 11, we see that symbolism, allegory and metaphor being employed quite extensively to permit God to conceal His true meaning from His non-elect, while revealing it to His elect.

Who are God's two witnesses? I think it's quite likely that they are not two individual men, just as the Antichrist is not one individual man, but rather that they represent the two kingdoms of ancient Israel and Judah who make up the 12 Hebrew tribes of Abraham, Isaac and Jacob, whom God is bringing together at the climax of all of world history to testify to the truth and reveal the events to come.

At the beginning of Chapter 7, 12,000 from each of the 12 Hebrew tribes are sealed. For what purpose? I believe it is so that they might prophecy for 1,260 out of the 1,290 days of the great tribulation, as Revelation 11:3 describes. To be clothed in sackcloth means to be in mourning and sorrow for what is to come soon.

In several places in the New Testament, Paul and Jesus refer to the olive tree and grafting in the wild olive branches (born again Gentiles) to the true olive tree of Israel of the Hebrews. Likewise, the symbol of candlesticks is used in Revelation 1:20 to designate the seven churches in Asia Minor (modern day Turkey). Here that same metaphor is being employed to designate born again Christians who are descended from the 12 Hebrew tribes who are sealed in Chapter 7 and who embody the heart of God's true church of the born again elect.

The spiritual power, which these witnesses have to cause it not to rain, to turn water into blood and smite the earth with plagues as often as they will, is quite likely to be in effect right now, and may be put into effect from time to time by select members of the sealed 144,000, as an answer to their prayers, which we simply don't know about. At the end of their 1,260 day prophecy, the beast that ascends out of the bottomless pit (first referenced in Chapter 9) will make war against the two witnesses, shall overcome them, and will kill them. Is this beast the same as the angel of the bottomless pit, whose Hebrew name is Abaddon and whose Greek name is Apollyon (or Destroyer)? Or could this beast be the first beast of Revelation 13? Scripture is not definitive here.

Furthermore, it's not clear to me that killing the two witnesses will occur literally (although it might, and probably will, at least for some of the 144,000, but not necessarily for all). It could mean that they are effectively silenced. Their dead bodies (of some) will not be buried, but will be left to be viewed by the pagan heathens who oppose God and God's people, in the city which is spiritually called Sodom and Egypt, both of which are symbols of sin and bondage, and this city is further described as the city where Yahushua was crucified, namely Jerusalem, the capital of the modern day rogue terrorist state of modern-day faux Israel, and the capital of the global elites' intended one world government, or New World Order.

Those who are the enemies of God and God's people will rejoice over the silencing and deaths of martyrs for the truth and for Christ for three and a half days. This seems to be symbolically referring to the three and a half year great tribulation in which God's elect are persecuted, tested and tried for their faith, revealing the truths I reveal in this book, and perhaps many more, thus tormenting the people of the lie, who serve the father of lies, the devil.

What other explanation makes sense out of the time period being a specific three and a half days? Those who are of the lie are tormented by the truth and during this period of the great tribulation, the truth is being revealed to a much larger audience than at any other time in all of world history, and it has the effect of driving God's non-elect crazy. Yahushua tells us this in Matthew 10:26-28:

> *"Fear them not therefore: for there is nothing covered, that shall not be revealed; and hid that shall not be known. What I tell you in darkness, that speak ye in light: and what ye hear in the ear, that preach ye upon the housetops. And fear not them which kill the body, but are not able to kill the soul: but rather fear him which is able to destroy both soul and body in hell."*

Then we see in verse 11 the Spirit of life entering into the two witnesses, a great fear falls on them which see them, and they are gathered up to heaven in a cloud, while their enemies behold them. Does this not sound much like the gathering described in Matthew 24:30-31, 1 Thessalonians 4:13-17 and 1 Corinthians 15:51-55? It most certainly does!

Finally, the earthquake which kills seven thousand people and causes a tenth part of the city of Jerusalem to fall and causes the rest to fear and give glory to God closely parallels the fourth of the four celestial events described in Matthew 24:29. Clearly, this Chapter seems to be referring to a portion of the sixth trumpet judgment in which God's elect, of the 144,000 of the 12 Hebrew tribes, have not yet been gathered to God, until the end of it, which concludes the second woe.

Perhaps this vision of the two witnesses is a flashback for the wicked to the time of the great tribulation which has already been concluded. Such an explanation is the only thing I can think of that might explain this passage occurring as part of the sixth trumpet judgment and second woe, as Revelation 11:14 reveals it to be.

Chapter 11 concludes with the seventh angel blowing his trumpet that ushers in great rejoicing in heaven saying the kingdoms of this world have become the kingdoms of our Lord (YHWH), and of his Christ (Yahushua) and he shall reign for ever and ever. The 24 elders in heaven sitting before God on their seats, fall upon their faces and worship and give thanks to God because he has taken to himself his great power and has reigned over all the earth and creation. These elders go on to reveal that the nations of the earth were angry (at God) and that God's wrath has come (upon the wicked) and that the dead should be judged so that God will give reward to his servants the prophets and to the saints (all born again elect believers), those both small and great who fear his name, and destroy those who destroy the earth, namely all those who oppose God and thus are wicked.

The passage concludes with the temple of God in heaven being opened and John sees the ark of his (God's) testament. Is this the same ark which sat in the holy of holies inside the Temple in Jerusalem before it was sacked by the Babylonian King Nebuchadnezzar and his army in 586 B.C.? It appears to be so. This revelation of John's vision is accompanied by voices, thunder and lightning, an earthquake and great hail.

10. The Rest of God's End Times Story

At this point in the story, John's vision takes a step back and gives us visibility into the broader story of God's perfect plan which has unfolded over the course of world history for the past 6,000 years:

> *"And there appeared a great wonder in heaven; a woman clothed with the sun, and the moon under her feet, and upon her head a crown of twelve stars: And she being with child cried, travailing in birth, and pained to be delivered. And there appeared another wonder in heaven; and behold a great red dragon, having seven heads and ten horns, and seven crowns upon his heads. And his tail drew the third part of the stars of heaven, and did cast them to the earth: and the dragon stood before the woman which was ready to be delivered, for to devour her child as soon as it was born. And she brought forth a man child, who was to rule the nations with a rod of iron: and her child was caught up unto God (Eloah), and to his throne."*
> Revelation 12:1-5

Who is this woman and who does she symbolize? Her crown of twelve stars symbolizes that she is a queen and the twelve stars indicate that she represents God's chosen people, who initially were the 12 Hebrew tribes of Abraham, Isaac and Jacob who made up the ancient (not modern) nation of Israel, through whom God blessed the whole world. Her being with child refers to the Messiah, Yahushua (Jesus Christ) who would be given birth by her, and indeed He was, through his mother Mary, who was a descendant of David, of the tribe of Judah (one of the 12 Hebrew tribes) and of the ancient nation of Israel.

The woman is opposed by the great red dragon, who represents Lucifer, a.k.a. Satan. The dragon's tail drawing a third of the stars of heaven and casting them to earth refers to one third of the angels in heaven who sided with Lucifer in his rebellion against God. These fallen angels have been demon spirits who have sought to do Satan's bidding to bring, pain, suffering destruction, death and eternal damnation to as many humans as possible for the last 6,000 years.

315

When Christ was about to be born, Satan sought to destroy him, using King Herod as his first agent to do so. In Matthew 2:16, the Bible tells us that King Herod, hearing of the birth of the Messiah in the town of Bethlehem from the three wise men from the east, directed his soldiers to slaughter every child two years of age and under in the town in order to see to it that the "King of the Jews" would not grow up to threaten or challenge Herod's earthly kingly rule. Then in Yahushua's ministry, the devil used the scribes and Pharisees to try (unsuccessfully) to oppose and discredit Him, and eventually had Him crucified, thinking that it would shut Him up and with Him the truths that He was teaching.

Satan, and the scribes and Pharisees who served him, mistakenly thought they had won. But Yahushua (Jesus) rose from the dead and ascended (was caught up) to heaven where He sits today at the right hand of God.

Verse 6 continues,

> *"And the woman fled into the wilderness, where she hath a place prepared of God (Eloah), that they should feed her there a thousand two hundred and threescore (1,260) days."*
> Revelation 12:6

Here we see the true spiritual nation of Israel, namely God's born again elect followers of Yahushua, fleeing into the wilderness where she is fed for 1,260 days, the exact same number of days that the two witnesses of Chapter 11 testify and prophecy, and just 30 less than the 1,290 days of the great tribulation's duration revealed to us in Daniel 12:11. In Matthew 24:16, in response to seeing the abomination of desolation, spoken of by Daniel the prophet, stand in the holy place, Yahushua commands God's elect,

> *"Then let them which be in Judaea flee into the mountains . . . For then shall be great tribulation, such as was not since the beginning of the world to this time, no, nor ever shall be."* Matthew 24:16 & 21

Fleeing into the wilderness and into the mountains essentially refers to the same thing. Today, God's elect have, in many instances that I know of, fled to and are living in the mountains away from populous metropolitan areas in America, all of which have gone quite dark and demonic and are no longer safe places to live, especially for God's true born again elect, represented by the woman of Revelation 12.

The chapter goes on to further describe the war in heaven which resulted in the great dragon, the devil, being cast out of heaven to earth:

> *"And there was war in heaven: Michael and his angels fought against the dragon; and the dragon fought and his angels, And prevailed not; neither was their place found any more in heaven. And the great dragon was cast out, that old serpent, called the Devil, and Satan, which deceiveth the whole world: he was cast out into the earth, and his angels (demon spirits) were cast out with him."* Revelation 12:7-9

Michael is the archangel Michael who led two thirds of the angels in heaven against the devil and a third of the angels who sided with him, in which the devil and his fallen angels (demon spirits) were cast from heaven to earth. Notice that Satan is described as one who deceives the whole world, and quite effectively, as we have seen from my revealing earlier some of the most powerful lies and frauds of the last hundred years, which deceive the vast majority of mankind to this day, and will continue to do so until the second coming of Christ and beyond.

> *"And I heard a loud voice in heaven, Now is come salvation (through faith in Christ), and strength, and the kingdom of our God (Eloah), and the power of his Christ (Messiah): for the accuser of our brethren is cast down, which accused them before our God (Eloah) day and night. And they overcame him (the devil) by the blood of the Lamb (Yahushua), and by the word of their testimony; and they loved not their lives unto the death. Therefore rejoice, ye heavens, and ye that dwell in them. Woe to the inhabiters of the earth and of the sea! for the devil is come down unto you, having great wrath, because he knoweth that he hath but a short time. And when the dragon saw that he was cast unto the earth, he persecuted the woman which brought*

forth the man child. And to the woman were given two wings of a great eagle, that she might fly into the wilderness, into her place, where she is nourished for a time, and times, and half a time (three and a half years), from the face of the serpent. And the serpent cast out of his mouth water as a flood after the woman, that he might cause her to be carried away of the flood. And the earth helped the woman, and the earth opened her mouth, and swallowed up the flood which the dragon cast out of his mouth. And the dragon was wroth (angry) with the woman, and went to make war with the remnant of her seed, which keep the commandments of God (Eloah), and have the testimony of Jesus Christ (Yahushua)." Revelation 12:10-17

The salvation referred to at the opening to this passage, refers to the the salvation available to God's people, His elect, through trust in the person and work of Yahushua on the cross, which defeated the devil, the father of lies, the accuser and the prince of this world, as he is variously referred to in the Bible, once and for all. When Christ died on the cross, shedding the blood of the Lamb, which paid the price for the sins of God's elect, which we deserve to pay, by confessing Yahushua (Jesus) as Lord over our lives and wills in every respect, all born again elect believers overcome and defeat the devil who seeks to destroy all of us and keep us on the path we are all born into: headed to torment and agony in hell for the sins we have committed in this life.

The term "they loved not their lives unto the death," means that all true born again elect and therefore saved believers in Yahushua die to their selfish wants and wills and submit and surrender their lives and wills to the perfect will of YHWH and Yahushua for their lives. Those who refuse to fully submit and surrender their lives and their wills to Yahushua choose eternal death in hell, separated from the eternal life in Christ. In other words, placing greater value on comforts and riches in this life, will always result in eternal death, separated from true life in God for all eternity. Is such a tradeoff worth it? No, of course not! But the power of the devil to deceive all but God's elect is so strong that the non-elect lack the ability to see what seems so obvious and sensible to those of us who number among God's elect. If this phenomenon doesn't prove the reality of spiritual warfare, the devil, demons and deceit in all of our lives, nothing ever will.

The bottom line to all of life is that the devil, having lost his place in heaven, is filled with anger and hatred for God, whom he cannot touch, so the devil tries to hurt God by persecuting God's people, His elect, spiritual Israel, the woman of Revelation 12. This is why Yahushua tells us in John 16:33,

> "... In the world ye shall have tribulation: but be of good cheer; I have overcome the world."

Tribulation is distinctly different than the wrath of God which He intends to pour out upon the wicked. Tribulation, meaning troubles, trials, struggles, affliction and opposition has been orchestrated by God to refine, test, strengthen and mature the faith and wisdom of God's elect, by subjecting us to the scorn, abuse, mockery, hatred, injustice and persecution of this world, which teaches us not to put our faith and trust in this world, but rather trust YHWH and Yahushua to protect us from harm and provide for our every need.

This can only come from a long, intimate and personal relationship with Yahushua in which He comes through for us time and time again, even when circumstances look dire, bleak and hopeless. God orchestrates these sort of circumstances in the lives of each of His elect, to lead us into a deeper love for and trust in Him in all circumstances.

This ends up becoming the precise opposite of man exercising his mythical "free will," which you will never find taught in Bible Scripture. Such a concept is a bald-faced lie, and we need to drive it out of our thinking once and for all. God does it all; we do nothing but trust (believe) Him so that God, and not man, gets all the glory for it.

Many forms of false organized religion teach this "free will" doctrine of devils which suggests that God will not or is powerless to resist the free will of man to accept or resist His free offer of grace and salvation. That is not the experience of those of us who are truly born again in the Spirit with a love for the truth and a love for the long term best interests of our fellow man. God is sovereign. What God wills, He gets 100% of the time:

> *"There is no wisdom nor understanding nor counsel against the LORD (YHWH)."* Proverbs 21:30

For God's true elect, this is very good news. It means that YHWH and Yahushua are all-powerful and fully in control over all things, no matter how bleak and discouraging they may seem at times.

The doctrine of devils of "free will" Arminianism taught in most forms of apostate organized religion today has the effect of elevating man's alleged "free will" over the sovereignty of almighty God, reversing the power and might of God vs. man. It is a complete abomination to God that teaches a form of works-based salvation, inasmuch as man has the ability to exercise his "free will" over the sovereign will of almighty God. It is patently absurd and makes a mockery of the character, nature, brilliance and majesty of almighty God. But for those who do not number among God's elect, it appeals to their pride that they can earn their way to salvation through the work of exercising their free will to accept the gift of salvation offered by God only to His elect.

When the "Hound of Heaven" decides to tree one of His elect, His elect have very little choice in the matter. God will break His elect and bring them broken, desperate, humbled and out of answers to the foot of the cross, with no other viable options left, just as He did in my life. But my desperate state was orchestrated by God, who brought me fully submitted, surrendered, humble and teachable concerning the character, nature, thoughts and ways of God as He truly is, rather than based on some fictitious imaginings and wishes I might wish God to be. I was prepared to shut up and learn from Him directly through His Word, with no human filters between me and God.

Ephesians 2:1 makes it very clear that in our sinful state, we all are dead in our sins, have no spiritual life in us, and therefore God must do it all, so that He gets all the glory and we have no room to boast that we did anything to warrant being saved, because none of us did. God did it all: period!

> *"And you (God's born again elect) he hath quickened (made alive), who were dead in trespasses and sins."* Ephesians 2:1 (parentheticals added)

We further see in this passage from Chapter 12 that the woman (spiritual Israel, composed of all true born again elect submitted followers of Yahushua) flies into the wilderness for three and a half years, which repeats and therefore emphasizes the 1,260 days of sanctuary in the wilderness referenced in verse 6 of Chapter 12. 360 days per Biblical year (30 days per month X 12 months = 360) X 3.5 years equals 1,260 days, thereby confirming that verses 6 and 14 of Chapter 12 refer to the same time period, which overlaps with the first 1,260 days of the 1,290 day great tribulation of Daniel 12:11.

From verse 17, we see that the devil makes war with the remnant of the woman's seed, where her seed represents Yahushua or Jesus; hence the remnant of her seed refers to the small number of obedient born again followers of Christ who keep God's commandments and have the testimony of Jesus Christ, as manifested in their example of honesty, integrity and agape (sacrificial) love for their fellow man during this time of the great tribulation in which the far more numerous earth dwellers (God's non-elect and the wicked), who knowingly or unknowingly serve the devil, the father of lies, will seek to endlessly suppress and silence the inconvenient truth. We know they will not succeed in the end, but they will certainly try to do so.

In Chapter 13, Paul describes the emergence of two beasts, representing the Antichrist and the false prophet who are the agents of and empowered by the dragon of Revelation 12, or the devil. Paul stands on the sand of the sea and sees a beast (the first beast or Antichrist) rise up out of it, having seven heads and ten horns, and upon his heads the name of blasphemy. The sea represents the nations of the world and the political and military power which those nations wield. The first beast has the appearance of a leopard, the feet of a bear and the mouth of a lion and the dragon (the devil) gives him his power, position and great authority. A number of Bible pundits have noted that the leopard is the symbol of Germany and the Panzer tank of WWII, the bear is the national symbol of Russia and the lion is the symbol of the British Empire and the UK and that this Antichrist figure is symbolic of the New World Order one world government which the world's Jewish Illuminati Freemason Zionist global elite conspiracy has been working toward for centuries. Perhaps this symbolism is accurate; I don't know for certain, but I do not believe it's overly important. What is important is that the identity of this first beast, the Antichrist, has now been revealed to some of us who number among God's elect. This beast is a multi-headed monster: the people falsely claiming to be Jews who adhere to the beliefs and occult practices of the Babylonian Talmud and Zohar Kabbalah, who arrogantly profess themselves to be God's chosen people, when in reality their god is Lucifer, Satan or the devil himself, by the admission of some of their own leaders.

> *"And I saw one of his heads as it were wounded to death; and his deadly wound was healed: and all the world wondered after the beast. And they worshipped the dragon (the devil) which gave power unto the beast (the Antichrist): and they worshipped the beast, saying, Who is like unto the beast? who is able to make war with him? And there was given unto him a mouth speaking great things and blasphemies; and power was given unto him to continue forty and two months. And he opened his mouth in blasphemy against God (Eloah), to blaspheme his name, and his tabernacle, and them that dwell in heaven. And it was given unto him to make war with the saints, and to overcome them: and power was given him over all kindreds, and tongues and nations."* Revelation 13:3-7

In this passage, heads may refer to leaders or to nations or empires. In this context it appears to refer to empire: either the reconstituted Roman Empire in the form of the European

Union (EU), the form of the British Empire, or by the impostors posing as Jews who are falsely alleged to have received a deadly wound in the form of the fraud of the holohoax. I am inclined to think it's the latter, since the global conspiracy is, for all intents and purposes, headquartered out of a separate legal entity known as the City of London, which is the seat of finance and central banking power through which the Jewish global conspiracy controls the entire world. America and the UK are clearly at the epicenter of the global conspiracy, and these nations have been hijacked and are ruled by the Jewish Illuminati Freemason Zionist global elite conspiracy.

Thus it seems more likely that the wounded power which has been healed refers to the impostors posing as Jews, rather than the EU or the reconstituted Roman Empire. This Antichrist beast (the impostors posing as Jews and the global elite conspiracy in particular) has great power to speak great blasphemies through its lock tight control over the world's media outlets and to censor, suppress and often silence those who are courageous enough to try to expose the truth to the world of the global conspiracy and its many obvious implications for the fulfillment of end times Bible prophecies.

Notice that the beast, the Antichrist, the impostors posing as Jews, are given power to operate largely unopposed and for 42 months to make war against God's born again elect, and to overcome them. Once again, this is the three and a half years or 1,260 days (42 months X 30 days per month = 1,260 days) that make up the preponderance of the 1,290 day great tribulation foretold in Daniel 12:11. Furthermore, is it not painfully obvious that the Jewish banking power, comprised of global elites who secretly practice the occult, rules our entire world today, just as verse 7 describes? It most certainly is for those of us who have not been sent a strong delusion by God, in fulfillment of the prophecy of 2 Thessalonians 2:10-12 upon the wicked and God's non-elect (really one and the same thing).

Chapter 13 continues,

"And all that dwell upon the earth shall worship him (the beast or Antichrist, the impostors posing as Jews), whose names are not written in the book of life of the Lamb slain from the foundation of the world. If any man have an ear, let him hear. He that leadeth into captivity shall go into captivity: he that killeth with the sword must be killed with the sword. Here is the patience and the faith of the saints." Revelation 13:8-10

This passage is explaining that those who do not number among God's elect, will bow and swear allegiance and loyalty to the beast, the impostors posing as Jews. Such people will include those who number among self-professed Christian Zionists who advance the lie that the modern day rogue terrorist state of faux Israel is one and the same with spiritual Israel referred to in end times Bible prophecy, which I have already demonstrated it most assuredly is not.

False teaching pastors such as John Hagee, Pat Robertson and many other prominent televangelists and the Pope of Roman Catholicism, who falsely teach their flocks of deceived followers that those posing as Jews are God's chosen people and the rightful heirs of the promises made to the true descendants of Abraham, Isaac and Jacob in Genesis 12:2-3, are teaching bald-faced lies which promote the Antichrist and feed billions of dollars of American foreign aid to the rogue terrorist state of Israel every year which advances the cause of Satan!

Nothing could be a greater abomination to almighty God. It is hideously wicked and evil! Those who cannot or will not see this obvious reality, are demonstrating that they are spiritually blinded, do not have their names written in the Lamb's (Yahushua's) book of life, and therefore do not number among God's elect, who can hope to be gathered in the gathering of Matthew 24:30-31, 1 Thessalonians 4:13-17 and 1 Corinthians 15:51-55.

Once again, we see how central the doctrine of election taught in the Bible truly is. Various forms of false organized religion teach the lie that if a person prays the sinner's prayer, he's saved and becomes a born again Christian. The Bible teaches no such thing! We can truly know that we are one of God's elect only once we are born again in God's Holy Spirit, which can occur at any time in our lifetimes up to the moment we die. For a person to be truly born again, his spirit must be able to confess that Jesus Christ (the Messiah) came in the flesh. Here's how the Apostle John explains it in his first epistle:

> *"Hereby know ye the Spirit of God (Eloah): Every spirit that confesseth that Jesus Christ (Yahushua the Messiah) is come in the flesh is of God (Eloah): And every spirit that confesseth not that Jesus Christ (Yahushua the Messiah) is come in the flesh is not of God (Eloah): and this is that spirit of the antichrist, whereof ye have heard that it should come; and even now already is it in the world."* 1 John 4:2-3

Furthermore, anyone who professes to be born again in the Spirit whose predominate behaviors remain the works of the flesh described by the Apostle Paul in Galatians 5:19-21, as opposed to the nine attributes of the fruit of the Spirit laid out for us in Galatians 5:22-23, ought to be highly suspect.

Finally, if a professed born again follower of Christ does not exhibit a distinct love for the truth and a love for the long-term well-being of his fellow man over his own wants and comforts, such a man is likely self-deceived, a fraud or both. False organized religion is filled with God's non-elect, His spiritual goats, who continue to lie, be selfish and sin like hell who wrongly think they have pulled one over on God and their fellow man. Soon, this fraud will be exposed for what it always has been.

Clearly, these sort of discussions make a number of people very nervous and some become downright angry and hostile over it. This is to be expected. Those who are living lives of deceit, don't like being exposed; it blows their cover! Nevertheless, God is a God of truth and in the end, He will not be mocked and He is never fooled. Those who are practicing false "feel good" religion in which "God is love, and that's all you gotta know," are misleading many others astray and those who know better and teach lies in spite of that are blaspheming the Spirit of God, thereby committing the only unforgivable sin.

The bottom line is that those who revere and swear allegiance to the impostors posing as Jews and/or the rogue terrorist state of modern day Israel are doing the work of Satan and thus are not of God's born again elect, no matter what they may claim or profess otherwise. This test alone will make it rather evident that the vast majority of those professing to be Christians today (probably in excess of 99% of those professing such a thing) simply are not, and on their day of judgment, they will hear the words of Yahushua of Matthew 7:23:

" . . . I never knew you: depart from me, ye that work iniquity."

Mankind has gotten away with playing games of make believe for a very long time. Those days are nearly over, and when they arrive, all those playing fast and loose with the truth, who are many, will live to regret it for all eternity. This is the sad truth and no false teacher will be there to rescue the self-deceived. It will be just them and Yahushua (Jesus) and they will be out of excuses.

In verse 10 of Chapter 13 John tells us that he who is marked for arrest must not resist and if we are to be killed, we are not to fight back. A day of reckoning from God is coming, and true born again believers who number among God's elect are to wait for that day. The point of this verse is to leave the fighting to God.

"And I beheld another beast coming up out of the earth; and he had two horns like a lamb, and he spake as a dragon. And he exerciseth all the power of the first beast before him, and causeth the earth and them which dwell therein to worship the first beast, whose deadly wound was healed. And he doeth great wonders, so that he maketh fire come down from heaven on the earth in the sight of men, And deceiveth them that dwell on the earth by the means of those miracles which he had power to do in the sight of the beast; saying to them that dwell on the earth, that they should make an image to the beast, which had the wound by a sword, and did live. And he had power to give life unto the image of the beast, that the image of the beast should both speak, and cause that as many as would not worship the

*image of the beast should be killed. And he causeth all, both
small and great, rich and poor, free and bond, to receive a mark
in their right hand, or in their foreheads: And that no man
might buy or sell, save he that had the mark, or the name of
the beast, or the number of his name. Here is wisdom. Let him
that hath understanding count the number of the beast: for it is
the number of a man; and his number is Six hundred threescore
and six (666)."* Revelation 13:11-18

This second beast, or false prophet, has two horns like a lamb.
These horns may refer to the two horned mitre of the Pope of
the Roman Catholic Church. We certainly see the current
Pope, Francis, using his bully pulpit to worship the impostors
posing as Jews, who we now know to be the Antichrist and the
first beast. Yet another possibility is that the false prophet is a
symbol or metaphor for the Jewish-owned and controlled
mainstream media, which is nothing more than a propaganda
mouthpiece and purveyor of graphic images, to serve the
deceptive aims of their global elite masters. The image of the
first beast referred to here need not be a literal image, statue or
idol. It is far more likely to be an image in the minds of those
who do not number among God's elect.

Likewise, the mark of the beast, bearing his name or number
(666) is not *on* people's foreheads or hands, but rather *in* them.
This subtle distinction implies that the mark of the beast is
metaphorical and refers to whoever one works for with his
mind or his hands and to whom he is ultimately loyal and
swears allegiance. The number of the beast, 666, is a reference
to God having created man on the sixth day of creation, in
which mankind attempts to usurp the authority of God the
Father, God the Son and God the Holy Spirit and replace it
with a man-centered philosophy of man, over the infinite and
sovereign God as ruler of the universe.

When man attempts to do such a foolish thing, man attempts
to redefine right and wrong, justice and morality in the
imperfect image of man and that which is evil gets redefined
as good and that which is good gets redefined as evil. This is
precisely what we see happening today in which the righteous

man of integrity, character and courage who becomes angry at cruelty, lies and injustice, is branded as hateful, racist, bigoted and a dangerous right wing extremist and terrorist, when nothing could be further from the truth! This reverse of logic and common sense is being pushed so that wicked criminals can go on persecuting their innocent victims without any consequences or any justice for their victims. It is completely absurd, and the exact opposite of what constitutes a healthy culture or society.

Here's how one clear thinker once described what has become commonplace today:

> *"He who is not angry when there is just cause for anger is immoral. Why? Because anger looks to the good of justice. And if you can live amid injustice without anger, you are immoral as well as unjust."*—St. Thomas Aquinas (1225-1274)

Yet today, the few of us who dare to show our outrage, fury and anger at lies, deceit, treachery, extortion and murder are vilified and demonized as mentally unstable and downright dangerous to others. As such, the world has proven that it is stark raving mad, unjust and grossly immoral. What further evidence does anyone in his right mind need to prove that we are living in the final days of the great tribulation? Not a damn thing! Anyone who fails to get this today, is not in his right mind. It's that simple.

In Chapter 14, John had yet another vision that provides yet another overview of the end times:

> *"And I looked, and lo, a Lamb stood on mount Sion, and with him an hundred forty and four thousand (144,000), having his Father's name (YHWH) written in their foreheads. And I heard a voice from heaven, as the voice of many waters, and as the voice of a great thunder: and I heard the voice of harpers harping with their harps: And they sung as it were a new song before the throne, and before the four beasts, and the elders: and no man could learn that song but the hundred and forty and four thousand, which were redeemed from the earth. These are they which were not defiled with women; for they are*

virgins. These are they which follow the Lamb withersoever he goeth. These were redeemed from among men, being the firstfruits unto God (Eloah) and to the Lamb. And in their mouth was found no guile: for they are without fault before the throne of God. "Revelation 14:1-5

In this passage, John sees the 144,000 from Chapter 7 who are with the Lamb (Yahushua or Jesus) who stands on mount Sion (a metaphor for God's abode) and who have the name of the Lamb's Father (YHWH) written *in* their foreheads. In other words, God is the first thing on their minds and they belong to Him. This group of 144,000 is uniquely honored by being the only ones capable of learning and singing a new song of worship and praise to YHWH (God) before His throne.

Their having been redeemed from the earth means that they were part of the gathering that occurs right after the great tribulation is over. These specially honored members of God's born again, gathered elect embody purity and integrity in their conduct. It suggests that they never married and they never committed sexual immorality with women. But it could also mean that they have been cleansed of any defilement due to sexual immorality and thus are viewed by YHWH as spiritual virgins, but are not necessarily literal ones. These 144,000 men faithfully followed Yahushua wherever he led them. They are the first fruits, the unblemished sacrifices to YHWH and Yahushua, who were foreshadowed by the animal sacrifices of the Mosaic law of the Old Testament, in which only young animals without blemish qualified as suitable animal sacrifices to God for the sins of man.

Finally, this same group of honored elect, are described as being without guile, meaning without cunning or deceit. As such, these 144,000 manifest the holiness and righteousness of God and Jesus. And isn't it interesting to note that in 2015, for someone to be described as "without guile," is not a compliment at all? In our twisted and depraved culture, it implies a lack of sophistication and is used to refer to someone who is viewed as hopelessly naive. Clearly, God sees things exactly the opposite of the way the world sees things.

Chapter 14 continues by describing the rest of John's overview of the end times vision and what is soon to follow in the way of God's wrath upon the wicked:

"And I saw another angel fly in the mist of heaven, having the everlasting gospel to preach unto them that dwell on the earth, and to every nation, and kindred, and tongue, and people. Saying with a loud voice, Fear God (Eloah), and give glory to him; for the hour of his judgment is come: and worship him that made heaven, and earth, and the sea, and the fountains of waters. And there followed another angel, saying, Babylon is fallen, is fallen, that great city, because she made all nations drink the wine of the wrath of her fornication. And the third angel followed them, saying with a loud voice, If any man worship the beast and his image, and receive his mark in his forehead, or in his hand, The same shall drink of the wine of the wrath of God (YHWH), which is poured out without mixture into the cup of his indignation; and he shall be tormented with fire and brimstone in the presence of holy angels, and in the presence of the Lamb: And the smoke of their torment ascendeth up for ever and ever: and they have no rest day or nor night, who worship the beast and his image, and whosoever receiveth the mark of his name. Here is the patience of the saints: here are they that keep the commandments of God (Eloah), and the faith of Jesus (Yahushua). And I heard a voice from heaven saying unto me, Write, Blessed are the dead which die in the Lord (our Adon) from henceforth: Yea, with the Spirit, that they may rest from their labours; and their works do follow them. And I looked and behold a white cloud, and upon the cloud one sat like unto the Son of man, having on his head a golden crown, and in his hand a sharp sickle. And another angel came out of the temple, crying with a loud voice to him that sat on the cloud, Thrust in thy sickle, and reap: for the time is come for thee to reap; for the harvest of the earth is ripe. And he that sat on the cloud thrust in his sickle on the earth; and the earth was reaped. And another angel came out of the temple which is in heaven, he also having a sharp sickle. And another angel came out from the altar, which had power over fire; and cried with a loud cry to him that had

the sharp sickle, saying, Thrust in thy sharp sickle, and gather the clusters of the vine of the earth; for her grapes are fully ripe. And the angel thrust in his sickle into the earth, and gathered the vine of the earth, and cast it into the great winepress of the wrath of God (Eloah). And the winepress was trodden without the city, and blood came out of the winepress, even unto the horse bridles, by the space of a thousand and six hundred furlongs." Revelation 14:6-20

The first angel appearing in this passage, who has the gospel message of salvation by grace alone through the atoning sacrifice of Yahushua on the cross, who bore the punishment for our sins, so that we might have His righteousness imputed to us, makes it clear that the wicked, those who dwell on the earth, ought to fear God and give Him glory because now the hour of judgment has arrived, in which the righteous shall receive rewards, and the wicked shall receive the punishment they so richly deserve. Time is over, is what this portion of the passage is telling us.

The second angel announces that Babylon, which symbolizes the Vatican and the City of Rome where the Roman Catholic Church is headquartered, has fallen, because she has been responsible for making all nations suffer from her fornication, both literally, and metaphorically. I'll have a lot more to discuss on this matter when we come to Chapters 17 and 18 of the Book of Revelation in which much more is revealed about this matter.

The third angel in heaven announces with a loud voice that those who have worshipped the beast, the Antichrist, the impostors posing as Jews and the Jewish Illuminati Freemason Zionist global elite conspiracy and received the mark of the beast *in* their foreheads or *in* their hands, thus demonstrating their allegiance to the beast system, will be tormented and damned in the burning lake of fire and brimstone, the successor place to hell. God is not bashful here.

The passage tells us that the wrath of God will be poured out full force upon such people, who make God indignant. All such people will be tormented with fire and brimstone (a form of volcanic stone that becomes negatively charged when heated) in the presence of the angels and Yahushua. It tells us that those wicked (resurrected) people will have no rest day or night without end, such that the smoke of their torment will never cease. It is an end of unspeakable horror and terror. Because God, in His brilliance, seeks to bring every sinner to repentance and submission to His son, Yahushua as Lord, by creating an eternity so ghastly for the rebellious, that only a blind fool would choose such an end.

And yet, in the end, we know that the vast majority of those alive on this earth today will choose this end over submitting their lives to the lordship of Jesus. It seems absolutely insane, because it is. But this is what God tells His elect will happen in the end times. We ignore this horrible warning at our eternal peril.

Think about it: eternal torment with no rest day or night! Is this not more awful than anyone can possibly imagine? Who in his right mind would ever choose such a hideous and terrifying end? And that's just the point: no one in his right mind would make such a choice. And so it points to the power of the spiritual realm over all our lives and the essential nature of God's election as one of His own. Without it, all of mankind is completely without hope and completely screwed.

In verse 12, the passage explains that the patience of the saints (all true born again adopted sons and daughters of God, who thus evidence their election by God) is manifested by their keeping the commandments of God – all of them, and keeping the faith (trust in God) *of* Jesus (Yahushua). These traits distinguish the righteous from the wicked.

In verse 13, the voice from heaven that tells John to write Blessed are those who die in the Lord (Yahushua) from henceforth, because they may then rest from their labors and they will be rewarded for their good works in due time, refers to all followers of Christ who read the revelations of John from his Book of Revelation from the time it was written in 95 A.D. until the end.

10. The Rest of God's End Times Story

Finally, this passage turns to the harvesting of the earth at the end. First, the one sitting on the cloud like the Son of man refers to Yahushua or Jesus, wearing a golden crown (as King of kings and Lord of lords) and holding a sharp sickle used for harvesting grain or wheat. An angel comes out of the temple and tells Yahushua to thrust in His sickle and reap for the harvest of souls is now ripe. Yahushua does this and reaps the earth, which metaphorically refers to His gathering described in Matthew 24:30-31, 1 Thessalonians 4:13-17 and 1 Corinthians 15:51-55.

Next, another angel comes out of the temple, also carrying a sharp sickle, and yet another angel having power over fire cries with a loud voice telling the angel with the sharp sickle to also thrust in his sickle and gather the clusters of the vine of the earth (the earth dwellers, or the wicked), for they too are fully ripe. The angel with the sickle does as he is commanded, gathers the vine of the earth (the wicked) and casts it into the great winepress of the wrath of God, a term which appears yet again in Chapter 19 of the Book of Revelation.

Verse 20 tells us that the winepress is trodden outside the city, which in the books of Moses signified that the things were unclean and sinful. Blood comes out of the winepress up to the bridles of horses (about five feet deep) and 1,600 furlongs or 200 miles long and 200 miles wide. In other words, there will be a large number of the wicked who will die rather horrifically, as will soon be described in Chapters 15 and 16 of the Book of Revelation.

Chapter 15 introduces us to the final seven vial judgments to be poured out upon the wicked of the earth, which fulfill the prophecy and vision of John with which Chapter 14 has just concluded:

> *"And I saw another sign in heaven, great and marvelous, seven angels having the seven last plagues, for in them is filled up the wrath of God (Eloah). And I saw as it were a sea of glass mingled with fire: and them that had gotten the victory over the beast, and over his image, and over his mark, and over the number of his name, stand on the sea of glass, having the harps*

of God (Eloah). And they sing the song of Moses the servant of God (Eloah), and the song of the Lamb (Yahushua), saying, Great and marvelous are thy works, Lord God Almighty (Adonai YHWH); just and true are thy ways, thou King of saints. Who shall not fear thee, O Lord (YHWH), and glorify thy name? for thou only art holy: for all nations shall come and worship before thee; for thy judgments are made manifest. And after that I looked, and behold, the temple of the tabernacle of the testimony in heaven was opened: And the seven angels came out of the temple, having the seven plagues, clothed in pure and white linen, and having their breasts girded with golden girdles. And one of the four beasts gave unto the seven angels seven golden vials full of the wrath of God (Eloah), who liveth for ever and ever. And the temple was filled with smoke from the glory of God (Eloah), and from his power, and no man was able to enter into the temple, till the seven plagues of the seven angels were fulfilled." Revelation 15:1-8

In this Chapter, we cannot help but understand that YHWH (God), the almighty and sovereign creator of the universe and all that is in it, is filled with wrath, anger and fury at the wicked and deceitful acts of the earth dwellers of the world. Just as He was in the days before Noah's flood, God is seething with rage at the injustices of mankind which he sees everywhere.

None of this surprises God; after all, He has been allowing and orchestrating all events in all of world history leading up to this climax to His story (history). But when we understand the holy and just nature of God, as He reveals Himself to His elect in Scripture, only then can we come to have a hint at the seemingly endless patience, mercy and grace that He has shown mankind up to now, so as to ensure that no one goes to hell for all eternity by any form of accident.

Yet God's patience is not without limit. He too has His limits and we are nearly there today. God would be entirely within His rights to send every last one of us to the eternal fires of hell the instant we sin. He is that holy and abhors all sin that much. But His nature is far more grand than that, and He seeks to grow His elect to become saints who manifest the character of Yahushua willingly and naturally. Such a result can only come through numerous trials, suffering and refining fires, many of them brought upon His elect at the hands of the wicked, who God has created for just this purpose. Now, at the end, God seeks to cleanse and purify the world of evil once and for all through His scorching and refining fires.

Those gathered saints who have been victorious over the beast during the great tribulation stand on a sea of glass in heaven and sing praises to YHWH for His marvelous works, His just and true ways, His holiness and His power and might. After this, the seven angels emerge from the temple, clothed in pure and white linen (symbolizing holiness and purity) with gold sashes (symbolizing that they represent royalty), carrying the seven plagues and one of the four beasts gives them seven golden vials full of the wrath of God to go with the plagues that they will soon pour out upon the wicked.

The final verse 8 describes the temple of God in heaven, filled with smoke from the glory and power of God, which is so overwhelming that no man may enter into the temple until the seven plagues from the seven vials are poured out upon the earth. In other words, God is furious beyond belief! Let the whole earth tremble when God gets angry! And He is right now!

In Chapter 16, a voice from the temple, presumably from YHWH (God), directs the angels to go their ways and pour their vials of plagues and YHWH's wrath upon the earth. The first angel does so and violent and painful sores afflict the men of the earth who have taken on the mark of the beast and worshipped his (the Antichrist's) image. Remember that this mark of the beast is not at all likely to be literal. It is likely to be a symbol for those who are of the lie, selfish and unloving – the opposite of the core traits of Yahushua.

The second angel pours his vial out upon the sea and it becomes like the blood of a dead man and every living thing in it dies.

335

The third angel pours his vial out upon the rivers and foundations of waters (springs, wells, underground aquifers) and they become blood. And an angel of the waters declares YHWH right and just for doing so, because the wicked of the earth have shed the blood of the saints (followers of Christ) and the prophets, so now God has given the wicked blood to drink and they deserve it (they are worthy). Yet another angel out of the altar affirms to YHWH that His judgments are both true and right.

The fourth angel pours out his vial upon the sun and power is given to him (the sun) to scorch men with fire. This could very easily be a set of massive solar flares of some sort, which scorch the earth with heat and intense solar radiation.

In response, the men of the earth (the wicked who are remaining) are scorched with great heat and blaspheme the name of God (YHWH) who has power over these plagues; yet they refuse to repent of their sins and wickedness that would give glory to YHWH.

The fifth angel pours out his vial upon the seat (headquarters) of the beast (meaning the Antichrist) and the kingdom of the beast becomes dark and the wicked of the earth gnaw their tongues in pain, blaspheme God for their pains and their sores, but refuse to repent of their evil deeds.

The sixth angel pours out his vial upon the great river Euphrates and the river thereof is dried up, that the way of the kings of the east (China perhaps?) might be prepared for invasion and war. John sees three unclean spirits or demons, like frogs, coming out of the mouths of the dragon (the devil), the beast (the Antichrist or the impostors posing as Jews), and the false prophet (the Roman Catholic Pope and/or the Jewish-owned and controlled media). John goes on to explain that these unclean spirits of frog-like appearance (reminiscent of the frogs of the 10 plagues God wrought upon Egypt and the Pharaoh in the days of Moses) work miracles (have spiritual powers) which go forth into the wicked kings of the earth and into the whole world, to gather the wicked, God's non-elect, His spiritual goats, to the battle of the great day of Almighty

YHWH (God). Then Yahushua (Jesus) speaks, reminding us of His Words of warning to His elect in Matthew 24 and 25:

*"Behold, I come as a thief, **Blessed** is he that watcheth, and keepeth his garments, lest he walk naked, and they see his shame."* Revelation 16:15 (emphasis added)

Here Yahushua (Jesus) is speaking to His elect, reminding us that we must remain watchful of the signs of his second coming and be ready to be gathered with Him in His gathering of Matthew 24:30-31. The keeping of his garments so as to avoid shame is a symbol for remaining righteous and ready for His second coming which finds its parallel in Matthew 24:17-18:

"Let him which is on the housetop not come down to take any thing out of his house: Neither let him which is in the field return back to take his clothes."

He (Yahushua or YHWH) gathers them (the wicked of this world) into a place in the Hebrew tongue or language called Armageddon, which Strong's 4023 translates for us as Megiddo, which is a valley in northern Israel today known as the Valley of Jezreel.

Finally, the seventh angel pours out his vial into the air, and John hears a loud voice from heaven, from the throne (of God) saying, "It is done." John witnesses voices, thunders, lightning and a massive earthquake greater than any earthquake ever witnessed before by mankind. In verse 19, the great city, probably referring to Jerusalem, is divided into three parts (perhaps the Jewish, Muslim and Christian quarters?) and the cities of the nations, presumably all of them, fall, while great Babylon (the city of Rome and the headquarters of the Vatican of the Roman Catholic Church) is remembered by YHWH (God) to give to her "the cup of the wine of the fierceness of his wrath."

Treading the grapes and pouring out the cup of wine of God's wrath is a frequent metaphor the Bible employs to describe the wrath God plans to pour out upon the wicked of this world at the end of the age. As a result of the massive and global earthquake, every island and mountain is destroyed (eliminated) and a great hail falls upon mankind, with every hail stone weighing a talent, which is roughly 113 pounds.

Once again, in response to the exceedingly great hail storm, the wicked of the world blaspheme YHWH (God) and refuse to confess and repent of their evil and wicked deeds. Clearly, these wicked men are so depraved and reprobate that nothing will deter or turn them from doing that which is evil and wicked in the sight of YHWH (God) and from rebelling against Him.

Chapter 17 changes the scene and fades back to provide us with insight into the vision John was given of the fate of the "great whore that sitteth upon many waters" which, as we will soon see, is the Roman Catholic Church: the seat of fornication, idolatry, deceit and treachery for the last 1,700 years. How this truth could have been embedded in the verses of Chapter 17 of the Book of Revelation for so long without the Roman Catholic Church being identified as the mother of harlots and abominations of the earth, is truly remarkable. It is a testimony to the power of the spiritual realm to conceal the truth from the people of the world until God chooses to reveal it to a few of His elect who, in turn, might reveal it to others, as I am doing here. As we unpack the verses in this chapter of Revelation, it is helpful to keep in mind that this chapter is indeed referring to the acts and history of the Roman Catholic Church since its inception.

> *"And there came one of the seven angels which had the seven vials, and talked with me, saying unto me, Come hither; and I will shew unto thee the judgment of the great whore that sitteth upon many waters: With whom the kings of the earth have committed fornication, and the inhabitants of the earth have been made drunk with the wine of her fornication. So he carried me away in the spirit into the wilderness: and I saw a woman sit upon a scarlet coloured beast, full of names of blasphemy, having seven heads and ten horns. And the woman was arrayed in purple and scarlet colour, and decked with gold and precious stones and pearls, having a golden cup in her hand full of*

abominations and filthiness of her fornication: And upon her forehead was a name written, MYSTERY, BABYLON THE GREAT, THE MOTHER OF HARLOTS AND ABOMINATIONS OF THE EARTH." Revelation 17:1-5

Here we have one of the angels of the seven vial judgments inviting John to see the judgment and end of the Roman Catholic Church, which the angel minces no words in describing as "the great whore that sittest upon many waters." A whore is an immoral woman who engages in lustful promiscuity and sexual immorality with men for money, and that is precisely what the angel is describing the Roman Catholic Church as. The reference to sitting upon many waters is a metaphor for many nations or people groups.

The Roman Catholic Church clearly has the broadest reach of any form of organized religion which claims (falsely or otherwise) to follow Yahushua (Christ) and the teachings of the Bible in their entirety, since its founding under the Roman Emperor Constantine in approximately 310 A.D. According to Pew Research Center, Catholics account for 1.1 billion out of the 2.2 billion people worldwide who identify themselves as Christians, or about 50% of the total, with Protestants of various denominations accounting for roughly 800 million people (37%), Eastern Orthodox accounting for 260 million people (12%) and other allegedly Christian denominations accounting for roughly 30 million people (1%). As we shall see in the following chapter, the practices, rituals and teachings of the Roman Catholic Church have always departed materially from and conflicted with many of the important and core teachings of the Bible. As such, it cannot possibly be of God, Christ or the Bible, but is, in reality, ruled by Satan and demonic spirits.

The angel goes on to expose this whore as having committed fornication with the kings of the earth, and we know from a study of world history that the political rulers, especially of Europe throughout the centuries, have conspired and colluded with the Catholic Church to keep the popular masses under their joint manipulations and control through deception, lies and intense social and political pressure to conform to the popular culture which these two institutions, political and ecclesiastical, have controlled to suppress and deceive the masses.

Similarly, it is no secret to many that the Roman Catholic priesthood has committed endless fornication and sexual molestation with vulnerable young women and boys, which invariably results in demon spirit infestation and possession leading to early promiscuity, homosexuality and other forms of sexual immorality that has ruined billions of lives over the last 1,700 years.

John is carried away in the spirit into a wilderness where he sees a woman (the whore) sitting atop a scarlet colored beast. It would seem that this beast is the same beast as the first beast of Revelation 13, namely the Antichrist, who we now have identified as impostors posing as Jews, led by the dynamic investment and central banking family of the Rothschilds. Rothschild means "Red Shield" in German. Similarly, Communism, an invention of the lodges of Jewish Illuminati Freemasonry, which the *Protocols of the Learned Elders of Zion,* boldly boasts the leaders of Zionism (another invention of Jewish Freemasonry) aggressively promoted, is symbolized by the color red. None of this is any accident. It is all quite deliberate and intentional. Red is also a symbol and the color of blood, which the Jews and Communists have shed in abundance during the 20th century.

The beast, which has the seven heads and ten horns, is explained further in later verses in this chapter. Notice that the woman herself is arrayed in purple and scarlet and decked with gold, precious stones and pearls. Purple and scarlet are the colors of the robes of archbishops and cardinals, who make up the leadership of the Roman Catholic Church under the Pope. Moreover, the Vatican is widely known to be one of the wealthiest institutions in the world, as manifested in the numerous jewels worn by the leaders of the Catholic Church in their various formal rituals and ceremonies to impress the masses.

The name on her forehead is Mystery (as in of the occult and magic), Babylon the Great, in which Babylon symbolizes evil and the practice of the occult and Mother of Harlots and Abominations of the Earth suggests that she has spawned children of like character; and indeed she has in the form of virtually every form of Christian denomination, be it Catholic, Protestant or Eastern Orthodox. They all employ the same gimmicks and tricks to suppress and silence the truth and subdue the masses psychologically and socially, which we will examine in much further detail in the following chapter.

> "And I saw the woman drunken with the blood of the saints, and with the blood of the martyrs of Jesus (Yahushua), and when I saw her, I wondered with great admiration. And the angel said unto me, Wherefore didst thou marvel? I will tell thee the mystery of the woman, and of the beast that carrieth her, which hath the seven heads and ten horns. The beast which thou sawest was, and is not; and shall ascend out of the bottomless pit, and go into perdition: and they that dwell on the earth shall wonder, whose names were not written in the book of life from the foundation of the world, when they behold the beast that was, and is not, and yet is. And here is the mind which hath wisdom. The seven heads are seven mountains, on which the woman sitteth. And there are seven kings: five are fallen, and one is, and the other is not yet come; and when he cometh, he must continue a short space. And the beast that was, and is not, even he is the eighth, and is of the seven, and goeth into perdition. And the ten horns which thou sawest are ten kings, which have received no kingdom as yet, but receive power as kings one hour with the beast. These have one mind, and shall give their power and strength unto the beast. These shall make war with the Lamb, and the Lamb shall overcome them: for he is Lord of lords, and King of kings: and they that are with him are called, and chosen, and faithful. And he saith unto me, The waters which thou sawest, where the whore sitteth, are peoples, and multitudes, and nations and tongues. And the

ten horns which thou sawest upon the beast, these shall hate the whore, and shall make her desolate and naked, and shall eat her flesh and burn her with fire. For God (Eloah) hath put in their hearts to fulfill his will, and to agree, and to give their kingdom unto the beast, until the words of God (Eloah) shall be fulfilled. And the woman which thou sawest is that great city, which reigneth over the kings of the earth." Revelation 17:6-18

Those who have studied world history, especially European history, know that the Roman Catholic Church has a long and sordid history of persecuting and torturing their opponents who challenged the absolute authority of the Pope, often with the full backing and support of kings and other political rulers. The Inquisition was one such chapter in Catholic history in which anyone who dared to challenge the practices and teachings of the Catholic Church were hideously tortured and often burned at the stake as heretics and witches, in a campaign of terror to intimidate anyone who dared challenge Rome's authority and to suppress and silence the truth of the full teachings of the Bible which, until the advent of the printing press, was tightly controlled by the Catholic priesthood and only they interpreted its contents for the masses, with many distortions, corruptions and abuses of the true teachings of the Bible.

The Jesuit order, founded out of the Alumbrados of Spain by Ignatius Loyola, a crypto-Jew, and primarily composed of fellow crypto-Jews, swore oaths reminiscent of the blood oaths of Jewish Freemasonry which followed it, swearing allegiance to the Pope on pain of death, as the Pope's assassins.[65] Today's Pope Francis is himself a Jesuit.

The Vatican has secretly been founded and ruled by crypto-Jews of the Babylonian Talmud since its inception, under a shroud of secrecy and intrigue that would boggle the minds of

---

[65] Hendrie, Edward. *Solving the Mystery of Babylon the Great: Tracking the Beast from the Synagogue to the Vatican.* 2010. pp. 51-52.

most people. This is the institution of fraud which has murdered millions of saints and martyrs for Christ and suppressed and silenced the truth over the centuries. To drink the blood of the saints alludes to the occult practice of human sacrifice and drinking of human blood, which is secretly practiced inside the highest levels of the Roman Catholic Church and the occult secret societies of the Jewish Illuminati Freemasons today.

John tells us that he wondered at the woman (the Catholic Church) with great admiration. On the outside it manifests the form of pious religiosity, wealth and power that has deceived countless many adherents of Catholicism over the centuries. Yet the angel tells John not to marvel and that he will reveal her mysteries and secrets, along with those of the beast on which she rides. Remember, the beast is the Antichrist, those impostors posing as Jews, led by the Jewish Illuminati Freemason Zionist global elite conspiracy, which has hijacked our world under a satanic cult today, employing the dark spiritual forces of the occult to enslave the majority of mankind under their satanic spell. This beast held power in Judea during the time of Jesus' ministry and was, by 95 A.D., when John wrote the Book of Revelation, defeated and dispersed by the Roman General Titus in 70 A.D., when Jerusalem and the Temple was destroyed by the Roman army in response to the rebellion and sedition of the Jewish leaders and their followers.

So at the time of John's visions, the power of the Jewish leadership was no longer, yet the angel tells John that this same power shall ascend out of the bottomless pit (a metaphor for hell) and go into perdition (ruin or destruction). That portion of the story of Revelation has not yet been fulfilled. Those that dwell on the earth, or earth dwellers, are not all human beings. They are the wicked, God's spiritual goats, His non-elect, whose names were never written in the Lamb's book of life since the foundation of the world, as are the names of all of God's elect, His chosen ones, His spiritual sheep.

Thus, we are told here that those who do not number among God's elect, will wonder at the beast, the Antichrist, and will worship him over God and Jesus. Today, we see just this happening as the world fawns over those professing to be Jews and over the rogue terrorist state of faux Israel.

The angel then explains to John that the seven heads of the beast on which the woman is riding represent the seven hills or mountains on which the woman (the Vatican or the Roman Catholic Church) sits. Rome is known as the city of seven hills, made up of the Aventine, Caelian, Capitoline, Esquiline, Palatine, Quirinal and Viminal Hills and the Vatican, the seat of the Roman Catholic Church, is located within the confines of Rome, the former capital of the Roman Empire. There is no other city in the world that has been known for the last 2,000 years as the city of seven hills other than Rome. Verse 18 clearly elaborates that the woman that John saw is that great city, which has reigned and continues to reign over the kings of the earth. In the days of John, the Roman Empire, whose capital was Rome, was the most powerful empire the world had ever seen. What could be a greater city, from John's historical perspective, than Rome? None, is the simple answer.

The angel further reveals to John that the seven heads represent and symbolize kings or empires. The angel tells John that five of these empires have come and gone, one (the Roman Empire) is in power and the seventh (the British and/or British/American Empire) has not yet come. The five empires that had come and gone by 95 A.D. likely consisted of Egypt, Assyria, Babylon, Medo-Persia and Greece. The angel further explains that the eighth head is part of the seven before it and that it (the Antichrist) goes to perdition or destruction. Moreover, the ten horns, which symbolize political and military power, symbolize ten rulers or kings who have not yet come to power, but which will receive power as kings with the beast for a short time (the passage describes it as one hour, which is not to be taken literally, but rather figuratively). The globalist's plan for a New World Order calls for ten regional governments and it is likely that this is the ten rulers and regions that this passage is referring to. It goes on to explain that these 10 regional rulers will give their power and strength to the beast, a.k.a. the Antichrist, or the Jewish Illuminati

Freemason Zionist global conspiracy, and this is what we are witnessing in our nation and world today, masked by the endless lies and foolish nonsense of our media. Few understand it for what it is, but this is what is truly going on. These, the 10 regional governments and the Jewish global conspiracy, are today waging war with the Lamb, namely Yahushua, and it tells us that Yahushua will overcome the global conspiracy, for as the passage tells us, Yahushua (Jesus) is Lord of lords and King of kings and those of us who will be with Him, as gathered and resurrected saints, are called, chosen (elect) and faithful to YHWH and to Yahushua.

Figure 2 reflects the likely 10 regional governments referred to in this passage, although in 2005 President George W. Bush illegally signed agreements with Canada and Mexico intended to merge the United States with those two countries to form the North American Union, whereas the chart depicts Mexico as part of a Central and South American region (6).[66]

Figure 2

Kingdom #	Description
1	Canada and the United States of America
2	European Union - Western Europe
3	Japan
4	Australia, New Zealand, South Africa, Israel and Pacific Islands
5	Eastern Europe
6	Latin America - Mexico, Central and South America
7	North Africa and Middle East *(Moslems)*
8	Central Africa
9	South and Southeast Asia
10	Central Asia

The angel concludes this chapter by revealing that the ten horns or regional political and military rulers upon the beast will hate the whore (the Roman Catholic Church) and will make her naked (will shame and disgrace her), eat her flesh and burn her with fire and that all this will occur because God will put it in their hearts to do such things and give their power to

---

[66] http://www.ubm1.org/tenkings.gif.

the Antichrist (the Jewish global conspiracy) until the words of the end time prophecies of God are fulfilled. The angel reveals in verse 18 that the woman, the whore, which John sees is the great city Rome which has reigned over the kings of the earth for the last 17 centuries.

Chapter 18 continues where Chapter 17 left off in revealing the destruction of Babylon the Great, the Roman Catholic Church:

> *"And after these things I saw another angel come down from heaven, having great power; and the earth was lightened with his glory. And he cried mightily with a strong voice, saying, Babylon the great is fallen, is fallen, and is become the habitation of devils, and the hold of every foul spirit, and a cage of every unclean and hateful bird. For all nations have drunk of the wine of the wrath of her fornication, and the kings of the earth have committed fornication with her, and the merchants of the earth are waxed rich through the abundance of her delicacies. And I heard another voice from heaven, saying, Come out of her, my people, that ye be not partakers of her sins, and that ye receive not of her plagues. For her sins have reached unto heaven, and God (Eloah) hath remembered her iniquities."* Revelation 18:1-5

Here, an angel of light and glory loudly announces once again that Babylon the great, who we now know to be the Roman Catholic Church, is fallen and he repeats himself, adding further emphasis to his words. He goes on to reveal that the Catholic Church is a habitation of devils, or demon spirits. Foul spirits and unclean and hateful birds are simply other ways of describing demon spirits that infest and rule the Catholic Church.

The passage goes on to repeat the revelation that all nations and earthly rulers (kings) have slept with the Catholic Church and committed immorality (fornication) with the whore of Babylon, where Babylon is a metaphor for the occult, paganism and sin.

Similarly, the Catholic Church is widely known to be rich beyond description and with that wealth it has made the merchants of the earth rich selling luxurious goods and services (delicacies) to her.

Then another voice from heaven warns God's people, the elect, to come out of the harlot church; otherwise, they will share in her sins and receive the same plagues that will be poured out upon the church of Babylon. This applies not just to those trapped inside the satanic cult and whorehouse of Roman Catholicism, but applies equally to all forms of organized religion today, which have modeled themselves after the practices of the great whore, and teach doctrines of devils that deceive the masses trapped inside of them. I will have more to reveal and say about these harlot children of the mother of harlots, the Catholic Church, in the following chapter.

As in Chapter 16, we are reminded that God has seen the sins of all forms of organized religion, and has remembered them and intends to bring punishment to them, which they so richly deserve, for misleading and deceiving so many people over the centuries.

Such fraud, deceit, betrayal and treachery on the part of all forms of organized religion ought to rightly cause the holy and the just people of God to become furious with rage over such a reprehensible abomination. The fact that few people are rightly angered over the immense evil reveals just how few people who profess to be be Christians, truly are what they claim to be. The good news is that justice is coming!

"Reward her even as she rewarded you, and double unto her double according to her works: in the cup which she hath filled fill to her double. How much she hath glorified herself, and lived deliciously, so much torment and sorrow give her: for she saith in her heart, I sit a queen, and am no widow, and shall see no sorrow. Therefore shall her plagues come in one day, death, and mourning, and famine; and she shall be utterly burned with fire: for strong is the Lord God (Adonai YHWH) who judgeth her. And the kings of the earth, who have committed fornication and lived deliciously with her, shall bewail her, and lament for her, when they shall see the smoke of her burning.

Standing afar off for the fear of her torment, saying, Alas, alas that great city Babylon, that mighty city! for in one hour is thy judgment come. And the merchants of the earth shall weep and mourn over her, for no man buyeth their merchandise any more: The merchandise of gold, and silver, and precious stones, and of pearls, and fine linen, and purple, and silk, and scarlet, and all thyine wood, and all manner vessels of ivory, and all manner vessels of most precious wood, and of brass, and iron, and marble, And cinnamon, and odours, and ointments, and frankincense, and wine, and oil, and fine flour, and wheat, and beasts, and sheep, and horses, and chariots, and slaves, and souls of men. And the fruits that thy soul lusted after are departed from thee, and all things which were dainty and goodly are departed from thee, and thou shalt find them no more at all. The merchants of these things, which were made rich by her, shall stand afar off for the fear of her torment, weeping and wailing, And saying, Alas, alas that great city, that was clothed in fine linen, and purple, and scarlet, and decked with gold, and precious stones, and pearls! For in one hour so great riches is come to nought. And every shipmaster, and all the company in ships, and sailors, and as many as trade by sea, stood afar off. And cried when they saw the smoke of her burning, saying, What city is like unto this great city! And they cast dust on their heads, and cried, weeping and wailing, saying, Alas, alas that great city, wherein were made rich all that had ships in the sea by reason of her costliness! for in one hour is she made desolate." Revelation 18:6-19

Here, the angel calls out to God to reward the Catholic Church and all other forms of apostate organized religion as they have rewarded Him, which is not at all, and to punish them double according to their works of evil, wickedness and immorality.

The angel goes on to decry how arrogantly they have glorified themselves and lived luxuriously at the expense of their many misled followers and boasted to themselves that they are like royalty and will never live to regret it. As a consequence, verse 8 tells us that God will pour out the plagues of death, mourning, famine and intense fire upon them in a single day.

This may not be literally one earthly day, but we can be sure that it will come suddenly and occur with remarkable swiftness.

The balance of this passage repeats multiple times the wailing by the merchants of the earth, who profited richly from selling luxuries to the Catholic Church and others. Clearly, in the end, the wealth of the Roman Catholic Church will be destroyed in an instant and be of no value.

The final verses of Chapter 18 turn and speak to God's elect, celebrating the justice of Almighty God which will be poured out upon the wicked, and revealing to the Catholic Church and all who are trapped inside her that her glory will be completely destroyed in the end, and her guilt over her murder of the prophets and saints of God will be completely exposed and revealed:

> "Rejoice over her, thou heaven, and ye holy apostles and prophets; for God (Eloah) hath avenged you on her. And a mighty angel took up a stone like a great millstone, and cast it into the sea, saying, Thus with violence shall that great city Babylon be thrown down, and shall be found no more at all. And the voice of the harpers, and musicians, and of pipers, and trumpeters, shall be heard no more at all in thee; and no craftsmen, of whatsoever craft he be, shall be found any more in thee; and the sound of a millstone shall be heard no more at all in thee; And the light of a candle shall shine no more at all in thee; and the voice of the bridegroom and of the bride shall be heard no more at all in thee: for thy merchants were the great men of the earth; for by thy sorceries were all nations deceived. And in her was found the blood of the prophets, and of saints, and of all that were slain upon the earth." Revelation 18:20-24

Chapter 19 continues with the voices of many in heaven giving praise, honor and glory to God for His fair and just judgments and wrath poured out upon the whore of Babylon, the Roman Catholic Church, and her spawn of all other forms of apostate and fraudulent organized religion:

"And after these things I heard a great voice of much people in heaven, saying Alleluia; Salvation, and glory, and honour, and power, unto the Lord our God (Eloah): For true and righteous are his judgments: for he hath judged the great whore, which did corrupt the earth with her fornication, and hath avenged the blood of his servants at her hand. And again they said, Alleluia. And her smoke rose up for ever and ever. And the four and twenty elders and the four beasts fell down and worshipped God (Eloah) that sat on the throne, saying, Amen; Alleluia. And a voice came out of the throne, saying, Praise our God (Eloah), all ye his servants, and ye that fear him, both small and great. And I heard as it were the voice of a great multitude, and as the voice of many waters, and as the voice of mighty thunderings, saying, Alleluia: for the Lord God (Adonai YHWH) omnipotent reigneth. Let us be glad and rejoice, and give honour to him: for the marriage of the Lamb is come, and his wife hath made herself ready. And to her was granted that she should be arrayed in fine linen, clean and white: for the fine linen is the righteousness of saints. And he saith unto me, Write **Blessed** *are they which are called unto the marriage supper of the Lamb. And he saith unto me, These are the true sayings of God (Eloah). And I fell at his feet to worship him. And he said unto me, See thou do it not: I am thy fellowservant, and of thy brethren that have the testimony of Jesus (Yahushua): worship God (Eloah): for the testimony of Jesus (Yahushua) is the spirit of prophecy."* Revelation 19:1-10 (emphasis added)

The marriage supper of the Lamb described in the second half of this passage occurs when Yahushua (Jesus), the bridegroom marries His bride, the true church, the body and community of born again believers and of God's elect, who have been previously gathered to Him in the gathering described in Matthew 24:30-31, 1 Thessalonians 4:13-17 and 1 Corinthians 15:51-55. The fine, clean and white linen in which the resurrected saints (believers) are arrayed symbolizes their righteousness, meaning their right relationship with YHWH (God).

10. The Rest of God's End Times Story

Notice here that John is commanded by a being in heaven to write "***Blessed*** are they which are called unto the marriage supper of the Lamb." This is an important clue which links back to Daniel 12:12 which describes a day, 1,335 days after the start date of the great tribulation, which began on March 22, 2013, namely November 16, 2016, which I refer to as the blessing date. This is why I believe that during the 45 day window after the end of the great tribulation up to, and possibly including, the blessing date, both the the prophecy of the gathering of Matthew 24:30-31 and the marriage supper of the Lamb of Revelation 19:7-9 must be fulfilled.

As I have revealed previously, now that we know that March 22, 2013 signaled the start of the great tribulation, via the fulfillment of the prophecy at Matthew 24:15, and knowing from Daniel 12:11-12 that the great tribulation will last 1,290 days and the blessing date will occur 1,335 days after the start (and thus 45 days after the end) of the great tribulation, we can now calculate the end date as October 2, 2016 and the blessing date as November 16, 2016, by which time the three prophecies consisting of the four celestial events described in Matthew 24:29, the gathering described in Matthew 24:30-31 and the marriage supper of the Lamb described in Revelation 19:7-9 will all be fulfilled.

Notice at the end of the above passage that the testimony of Jesus (Yahushua) is the spirit of prophecy. This appears to indicate that those who manifest the truth and love of Jesus in their lives are blessed with the the spirit or gift of prophecy. In my own case, this is at the root of what permits me to properly comprehend what end times Bible prophecy is telling us and to connect the dots between the prophecies and events which we are witnessing in our world today.

Chapter 19 then proceeds to describe the second coming of Christ (Yahushua) with His resurrected saints:

> *"And I saw heaven opened, and behold a white horse; and he that sat upon him was called Faithful and True, and in righteousness he doth judge and make war. His eyes were as a flame of fire, and on his head were many crowns, and he had a*

name written, that no man knew, but he himself. And he was clothed with a vesture dipped in blood: and his name is called The Word of God (Eloah). And the armies which were in heaven followed him upon white horses, clothed in fine linen, white and clean. And out of his mouth goeth a sharp sword, with it he should smite the nations: and he shall rule them with a rod of iron: and he treadeth the winepress of the fierceness and wrath of Almighty God (Eloah). And he hath on his vesture and on his thigh a name written, KING OF KINGS, AND LORD OF LORDS." Revelation 19:11-16

John witnesses heaven being opened and Yahushua (Jesus) riding on a white horse prepared to judge the nations and wage war upon the wicked. Here Yahushua is referred to by a number of names by which He is known and which defines His true character and authority bestowed upon Him by God: Faithful and True, The Word of God, King of kings and Lord of lords.

Notice that the armies in heaven which follow Yahushua are riding white horses and wearing garments described with identical words to those employed in Revelation 19:8. This is how we are able to discern that these souls are one and the same with the resurrected saints from the gathering and the marriage supper of the Lamb.

Verse 15 clearly reveals that Yahushua will tread the winepress of the fierceness and wrath of Almighty God upon the wicked of the earth who have been gathered together in the Valley of Megiddo (Jezreel) to oppose YHWH, Yahushua and the saints. What follows is not at all close to an even fight. The armies of the beast (the Antichrist) are annihilated by Yahushua, leaving no doubt who has been in control of world events all along: Almighty YHWH.

"And I saw an angel standing in the sun; and he cried with a loud voice, saying to all the fowls that fly in the midst of heaven, Come and gather yourselves together unto the supper of the great God (Eloah); That ye may eat the flesh of kings, and the flesh of captains, and the flesh of mighty men, and the flesh of horses, and of them that sit on them, and the flesh of all men, both free

and bond, both small and great. And I saw the beast, and the kings of the earth, and their armies, gathered together to make war on him that sat on the horse, and against his army. And the beast was taken, and with him the false prophet that wrought miracles before him, with which he deceived them that had received the mark of the beast, and them that worshipped his image. These both were cast alive into a lake of fire burning with brimstone. And the remnant were slain with the sword of him that sat on the horse, which sword proceeded out of his mouth: and all the fowls were filled with their flesh."
Revelation 19:17-21

Here we see the fowls and carrion birds of the air called by the angel standing in the sun to gather together to feast on the dead bodies of those who make up the enemies of YHWH, using the same words used to describe the elites and enemies of YHWH who hide in the rocks in Revelation 6:15.

Here, we see the beast, the kings of the earth and their armies gathered in the Valley of Megiddo (Armageddon) to make war against Yahushua and His army of resurrected saints, who follow him on white horses. Notice that there is no protracted battle. Verses 20 and 21 employ the passive voice that implies that Yahushua is the sole actor here who takes the beast (the Antichrist, the impostors posing as Jews) and the false prophet (the Roman Catholic Pope and/or the Jewish-owned and controlled media) and hurl them alive into a burning lake of fire and brimstone (a form of volcanic scorching hot rock). Then Yahushua slays the remaining army which opposes Him with a sword, which symbolizes the Word of God and the vultures and carrion birds of heaven gorge themselves on their dead bodies. It is clearly a picture of horrible death and destruction in which there is no contest. The remaining wicked of the world are annihilated in an instant.

Such a vision ought to take our breath away. Moreover, since it is all a part of God's inspired words of His Bible, it all has to be true! From what I have revealed here previously, we now know that these prophecies are on the brink of being fulfilled in just a few short years. As such, it is highly relevant to every one of us alive on the planet today. Nothing could be more important!

Once the wicked of the world have been slain by Yahushua, Chapter 20 addresses their eternal judgment. Six times in Chapter 20, Scripture refers to a thousand year reign of Christ and the souls of those who were beheaded (martyred) for their witness of Yahushua and who had not worshipped the beast (the Antichrist, namely the impostors posing as Jews, especially the Jewish Illuminati Freemason Zionist global conspiracy) or his image and had not taken the mark of the beast in their foreheads or in their hands. The language of this chapter is intentionally rather complex and is not properly understood by taking it literally. Not once does Chapter 20 say that Yahushua (Jesus) returns to earth or reigns here, although many have read this passage somewhat carelessly and assumed, without supporting evidence in Scripture to back it up, that this is what the passage means or implies. Additionally, the six references to a thousand year period in this chapter is a hint or clue that it is a symbol and metaphor and not to be understood literally, which can only be properly understood by referring to 2 Peter 3:3-13:

> *"Knowing this first, that there shall come in the last days scoffers, walking after their own lusts, And saying, Where is the promise of his coming? for since the fathers (the patriarchs) fell asleep (died), all things continue as they were from the beginning of creation. For this they willingly are ignorant of, that by the word of God (Eloah) the heavens were of old, and the earth standing out of the water and in the water: Whereby the world that then was, being overflowed with water (from Noah's flood), perished: But the heavens and the earth, which are now, by the same word (of God) are kept in store, reserved unto fire against the day of judgment and perdition (ruin) of ungodly men. **But, beloved, be not ignorant of this one thing, that one day is with the Lord (YHWH) as a thousand years, and a thousand years as one day.** The Lord (YHWH) is not slack concerning his promise, as some men count slackness; but is longsuffering to us-ward, not willing that any should perish, but that all should come to*

repentance. But the day of the Lord (YHWH) will come as a thief in the night (without prior warning and announcement); in which the heavens shall pass away with a great noise, and the elements shall melt with fervent heat, the earth also and the works that are therein shall be burned up. Seeing then that all these things shall be dissolved, what manner of persons ought ye to be in all holy conversation and godliness, Looking for and hasting unto the coming of the day of God (Eloah), wherein the heavens being on fire shall be dissolved, and the elements shall melt with fervent heat? Nevertheless we, according to his promise, look for new heavens and a new earth, wherein dwelleth righteousness." 2 Peter 3:3-13 (parentheticals and bold face added for emphasis and further clarity)

Note the bold face portion of Scripture in the above passage. It is alerting us, in the context of end times prophecy, to understand that what Scripture refers to as a thousand years, may be only as long as one 24 hour day and likewise, the reference to a day, may be as long as a thousand years. Thus, we ought to understand Chapter 20's reference to a thousand years, repeated six times, as a clue that there will be a period of time, but it is very unlikely that it will last a literal one thousand years, and it is not at all likely that it will be on earth, after the earth has been scorched by the fires of the seven vial judgments described in Chapters 16 and 17 of Revelation.

With this thinking in mind, let's examine now what Chapter 20 reveals to us:

"And I saw an angel come down from heaven, having the key of the bottomless pit and a great chain in his hand. And he laid hold on the dragon, that old serpent which is the Devil, and Satan, and bound him a thousand years (this is the first reference to a thousand years). And cast him into the bottomless pit, and shut him up, and set a seal upon him, that he should deceive the nations no more, till the thousand years (second occurrence) should be fulfilled: and after that he must be loosed a little season. And I saw thrones, and they that sat upon them (the twenty four elders of Revelation 4), and judgment was given unto them: and I saw the souls of them that were beheaded for

the witness of Jesus (Yahushua), and for the word of God (Eloah), and which had not worshipped the beast, neither his image, neither had received his mark upon their foreheads, or in their hands; and they lived and reigned with Christ (the Messiah) a thousand years (third occurrence). But the rest of the dead lived not again until the thousand years (fourth occurrence) were finished. This is the first resurrection (the gathering of God's elect described in Matthew 24:30-31 and elsewhere). Blessed and holy is he that hath part in the first resurrection: on such the second death (spiritual death in the lake of fire and brimstone) hath no power, but they shall be priests of God (Eloah) and of Christ (the Messiah), and shall reign with him a thousand years (fifth occurrence). And when the thousand years (sixth occurrence) are expired, Satan shall be loosed out of his prison (the bottomless pit where he is bound with a great chain), And he shall go out to deceive the nations which are in the four quarters of the earth, Gog and Magog, to gather them together to battle: the number of whom is as the sand of the sea. And they went up on the breadth of the earth, and compassed the camp of the saints about, and the beloved city: and fire came down from God (Eloah) out of heaven, and devoured them. And the devil that deceived them was cast into the lake of fire and brimstone, where the beast and the false prophet are, and shall be tormented day and night for ever and ever." Revelation 20:1-10

This passage appears to start by describing many events that, from today's perspective, have already been fulfilled. John's vision of an angel coming down from heaven having the key to the bottomless pit and a great chain in his hand, is a vision of Yahushua. Upon his death on the cross, Yahushua bound the devil, Satan for a figurative thousand years. In reality, it has been nearly two thousand years since Yahushua died on the cross and defeated his arch-enemy, the devil, by doing so. Yahushua's perfect sacrifice of the Lamb of God put a lid on evil and wickedness since that time, until the great tribulation began on March 22, 2013, which will last 1,290 days. This appears to be the "little season" that Satan must be loosed into.

Next we see the 24 elders (the 12 patriarchs and the 12 Apostles) who reign with Christ in heaven (not necessarily on earth) for the next 2,000 years, which this passage describes as a figurative thousand year reign, which concludes with the gathering of the saints (God's elect) described in Matthew 24:30-31 and elsewhere, which is described as the "first resurrection" here. For those of us who are gathered right after the end of the great tribulation, our reign with Yahushua will be quite brief: well less than a literal one thousand years.

The rest of the dead who do not live again until the thousand years are finished are the wicked, God's non-elect, His spiritual goats, who will be judged at the great white throne judgment we are about to examine together.

Then we see Satan loosed out of his prison, the bottomless pit at the end of the thousand years, to deceive the nations (a description consistent with the one Yahushua gives us for the great tribulation) to gather them together, which is consistent with the descriptions of Revelation 16:16 and 19:19 of the gathering of all those opposed to Yahushua and His army of saints in the Valley of Megiddo, or Armageddon. The passage describes this army of God-haters who surround the camp of the saints (God's elect, born-again Christians) and the beloved city (a reference to spiritual Jerusalem, where God's people dwell in spirit).

Now we see how the army of Satan and the Antichrist will be destroyed in the end that is referred to in the passive voice in Revelation 19:21: fire will come down from God (YHWH) out of heaven and devour them. At the conclusion of this battle of Armageddon against the armies of Gog and Magog (a likely reference to the king of Magog and his country which appears to be an allegorical reference to Khazaria, the true ancestral homeland of those impostors who claim to be Jews today, and are not), Satan is cast into the burning lake of fire and brimstone where the beast (the Antichrist who are impostors posing as Jews, led by the Jewish Illuminati Freemason Zionist global elites) and the false prophet (the Roman Catholic Pope and/or the Jewish-owned and controlled media) have already been thrown, where all three of them will be tormented day and night for ever and ever. This fate is fitting justice for the unending wickedness, injustices, cruelty, treachery, deceit and betrayals that these foul rulers of mankind have perpetrated upon all of humanity for centuries.

YHWH is a God of holiness and justice and in the end, His wrath poured out upon the wicked avenges the deaths, oppression and affliction that these scum of the earth have perpetrated upon God's elect, His people, throughout the last 6,000 years. Justice will finally be done.

In the last five verses of Chapter 20, we see what will happen to the wicked, who opposed God and His people during their lifetimes:

> *"And I saw a great white throne, and him that sat on it, from whose face the earth and the heaven fled away; and there was found no place for them. And I saw the dead, small and great, stand before God; and the books were opened: and another book was opened, which is the book of life: and the dead were judged out of those things which were written in the books, according to their works. And the sea gave up the dead which were in it; and death and hell delivered up the dead which were in them: and they were judged every man according to their works. And death and hell were cast into the lake of fire. This is the second death. And whosoever was not found written in the book of life was cast into the lake of fire."* Revelation 20:11-15

This passage is describing the great white throne judgment of God in which all those who have ever lived, who did not number among God's born again adopted sons and daughters, His elect, His spiritual sheep, namely the wicked who are God's non-elect and His spiritual goats, are judged by God according to their works (deeds) done while they lived.

YHWH's face and countenance is so powerful and fearsome that the earth and heaven flee from his presence and are no more; there is no place for them in YHWH's creation any longer and there is no place for the wicked to hide. Then John sees the dead of the non-elect who are resurrected in immortal bodies, much as God's elect are raised in immortal, resurrected bodies in the gathering that precedes this great white throne judgment upon the wicked. All the works of the wicked are written in books before God, and the book of life of the Lamb of God, containing all the names of God's elect since before the world began, is opened. Anyone whose name is not written in the book of life (signifying that they are one of God's elect), are thrown into the lake of fire where the beast (the Antichrist), the false prophet (the Roman Catholic Pope and/or the Jewish-owned and controlled media) and the devil were thrown before, to be subjected to torment day and night for ever and ever.

Such an eternity is more horrible than anyone can possibly imagine. And yet mankind, in their state of total depravity, without God's Holy Spirit in them, universally are incapable of doing that which is good, true, loving and kind and since all of us have sinned and fall short of the glory of God, and since the wages of sin is death, we all deserve the burning lake of fire and brimstone.

Only God's elect, with God's Holy Spirit in us, are seen by God as righteous, not because of anything we did to deserve it, but because He chose us to receive His free gift of grace and mercy and to enjoy the righteousness of Christ imputed to us, as He bore the punishment for our sins — all of them! In verse 14, even death and hell are thrown into the lake of fire, thus putting an end to death and hell (a holding area for the wicked who have died) forever.

Chapter 21 begins to reveal what God's elect, His resurrected people, can expect to experience once the end times are over.

> *"And I saw a new heaven and a new earth: for the first heaven and the first earth were passed away; and there was no more sea. And I John saw the holy city, new Jerusalem, coming down from God ((Eloah) out of heaven, prepared as a bride adorned for her husband. And I heard a great voice out of heaven saying, Behold, the tabernacle of God (Eloah) is with men, and he will dwell with them, and they shall be his people, and God (Eloah)*

*himself shall be with them, and be their God (Eloah). And God (Eloah) shall wipe away all tears from their eyes; and there shall be no more death, neither sorrow, nor crying, neither shall there be any more pain: for the former things are passed away. And he that sat upon the throne said, Behold, I make all things new. And he said unto me, Write: for these words are true and faithful. And he said unto me, It is done. I am Alpha and Omega, the beginning and the end. I will give unto him that is athirst of the fountain of the water of life freely. He that overcometh shall inherit all things; and I will be his God (Eloah), and he shall be my son. But the fearful, and unbelieving, and the abominable, and murderers, and whoremongers, and sorcerers, and idolaters, and all liars, shall have their part in the lake which burneth with fire and brimstone: which is the second death. "*Revelation 21:1-8

We are told in several places in the Bible that this earth will not last forever; that it is perishing, and indeed it is. But we need not despair. God has had a plan all along for this heaven and earth to pass away and that He will create a new heaven and earth in their places in which YHWH (God) Himself will reside with His resurrected saints (born again elect believers).

Verse 4 tells us that the new earth will not be like the present one. God promises to do way with all tears, sadness, death and pain which were necessary in this life to discipline, chasten, test, refine and mature His elect into the likeness of the character of His son, Yahushua (Jesus). YHWH tells John to write that He is the Alpha and the Omega, the first and last letters of the Greek alphabet, signifying that God is the beginning and end of all things and that anyone who seeks life, God will freely and abundantly supply it to them from the fountain of the water of life, a symbol or metaphor for the source of all life.

God goes on to tell John that those who overcome (meaning to overcome the world, the flesh and the devil) shall inherit all things and God will be his God and he shall be God's adopted son forever.

Then God contrasts the eternal destination of and promise to His elect, with the attributes of those who must suffer the second (spiritual) death in the burning lake of fire and brimstone. Those who are fearful (cowardly), unbelieving (of God and all He says), those who commit sins that God's Word deems abominations (homosexuality comes to mind here), murderers, whoremongers (pimps), those who engage in the occult and the magic arts, and all liars will end up in the burning lake of fire, He tells us.

Notice how God makes it very clear that all liars will find their end in this place of eternal torment. Once again, this underscores and reveals how the truth and God are inseparable, and how lies, liars and the devil are equally inseparable. The blessing of those of us who are of the truth is eternal life. The fate of those who lie and deceive others, is eternal death, torment, shame, disgrace and damnation.

Can anything justify making a choice in favor of lying and experiencing the hideous and unending consequences that are attached to such a choice? Absolutely not! Nothing could be more foolish! Yet the vast majority of mankind that has ever lived, has chosen the path of eternal and spiritual death, separated from a loving and right relationship with God, the creator of all things! Something is clearly twisted and broken in the psyche of man and it is! We are all totally depraved, the heart is desperately wicked and there is no good thing in us, apart from the love of Yahushua (Jesus Christ), the Bible tells us in Jeremiah 17:9.

The eternal fate of the majority of mankind proves decisively, that without God having chosen us since before the world began, we are eternally screwed. Hence, those of us blessed enough to become born again in God's Holy Spirit, who walk in truth and in agape love are in the distinct minority of all of mankind and have every reason to be eternally grateful to God who did it all for us, so that we might live with Him in love, peace, joy and fellowship forever.

None of us did anything to earn this free gift, and hence, we have no room for pride or boasting. The only suitable response is eternal gratitude to and love for God who chose us from the beginning of the world. It is almost too wonderful to grasp! And who gets all the honor, praise and glory in all of this? YHWH (God) does, of course, as He so richly deserves!

John continues,

> *"And there came unto me one of the seven angels which had the seven vials full of the seven last plagues, and talked with me, saying, Come hither, I will shew thee the bride, the Lamb's wife. And he carried me away in the spirit to a great and high mountain, and showed me that great city, the holy Jerusalem, descending out of heaven from God (Eloah), Having the glory of God (Eloah): and her light was like unto a stone most precious, and even like a jasper stone, clear as crystal; And had a wall great and high, and had twelve gates, and at the gates were twelve angels, and names written thereon, which are the names of the twelve tribes of the children of Israel: On the east three gates; on the north three gates; on the south three gates; and on the west three gates. And the wall of the city had twelve foundations, and in them the names of the twelve apostles of the Lamb. And he that talked with me had a golden reed to measure the city, and the gates thereof, and the wall thereof. And the city lieth foursquare, and the length is as large as the breadth: and he measured the city with the reed, twelve thousand furlongs. The length and the breadth and the height of it are equal. And he measured the wall thereof, an hundred and forty four cubits, according to the measure of a man, that is of the angel. And the building of the wall of it was of jasper: and the city was pure gold, like unto clear glass. And the foundations of the wall of the city were garnished with all manner of precious stones. The first foundation was jasper; the second sapphire; the third, a chalcedony; the fourth an emerald; The fifth, sardonyx, the sixth, sardius; the seventh, chrysolite; the eighth, beryl; the ninth, a topaz; the tenth, a chrysoprasus; the eleventh, a jacinth; the twelfth, an amethyst. And the twelve gates were twelve pearls; every several gate was of one pearl: and the street of the city was pure gold, as it were transparent glass. And I saw no temple therein: for the Lord God Almighty (Adonai YHWH) and the Lamb are the temple of it. And*

the city had no need of the sun, neither of the moon, to shine in it: for the glory of God (Eloah) did lighten it: and the Lamb is the light thereof. And the nations of them which are saved shall walk in the light of it: and the kings of the earth do bring their glory and honour into it. And the gates of it shall not be shut at all by day: for there shall be no night there. And they shall bring the glory and honour of the nations into it. And there shall in no wise enter into it any thing that defileth, neither whatsoever worketh abomination, or maketh a lie; but they which are written in the Lamb's book of life." Revelation 21:9-27

In this passage, John gives us a vision of the city of new Jerusalem, which one of the angels which had carried the seven vial judgments describes as the wife of the Lamb (Yahushua), from the marriage supper of the Lamb, which is described in Revelation 19:7-9 which we have already looked at. The metaphor of the wife of the Lamb reveals the harmony and unity with which Yahushua and all resurrected born again saints and the elect of God enjoy with one another.

John goes on to describe the city as having a high wall and twelve gates, three on each side of the city that he describes as a cube of equal width, depth and height of 12,000 furlongs or 1,500 miles per side. The walls are described has having a height of 144 cubits or 216 feet. Each of the twelve gates bears the name of one of the twelve Hebrew tribes of the children of Israel or Jacob, and the walls of the city have twelve foundations bearing the names of the twelve apostles of the Lamb (Yahushua or Jesus). Twelve is a number of completeness and wholeness. John describes the foundations, the walls, gates and the streets of this new Jerusalem to be made out of precious stones, pearls and gold, respectively, and God and Jesus (Yahushua) are the source of perpetual light in it. There is no night (symbolizing darkness and sin) and the only ones who come into it will be God's elect, whose names are written in the Lamb's book of life and nothing that might defile it, make an abomination or a lie will be able to enter it.

Chapter 22 continues John's story:

"And he showed me a pure river of water of life, clear as crystal, proceeding out of the throne of God (Eloah) and of the Lamb. In the midst of the street of it, and on either side of the river, was there the tree of life, which bare twelve manner of fruits, and yielded her fruit every month: and the leaves of the tree were for the healing of the nations. And there shall be no more curse: but the throne of God (Eloah) and of the Lamb shall be in it; and his servants shall serve him: And they shall see his face; and his name shall be in their foreheads. And there shall be no night there; and they need no candle, neither light of the sun; for our Lord God (Adonai YHWH) giveth them light: and they shall reign for ever and ever. And he said unto me, These sayings are faithful and true: and the Lord God (Adonai YHWH) of the holy prophets sent his angel to shew unto his servants the things which must shortly be done. Behold, I come quickly: blessed is he that keepeth the sayings of the prophecy of this book. And I John saw these things, and heard them. And when I had heard and seen, I fell down to worship before the feet of the angel which showed me these things. Then saith he unto me, See thou do it not: for I am thy fellowservant, and of thy brethren the prophets, and of them which keep the sayings of this book: worship God (Eloah). And he saith unto me, Seal not the sayings of the prophecy of this book: for the time is at hand. He that is unjust, let him be unjust still: and he which is filthy, let him be filthy still: and he that is righteous, let him be righteous still: and he that is holy, let him be holy still. And behold, I come quickly; and my reward is with me, to give every man according as his work shall be. I am Alpha and Omega, the beginning and the end, the first and the last. Blessed are they that do his commandments, that they may have right to the tree of life, and may enter in through the gates to the city. For without are dogs, and sorcerers, and whoremongers, and murderers, and idolaters, and whosoever loveth and maketh a lie. I Jesus (Yahushua) have sent mine angel to testify unto you those things in the churches. I am the root and the offspring of David, and the bright and morning star. And the Spirit and the bride say, Come. And let him that is athirst come. And

whosoever will, let him take the water of life freely."
Revelation 22:1-17

Here we are being given a glimpse into the new earth in which YHWH (God) and Yahushua (Jesus the Lamb of God) will live with all of God's resurrected elect which is a picture of life with the river of life flowing out of the throne of God and on either side of it are the tree of life which bears a different fruit every month for twelve months of the year. This appears to be the same tree of life that appears in the Garden of Eden referred to in Genesis 3:22-24 which God drove man from after the fall of Adam and Eve. Now it is being restored to God's chosen people. Likewise, we are told that there will be no more curse from the fall. This means that husbands and wives will no longer compete with one another for control in marriage, man shall no longer labor with the sweat of his brow for his daily sustenance from the earth and women will no longer suffer pain in childbirth. Now God and Jesus will be in the midst of His people, who will serve Him, they shall see His face and His name shall be in their foreheads, meaning foremost on their minds and hearts. We are further told once again that there will be no need of the sun, for God will be their light and they will reign (as kings) for ever and ever.

We clearly see the angel telling John that in this present world there will continue to be the unjust and the filthy and the righteous and the holy and that when Jesus returns He will give to each man the rewards and punishments that his works deserve. We see that only those who do or obey the commandments of Jesus will be blessed, have access to the tree of eternal life and be permitted to enter in through the gates to the holy city described here. Outside the city will be those who we were told previously will be thrown into the burning lake of fire and brimstone described as dogs, sorcerers, whore mongers murderers, idolaters and all those who love and speak lies.

Finally, the Book of Revelation leaves us with this stern and grave warning:

"For I testify unto every man that heareth the testimony of the prophecy of this book, If any man shall add unto these things, God (Eloah) shall add unto him the plagues that are written in this book: And if any man shall take away from the words of the book of this prophecy, God (Eloah) shall take away his part out of the book of life, and out of the holy city, and from the things which are written in this book." Revelation 22:18-19

God's flawless, complete and inspired words of the Bible are telling those of us who are His born again elect, who embody integrity and are of the truth, that there are no more prophecies of what is to come. This is it! Moreover, anyone who dares add to it or subtract from it will not enjoy eternal life on the new earth in the new Jerusalem with YHWH (God), Yahushua (Jesus) and His resurrected born again elect. It's really that simple!

Yet in the last 150 years we have seen a reported 33,000 different allegedly Christian denominations arise, all of whom claim, falsely we shall see, exclusivity to the truth of God and of the Bible and what it says, means, and how it applies to our lives. The logical law of contradiction reveals that at most one of them can be true, since they all conflict with each other. Those who think or claim otherwise, simply are not thinking clearly or logically and in the end will find themselves eternally separated from God, Jesus and the resurrected believers in Christ from all time, and from eternal life. This is what God's flawless and inspired words tell us: no liars allowed!

We are told by Jesus in Matthew 22:14 that "many are called, but few are chosen." Chosen, elect, with their names written in the Lamb's book of life since before the world began are all synonyms for those whom God chose by His mercy and grace alone, to one day become His born again adopted sons and daughters, at a time and in a manner of His choosing, and at His initiative – not ours – so that no man may boast that he did anything to deserve salvation and eternal life. None of us ever did, other than Jesus. Such a proper understanding of what the Bible clearly teaches can only result in humility and profound gratitude beyond words, to those of us who are blessed enough to have been chosen by God from all the billions of people who have ever lived on the planet over the past 6,000 years.

The reality that the vast majority of humanity, including those trapped, deceived and misled in all forms of apostate organized religion today, were created by God to afflict and oppress His elect during their lifetimes, and then to ultimately be thrown into the burning lake of fire and brimstone for the wicked deeds they did in life is very sad. In fact, it breaks my heart. But I now understand that there was no other way to test, refine, discipline, mature and make wise God's elect through trials, suffering, persecution and the hatred of the world. Such is the divine purpose of the great tribulation, in which we are now living, which only the wise can understand. Daniel 12:10 tells us just this:

> *"Many shall be purified, and made white, and tried (meaning God's elect); but the wicked (meaning all others who number among God's non-elect) shall do wickedly:* **and none of the wicked shall understand; but the wise shall understand.***"*

Those forms of organized religion that have added to the prophecies of the Book of Revelation, as have the Mormons with their Book of Mormon, Pearl of Great Price and Doctrine and Covenants, are clearly in defiance of and in disobedience to Revelation 22:18-19. God makes it very clear in His Word what the eternal consequences are to those who disobey the commandments of God and of Jesus: it is always spiritual death. Likewise, many modern day translations of the Bible (other than the 1611 KJV) which are idea-for-idea translations or paraphrases of the original Hebrew and Greek manuscripts of the Bible are equally guilty of adding to or subtracting from or in some way distorting the teachings of God from His holy words, which are faithful, true and flawless in every regard. While verses 18 and 19 of Chapter 22 refer to anything which adds to or subtracts from this book, meaning the Book of Revelation, God chooses His every word deliberately and carefully and so it seems quite apparent to me that He intends His warnings here to include all 66 books of the Old and New Testament of the Bible in a sweeping warning. This view is further supported by the warning of Proverbs 30:5-6:

> *"Every word of God (YHWH) is pure: he is a shield unto them that put their trust in him.* **Add thou not unto his words, lest he reprove thee, and thou be found a liar.***"*

The bottom line is that God is sovereign, all-wise, all-powerful, all-knowing, all-seeing, holy, just, loving, merciful, kind, long-suffering and the source of all truth. His Word tells us repeatedly to fear God. That's no mistake in translation or in our understanding of that word. We are not to live in terror of God. He is neither arbitrary, nor capricious. But God is not to be trifled with or taken as a fool, either. He is most assuredly no fool and He has zero tolerance for anyone trying to test Him or con Him.

Most of Christendom today does just this: it tries to redefine God into its own desire for God to be an indulgent and rather impotent father who is too weak and stupid to hold his errant children accountable for their wicked and hurtful actions and words. Yet that is not at all the nature and character of the perfect God of the universe who has created all things merely by speaking them into existence. Unlike sinful man, God is of perfect honesty, integrity and wisdom and has zero tolerance for those who try to remake Him in the image of their wishful thinking or who seek to twist and distort His nature and any doctrine which He has clearly revealed in Scripture to mankind. Anyone trying to do such a thing is walking on very thin ice, dishonors and disrespects God and is likely to break through and drown.

John concludes the Book of Revelation with these words:

> *"He which testifieth these things saith, Surely I come quickly. Amen. Even so, come, Lord Jesus (Adon Yahushua). The grace of our Lord Jesus Christ (Adon Yahushua the Messiah) be with you all. Amen."* Revelation 22:20-21

These words were penned by the Apostle John over 1,900 years ago. By man's standards, that's hardly evidence of Jesus coming quickly. But we must remember that to God and to Jesus, a day is like a thousand years and a thousand years is as if it were a day. In the context of eternity, 1,900 years is but an instant of time. Yet just as in our day in which true believers in Christ are longing for Jesus' second coming to occur quickly, John is calling upon Him in his day to come quickly. For the last 2,000 years, God's elect have longed for the coming of Yahushua. Today, we are on the brink of that happening, in less than 20 months! In an instant, that day will be here, at last.

11. Revealing the Apostasy and Fraud of Organized Religion

In my own spiritual journey over the past ten years I have spent time within ten separate institutional churches or para-church organizations. Every one of them revealed themselves to be teaching and living out false doctrines which overtly conflicted with one of more teachings of the Bible, or in which the leader suffered from a serious case of pride and a need to control and manipulate his flock to bring honor and glory to himself, rather than to Jesus. This latter evidence of a deficient and immature character of most, if not all, leaders of any form of organized religion is no accident. The Bible predicts this will happen in the end times right before Yahushua returns, in three places:

> *"Let no man deceive you by any means: for that day (the day of the second coming of Yahushua) shall not come,* **except there come a falling away first,** *and that man of sin be revealed, the son of perdition;"* 2 Thessalonians 2:3

> *"This know also, that* **in the last days perilous times shall come.** *For men shall be* **lovers of their own selves,** *covetous, boasters,* **proud,** *blasphemers, disobedient to parents, unthankful, unholy,* **Without natural affection,** *trucebreakers,* **false accusers,** *incontinent, fierce,* **despisers of those that are good,** *Traitors, heady, highminded, lovers of pleasures more than lovers of God (Eloah);* **Having a form of godliness but denying the power thereof: from such turn away.** *For of this sort are they which creep into houses, and lead captive silly women laden with sins, led away with divers lusts, Ever*

learning, and never able to come to the knowledge of the truth."
2 Timothy 3:1-7

"For the time will come when they will not endure sound doctrine; but after their own lusts shall they heap to themselves teachers, having itching ears; **And they shall turn away their ears from the truth, and shall be turned unto fables.***"* 2 Timothy 4:3-4

One of the two things that must happen before Yahushua returns in His second coming is that a falling away or apostasy of all forms of organized religion must occur in which the teachings of those institutional churches depart from and conflict materially with what the words of Scripture say, mean and teach. This is what 1 Thessalonians 2:3 teaches us and my own experience proves this with 100% of those churches or para-church organizations I have been a part of over the past decade, proving themselves to not be of the truth and to lack sacrificial love for their fellow man. As such, every one of those forms of organized religion serves the devil, and not Jesus.

2 Timothy 3:1-7 reveals that many in the last days (the end times) will have a form of godliness, but be frauds and fakes and Paul tells his disciple Timothy, and us, to have nothing to do with them. This passage goes on to reveal that these demon-controlled frauds of false religion will creep into houses and lead silly women astray. Why does Paul single out women here? Because he knows that women are the weaker vessel and easier to deceive than men are. And we see this in virtually all forms of false religion today in which the women are flattered by the church leadership and the men are emasculated and passive do-nothings who fail to protect their women and children from harm and error.

In 2 Timothy 4:3-4, we see that sound doctrine will be rejected in favor of "feel good" messages of false teachers who tell their deceived flocks what they want to hear rather than the truth of what God's Word, the Bible, says. Televangelist pastors today, such as Joel Osteen and Rick Warren, are disgraceful examples of this very phenomenon, which is far more the rule, than the exception, today.

In August 2013 God spoke these very words to me:

"All forms of organized religion are, and always have been, demonic."

At first, this struck me as a bit of an over-reach. But as I sat and contemplated what He had just told me, reflecting on my own numerous unfortunate experiences with organized religion, and having studied its serious structural flaws, which doom virtually any church to fall into the hands of demonic spirits sooner or later, I realized that once again, He was right. Here's why:

1. Organized religion, which took its lead from the formation of the Roman Catholic Church in 310 A.D. under the Roman Emperor Constantine, who declared Roman Catholicism to be Christianity (it wasn't) and declared Christianity (and therefore Roman Catholicism) to be the official religion of the Roman Empire, almost universally reflects several attributes which enable it to manipulate, control and deceive its followers quite effectively:

    a. A full time paid and educated clergy class leads the church rituals, ceremonies and teachings, to whom the lay people (everyone else) defer and whom they obey.

    b. A building is secured in which church ceremonies are conducted which carries its own financial overhead in terms of a mortgage, maintenance and ongoing operating expenses.

    c. The financial overhead of a paid clergy and building mortgage dictates the need to solicit the lay people for contributions of money in the form of tithes and offerings.

    d. Whenever money is involved, a committee of men determines how much cash can be spent based on how much is collected. Whenever cash in is less than cash out, this committee or board of men must figure out how to increase giving. The easiest way to do this, is to water down the truth of the message and preach lies that tickle the ears of their hearers.

In short, whenever men, money and power come together, human nature and the total depravity of man dictates that corruption cannot be far behind. This paradigm explains virtually all forms of organized and fraudulent religion today. It is designed to fail and to deceive and it accomplishes just what it is designed to do!

2. Additionally, most forms of organized religion in America are agents of our corrupt and deceitful government and the global elites who control it. This is accomplished through the income tax law (which was never legitimately and properly ratified as the 16th Amendment to the U.S. Constitution) and the operations of the Internal Revenue Service (IRS), which grants tax exempt status to both churches and clergy in the form of 501c3 tax exempt status for non-profit corporations of a religious nature, provided that they agree to comply with a number of terms dictated by the IRS. I urge all readers to go to the following link and read the entire article by Lorraine Day, M.D.:

http://goodnewsaboutgod.com/studies/spirit ual/the_organized_church/501c3.htm.

Here is the list of things which any 501c3 organization is prohibited from doing to maintain its 501c3 IRS status, which no church needs anyway, because of the protections of the First Amendment of the United States Constitution, derived from Dr. Day's article:

According to the IRS, 501c3 Christian churches, ministries, and organizations may NOT do any of the following:

1. Expose conspiracies.

2. Criticize the New World Order

3. Say or publish anything negative about ANY politician, Republican or Democrat.

4. Criticize government agencies and bureaus – the IRS, FBI, BATF, CIA, EPA, DEA, OSHA, DOJ, etc.

5. Criticize an institution of government such as the White House, the Congress, the Federal Reserve Board (even though this is a private corporation) or the Supreme Court.

6. Encourage citizens to call or write their congressman, senator, governor, mayor, or other public official.

7. Criticize any proposed or pending bill or legislation that would take away the rights and freedoms of the people.

8. Make disparaging remarks about, or criticize, any other faith group, cult, or religion.

9. Expose or criticize the New Age Movement.

10. Support or encourage a law-abiding citizens' militia (even though this is constitutional).

11. Support or encourage the Second Amendment, the right of the people to keep and bear arms.

12. Discourage young women from getting an abortion, or endorse the pro-life movement.

13. Teach that abortion, especially partial birth abortion, is murder and is the killing of innocent babies.

14. Identify homosexuality as a sin and an abomination to God.

15. Express an opinion on any subject or issue.

16. Appeal to peoples' emotions by employing an evangelization method (such as "fire and brimstone" preaching) not considered a "reasoned approach" by the IRS.

17. Discuss or identify threats to Christianity.

18. Discuss subjects or topics the IRS deems "sensationalist."

19. Criticize well-known public figures or institutions the IRS deems "worthy," such as the super-rich elite, international bankers, the Hollywood movie industry, etc.

20. Publish or broadcast information on any topic without giving credence to the opposing viewpoints of Christ's enemies.

21. Publish and offer books, tapes, or products that expose the elitist plot against humanity and God.

22. Criticize the Pope or the Vatican, or contrast the New Catholic Catechism with the truths found in the Holy Bible. (Note: only liberal churches are permitted by the IRS to criticize the Catholic Church).

23. Criticize the United Nations or such globalist groups as the Council on Foreign Relations, the Bilderbergers, and the Trilateral Commission.

24. Criticize the Masonic Lodge, the Order of Skull & Bones, or other secret societies.

25. Highlight or otherwise bring attention to immorality of public officials or corruption in government.

26. Complain of government wrongdoing or injustice, such as happened at Waco, Ruby Ridge, and elsewhere.

27. Criticize the Jewish ADL or other Jewish lobby groups.

28. Say anything positive about the "religious right" or the "patriot movement."

29. Support home schooling, home churches, or unregistered churches.

30. Spend money on missionary projects or charitable causes not approved by the IRS.

31. Promote or encourage alternative healthcare (herbs, vitamins, etc.).

32. Expose false teachings of any kind by anyone.

33. Support or encourage persecuted Christians suffering under anti-Christian regimes in Red China, Cuba, Russia, Israel, Saudi Arabia, the United States, and elsewhere.

34. Ordain a pastor whose training or qualifications are not approved by the IRS.

35. Advocate or teach any Bible doctrine that is politically or religiously incorrect, or is inconsistent with any "public policy" (abortion, feminism, gay rights, etc.) currently being enforced by the IRS.

Additional requirements for 501c3 churches are found in the Department of the Treasury Internal Revenue Service Publication 1826 (9-94) Cat. No. 21096G, in which churches must:

36. Have a recognized creed and "IRS approved form of worship."

37. Have "IRS approved code of doctrine and discipline."

38. Have ordained ministers educated in "state accredited colleges."

39. Pastor must answer to the IRS as to "daily activities of the church."

40. The IRS must be privy to "all financial transactions" of the church.

41. Pastor must supply "names of all donors" – make books, records available.

42. Be neutral on political issues.

43. Be engaged in activities furthering exclusively public purposes.

44. Open its services to the public.

45. Submit names of all church workers; pastors, teachers, clerks, counselors, educational directors, office help, associates, and maintenance personnel.

46. Not publicly oppose licensing of church ministries.

47. Give unlimited submission to civil magistrates pertaining to all laws – federal, state, and local – including public policy.

48. May only use "IRS approved" fundraising methods.

49. Pastor will be "called to account over any stand taken against the tax system."

50. Church "must advocate and support racial integration." (Multiculturalism)

51. May NOT engage in activities "opposing pornography."

52. May NOT support legislation saying "children belong to parents" rather than "the state."

53. May NOT form a Political Action Committee nor support legislation "opposing lotteries and gambling activity."

54. May not "oppose the public school system."

55. May "not publicly declare" we are to "obey God rather than the government."

56. May not advocate support of the United States or state constitutions as the supreme law of the land. (Public policy takes precedence).

In other words, as Dr. Day has rightly concluded from this reprehensible list of restrictions most "Christian" churches have agreed to comply with,

> **The "Christian" Church has been gutted.** It has had its "heart" and all of its inward parts removed just as completely as a slaughter-house

animal on its way to being dismembered for market. The "Church" can SAY nothing and DO nothing."

Any church leadership which agrees to these terms has sold its soul to the enemy, the devil, the father of lies, and is ruled by demon spirits today. It's that simple and this serious!

3. To add insult to injury, credible reports on the internet indicate that a DHS or FEMA program has existed since 2006 or earlier, in which one or both of these federal agencies is paying 25,000 to 50,000 pastors $40,000 a year to spy on the members of their congregations and report any "suspicious activity" to federal antiterrorist agencies, when in reality, it is our federal government and the Jewish Illuminati Freemason Zionist global elite conspiracy which is terrorizing law-abiding patriotic Americans who want no part of their hell on earth New World Order horror.

To state plainly that America's pastors are traitors, frauds and servants of the father of lies, the devil, is no understatement in the least. Every man, woman and child in America ought to be outraged by these fraudulent pastors for their immorality, their deceit and their lack of integrity! This reason alone is more than sufficient reason to leave all forms of organized religion immediately and force them to close their doors because they have no paying customers.

Now let us turn and examine just how far some of the largest, well-known and one of the fastest growing churches of organized religion in America have departed from the truth of the teachings of the Bible in their entirety, which will prove conclusively that the falling away of the end times prophecy of 2 Thessalonians 2:3 has indeed occurred with hair-splitting accuracy. The sad reality is that all forms of organized religion are so corrupt and deceitful, that they are beyond saving. They are nothing more than whore houses which are doing the work of the devil to deceive many with false "feel good" messages that are keeping the spiritual goats trapped inside those houses of ill-repute on the road to hell that we all were born into. Imagine these people's sense of anger and betrayal when they discover how badly they have been misled by these false teachers and false prophets of fraudulent organized religion! Their treachery and deceit is beyond comprehension or excuse and the Apostle Paul teaches in Galatians 1:8-9 what their eternal fate will be:

> *"But though we, or an angel from heaven, preach any other gospel unto you than that which we have preached unto you, **let him be accursed.** As we said before, so say I now again, If any man preach any other gospel unto you than that ye have received, **let him be accursed.**"*

This is also why the voice in heaven in Revelation 18:4-5 urges all of God's people to come out of the harlot church of Roman Catholicism, which pertains to all the other harlot churches of organized religion today as well:

> *"And I heard another voice from heaven, saying, Come out of her my people, that ye be not partakers of her sins, and that yet receive not of her plagues. For her sins have reached unto heaven, and God (Eloah) hath remembered her iniquities."*

In a moment we will examine a few specific examples of harlot churches to examine their common tricks, treacheries and false teachings that contradict the teachings of the Bible in its entirety, and thus, according to the logical law of contradiction, cannot possibly be true. As such, they have to be lies from the father of lies, the devil himself, and will save nobody. Our methodology for challenging several major denominations of false organized religion is quite simple. We start by accepting the Bible to be precisely what it claims to be: the pure and inspired words of God to mankind. Then we will examine some of the core teachings of select denominations of allegedly Christian churches which from my studies I know to be at odds with what the Bible teaches and explain what the differences are so that you, my readers, can see just how fraudulent these harlot churches truly are. What is vitally important for you to grasp is that none of this is any accident: it is deliberate and intentional. These harlot churches are ruled by demon spirits who have taken over the leadership of these various churches and secretly serve the devil, and not Jesus Christ at all!

According to the Pew Research Center, as of December 2012, self-professed Christians number 2.2 billion people, or roughly 32% of the world's population of roughly 7.0 billion people. Roughly half (50%) of this 2.2 billion, or 1.1 billion people, are Catholic, 37% or 800 million belong to the Protestant tradition, broadly defined to include Anglicans as well as independent and nondenominational churches. The Orthodox Communion, including the Greek and Russian Orthodox, make up 12% or 260 million of this number. People who belong to other traditions that view themselves as Christian (including Christian Scientists, Mormons and Jehovah Witnesses) make up about 1% or 30 million of the global Christian population.

What I hope to demonstrate here is that the vast majority of the 2.2 billion people who view themselves to be followers of Christ, and hence Christians, are not that at all: instead, the vast majority of these people are affiliated with various forms of religious cults which are fraudulent forms of Christianity, that save no one. In his book, *New Age Cults and Religions*, author Texe Marrs, who has written extensively on the New Age and many aspects of the global conspiracy, defines a cult as *"a body or organized group of activists or believers who have involved themselves in a social movement in opposition to the clear and direct Word of God."* By this clear standard, the vast majority of self-professing Christians are cult members and not true born again followers of Christ of the Bible at all! This conclusion has serious ramifications for the vast majority of self-professing Christians on the planet today who falsely believe they are saved, when in fact they are not. Instead, they are deeply deceived and defrauded by the charlatans of all forms of false, apostate organized religion and the harlot church. There is only one remedy for this:

> *"Having a form of godliness, but denying the power thereof:* **from such turn away.**" 2 Timothy 3:5

11. Revealing the Apostasy and Fraud of Organized Religion

For many people who have spent much time as part of any form of organized religion, such a thing as walking away from a church community is almost too psychologically and emotionally painful to consider. But this is precisely how Satan, the devil, has so effectively deceived so many, for so long. These whore houses of false religion appeal to our emotions and our hearts and seek to bypass our critically thinking minds, because God has designed all of us to be in relationship with others.

The key here to our avoiding being harmed is to develop the discernment to recognize the difference between safe and genuine communities of people who are both loving and of the truth, and those who pretend to embody those qualities, but in reality, do not. Bad company, corrupts good character, and wisdom and maturity result from our learning how to recognize bad company when we see it, and having nothing to do with it.

This ability to discern between good and evil is not intrinsic to our overly-feminized culture that appeals to our feeling gates and tries to circumvent our thinking minds. Thus, the primary burden for discerning the dangers of organized religion for what they are falls to men discovering and living out their callings by God to provide, protect, teach and lead their wives and children and to lead them out of psychologically manipulative and controlling social settings and the harlot churches of organized religion, and back to the home church movement of the first century churches of the Book of Acts meeting in people's homes and studying God's Word without the baggage of the institutional church to manipulate, control and deceive them.

Let's start by examining the model for the church, the body of believers in Christ, which the Apostles of Jesus planted during the first few decades after Christ's death on the cross. Much of the teaching here comes from the writings of Frank Viola and George Barna, from books such as *Pagan Christianity?* and others on this subject (all of which are referenced in the bibliography under Viola). Viola explains, and we can see in the writings of Luke in the Book of Acts, that the early church was an informal home church movement in which people met in people's homes, usually over food and with plenty of fellowship and social interaction and these groups became genuine communities which cared for and about one another, prayed for one another and sought to learn the ways and teachings of Jesus who came to teach us the thoughts and ways of God and to testify to the objective truth which was under attack 2,000 years ago, just as it is today.

These communities met in people's homes at least once a week, quite likely on the sabbath (Saturday), broke bread together (which is always conducive to developing friendships) and learned from one another, with the older and more spiritually mature men of the community teaching from God's Word, and from the first hand reports of the Apostles (the earliest church planters) who had walked and lived with Jesus during His three and a half year ministry. There were no church buildings with the financial burdens of debt service on a mortgage and there were no paid clergy and no one was in formal authority over these home churches.

Around 310 A.D, the Roman Emperor Constantine, in collaboration with a number of crypto-Jews (people who pretended to have converted to Christianity, but who secretly believed and practiced the various rituals of the Pharisees of Talmudic Judaism) sought to co-opt the growing sect of Christianity by merging the beliefs and practices of Babylonian, Greek, and Roman paganism with Biblical Christianity to give birth to the harlot church of Roman Catholicism and to declare this corrupted religious stew as true Christianity and the official religion of the Roman Empire. In other words, from its very inception, Roman Catholicism has been ruled by crypto-Jews who have intentionally and deliberately distorted the true teachings of the Bible to mislead people, and keep them on the road to hell that we are all born into.

Constantine donated excess government buildings to his creation of Roman Catholicism and many of the rituals and pomp and ceremonies that promoted the power of the government of the Roman Empire over its subjects were introduced by a new class of priests or clergy, who were promoted as having the keys to the knowledge of God and of true Christianity. Nothing was further from the truth, but most of the people of the Roman Empire at that time had few ways of knowing that.

What copies of the Bible that did exist, were written in Latin, and their access was confined to the clergy, who told the people what they chose to tell them. Often, what they chose to tell the people, and what the Bible, in its entirety taught, were in sharp conflict with one another, but very few people outside of the Catholic clergy had a clue that this fraud was going on.

Furthermore, this early form of organized religion (as opposed to the home church movement) served to maintain surveillance over its practitioners. The confession booth, in which adherents would confess their sins to a Roman Catholic priest, was a very effective tool to keep virtually every member of Roman Catholicism in line with the implied threat of exposure of a person's sins, and with the ability to extort money and allegiance to the church out of those members in exchange for the priest's keeping those confessions confidential. To believe that such knowledge and insights into peoples' indiscretions were not abused and used to coerce all sorts of things out of the adherents of the Roman Catholic Church would be hideously naive, gullible and foolish.

Clearly such abuses must have happened all the time to enhance the power of the Roman Catholic clergy over the rest of the populace. The Catholic clergy owed their power to and were in cahoots with the political leaders of the Roman Empire, who collectively manipulated and controlled the populace with endless lies and trickery. Roman Catholicism taught the populace to submit to secular, political and church leaders, at the risk of being excommunicated, and even murdered, if anyone dared to challenge or defy church authority. As a result, very few people dared to challenge the awesome power and authority of the Catholic Church for over 1,200 years.

In 1517, Martin Luther, a Roman Catholic priest, read the Bible and properly concluded that the Roman Catholic Church was teaching and practicing rituals which were in direct conflict with what the Bible clearly said and posted his 95 theses on the door of the Wittenberg Church in Germany, which set off the Protestant Reformation. Around that same time, Guttenberg invented the printing press, which enabled Bibles to be printed in the common languages of Europe, making the words of the Bible widely accessible to the common man for the first time. Clearly, God was orchestrating world events and history to expand Biblical Christianity in the western world and many of its new adherents, seeking to escape the oppression of organized state religion in Europe, fled to the New World and America.

Yet the vast majority of the practices of the Roman Catholic Church as a form of organized religion were left intact in Protestant churches, leaving undue power and influence over church congregations in the hands of their pastors, ministers and priests, who employed more subtle forms of manipulative and controlling behaviors and deception to control their flocks. These congregations continued to place an undue and unwarranted amount of trust and confidence in their church leaders, and not enough on reading and obeying the teachings of the Bible in its entirety for themselves.

The Reformation brought with it religious universities, colleges and seminaries to train paid full-time clergy who, puffed-up with pride and a certain amount of gnosticism, falsely taught many of their flocks that no one could properly understand the Bible unless one was properly trained in a seminary, as they were. These seminaries in turn, became staffed with faculty who were not of the truth or of agape love, and they recruited seminary students who were more drawn to the power and influence they might have over others, than they were drawn to learning the truth of the Bible, living it out faithfully, and teaching and leading others to it by their own godly examples.

Today, there are over 33,000 separate and distinct Christian denominations, all of which boldly claim that they teach the

384

truth and that every other denomination is in error. In truth, they are all in error. Every last one of these harlot churches is dysfunctional. They use the appearance of love to manipulate and control others and to evade and hide the truth. At a spiritual level, this is because every form of organized religion is, and always has been, ruled by demon spirits of deception, and serve the agenda of the devil and not Christ, their claims to the contrary, notwithstanding.

Organizationally, at least in America, most of these whore houses of false religion are structured as IRS 501c3 tax exempt organizations who have willingly agreed to comply with the list of 501c3 restrictions I have revealed earlier in this chapter. As such, those 501c3 church pastors and elders have willingly and knowingly conspired to suppress and silence the truth. There is no nice way to say this: as a result, those church leaders are of the lie, serve the father of lies, the devil, and are doing his work, and in no way are led by God's Holy Spirit.

It hardly takes a rocket scientist to figure out that the Spirit of God has left those godless churches and all that is left in them are spiritually dead people, most of them numbering among God's non-elect, His spiritual goats, created by God for their day of evil and destruction, to bring ultimate glory to God.

Such churches all have two things in common: they are not of the truth and they exhibit little or no genuine agape (sacrificial) love for one another or for their fellow man. They are demon-ruled frauds, one and all! In light of the reality that the prophecies of 2 Thessalonians 2:3A and 2 Timothy 3:1-7 and 4:3-4 have now been fulfilled with hair-splitting accuracy, this assessment of reality concerning the harlot churches ought not to surprise any of God's elect, while leaving those who do not number among God's elect entirely in the dark and clueless as to what has been going on in these viper pits of the devil for decades.

Roman Catholic Church

As I have revealed in the last chapter, the Roman Catholic Church is Mystery, Babylon the Great, Mother of Harlots and Abominations of the Earth of Revelation 17 and 18 and the Catholic Pope or the Jewish media is likely the false prophet of Revelation 13. Here are just a few of the teachings of the Roman Catholic Church which fly in the face of the pure (flawless and true) and inspired words of God of the Bible:

1. The Catholic Church teaches that the Pope, a mere man, is the Vicar of Christ. According to *Noah Webster's 1828 American Dictionary of the English Language*, a vicar is "a person deputed or authorized to perform the functions of another; a substitute in office. The pope pretends to be vicar of Jesus Christ on earth."

   a. There is no such position revealed in all of Scripture. In fact, in Hebrews 4, we are told,

      "Seeing then that we have a great high priest, that is passed into the heavens, Jesus the Son of God (Yahushua the Messiah, the Son of Elohim), let us hold fast our profession (of faith and trust in Him). For we have not an high priest which cannot be touched with the feeling of our infirmities; but was in all points tempted like as we are, yet without sin. **Let us therefore come boldly unto the throne of grace** *(of Yahushua), that we may obtain mercy, and find grace to help in time of need."* Hebrews 4:14-16

      The Bible is clearly telling us that we no longer have a human high priest entering into the holy of holies once a year on the Day of Atonement on behalf of Biblical Israel, as was the case under the law of Moses. Now we have a direct, personal and intimate relationship with Yahushua (Jesus) and no need for any human being, pope or otherwise, to serve as a mediator on our behalf with YHWH (God). Jesus taught and modeled to us how to pray (talk) directly to God the Father, in the name of Yahushua (Jesus) and YHWH has given us His flawless and inspired words of the Bible through which He speaks to us, revealing Himself, His thoughts and ways and the truth to His elect.

2. The Catholic Church teaches that in the ritual of the Holy Eucharist (a distorted form of Holy Communion), that the priest invokes his spiritual power to summon the spirit, the body and the divinity of Jesus Christ to inhabit man-made wafers of bread and cups of wine, as the literal body and blood of Jesus, and that these "transubstantiated" items are to be worshiped in a physical procession and after the Eucharist is observed, the remainder of the bread and the wine is to be housed in a box on an altar in the front of Catholic churches and adored and worshiped as Christ himself. The document of the Council of Trent, which teaches this absurd notion, goes on to proclaim that anyone who denies these teachings, "let him be anathema" (meaning accursed).

a. Jesus himself revealed His whole intent for commemorating the Lord's Supper on the night He was betrayed as follows:

> *"And when he had given thanks, he brake it, and said, 'Take, eat: this is my body, which is broken for you: this do in remembrance of me. And after the same manner also he took the cup, when he had supped, saying, This cup is the new testament in my blood: this do ye, as oft as ye drink it, in remembrance of me." For as often as ye eat this bread, and drink this cup, ye do shew the Lord's (our Adon's) death till he come. Wherefore, whosoever shall eat of this bread, and drink this cup of the Lord (YHWH), unworthily, shall be guilty of the body and blood of the Lord (Yahushua)."*
> 1 Corinthians 11:24-27

Throughout His ministry, Yahushua spoke in parables, so that those who did not number among God's elect, would hear His Words, but not

387

understand the spiritual truths He was seeking to convey to those whom God had chosen for Him. This clearly is one of those instances. Just as the Pharisees and other Jewish leaders wore phylacteries, consisting of small metal boxes strapped upon their foreheads in which passages of Old Testament Scripture were placed, so that the words of God were on their minds, so too church leaders throughout the ages have grossly misunderstood the intent of God's Word and made a mockery of its teachings in the process. The fraud of the Holy Eucharist is one of the most blatant examples of this.

The practice of summoning the body and spirit of Christ into the bread and wine, respectively, amounts to sorcery, divination and witchcraft, all of which the Bible warns us repeatedly, we are to have nothing to do with. These practices amount to occult rituals summoning up demon spirits. Furthermore, the worship and adoration and the procession about the church directed at the alleged transubstantiated bread and wine is a form of worshiping graven images and idolatry which are also expressly forbidden throughout the Bible, and in particular by the first and second commandments at Exodus 20:3-4:

> *"Thou shalt have no other gods before me. Thou shalt not make unto thee any graven image, or any likeness of any thing that is in heaven above, or in the earth beneath, or that is in the water under the earth."*

Finally, eating the body and blood of Christ, if taken literally, amounts to a form of spiritual cannibalism and the drinking of blood, the latter of which is expressly prohibited in the Book of Leviticus:

> *"And whatsoever man there be of the house of Israel, or of the strangers that sojourn among you, that eateth any manner of blood;* **I will even set my face against that soul that eateth blood, and will cut him off from among his**

> **people.** *For the life of the flesh is in the blood: and I have given it to you upon the altar to make an atonement for your souls: for it is the blood that maketh an atonement for the soul.*" Leviticus 17:10-11

It is common practice among those who practice witchcraft and the occult to engage in human sacrifice and drinking human blood, in direct violation of this specific prohibition against doing so by YHWH (God) in this passage. The so-called Holy Eucharist of Roman Catholicism smacks of the practices of the occult. Those who practice the occult, serve the devil and engage in such practices in order to gain spiritual powers over others.

3. The Catholic Church canon states that Catholics are to pray to, communicate with, and ask the spirits of dead people to intercede for them with God. Moreover the intercession of Mary is a central doctrine of the Catholic Church. These prayers to and communion with dead spirits is no different than occult séances which are held to summon spirits of dead people to obtain their help. The Bible expressly forbids such communication, which is referred to as necromancy:

> *"There shall not be found among you any one that maketh his son or his daughter to pass throughout the fire (child sacrifice), or that useth divination, or an observer of times (astrology), or an enchanter (sorcery), or a witch, Or a charmer, or a consulter with familiar spirits, or a wizard,* **or a necromancer.**" Deuteronomy 18:10-11

We are to have **one** mediator between God and men – Yahushua, or Jesus Christ of the Bible.

> *"For there is one God (Eloah), and one mediator between God (Eloah) and men, the man Christ Jesus (Yahushua the Messiah); Who gave himself a ransom for all, to be testified in due time."* 1 Timothy 2:5-6

The Bible does *not* give us permission to contact the dead at any time! To do such a thing is pure witchcraft and is strictly forbidden in the Bible.

4. The Catholic Church teaches that Mary, the mother of Yahushua (Jesus) was, like her son, immaculate, meaning without sin, both in her conception, and in her heart. Rebecca Brown, in her book, *Prepare for War*, chronicles the comical theater and fraud which was perpetrated by a cardinal and Pope Pius IX on December 8, 1854 in which Pius IX declared that Mary was immaculate in her conception and that anyone failing to believe this fraudulent dogma is not saved.[67]

5. The Catholic Church actively teaches and practices idolatry by worshipping graven images in the form of statues and other images created by man. The Catholic Church attempts to conceal this forbidden practice by redefining the Ten Commandments so that the second commandment which reads,

    "Thou shalt not make unto thee any graven image, or any likeness of any thing that is in heaven above, or that is in the earth beneath, or that is in the water under the earth." Exodus 20:4

is displayed in Catholic churches as being a subordinate clause to the first commandment, which reads,

    "Thou shalt have no other gods before me." Exodus 20:3

Then, to conceal this sleight of hand of the Catholic Church from its adherents, it splits the tenth commandment into two commandments, such that the ninth commandment commands Catholics not to covet their neighbor's property and the tenth commandment commands them not to covet their neighbor's wife.

6. The Catholic Church actively teaches works-based salvation, in direct contradiction to the doctrine of

---

[67] "Brown, Rebeca, M.D. *Prepare for War*. 1987. pp. 167-168.

salvation by grace alone which is clearly spelled out for us in Ephesians 2:8-9:

> *"For by grace are ye saved through faith; and that not of yourselves: it is the gift of God (Eloah): Not of works, lest any man should boast."*

Throughout its long and sordid history, the Catholic Church has sold indulgences and commanded its adherents to pray the rosary and pray repetitiously Hail Mary, to redeem themselves from sins. This often is the outgrowth of times spent by adherents confessing their sins in the confession booth to their local Catholic priest, who then seeks to use this insight into his parishioner's private life to pressure him into making generous gifts of value to the Catholic Church. It amounts to nothing more than spiritual extortion, which finds no support for such practices in the Bible.

In fact, this doctrinal dispute was at the heart of the conflict between the Catholic Church and Martin Luther who ignited and launched the Protestant Reformation. Today, this teaching of the Catholic Church, a variant on the false teaching of Arminianism, which falsely teaches that to be saved, a person must exercise one's mythical "free will," to accept the free gift of grace offered to all people, negates the doctrine of God electing His chosen people and replaces it with man choosing or rejecting God's free gift of salvation, thus reversing the sovereignty of God and replacing Christ's gospel of grace with the anti-gospel false notion of the sovereignty of man.

7. Catholics commit blasphemy by referring to the Pope as the Holy Father and referring to parish priests by the title of Father, a name that the Bible only uses to refer to YHWH (God) himself. This has the psychological effect of placing the Catholic priest in a position of deference, respect and authority that usurps man's relationship with Christ and with God:

"...I will receive you, And will be a Father unto you, and ye shall be my sons and daughters, saith the Lord Almighty (YHWH)" 2 Corinthians 6:17-18

"But I would have you know, that the head of every man is Christ (the Messiah); and the head of the woman is the man, and the head of Christ (the Messiah) is God (Eloah)." 1 Corinthians 11:3

Where is there provision in the Bible for any man, priest or otherwise, to usurp the title and authority of Father from YHWH (God)? It's nowhere to be found, and thus the practice of the Roman Catholic Church is nothing more than a manipulative and cunning fraud and trick used to induce the naïve and gullible to submit themselves to the authority of church leaders, which has been subject to extensive abuse over the centuries, and continues to this day.

8. Finally, the practice of Catholic Church adherents confessing their sins in a confession booth to their local parish priest has been been used to hideously abuse many people. A friend of mine who grew up in Guatemala revealed to me that in her local village, it was widely known which children in the village were the children of the different parish priests. Moreover, the homosexual molestation of boys is widely known and no secret anymore and is a direct outgrowth of the practice of the Catholic Church which requires all Catholic priests to be unmarried, thus attracting homosexuals, pedophiles and fornicators to the ranks of the Roman Catholic priesthood, whose sexual immorality and promiscuity has led to widespread demon spirit infestation of the vast majority of these unfortunate children, whose trust was violated by sexual predators with the full knowledge and tacit allowance of the Catholic Church hierarchy, which secretly serves the devil, and not Christ at all!

For further reading on the corrupt practices of the Roman Catholic Church, I direct readers to the following sources:

Prepare for War, by Rebecca Brown M.D., Chapter 11

Solving the Mystery of Babylon the Great: Tracking the Beast from the Synagogue to the Vatican, by Edward Hendrie

The Anti-Gospel: The Perversion of Christ's Grace Gospel, by Edward Hendrie

From the preceding expose of the fraud of the Roman Catholic Church and the revelation that it is the mother of all harlot churches of Revelation 17 and 18, we may safely conclude that virtually all of those reported to be Catholics by the Pew Research Center, totaling 1.1 billion people, or 50% of all those professing to be followers of Christ are, in reality, not saved and not Christians, as they falsely claim to be. In most cases, this is true out of complete ignorance on the part of of its adherents. Yet ignorance and blindness to the truth, in no way alters objective reality. Clearly, we can see from this that the agents of Satan have made major inroads into corrupting the churches of organized religion. And it gets worse: much worse, as we will see below.

Mormon or LDS Church

Much of my material for the Mormon Church comes from two sources: 1) *New Age Cults and Religions*, by Texe Marrs and *Mormonism, Masonry and Godhood*, by Dr. Cathy Burns. According to the Pew Research Center, the Mormon Church has roughly 15 million members worldwide.

The Mormon Church, officially known as the Church of Jesus Christ of Latter Day Saints (LDS) was founded in the 1830s by American Joseph Smith, who was both a 33rd degree Mason and a practitioner of witchcraft, divination and the occult. Historians of Mormonism have chronicled that Smith's entire family was deeply involved in the occult.

One of my sources who is close to the great-great-grandson of one of Smith's bodyguards revealed to my source that his grandfather told him unabashedly that his grandfather was there at the founding of the Mormon Church and that they just made it all up! I am not at all surprised by this fact, though I am a bit surprised that anyone would dare break ranks and openly admit it to anyone outside the inner circle of Mormonism; instead, I would have expected every last one of them to take such a secret to their grave. And certainly, for most of them, that is precisely what they did, probably out of fear of their being murdered in a Masonic ritual killing if they dared do such a thing, in violation of their secret loyalty oaths to the lodge of Freemasonry, required of all Masons.

As a result of Joseph Smith's involvement with the occult and Freemasonry (which in reality is the secret society of the Illuminati concealed inside the secret society of Freemasonry, whose top leaders secretly worship Satan and practice the rituals of the Jewish Zohar Kabbalah of the occult), Mormonism amounts to disguised Satanism and promotes numerous false and heretical teachings which overtly conflict with many important doctrines of the Bible. Here are some of those heretical teachings of Mormonism:

1. Mormonism falsely claims that all men are potential gods and that God was once an exalted man who is not an eternal being. Instead, He worked himself up to godhood. In fact, the core Mormon teachings and credo is: "As man is, God once was: As God is, man may become."

2. For anyone who has even the remotest understanding of the infinite, eternal, divine and sovereign nature and attributes of almighty YHWH (God), creator of the universe and all that is in it, such a belief held by the Mormon Church concerning the personhood of God is patently absurd; so much so, that one must marvel how anyone in his right mind could hold to such a view and conduct him or herself with any degree of truth and integrity and claim that he/she is a follower of Christ. Clearly, the Jesus Christ of Mormonism bears little resemblance to Yahushua (Jesus) of the Bible and for Mormons to imply or claim otherwise, is patently dishonest and fraudulent on many levels.

   a. In this jumbled and occult belief system, the doctrine of works is heavily taught and practiced. As such, it directly contradicts the teachings of salvation by grace alone, taught very clearly in Ephesians 2:8-9. In fact, Mormons even reject the notion of the existence of hell.

3. Mormonism claims that Jesus is not unique from other men. It denies the virgin birth of Jesus (which establishes His divinity and sonship with God). Instead, it teaches that Jesus was begotten in the flesh sexually by God, who is also a fleshly being, that Jesus was married to the two sisters of Lazarus (Martha and Mary) and also to Mary Magdalene, and that His wives and children were present at His crucifixion.

   a. It hardly takes a rocket scientist to see the extensive fraud being perpetrated by the Mormon Church upon its adherents, and upon those outside Mormonism, who innocently and naively assume that Mormonism is merely another Christian denomination. Nothing could be further from the truth! The Jesus Christ of Mormonism has few, if any similarities with Yahushua of the Bible!

4. Mormons teach that Jesus and Satan are brothers and that he became Savior only after his salvation was approved by a vote of the Council of gods.

5. Mormons teach that our souls have eternally been in heaven with God and that when we are born, we come to earth like Jesus, receive a physical body, live, die and return to heaven to be with God and other souls for all eternity. This is "feel good" false religion at its finest, with no accountability and no consequences for the many sins committed while in this body and no hell for those who fail to surrender their lives and their wills to the Jesus of the Bible (Yahushua) in this life. All this, in spite of the teaching of Yahushua at John 14:6 that He is the way, the truth and the life and that *no one* comes to the Father (YHWH) but through Him. Someone is lying through their teeth here folks! Hint: it ain't Yahushua of the Bible!

6. Men who are Mormons, who follow the Mormon teachings and are initiated into a higher state (which sounds very similar to initiation into higher degrees of Freemasonry which practices the occult), are taught that they become gods of their own planets. Further, they are taught that as gods, they may have millions of wives and enjoy endless sex.

   a. In its early years, Mormons routinely practiced polygamy (being married to multiple wives). Moreover, Joseph Smith clearly was obsessed with having sex with as many women as he possibly could, as evidenced by his routinely wearing a talisman (a medallion) picturing the Roman god Jupiter, which he referred to as his "Masonic Jewel," and which he claimed enhanced his sexual prowess. Obsession with sex with multiple partners is a common trait of those who are demon possessed and active practitioners of the occult, witchcraft and Satanism, all of which appear to be secret practices of Mormonism, which are concealed by its leaders and practitioners from the outside world.

   b. Any man who has been married for any length of time ought to be able to figure out that being married to multiple women would be a curse, not a blessing, and that multiple wives can only lead to cat fights and endless conflict in the home. Why would anyone in his right mind be attracted to such a living hell? Frankly speaking, the very notion itself is the mark of complete foolishness and blind insanity.

7. In Mormonism, salvation is not possible except through the prophet of the Mormon Church, namely Joseph Smith, a practitioner of the occult, and an apparent sexual deviant. Thus Joseph Smith functions as a human gatekeeper between God and Mormons, just as the pope falsely claims to do for all Catholics, both of which are contradicted by the passage of Hebrews 4:14-16 quoted previously in connection with the pope.

8. According to Mormonism, there is a Mother in heaven as well as a Father. Sounds like the unholy trinity of Babylonian King Nimrod, his voluptuous and promiscuous wife, Semiramis, and the son who was the offspring of their union, whose name was also Nimrod, to me, but hey, what do I know?

9. Mormons claim (falsely I might add) that the Old and New Testaments of the Bible are flawed, imperfect, inaccurately translated into English and inferior to the works of Joseph Smith, which include *The Book of Mormon, Doctrines and Covenants, and Pearl of Great Price*, along with a book which provides alternative alleged (and fraudulent) translations of the KJV of the Bible which Smith claimed to be in error. This latter alleged correction of flawed translations does not come anywhere near close to resembling the various translations of the original Hebrew and Greek manuscript autographs into English with which I am quite familiar, the KJV, NIV, NASB among them. It is painfully obvious to me that these alleged correct translations, professed by the Mormons, are nothing more than a con job and a complete fraud pulled off by Joseph Smith and his fellow charlatans.

10. Mormons teach and expect that their adherents will tithe, donating 10% of their income each year to the LDS Church. This has greatly enriched the LDS Church as an institution, with financial assets totaling billions of dollars under their control. This makes the LDS Church a financial and political power house to be reckoned with, and they most assuredly use this power in very worldly and ungodly ways to advance their cult's agenda and to promote their public relations image as a wholesome and family-oriented brand of Christianity. The truth is quite the opposite of this.

11. After they themselves have been baptized into the Mormon Church, many Mormons engage in the practice of being baptized for the dead who were not baptized into the Mormon Church during their lifetimes. The Mormons believe that such a practice is a prerequisite for the

397

deceased getting into paradise. As such, it is one of many works that save no one. The author of the Book of Hebrews put it directly this way:

"And as it is appointed unto men once to die, but after this the judgment:" Hebrews 9:27

Nowhere in the Bible does it support such a notion of works-based salvation or of any second chances after one has died. In fact, if a person has not become born again in the Spirit by the time one dies, we can be quite sure that such a person was not one of God's elect. Yet that in no way stops the Mormon Church from preying on this scam to further confuse and deceive their members and lead them away from the teachings of the Bible.

12. Mormons refer to non-Mormons as Gentiles behind our backs and secretly regard us with disgust and disdain as little better than dogs. This bigoted way of thinking comes directly out of the Jewish Babylonian Talmud and Zohar Kabbalah, which form the core teachings of Freemasonry, which in turn is the foundation of the core teachings of Mormonism. All three religions of the occult are, in substance, derived from the same source, although the members of the Mormon Church generally are quite unaware of this underlying reality, as a result of the church's unending barrage of public relations hype, mind-control programming and psychological warfare ploys in which it engages to deceive its members and conceal the truth.

The Talmud teaches impostors posing as Jews that non-Jews are goyim, or cattle, to be used and abused by Jews to whatever extent they can get away with it, without bringing shame to the Jewish community. We can safely assume that Mormons regard non-Mormons in much the same way and engage in business with non-Mormons in deceitful ways that they refuse to own up to.

   a. Several years ago, I served on the executive board of a non-profit organization dedicated to trying to keep

LGBT indoctrination out of the public schools, starting in California, which was founded by two wealthy and politically active Mormons. Within a few months, these two Mormons revealed themselves to back slide on prior commitments they had made to the fourth member of our executive board. Subsequently, the Mormon attorney and chairman of the non-profit tried to extort $400 from me by falsely alleging that he had sent me two checks for expenses I had incurred on behalf of the non-profit for which he was reimbursing me. The truth was, he never reimbursed me for those expenses and I had to eat it. When I informed him that I believed him to be in error and could find no such record of any deposits in my bank account and asked him to furnish me with a copy of his canceled check, he faxed me the back of a check that was completely illegible and when I confronted him on this, he merely ignored me and went silent. I don't believe this was any isolated incident. When I had previously visited him at his house in southern California, he was intent on showing me his many religious icons and idols scattered about his home. Clearly his "stuff" and mammon owned him, and was the god he served, and not YHWH and Yahushua of the Bible at all! Since I was merely a "Gentile," in his mind, I was a legitimate target for his attempt to defraud me, and I have no doubt that this is a routinely practiced behavior by many Mormons, who get away with it with impunity.

There is no question that Mormons have been very effective at public relations to convince the American public that they are a family-oriented organization. This has permitted Mormons to deceive many, because many Americans remain strongly attracted and committed to healthy marriages and healthy family values that the Mormons skillfully employ to their advantage. Yet real authentic masculine men of America need to wake up to reality and tell it like it is: Mormonism is a spinoff from Freemasonry, which is rooted in the occult teachings of the Jewish Kabbalah. Mormonism is of the occult, is very dangerous and not at all what it purports to be. As such, we can safely assert that those who purport to be Mormons most assuredly are not born again Biblical Christians and thus, are not any more saved than Catholics are.

Calvary Chapel System

Chuck Smith, founder of Calvary Chapel in Costa Mesa in southern California, founded his denomination in the 1970s out of the Jesus Movement. Today, the Calvary Chapel system or movement claims 25 million followers worldwide. Chuck Smith, who died in late 2013, was a lightning rod of controversy during his lifetime. A number of books and radio talk show hosts have sharply denounced Smith's beliefs, teachings and practices that in many ways were quite unorthodox, but which served to position Smith as the unchallenged authority on all doctrines taught within the Calvary Chapel franchise. In short, Smith functioned in much the same capacity as the pope of the Roman Catholic Church. Calvary Chapel was Chuck Smith's church and any challenges to his teachings or authority were simply not tolerated or permitted within his system. All such challenges were simply ignored and dismissed by its pastors and elders. The principle they follow is "He who controls the mike (the microphone) has the power" and they use that to control and limit what is, and is not, permitted to be talked about.

Smith's book, *Calvary Chapel Distinctives*, summarizes what Calvary Chapel's founder and CEO regarded as the core teachings of his church which make it distinct and unique from other allegedly Christian denominations, and it is from this source that I draw most heavily in my critique of this brand of false organized religion. The following are the major points of departure and difference between what the Bible says and what Chuck Smith taught and his church teaches today:

1. In spite of his claiming to be neither a Calvinist nor an Arminianist concerning the Biblical doctrine of election, Smith and Calvary Chapel aggressively promote the

doctrine of devils and anti-gospel teachings of Arminianism, which holds that it is possible for all people to become saved and born again Christians, provided that we exercise our mythical and unbiblical "free will" to accept the free gift of salvation offered to us by the death of Yahushua (Jesus) on the cross in our place, so that His righteousness might be imputed or credited to us. This false gospel is nothing short of abject heresy and blasphemy, relative to what God's Word, the Bible teaches us in a number of passages:

> *"**As it is written, Jacob Have I loved, but Esau have I hated.** What shall we say then? Is there unrighteousness with God (Eloah)? God forbid. For he saith to Moses, I will have mercy on whom I will have mercy (meaning God's elect), and I will have compassion on whom I will have compassion. **So then it is not of him that willeth, nor of him that runneth, but of God (Eloah) that sheweth mercy.** For the scripture saith unto Pharaoh, Even for this same purpose have I raised thee up, that I might shew my power in thee, and that my name might be declared throughout all the earth (from the destruction of Pharaoh and the Egyptian army who were drowned in the Red Sea, pursuing Moses and the 12 Hebrew tribes out of Egypt). Therefore hath he mercy on whom he will have mercy (meaning His elect), and whom he will (meaning God's non-elect) he hardeneth. Thou wilt say then unto me, Why doth he yet find fault? For who hath resisted his will? Nay but, O man, who art thou that repliest against God (Eloah)? Shall the thing formed say to him that formed it, Why hast thou made me thus (i.e. one of Your non-elect)? Hath not the potter (God) power over the clay (man), of the same lump to make one vessel unto honour (His elect), and another unto dishonour (His non-elect)? What if God (Eloah), willing to shew his wrath, and to make his power known, endured with much longsuffering the vessels of wrath fitted to destruction: And that he might make known the riches of his glory on the vessels of mercy, which he had afore (before*

the world began) prepared unto glory, Even us, whom he hath called, not of the Jews only, but also of the Gentiles?" Romans 9:11-24 (parentheticals added for clarity; bold face added for emphasis)

This passage clearly contradicts and proves false the teaching of Arminianism that God creates all of us alike and loves all of mankind. That is simply not the case and any honest reading of this passage alone ought to make this truth abundantly clear. Yet this is precisely what Chuck Smith and his Calvary Chapel churches teach relentlessly, and they suffer and tolerate no challenges to it, employing psychologically controlling and manipulative tactics which give no fair airing of the truth: the Biblical teaching of the doctrine of election.

Here are two further passages from Scripture which prove beyond a shadow of a doubt the truth of God's electing some, but not all (not even most), to become His born again adopted sons and daughters at a time and in a manner of His choosing and at His initiative:

"According as he (God) **hath chosen us in him before the foundation of the world,** *that we should be holy and without blame before him in love:* **Having predestinated us unto the adoption of children by Jesus Christ** *(Yahushua the Messiah)* **to himself, according to the good pleasure of his will,"** Ephesians 1:4-5 (parentheticals added for clarity; bold face added for emphasis)

"And you hath he quickened (made alive), who were dead in trespasses and sins (spiritually dead people are incapable of doing anything to save themselves — they are without life!); Wherein in time past ye walked according to the course of this world, according to the prince of the power of the air (the devil), the spirit that now worketh in the children of disobedience: Among whom also we all had our conversation in times past in the lusts of our flesh, fulfilling the desires of the flesh and of the mind; and were by nature the children of wrath, even as others. But God (Eloah),

> *who is rich in mercy, for his great love wherewith he loved us (but not all men), Even when we were dead in sins, hath quickened us together with Christ (the Messiah), (by grace ye are saved;) and hath raised us up together, and made us sit together in heavenly places in Christ Jesus (Yahushua the Messiah): That in the ages to come he might shew the exceeding riches of his grace in his kindness toward us (but not to all men) through Christ Jesus (Yahushua the Messiah).* **For by grace are ye saved through faith; and that not of yourselves; it is the gift of God (Eloah): Not of works** *(exercising one's mythical "free will" would be a work)***, lest any man should boast. For we are his workmanship, created in Christ Jesus (Yahushua the Messiah) unto good works, which God (Eloah) hath before ordained that we should walk in them."** Ephesians 2:1-10 (parentheticals added for clarity; bold face added for emphasis)

The bottom line is that God's Word, the Bible, reveals to us that God creates two classes of people: His elect (His spiritual sheep) and all others (His non-elect and spiritual goats). Until one of His elect is born again in His Holy Spirit, God's spiritual sheep will often behave much like spiritual goats, being selfish, deceitful, unkind and sinning with abandon. But the moment that God chooses to draw His elect to Himself, He will do it all: He will put His Holy Spirit in that person, orchestrate events so that he hears the gospel preached, he will believe it, and is thus saved and becomes born again in God's Holy Spirit, who gives the born again believer the ability, over time, to understand the thoughts and ways of God as He has revealed Himself to us in Scripture.

All others will read the same words of Scripture and not arrive at a coherent understanding of what the words say, what they mean and how they should apply to our lives. Above all, all true believers will evidence a dedication to the truth and a loving spirit, which places the long-term best interests of others ahead of their own selfish wants and comforts.

These are the two traits which the apostle John, who was the favorite of Jesus, emphasizes repeatedly in the epistles of 2 John and 3 John: truth and love. Without both, a person professing to be a follower of Christ is self-deceived, a fraud or both. In light of the fact that Calvary Chapel suppresses the truth of the doctrine of election, and does so in some very unloving and under-handed ways, we can safely conclude that the Calvary Chapel system serves the devil, the father of lies, and not Yahushua (Jesus Christ) of the Bible.

2. Smith and Calvary Chapel teach the fraud and doctrine of devils of a pre-trib rapture. They claim that the Bible teaches that before the great tribulation (spoken of in Daniel 12 and Matthew 24) arrives, that all true believers will be gathered into the clouds to be with Jesus. Nothing could be further from the truth! As I have revealed in earlier chapters, Matthew 24 clearly spells out the sequence of events surrounding the timing of the great tribulation relative to the gathering described in Matthew 24:30-31. Matthew 24:15-28 reveals the nature of the great tribulation and the event which signals its start (in verse 15) and reveals quite clearly that God's elect will be here and will go through the great tribulation, rather than be rescued from it. Verse 29 begins: "Immediately after the tribulation of those days . . . " and goes on to describe four celestial events concluding with a global earthquake. Verse 30 begins, "And then . . . " and goes on to describe the gathering of the elect in that verse and verse 31. In other words, the Bible is crystal clear on this: the gathering is a post-trib gathering. Additionally, I have revealed earlier the substantial evidence that indicates that the great tribulation has already begun. If this fact is true, and I believe it most assuredly is, the pre-trib rapture notion has now been soundly disproven to be the fraud and doctrine of devils it has always been.

It is not difficult to figure why Smith and the church he founded teach and promote a pre-trib rapture and "free will" Arminian salvation. Calvary Chapel clearly is marketing itself to the non-elect, that is, to God's spiritual goats, who are vastly greater in number than God's elect, and who have no interest in hearing about the suffering and trials of God's elect.

As such, those who are drawn to the Calvary Chapel services and programs are quite comfortable in an environment that is heavily oriented toward entertainment with single direction communication from the performers' stage to the emoting audience: no thinking allowed! Modern day contemporary organized religion is big business and Chuck Smith and his followers have perfected the model to fill its church services with spiritually dead people and its offering plates with money. Those who attend, do so to be told what their itching ears want to hear, in fulfillment of the prophecy of 2 Timothy 4:3-4. They have little or no interest in the truth:

> "For the time will come when they will not endure sound doctrine; but after their own lusts shall they heap to themselves teachers, having itching ears; And they shall turn away their ears from the truth, and shall be turned unto fables."

3. Smith and Calvary Chapel promote the lie and agenda of Zionism. They falsely equate the rogue terrorist state of modern day Israel with the nation of Israel of the Bible, and the impostors posing as Jews as God's chosen people. Once again, nothing could be further from the truth! I have revealed the true identity of the impostors posing as Jews in an earlier chapter. The impostors posing as Jews are not at all what they falsely claim to be. They serve the father of lies, the devil, and follow a set of teachings of the rabbis out of the Babylonian Talmud and Zohar Kabbalah of the occult that are the most vile, disgusting, racist, bigoted, anti-Christ and anti-Christian teachings of a fanatical religious cult of the devil that the world has ever seen. In

405

short, the impostors posing as Jews are nothing less than the Antichrist and the first beast of end times Bible prophecy and any alleged Christian who supports the terrorism and deceit of the rogue state of Israel, or promotes the impostors posing as Jews as God's chosen people is doing the work of Satan and is worshipping the beast, just as end times prophecy in the Bible has predicted they would for thousands of years.

4. Smith founded Calvary Chapel and was one of the early pioneers in introducing Christian rock music to church services, replacing the traditional singing of hymns and praise music. This was no accident either. Much has been written by others concerning the dangers of rock music in creating emotional experiences for its listeners which bypasses the thinking mind and serves as a pathway for demon spirit influence and infestation. Edward Hendrie documents and chronicles in his book, *The Anti-Gospel: The Perversion of Christ's Grace Gospel*, how Chuck Smith received a gift totaling $8 million from the Illuminati to capitalize and support Smith's "Maranatha! Music" which pioneered in producing "Christian" rock and roll music. Smith vehemently denied the claims made by a messenger of the Illuminati, but Smith's denials lack credibility, especially when compared against the multiple false and misleading teachings promoted by Smith and Calvary Chapel for years. Where there's smoke, there's usually fire and Chuck Smith's brand of Christianity is most assuredly of the devil, and not at all what it purports to be on the surface.

Evangelical Covenant Church

The Covenant denomination, headquartered in Chicago, Illinois, claims to have 178,000 members and roughly 800 churches worldwide. Originally, the Covenant denomination was a spinoff of the Swedish Lutheran Church. While its number of adherents is not large, it serves as a good illustration of the practices of a number of more contemporary evangelical churches which depart materially from the spirit and the letter of what the Bible teaches concerning a healthy church community. My first adult experience with organized religion was in a Covenant denomination church from late 2004 to mid-2009 and during that time I had an opportunity to get to know the inner workings of that church and the denomination which it belonged to quite well. Here is what I observed while there:

1. A year after the new pastor and I arrived at that church, about a third of the church community met for a two day workshop to try to define its direction, purpose and mission. This church sought to be successful by the world's standards. Bill Hybel's Willow Creek Church in Ohio and Rick Warren's Saddleback Church in Orange County, California, well-known and highly successful mega-churches, were promoted by the church's new pastor as something to emulate and strive toward. Success was measured by both the pastor and his board of elders (referred to as "the leadership team") by the number of church attendees and members, dollar volume of offerings and donations, the number of staff on the payroll, the size of the church facility and the number of programs offered, as opposed to the qualities of transformed lives submitted and surrendered to the lordship of Christ.

    After months of debate, here's what their leadership team or board of elders came up with: "Our mission is to engage with the spiritually hungry, toward a life in Christ, that's intelligent, inspired and involved." A mission statement is supposed to define for any organization what it hopes to be when it grows up, that inspires and guides its members in its daily tactical and strategic decisions of what it chooses to do and not do. This one was pathetic and quite uninspiring! By all appearances, the church was already doing this, so now what?!?

    The church was located in a county with the lowest level of church participation I have ever heard of: only 2.7% of the county's residents had their rear ends in a church pew or seat on any given Sunday. Moreover, the county was quite affluent and was experiencing a divorce rate of 80%!

The community was in spiritual and marital shambles, and this is all that this church could come up with?!? I was under-whelmed! But it gave the pastors carte blanche to do whatever they wanted to amuse themselves, and they did just that.

Because of my expressed concerns about the church mission statement being so vague and uninspiring, the pastor invited me to a planning workshop directed to the leadership team on a Saturday in which the denomination's director of church planting gave an excellent talk on what needs to be in place before a church can even begin to think about defining a strategy (long term plan) for itself. This leader disclosed that it was well known within the denomination that this church in particular was dysfunctional and then he went on to define what he meant by the term.

He revealed that all dysfunctional organizations or systems use the appearance of love to manipulate and control its members and that our church in question employed just such tactics. I was dumb-founded that some of the members of the leadership team did not jump up and immediately demand an accounting from its pastor and a corrective action plan to resolve that sorry state of affairs once and for all. Instead, what I witnessed was complete silence, avoidance of the issue and the pastor side-stepped the issue by indicating that they would resume discussions at a later time.

Clearly, the head of the leadership team and the pastor were guilty of what had been revealed. But nothing ever came of it, in large part due to the fact that the women and feminized men on the leadership team were patsies of the pastor and would never consider challenging a pastor who had a controlling and manipulative personality, as this one most certainly did.

2. This same pastor shut down the men's support group which met once a week to offer support and encouragement to one another in the face of challenges

that various men were facing after the new leader of the group introduced me to a website defining the characteristics of a sociopath, with which I was having to deal at home. I later learned that this pastor went out of his way to direct this new leader to distance himself from and have no ongoing relationship with me and that he and 3-4 other men were "managing" my situation, unbeknownst to me at the time.

I was annoyed that the pastor had taken it upon himself to suppress and silence the truth from me on a matter which was directly pertinent to my understanding the depths of the serious challenges I was facing at home, but it never occurred to me that any pastor of any church might be deliberately and willfully doing the work of the devil to conceal the truth from me and keep me in the dark to my own very real harm. It was only after numerous other incidents had occurred that I could not help but arrive at this very disturbing conclusion.

3. The board of elders, or leadership team, was composed of at least as many women as men. The common denominator of all new additions to this group over my tenure there appeared to be that none of them possessed any real backbone, strong convictions or knowledge of what the Bible teaches and that they were easily influenced by the pastor's rather forceful and controlling personality. 1 Timothy 3 is very clear on the suitable qualifications for an elder or a deacon of any church. In no instance, are women permitted or encouraged to assume the role of elder or deacon in any Christian church. Here's what that passage teaches:

> *"This is a true saying, If a man desire the office of a bishop, he desireth a good work. A bishop then must be blameless, the husband of one wife, vigilant, sober, of good behaviour, given to hospitality, apt to teach; Not given to wine, no striker, not greedy of filthy lucre; but patient, not a brawler, not covetous; One that ruleth well his own house, having his children in subjection with all gravity; (For if a*

man know not how to rule his own house, how shall he take care of the church of God (Eloah)?) Not a novice, lest being lifted up with pride he fall into the condemnation of the devil. Moreover, he must have a good report of them which are without; lest he fall into reproach and the snare of the devil. Likewise must the deacons be grave, not doubletongued, not given to much wine, not greedy of filthy lucre; Holding the mystery of the faith in a pure conscience. And let these also first be proved; then let them use the office of a deacon, being found blameless. Even so, must their wives be grave, not slanderers, sober, faithful in all things. Let the deacons be the husbands of one wife, ruling their children and their own houses well. For they that have used the office of deacon well purchase to themselves a good degree, and great boldness in the faith which is in Christ Jesus (Yahushua the Messiah)." 1 Timothy 3:1-13

Is there any latitude in this teaching of the apostle Paul to his disciple Timothy concerning the qualifications of an elder (bishop) or a deacon to be a woman? No, there most assuredly is not. Elsewhere in Paul's writings, we see why not:

"Let the woman learn in silence with all subjection. But I suffer not a woman to teach, nor to usurp authority over the man, but to be in silence. For Adam was first formed, then Eve. And Adam was not deceived, but the woman being deceived was in the transgression. Notwithstanding she shall be saved in childbearing, if they continue in faith and charity and holiness with sobriety." 1 Timothy 2:11-15

"But I would have you know, that the head of every man is Christ (the Messiah); and the head of the woman is the man; and the head of Christ (the Messiah) is God (Eloah)." 1 Corinthians 11:3

"For the man is not of the woman; but the woman of the man. Neither was the man created for the woman; but the woman for the man." 1 Corinthians 11:8-9

"Wives, submit yourselves unto your own husbands, as unto the Lord (our Adon). For the husband is the head of the wife, even as Christ (the Messiah) is the head of the church (the body of believers — God's elect): and he is the savior of the body. Therefore as the church is subject unto Christ (the Messiah), so let the wives be to their own husbands in every thing. Husbands, love your wives, even as Christ (the Messiah) also loved the church, and gave himself for it (He died for us!);" Ephesians 5:22-25

What Paul is telling us is that God has designed distinct roles and responses for both men and women, if we are to learn to live together in harmony, and that these roles and responses to one another are different! Imagine that! Feminism is a demonic lie, designed to convince all of us that men and woman are the same, when in fact, we are very different, with different strengths and weaknesses in which men and woman are designed to complement one another; not compete with each other for dominance in the home!

Similarly, God has designed church to reflect these distinct roles and strengths of men and women and teach these behaviors to the men and women of each church community, so that it might bless their marriages and families. Men are to love, provide, protect, teach and lead their wives and children, and women are designed by God to support and respect their husbands.

In a church setting, this dictates that men step up and lead and teach others and that women yield and surrender to the authority of men, to teach others what godly womanhood and femininity looks like by their own wise and virtuous examples. This is why Paul forbids women to teach or to usurp authority over a man. Women are to submit to the authority of men in healthy relationships in which the men do not lord it over their wives, but live with their wives in an understanding way, that their prayers might not be hindered (see 1 Peter 3:7).

Thus, the Bible teaches us quite clearly that men have distinctly different teaching, protection and headship roles over women and children and that their ability to carry out their God-given roles is dependent upon the voluntary yielding, or submission, of their women and children to the headship of the husband and father. When women are permitted to assume the role of bishop (elder) or deacon in any church, that church is being willfully disobedient to the teachings of Paul which I have laid out here and to the overall caution of Paul at Romans 12:2:

> *"And be not conformed to this world: but be ye transformed by the renewing of your mind (by the reading, study and obedience to the Word), that ye may prove what is that good, and acceptable, and perfect, will of God (Eloah)."* (parenthetical added for clarity)

The world Paul is referring to here is the culture of the day, which in our day is defined by the demonic philosophy of feminism, which seeks to reverse the roles of men and women to create chaos and anarchy in the home, church and society at large, which Satan takes delight in, and which brings misery, dysfunction and suffering to men, women and children alike.

The hard truth is that women are far easier to manipulate and control by devious men ruled by demon spirits. The same thing applies to feminized and immature men. This was precisely the profile of the men and women nominated by the pastor of the Covenant church to become members of his board of elders, thus stacking the board with his patsies, which allowed him to operate with impunity and no accountability to what the Word of God says and clearly means. With no checks and balances, a pastor with a psychological inclination to control others will mislead his flock away from the truth of God's Word and into the the doctrines of devils and beliefs which are politically correct, dead wrong and of the devil.

4.   The pastor's eldest son who was in his twenties was hired in an inappropriate act of nepotism, as the music director

of the church. Nepotism in which the pastor's family and friends are hired onto the church payroll is always a red flag of deficient moral character of the pastor and of his board of elders who choose to look the other way and not bring correction to this dangerous practice. This son and music director introduced loud, to the point of jarring, rock music which appeared to be directed at driving a number of the older and more spiritually mature members of the church out. The music was so loud that the sound booth in the back of the church hall or sanctuary offered ear plugs for older members who struggled with hearing problems, which was both unloving and thoughtless.

As church attendance grew, the Sunday worship services were offered three times on Sunday morning, with the traditional music that appealed to the older members, offered at 8:00 a.m. in the morning, which was often a known struggle for the more elderly and infirm members of the church to get to that early. This also had the appearance of being quite deliberate and intentional on the part of church leadership, in order to discourage church participation by older, wiser and more mature members.

5. During my time attending this church, a friend of mine and I persuaded the pastors and leaders of the men's ministry in that church to permit us to host a three year long program of recorded materials directed at teaching men what it means to become authentic, wise, godly men of strategic vision for their homes and workplaces that was rooted in the accurate teachings of the Bible. That program almost got shut down by one of the pastors when some of the passages I have quoted from above were used to teach men that men and women are different and have different roles and responsibilities in the home. I was initially dumb-founded that any pastor could even contemplate such a thing. Later, I discovered a doctrinal paper published on the denomination's website, authored by a seminary-degreed pastor, which boldly stated that the verses of Ephesians 5:22-24 were three of the most abused verses in

all the Bible and because we lived in a more sophisticated and enlightened era, that such artifacts of first century Asia Minor no longer apply to us today.

It was the most brazen piece of nonsense I have ever read concerning how any teaching of the Bible is conditioned upon the cultural norms of the day, in direct violation of and disobedience to the teaching of Romans 12:2! Blind arrogance and pride does not begin to describe the fraud this so-called theologian was trying to pull over on the Covenant denomination, which its leaders had clearly embraced and endorsed.

From the date that the doctrinal paper was written and one other like it, it became obvious to me that the leaders of that denomination had sold out to the feminist movement hook, line and sinker in the 1970s and 80s and was continuing to promote and encourage women in every form of leadership in its denomination, in defiance of Biblical teaching.

The men's program continued for about four years and then quietly was allowed by its pastoral staff to die of neglect and lack of support from them. In retrospect, it is clear to me that had those pastors had their way, that men's teaching of Biblical manhood would never have been permitted to be presented in their church, had I not been so passionate and persistent in pushing for it, knowing full well how the psychologically emasculated men of that church desperately needed to learn what authentic Biblical manhood looks like and consists of.

The Illuminati and demon spirits had got there before me and were bound and determined to see to it that my attempt at bringing health and truth to the men of that community failed, since it flew in the face of the demonic agenda the entire denomination had embraced several decades earlier.

As I questioned and sought to bring correction to these Biblical errors with the pastors, I found them dodging, ducking, weaving and avoiding my open and transparent attempts to do so. Finally, I was directed by the lead pastor to make an appointment with his secretary to come see him, for what was obviously shaping up to be a beating behind the woodpile. At first, I ignored him, but finally decided to confront him in his office. He attempted to silence me every way he could, telling me to sit, down shut up and learn, because I didn't know anything. He was way off base, speaking lies, and he knew it and he was anything but loving and kind. It was about as worldly a performance of attempting to intimidate and silence me as I could imagine. He was further tacitly revealing to me that I would be marginalized and treated as a second class citizen in his church ever after that. Consequently, after several months of shopping for another church to join, I left his church.

6. Finally, this same pastor used other older men who I knew and initially respected to try to improperly claim that I was disobeying the teachings of the Bible by not submitting myself to the authority of church leaders who, by that point, I knew to be teaching lies and deliberately misleading me. One man in particular called me to dress me down in no uncertain terms that were verbally disrespectful to me to the point of verging on being abusive, and after warning him to back off and his failing to heed my warning, I hung up on him. His alleged coaching was neither truthful to what I knew the Bible teaches, nor was it at all loving or in my best long-term interests.

Other Signs of Dysfunctional Churches and Church Leaders

Other churches or home study groups which I have participated in have, over time, exhibited other signs which ought to be red flags which signal deviant behaviors and false teachings of its leaders: Here are a few of them:

1. One pastor who was a Biblically sound teacher exhibited significant pride and presumed things about me from very limited interaction with me which clued me in that this pastor suffered from undue pride and presumption to

415

know things about which he was grossly unqualified to express an opinion. Great talent and insight is often accompanied by excessive pride and arrogance in a number of pastors and church leaders. James 4:6 teaches us that "God opposes the proud, but gives grace to the humble." God is no respecter of persons: pride is a deadly character flaw that makes a man unteachable and incapable of accepting correction or learning from others. Flee from such men without hesitation! If you don't, they will burn you sooner or later.

2. Some church leaders and their wives have very clear unbiblical agendas that surface over time; thus revealing that they are not living in submission to the guiding of the Holy Spirit, but are under the influence of one or more demon spirits. In one instance I witnessed a husband and wife team who were convinced that any true Christian ought to sell his assets and give them to the poor and needy. When one of the group members objected and told them that she did not feel so led or called, this couple treated that woman in a rather dismissive and rude manner. That woman and her family properly did not return to that gathering of alleged Christians again.

3. In response to my attempting to bring private correction to one church pastor who was teaching the false doctrine of the pre-tribulation rapture, the pastor refused my multiple offers to get together privately to show him his Biblical error. Instead, he invited me to attend his next adult Sunday school class at which he announced that he and his fellow elders had decided to implement a "statement of faith" that they would ask all members of his church to sign which would include their belief in the rapture, but not necessarily a pre-trib rapture. However anyone entrusted with teaching in his church would be required to teach his error or a pre-trib rapture, thus making anyone who adhered to the truth of the Bible to become a second-class citizen in his church, who would always be viewed with suspicion and disrespect. Never

tolerate such trickery and psychological ploys; leave immediately when you see evidence of such a thing!

4. In response to my attempting to bring gentle correction to a pastor within the Calvary Chapel system, I encountered evasive language and behavior from him which amounted to his telling me, "I'm sorry you feel that way, but things aren't going to change here. This is my church and if you don't like it, you are always free to go elsewhere." This was after a friend he had invited to preach at his church had subjected his church community to a demonic attack against Calvinism, which amounted to a dishonest and disingenuous assault on the Biblical doctrine of election, in which anyone believing contrary to the speaker was depicted as being ignorant and close-minded. So much for modeling Biblical error and anti-love in his church which I found to be deeply offensive and outright heresy being falsely promoted as Biblical truth, with no opportunity for refutation or rebuttal of what was being wrongly taught.

When we factor into account the following factors:

1. The inherent structural flaws of all forms of organized religion rooted in the traditions introduced by the Roman Catholic Church over 1,700 years ago,

2. The truth silencing and suppressing impact of any church agreeing to comply with the outrageous demands of the IRS 501c3 tax-exempt status compliance rules, and

3. The extensive evidence that all forms of organized religion are frauds whose teachings contradict and disobey the teachings of the Bible in its entirety, are not of the truth, and lack genuine honesty and integrity,

we can safely conclude that the vast majority of the 2.2 billion people on the planet who profess themselves to be followers of Christ are, in reality, self-deceived or knowing frauds. True born again followers of Christ, who manifest their numbering among God's elect, are very few in number, and the Bible tells us this by describing the number of God's elect in the end times to be but a remnant, or a remaining small group.

The factors identified here and my illustrations of a number of fraudulent practices of false organized religion suggest that all denominations contain few, if any, true followers of Christ. In fact, given that we are less than 20 months away from the end of the great tribulation today, anyone of the truth, and thus of the elect, is unlikely to be affiliated with any form of organized religion today.

Is it any wonder then, that the world has become so deceitful, sinful, wicked, dishonest, foolish and downright insane? No, it should surprise no one who is of the truth who genuinely follows Yahushua (Jesus) and YHWH (God). We, the elect, are surrounded and far out-numbered. The power of God's holy people has already been largely scattered, just as the prophet Daniel told us it would be:

> "... and when he (God) shall have accomplished to scatter the power of the holy people, all these things shall be finished."
> Daniel 12:7

> "Many shall be purified, and made white, and tried; but the wicked shall do wickedly: and **none of the wicked shall understand; but the wise shall understand.**"
> Daniel 12:10

Let the wise understand.

12. How Ought We to Live During the Days of the Great Tribulation?

In this book, I have attempted to provide the extensive evidence and my sources for them which have led me to conclude that we are now living in the final days of the end times of Bible prophecy in what Daniel 12 and Matthew 24 describe as the days of the great tribulation, which Daniel 12:11 reveals to God's elect will last 1,290 days. At the end of this period of time, the Bible tells God's elect that the following events will occur in this order:

1. Four dramatic celestial events described in Matthew 24:29 will occur right after the days of the great tribulation will end, now revealed to be on October 2, 2016.

2. "And then . . . " the Son of man (Yahushua or Jesus) will be seen throughout the earth, coming in the clouds with power and great glory and all of God's elect from the last 6,000 years, first the dead, and then the living, will be transformed into resurrected bodies and will be caught up to join Jesus in the clouds in what is referred to as the gathering or rapture, that is described in Matthew 24:30-31, 1 Thessalonians 4:13-17, and 1 Corinthians 15:51-55.

3. The resurrected church of God's elect will be invited to participate in the marriage supper of the Lamb in heaven, in which Christ, the bridegroom will be married (joined in union) with His bride, the true church of God's elect believers, as described in Revelation 19:7-9. Revelation 19:9 tells us that those invited to this marriage supper of

the Lamb will be blessed and this blessing date appears to be the same day referred to in Daniel 12:12 that will come 1,335 days after the start (and 45 days after the end) of the great tribulation, now revealed to be November 16, 2016.

4. Yahushua, riding a white horse and wearing a robe dipped in blood, and followed by His army of resurrected saints, riding on white horses and clothed in clean white linen garments (symbolizing holiness, purity and righteousness) will tread the winepress of the fierceness and wrath of Almighty God upon the wicked, as described in Revelation 19:15, which will be manifested in the form of the seven trumpet and seven vial judgments and plagues described in Revelation Chapters 8, 9, 15 and 16, now revealed to occur immediately after November 16, 2016.

If the entirety of what I have revealed here is true, and I believe it is, it changes and should change everything, starting with our perspective on what is important and what is not. The absolute certainty that the global conspiracy that I have revealed here is true also reveals that 100% of the Bible is true and trustworthy and that it always has been. In other words, the global conspiracy proves the Bible to be precisely what it has always claimed to be: the inspired and true words of God to mankind. Thus anything which conflicts with what the Bible says in its entirety in any respect is, by definition, false and a lie and ought not to be trusted. The Bible tells us that this world is ruled by the father of lies and prince of this world, the devil and we now see this to be 100% true and that those who number among the Jewish Illuminati Freemason Zionist global conspiracy, which has hijacked our world today, are his agents and that nothing that they tell us can be trusted: nothing!

Our entire world is based on a fabricated set of lies so pervasive that it would cause most people to suffer extremely severe cognitive dissonance for quite some time before they came to grips with what the truth reveals and implies. And yet, God has, according to the prophecy of 2 Thessalonians 2:10-12, already sent a strong delusion on the vast majority of the people on this planet so that they will believe a lie, and so be condemned to hell for repeatedly rejecting the truth and delighting in unrighteousness. In other words, no matter how much those of us of the truth may speak the truth to a person of the lie, and provide hard evidence and sound logical reasoning from trustworthy authorities to back up our truth claims, a person of the lie will often be incapable of grasping and accepting such truths.

To be sent a strong delusion by God is a very serious thing. Yet how would anyone who has been sent a strong delusion by God even know it? If it is truly a delusion, they would never know it. To those of us who number among God's elect, who are of the truth and have a profound love for the long-term best interests of our fellow human beings, this is very distressing. And yet, this is the implication of the fulfillment of these end times Bible prophecies. The vast majority of the world's population is delusional and at least at some level, is insane: disconnected from and in denial of objective reality as it truly is and as God perceives it.

In these days of the great tribulation, in which our world is ruled by the Antichrist, the impostors posing as Jews, headed by the Jewish Illuminati Freemason Zionist global conspiracy, we have seen our world becoming increasingly chaotic and filled with conflict, lies and betrayals. Nothing is what it appears to be on the surface. Everything our leaders in every sphere of human endeavor are telling us are lies. There are no exceptions to this any longer. The father of lies today rules supreme in our world in which denials of the truth go on endlessly. It is enough to drive a person of the truth batty!

So what are those of us who number among God's elect, who are of the truth and who genuinely love our fellow man to do? How are we to live effectively in a world gone mad? What follows are the insights I have arrived at through much thought, contemplation and experimentation. I offer them as techniques we can use to remain sane and at peace in an insane and chaotic world:

1. First, recognize that God remains firmly in control of all events, thoughts and circumstances in each of our lives,

which He allows to teach us life lessons unique to each of us. God promises us that He will provide for our every need and up to this point in our lives, God has proven Himself entirely trustworthy in this regard. Not everything God allows is pleasant. Much of it can be quite painful. Yet we tend to learn the most when we are uncomfortable and experiencing some degree of struggle or affliction. It is a well-known principle of life that those who have achieved the greatest wisdom and maturity in life have often suffered hideously for it. God disciplines and chastens those whom He loves, just as a good father disciplines his children to teach them responsibility and develop their moral characters. Tribulation means troubles and the great tribulation is directed at chastening God's elect and molding our characters into the likeness of Christ. So we ought to expect troubles, affliction and opposition from a world that has gone over to the devil and his demon spirits.

2. Second, we must recognize that the vast majority of what we are witnessing in our world today, all of which is being orchestrated by God, is out of our control. No act of man is going to fix a spiritual condition which is global in scale and is designed by God to fulfill His perfect plan for His elect. What God wills, God always gets and His end times plan is clearly under way and unstoppable. For anyone to try to stop it is foolhardy.

3. Third, we need to stop listening to liars, if we are ever going to discover that which is objectively true and which is healthy for us, and then do those things. To begin with, we need to discover that which is true and completely reliable. Only God's Word, the Bible (preferably the KJV of the Bible, for those for whom English is their first language) meets this standard. If God and Jesus are real (and they are) and God has left his flawless and inspired words for mankind to live well, does it not follow that we ought to invest the time to become intimately familiar with what it says, what it means and how it applies to our daily lives and to come to know the true thoughts, ways and nature of

12. How Ought We to Live During the Days of the Great Tribulation?

God as He truly is, and not how our wicked and depraved world falsely portrays Him to be?

   a. Just as FBI anti-counterfeiting agents are taught to recognize counterfeit currency by exposing them to the real deals, so too ought all of God's elect to study and meditate on God's flawless and inspired words of truth so that whenever we hear or encounter a lie, we can instantly recognize it as error, reject it and expose it for what it is so that others are not deceived and misled by it.

4. Bad company corrupts good character. Proverbs 13:20 says it best: *"He that walketh with wise men shall be wise: but a companion of fools shall be destroyed."* Most of us have been hanging out with plenty of fools. Fools are people who are morally deficient. To become wise in an era such as ours requires great discernment and personal discipline to distance ourselves from those who are not of the truth and who show little or no love and compassion for their fellow man. In my own life, over the past three years, I have made a conscious choice to have nothing to do with over 95% of the people in my career and personal life who proved, over time, to be not at all what they purported to be. Today, I am very discriminating who I let into my life. I have been badly burned and betrayed in my 61 years of living and do not wish to repeat my errors in judgment from the past.

5. Our media and the technology of television are designed to deceive and manipulate us into believing endless lies being promoted by the Jewish Illuminati Freemason Zionist global elites in order to control and manipulate us into supporting actions aimed at achieving world domination by the impostors posing as Jews. Knowing that these Jewish globalists own and control all mainstream media outlets ought to be reason enough to cease listening to or watching any of the lying talking heads of the mainstream media. And there are no exceptions to this. FOX News, while more politically conservative than its

more liberal mainstream media competitors, is owned and controlled by Rupert Murdock, who is a member of the CFR and a close friend of the Rothschild banking dynasty family that sits at the top of the Rothschild-Zionist New World Order elites. We can easily see how stridently FOX News pushes the agenda of the rogue terrorist state of Israel at the expense of its Palestinian victims, painting the Antichrist impostors posing as Jews as morally above reproach. Their treachery and deceit is wicked, vile and pure evil!

Moreover, the technology of television includes a screen image that flickers every 60 seconds or so that allows television programmers to hypnotize viewers and in a hypnotized state, suggest subliminal messages which lodge in viewers' subconscious minds which can later be triggered or activated by the use of specific trigger words to induce an emotional response of some kind. This is mind-control programming at its finest, and it needs to stop!

The solution is obvious: stop reading newspapers, stop listening to radio news and talk shows and stop viewing television. I stopped viewing television over a decade ago and am very glad I did, especially in light of the more malevolent and intentional hypnotic design effects of television technology, which I have subsequently discovered.

  a. One exception I do still recommend reading is the weekly newspaper, American Free Press, which does a good job of openly reporting on the actions and movements of the global elites, even though they continue to write as though they believe our federal electoral process has any integrity to it and is worthy of our time and attention, whereas I am convinced it does not.

6. The Jewish global conspiracy is doing many things to undermine the health of the average citizen of the world in order to exterminate a large portion of the world's

population of 7.0 billion people. Monsanto and other global agriculture corporations beholden to the Jewish elites have been developing Genetically Modified Organism (GMO) crops which many scientific studies have indicated lead to increased risks of a multitude of chronic illnesses, cancer being among them. Our own U.S. Agriculture Department promotes a diet high in processed foods which benefit the profit motives of its corporate sponsors and lobbyists, but which encourage uninformed Americans to consume a preponderance of acid-forming foods which lead to an acidic body pH. Acidic body pHs are known to support the onset of a number of chronic diseases. These threats to Americans' health can be combatted with education and the personal discipline to alter one's diet to favor alkaline-forming foods and avoid acid-forming ones.

a. Appendix F provides a list of beneficial alkaline-forming foods to consume and acid-forming foods to avoid. I have used this protocol three times in the past two years with very positive results. I was easily able, just through these dietary changes, to change my body pH from 6.5 (which is acidic) to 8.0 (which is alkaline to a level in which cancer cannot survive in the body) in less than two weeks.

b. Periodically detoxing our bodies through colon, kidney, liver and blood cleanses reduces the buildup of toxins in our bodies through unhealthy eating and drinking habits and though our exposure to harmful chemicals we encounter in our daily lives, most of which we are seldom aware of. This includes detoxing for aluminum, barium and strontium in our atmosphere from chemtrails raining down on us.

c. Our dental work often is poisoning our bodies with the leaching of mercury, a highly toxic substance known to produce chronic disease from silver-amalgam fillings and posts under dental inlays, crowns and root canals which are composed of 50% mercury, which then leaches into our bodies for the rest of our lives. Root canals, which are dead teeth, contain over 3 miles of dentin tubules per tooth in which anaerobic bacteria produce highly toxic waste products which drain into our lymphatic and blood systems and are carried throughout our bodies with highly toxic effects to our immune systems. Additionally, these toxins often produce brain fog and a lack of mental clarity at a time in world history when we need all the wits about us we can possibly get.

Certain dentists, trained in bio-compatible dentistry and the safe removal of mercury-laden dental work are available to assist patients who seek to remove mercury-laden fillings and crowns, and extract root canal teeth and remove any cavitations, or holes in a patient's jaw bone where bacteria grow and emit their toxic waste products, created by the improper extraction of teeth in the past. I recently invested in such dental revision and removed the mercury that had leached into my body cells for decades with half a dozen rounds of Vitamin-C flushes under the guidance of my dentist who is trained in dental revision protocols and subsequent detoxing, in order to strengthen my compromised immune system (measured through blood and hair samples) and to enhance my mental alertness and clarity. Immediately after my dental revision procedure, I experienced a complete cessation of chronic back and neck pain which I had endured for nearly two decades that were connected with teeth that had mercury fillings in them.

d. America's cancer-treatment protocols and industry are a joke. The only treatments ever applied to the treatment of cancer in America is to cut, poison or irradiate the cancer patient's body (surgery, chemotherapy or radiation), all of which treat the symptoms of the cancer, while never addressing its root causes! This amounts to sheer insanity, gross incompetence and outright fraud on the part of the cancer-treatment industry in America.

Information available on the internet and elsewhere seems to indicate the the causes of cancer are a lot more well-known and better understood than the American public has been led to believe. An alkaline body pH of 7.5 inhibits the growth of cancer cells and a body pH of 8.0 or higher causes cancer cells and tumors to wither and die. Dr. Tullio Simonici in Italy has had great success applying baking soda delivered via catheter directly to cancer tumors to cure them and he contends that cancer is a fungus that baking soda eradicates.[68] It is likely no coincidence that baking soda is alkaline. Other cancer patients, consuming a cup of heated water with two teaspoons of baking soda and one teaspoon of organic maple syrup or molasses up to three times a day have been successful in curing their own stage four prostate cancers.[69]

Dr. Hulda Clark has written extensively on the effects of the common intestinal fluke that at certain stages in its life, if it comes in contact with isopropyl alcohol in the liver, produces cancer. Clark has identified a combination of black walnut hull extract, wormwood and common cloves that taken in certain concentrations kills intestinal flukes at the adult, adolescent and larvae stages to block the mutation of healthy cells into cancerous ones.

In states like California, it is illegal for any medical doctor to even mention any treatment beyond surgery, chemo or radiation or they may face jail time. Why? Because the cancer treatment industry is big business,

---

[68] *Dr Tullio Simonici Part 1 of 3.*
http://www.youtube.com/watch?v=69P-Cqy7OSk.
[69] Johnston, Vernon "Vito."
How to Make Baking Soda Molasses Cancer Protocol Solutions.
http://www.youtube.com/watch?v=Yl8Y8I_TsjI.

generating roughly $50 billion in revenues ($50,000 per cancer patient per year) to the oncology specialists and Big Pharma, which owns the patents to the very expensive and debilitating chemotherapy recipes to which cancer patients are routinely subjected.

It is widely known that it is quite common for cancer to come back. Now we know why: the cancer industry only treats symptoms and has no interest in developing and offering an effective cure for which there is very little money to be made. Who's behind this barbaric savagery and dark evil? Well, that would be the devil, the prince of this world and the father of lies and a medical establishment which has played dumb and remained silent in the face of known cures to cancer. This cowardice and silence of the oncology industry in the face of known cancer cures is about as wicked, immoral and as unjust as it gets.

7. Our political systems in America are completely rigged and corrupt to the core and few people have yet become aware of this colossal scam and con job. Anyone using any common sense and simple logical reasoning from known facts ought to be able to see this. So clearly, spiritual blindness plays an important factor in perpetuating the fraud of American politics.

Every couple of years, we witness a charade being played out in our lying and deceptive media that is owned and controlled by the Jewish global elites who have hijacked America decades ago. The deep-pocketed money elites who sit on the Council on Foreign Relations (the public and political arm of the Illuminati in America) select the candidates who will run in each electoral contest on behalf of the one party system with two branches (Democrat and Republican) just for show and theater, but both sides work for the same globalist New World Order satanic agenda. The Jewish owned and controlled media manufacture fraudulent polling numbers which the corrupt media then promotes through its lying talking heads to the naive and gullible American public who lap up the fraudulent theater like stupid puppy dogs.

All we are fed by our media are public relations images of political candidates who all secretly share two essential traits: 1) they lie well and get away with it, and 2) they have one or more embarrassing and compromising indiscretions in their pasts which the globalists are aware of and use to blackmail their puppets into doing their bidding. Not one of our political candidates has any truth or integrity to him, and this is by design to make a mockery out of our political system and to thumb their noses at those of us who finally figure this stuff out.

Before the elections take place, the globalists decide who they will declare the winner. The votes are taken and often in less than 30 minutes after the polls close, frequently with less than 0.5% of the votes allegedly having been counted, our corrupt and lying media informs us of the decision the globalists made before the elections occurred. Those of us who took a course in statistics in college can quickly figure out the impossibility of predicting a winner with such a small sample counted, but the globalists of our shadow government don't care about that: they know that the naive and gullible masses will go along with whatever they tell them to be true, even though it obviously is not.

In light of this reality, the simple truth is that votes don't matter, even though we have always been told (falsely) that they do. The only way to combat such wholesale voting fraud is to refuse to play their game. Why vote? Why lend any legitimacy and credibility to a system that is so hopelessly corrupt and dishonest? Instead, every last one of us ought to boycott the voting process and force the talking heads of the lying media to explain that one. Combined with our refusing to read, listen to or watch any media any longer, we expose the media-crony capitalism-government complex for being the corrupt fraud it always has been.

8. Our government-owned public schools have been used against the American people for decades to indoctrinate, brain wash, mind control program and subject our children to endless propaganda while defiling and corrupting their morals by promoting promiscuity, homosexuality, and anything goes morality so that our children believe that snow is black, good is evil and evil is good.

I know this all too well. All three of my twenty-something year old children are products of the public school system (as was I) and today they are indulged fools who are incapable of logical reasoning or coherent thought. They have been ruined for life, just as was the design of the Jewish Illuminati Freemason Zionist global elites, to create obedient, politically correct, unthinking slaves of their New World Order police state. As a result, my children have rejected my every attempt as their godly father to teach them the truth and true life wisdom that comes only from God, Jesus and the Bible. I was clueless that this was being done to me and my three children until it was too late. But that need not be the case for readers who are parents who still have kids living at home.

If you have any love at all for your kids and hope to spare them from the coming disaster less than a year from now, which will fall upon the wicked, I plead with you to pull your kids out of public school and home school them, no matter what it takes. Otherwise, I guarantee that you will lose your children to the corrupt, immoral, polluted and demonic culture that defines America today, just as I did, and you will have nobody but yourself to blame for it. I am dead serious about this!

9. In light of the fact that I have already revealed and demonstrated quite thoroughly that all forms of organized religion are, and always have been, ruled by demon spirits, I strongly urge all readers to leave and have nothing to do with any form of organized religion ever again. This may seem extreme at first, but I ask you to think very carefully about this. These spiritual whore houses are failing to teach

you the truth and are not loving, safe communities of true followers of Christ. They are frauds and misleading you and your families. Instead, consider organizing small Bible study or church groups in your homes, composed of you and other couples you trust who are of the truth and genuinely exhibit sacrificial love and compassion for their fellow man. Err on the side of caution concerning who you invite into your circles of friends. Seek out one or more mature and wise men to lead and facilitate your groups in accordance with the model of the first century church of the Book of Acts. Consider meeting at least weekly, sharing a meal together and sharing the teaching load out of the Bible between two or three men who have consistently exhibited the set of attributes which Paul tells his disciple, Timothy, to look for in both bishops (elders) and deacons in 1 Timothy 3. Above all, do not invite snakes into your homes. You will live to regret it if you do.

10. If at all possible, move out of densely populated metropolitan areas to more rural and less densely populated areas which are less likely to experience social strife, looting, riots and threats to your personal property and the lives of yourselves and your families in the event of globalist attempts to foment conflict, violence, chaos and anarchy. Invest some time and money in becoming better informed and prepared in the event of a natural disaster or man-made crisis. Seek to become as self-sufficient as you can, so that you and your family can survive for a minimum of two weeks, and preferably longer, in the event that all outside-supplied services (gas, electricity, water, and sewer) were cut off for an extended period of time.

Consider growing some of your own crops and raising livestock and securing a year's supply of dehydrated emergency food supplies. Consider securing firearms and learning how to use them to defend yourself and your family from looters and agents of the globalists seeking to confiscate or steal your property. Don't count on law enforcement to be able to respond in a timely manner to threats to your personal safety; if you are wrong it could cost you or your loved ones your lives.

11. Invest time and energy strengthening your close personal relationships with God and with those closest to you, beginning with your spouse. Feminism has done more to destroy healthy relationships, marriages and families than any other social development over the last century. Feminism is a demonic philosophy intentionally introduced into the modern day culture by the globalists, designed to destabilize the family in order to destroy it, and establish the structure of the State as the supreme authority over all society.

The way it has done this is to try to reverse the Biblical roles of men and women so that women compete with men for control and dominance in the home. In response, most men don't compete with their wives, they turn passive and effeminate and give way to their wives out of love for them. Wives in turn lose respect for passive and effeminate husbands and the inevitable result is social chaos in the home in which everyone is miserable.

This is all by deliberate and intentional design to destroy western civilization and replace it with a satanic New World Order in which every aspect of our lives is monitored and enslaved to serve the interests and deviancies of the super-rich Jewish Illuminati Freemason Zionist global elites through a brutal police state which they own and control. These satanic elites who rule our antichrist system today have failed to account for one thing: the inevitable second coming of Yahushua in late 2016.

In the meantime, those of us who number among God's elect, who are of the truth and love our fellow man, can resist the devil by strengthening our marriages and learning how to live effectively with our spouses to create joy, harmony and love in our homes. This is something which the globalists can do nothing to take from us unless we cooperate with their demonic plan of advancing the agenda of feminism, which is not in the best interests of women, men or children.

Once we have figured this out in our own lives, we can teach others what we have learned. For example, my new bride of one year and I have both come from past failed marriages in which our former spouses wanted nothing to do with God, chose to live selfishly, and became demon-possessed from their multiple sinful actions. We have chosen to learn from the past by marrying someone who is as equally yoked to God as we are, and living our lives according to what the Bible teaches. We are placing the health and integrity of our marriage second after our relationship with God. And how is it working so far? We are both thriving, growing and feeling safe and affirmed by one another and we both know we can count on and trust one another. We are learning how to constructively work out the inevitable differences that every couple encounters by seeking to make our relationship our number one priority and to understand the needs of one another, rather than seeking to get our way all the time.

12. When managing your finances, think in terms of a two year time horizon. You can't take it with you when you go and you won't need it when you do. Spend conservatively, but don't make investments with more than a two year time horizon that will get even shorter as we approach the blessing date of November 16, 2016. Don't permit money to be an idol of yours: it is a resource to live off of potentially, but make it last as long as you can, in case my understanding of God's Biblical timeline proves to be in error in some way. I don't believe it is, but I don't want you living as if that outlook is a certainty. Nothing is a certainty.

13. Use what opportunities you have to share this information with others who might heed it and benefit from it, but use wisdom when you do this. 99% of the people you encounter will not be able to process this information and will become highly distressed by it and quite possibly quite angry at and abusive toward you, if you try to do so. These

are common reactions I have encountered with a number of people I have shared this information with. Those who have grown up in some form of organized religion are the worst. They are heavily deceived by their false teaching pastors, ministers and priests, but think they know it all. It's much easier to teach someone with a blank slate and an open mind than it is to correct a deceived mind and then teach things that contradict and conflict with what they have been wrongly taught and believed all their lives. Their pride is often pricked and injured, and they struggle to admit they might have been wrong.

In instances where you encounter such resistance, keep your mouth shut and move on; you won't make any headway with such close-minded people who are in error until they are hurting sufficiently, such that the pain they are experiencing overcomes their pride and they are willing to seek out the truth and ask questions. Only then, are most people receptive to being taught much of anything.

14. If you have never studied the subject of spiritual warfare or been led through a spiritual cleansing and deliverance process, I strongly recommend that that you do so. My next book, planned for release in the second half 2015, will be addressing this very area in which I plan to condense and simplify a large body of knowledge out there that has been actively suppressed and silenced by most forms of organized religion and the global elites who engage in the occult. Many of these materials presuppose a greater knowledge and awareness of what the Bible teaches us about this subject than is justified by the knowledge base of the average reader today, even if he or she numbers among God's elect.

This advice only applies if you are already born again in the Spirit. If a person is not born again in the Spirit (and there are simple ways to test for this), going through a cleansing and deliverance process will quite likely make things much worse for anyone afflicted with demon spirits.

12. How Ought We to Live During the Days of the Great Tribulation?

The point I wish to leave readers with here is that virtually every person in America has been afflicted with demon spirits of some kind and most don't even know it or know that there is anything they can effectively do about it. The good news is that there is a great deal that true born again Christians can do about demon spirit infestation and control. Moreover, whenever a person becomes a born again Christian, he or she almost certainly still suffers from demon spirit affliction and opposition of some kind, which must be dealt with for that person to go on to live an abundant life free of oppression and affliction that is rooted in the spiritual realm, that is very real, and little understood by most people.

15. Related to the subject of spiritual warfare are a series of behaviors whose spiritual dangers we need to be aware of, so that we can tenaciously avoid them and urge our friends and family members to do the same. For young people who are easily influenced by social pressures to conform from their peers, much of this advice will seem counter-cultural and hopelessly out-of-date with today's world, because it is. Common practices in today's culture are very dangerous and we need to be aware of what these are. Here are a few of the most common and dangerous ones:

   a. Do not engage in sex with anyone outside of the covenant of marriage between one man and one woman for life. When we engage in sexual intercourse, we become one flesh, as Genesis 2:24 tells us. As one flesh, demon spirits in our sexual partners are free to pass from them to us, and vice versa. The more sexual partners a person has had, the more numerous and dangerous the demon spirits are likely to be which afflict him or her.

   This is the key principle which we see being vigorously promoted in our schools with our youth today, which is intentionally designed to encourage them to experiment with all forms of sexual encounters. The real goal of the satanic globalists who rule our world

435

today is to demonize our youth and take them captive to their satanic spells. Wake up parents and home school your kids for this reason alone!

b. Avoid taking on tattoos or any form of body piercings other than a single piercing for earrings in each ear for girls and women. Body piercings are frequently done to enhance the sexual pleasures of the wearers or their sexual partners, but it is a pathway for demon spirit infestation, as are tattoos of all sorts. The more tattoos and body piercings a person has, the more likely it is that they are infested with numerous and dangerous demon spirits which confuse their thinking and cause the infested person to exercise poor moral judgments.

c. Avoid hallucinogenic drug use. Hallucinogenic substances permit a user to see and communicate with the spirit world; something which is strictly forbidden in the Bible in the Old Testament, which still applies today.

d. Similarly, avoid all forms of practices in the occult, from ouija boards, fortune telling, palm reading, participating in séances and divination, necromancy (communing with the spirits of dead people), astrology, or engaging in any form of witchcraft or satanism, all of which inevitably lead to demon spirit infestation and control of the most pernicious kinds.

e. Avoid all forms of anti-Christian New Age practices, including transcendental meditation (in which you clear your mind, leaving it open for demon spirits to enter), yoga, use of crystals, bringing statues, masks, spears and idols into your home over which practitioners of the dark arts may have invoked a curse, or practicing martial arts, which at the higher levels require one to gain mastery over one's opponent using spirit power. This spirit power is always a form of demon spirit power.

12. How Ought We to Live During the Days of the Great Tribulation?

Summary and Conclusion

So there you have it, my dear readers. What I have shared with you in this book is some of the most shocking and taboo subject matter you could have ever laid your hands on. If you have read this far, you are to be commended greatly for it. Few have the integrity, character and courage to examine many of the issues I have revealed to you here. I don't doubt that you are likely to struggle with much of what I have shared with you here in these pages for some time. That certainly was my experience as I wrestled with a number of these revelations that were new to me at the time. I would advise you to go slow with this material and take your time processing it out in your mind and with trusted friends and loved ones who have examined the same evidence that you now have. Most of us experience what clinical psychologists refer to as cognitive dissonance. When we first discover these facts and circumstances, we become disoriented, anxious and confused as we reform our cognitive maps to integrate this new information into our worldview or understanding of truth and how the world really works, as opposed to how we were misled to believe it did work all our lives.

At some point, you are likely to experience considerable anger, directed at those who may have betrayed and deceived you. Anger is a healthy emotional response to that which is dangerous, unjust and immoral and it exists to protect us from harm. In my own experience, that anger has dissipated over time, but remains there in the background seeking justice for the wrongs done to me and to billions of other innocent people, by the enemy of all humanity, Satan himself.

Today I seek to channel that anger into my book writing and blogging to teach and warn others what I have learned so that they might benefit from it and effectively resist the devil, who is very real. If my writing and teaching reaches just one person who otherwise would have never discovered this information, then my efforts have been worth it.

For those of us who are blessed enough to number among God's elect, the next 12 months promise to be quite challenging and unsettling. And at the end of those 12 months, we have the very real hope and promise of being gathered to be with Yahushua (Jesus) in heaven with all other true believers in God and Christ for all time and to participate in the marriage supper of the Lamb in new resurrected bodies. From that point forward, there will be no more tears, pain or suffering and we are promised to be like Christ in character and to live in harmony with one another and with God and Jesus forever. These are amazing promises. They defy our ability to fully grasp, comprehend and believe. Yet I know our almighty, brilliant, kind and loving God and His nature and so I trust fully that all He promises will indeed come to pass.

I am grateful and humbled beyond words for the privilege He has blessed me with to serve Him as one of His prophets and a watchman on the wall in these final days of the great tribulation. I never knew this was even possible until the last several years of my life. "Why me?" keeps echoing through my head, even though I know the answer: because He chose me since before the world began to become one of his adopted sons. Nothing else in life comes close to comparing with this miracle. I am truly blessed; and so are you. We have much to hope in, be thankful for and look forward to!

To those who do not number among God's elect, I have very little to say. Few, if any of you, will have read to this point, for the truth is deeply offensive to you. I fully get that. But God is sovereign and He has chosen some vessels for honor and others for dishonor to bring ultimate glory to Himself. I know that this is not very satisfying for those of you who may be contemplating the burning lake of fire and brimstone for all eternity. I know that in light of this horrible future you are facing, that nothing I say is likely to make it any easier.

As much as a number of God's non-elect have hurt me deeply and brought me much pain and suffering over my lifetime, I now know it had to be that way to test, refine and mature and teach me godly wisdom and God's thoughts and ways to prepare me for this day. There was no other way to accomplish this in me. For those who inflicted those injuries on me, and in many cases took delight in doing so, I forgive you, for you knew not what you were doing. May God be merciful to you and may He keep you far from those of us who number among His elect.

Appendices

Appendices A, B and C reveal the behaviors and character disorder of psychopaths, sociopaths and those who are evil. All three terms are synonyms for one another. Virtually all those who rule our world and are leaders in almost every field of human endeavor in these days of the great tribulation in which we are living today possess and exhibit this character disorder. Thus, it is vitally important for all of God's elect to be able to quickly recognize those possessing and exhibiting the traits of this disorder, which is rooted in the spiritual realm of demon infestation and perhaps possession, and have as little as possible to do with them.

> *"Keep thy heart with all diligence; for out of it are the issues of life."* Proverbs 4:23

Appendix D documents 200 separate incidents in which the impostors posing as Jews were banned from their host countries for sedition and corruption. This information has been vigorously suppressed and silenced by these same psychopath impostors posing as Jews who have hijacked and own and control all major media outlets and sources of information, for what should now be obvious reasons.

Appendix E documents the range of estimates of exterminations of people by their own Communist governments during the first 87 years of the 20th century. In this book I have estimated the total deaths from four countries alone during the 20th century at 142 million innocent lives lost to the savage brutality of Jewish-inspired satanic Communism, which the Jewish Illuminati Freemason Zionist global elites are behind and for which they are guilty. Merely using the 142 million deaths figure is a number which exceeds all the deaths in all the wars of recorded human history. Appendix E reveals that it is quite possible that the actual number of deaths could have exceeded 259 million innocent lives lost to this pernicious evil.

Appendix F provides insights into which foods are alkaline-forming (good for us) compared to those which are acid-forming and provide a hospitable environment for chronic diseases such as cancer, heart disease and diabetes to thrive.

Appendix G identifies the eight end times prophecies which have been fulfilled with hair-splitting accuracy in recent years and the evidence for them. These fulfilled prophecies are symbolized by the eagles of Matthew 24:28 and the fig leaves of Matthew 24:32. Where the eagles are gathered, Yahushua tells us that the carcass, symbolizing His second coming, cannot be far removed. Likewise, when we see the fig tree putting forth its leaves, we know that summer, symbolizing His second coming yet again, cannot be far removed. Today, the second coming of Yahushua is less than a year away. It will be here before we know it.

Appendix A

"Profile of a Sociopath[70]

This website summarizes some of the common features and descriptions of the behavior of sociopaths.

- Glibness and Superficial Charm

- Manipulative and Conning
  They never recognize the rights of others and see their self-serving behaviors as permissible. They appear to be charming, yet are covertly hostile and domineering, seeing their victim as merely an instrument to be used. They may dominate and humiliate their victims.

- Grandiose Sense of Self
  Feels entitled to certain things as their "right."

- Pathological Lying
  Has no problem lying coolly and easily and it is almost impossible for them to be truthful on a consistent basis. Can create, and get caught up in, a complex belief about their own powers and abilities. Extremely convincing and even able to pass lie detector tests.

- Lack of Remorse, Shame or Guilt
  A deep seated rage, which is split off and repressed, is at their core. Does not see others around them as people, but only as targets and opportunities. Instead of friends, they have victims and accomplices who end up as victims. The end always justifies the means and they let nothing stand in their way.

- Shallow Emotions
  When they show what seems to be warmth, joy, love and compassion, it is more feigned than experienced and serves an ulterior motive. Outraged by insignificant matters, yet remaining unmoved and cold by what would upset a normal person. Since they are not genuine, neither are their promises.

---

[70] http://www.mcafee.cc/Bin/sb.html.

Appendix A

- Incapacity for Love

- Need for Stimulation
  Living on the edge. Verbal outbursts and physical
  punishments are normal. Promiscuity and gambling are
  common.

- Callousness/Lack of Empathy
  Unable to empathize with the pain of their victims,
  having only contempt for others' feelings of distress and
  readily taking advantage of them.

- Poor Behavioral Controls/Impulsive Nature
  Rage and abuse, alternating with small expressions of love
  and approval produce an addictive cycle for abuser and
  abused, as well as creating hopelessness in the victim.
  Believe they are all-powerful, all-knowing, entitled to
  every wish, no sense of personal boundaries, no concern
  for their impact on others.

- Early Behavior Problems/Juvenile Delinquency
  Usually has a history of behavioral and academic
  difficulties, yet "gets by" by conning others. Problems in
  making and keeping friends; aberrant behaviors such as
  cruelty to people or animals, stealing, etc.

- Irresponsibility/Unreliability
  Not concerned about wrecking others' lives and dreams.
  Oblivious or indifferent to the devastation they cause.
  Does not accept blame themselves, but blames others,
  even for acts they obviously committed.

- Promiscuous Sexual Behavior/Infidelity
  Promiscuity, child sexual abuse, rape and sexual acting
  out of all sorts.

- Lack of Realistic Life Plan/Parasitic Lifestyle
  Tends to move around a lot or makes all-encompassing
  promises for the future, poor work ethic but exploits
  others effectively.

- Criminal or Entrepreneurial Versatility
Changes their image as needed to avoid prosecution.
Changes life story readily.

Other Related Qualities:

1. Contemptuous of those who seek to understand them

2. Does not perceive that anything is wrong with them

3. Authoritarian

4. Secretive

5. Paranoid

6. Only rarely in difficulty with the law, but seeks out situations where their tyrannical behavior will be tolerated, condoned, or admired

7. Conventional appearance

8. Goal of enslavement of their victim(s)

9. Exercises despotic control over every aspect of the victim's life

10. Has an emotional need to justify their crimes and therefore needs their victim's affirmation (respect, gratitude and love)

11. Ultimate goal is the creation of a willing victim

12. Incapable of real human attachment to another

13. Unable to feel remorse or guilt

14. Extreme narcissism and grandiose plans

15. May state readily that their goal is to rule the world

The above traits are based on the psychopathy checklists of H. Cleckley and R. Hare.

NOTE: In the 1830s this disorder was called "moral insanity." By 1900 it was changed to "psychopathic personality." More recently it has been termed "antisocial personality disorder" in the DSM-III and DSM-IV. Some critics have complained that, in the attempt to rely only on 'objective criteria,' the DSM has broadened the concept to include too many individuals. The APD category includes people who commit illegal, immoral or self-serving acts for a variety of reasons and are not necessarily psychopaths.

DSM-IV Definition:

Antisocial personality disorder is characterized by a lack of regard for the moral or legal standards in the local culture. There is a marked inability to get along with others or abide by societal rules. Individuals with this disorder are sometimes called psychopaths or sociopaths.

Diagnostic Criteria (DSM-IV)

1. Since the age of fifteen there has been a disregard for and violation of the rights of others, those rights considered normal by the local culture, as indicated by at least three of the following:

   A. Repeated acts that could lead to arrest.

   B. Conning for pleasure or profit, repeated lying, or the use of aliases.

   C. Failure to plan ahead or being impulsive.

   D. Repeated assaults on others.

   E. Reckless when it comes to their or others' safety.

   F. Poor work behavior or failure to honor financial obligations.

   G. Rationalizing the pain they inflict on others.

2. At least eighteen years in age.

3. Evidence of a Conduct Disorder, with its onset before the age of fifteen.

4. Symptoms not due to another mental disorder.

Antisocial Personality Disorder Overview (Written by Derek Wood, RN, BSN, PhD Candidate)

Antisocial Personality Disorder results in what is commonly known as a Sociopath. The criteria for this disorder require an ongoing disregard for the rights of others, since the age of 15 years. Some examples of this disregard are reckless disregard for the safety of themselves or others, failure to conform to social norms with respect to lawful behaviors, deceitfulness such as repeated lying or deceit for personal profit or pleasure, and lack of remorse for actions that hurt other people in any way. Additionally, they must have evidenced a Conduct Disorder before the age of 15 years, and must be at least 18 years old to receive this diagnosis.

People with this disorder appear to be charming at times, and make relationships, but to them, these are relationships in name only. They are ended whenever necessary or when it suits them, and the relationships are without depth or meaning, including marriages. They seem to have an innate ability to find the weakness in people, and are ready to use these weaknesses to their own ends through deceit, manipulation, or intimidation, and gain pleasure from doing so.

They appear to be incapable of any true emotions, from love to shame to guilt. They are quick to anger, but just as quick to let it go, without holding grudges. No matter what emotion they state they have, it has no bearing on their future actions or attitudes. They rarely are able to have jobs that last for any length of time, as they become easily bored, instead needing constant change. They live for the moment, forgetting the past, and not planning the future, not thinking ahead what consequences their actions will have. They want immediate rewards and gratification. There currently is no form of psychotherapy that works with those with antisocial personality disorder, as those with this disorder have no desire to change themselves, which is a prerequisite. No medication is available either. The only treatment is the prevention of the disorder in the early stages, when a child first begins to show the symptoms of conduct disorder.

THE PSYCHOPATH NEXT DOOR (Source:
http://chericola57.tripod.com/infinite.html)

Psychopath. We hear the word and images of Bernardo, Manson and Dahmer pop into our heads; no doubt Ted Bundy too. But they're the bottom of the barrel — most of the two million psychopaths in North America aren't murderers. They're our friends, lovers and co-workers. They're outgoing and persuasive, dazzling you with charm and flattery. Often you aren't even aware they've taken you for a ride — until it's too late.

Psychopaths exhibit a Jekyll and Hyde personality. "They play a part so they can get what they want," says Dr. Sheila Willson, a Toronto psychologist who has helped victims of psychopaths. The guy who showers a woman with excessive attention is much more capable of getting her to lend him money, and to put up with him when he strays. The new employee who gains her co-workers' trust has more access to their check books. And so on. Psychopaths have no conscience and their only goal is self-gratification. Many of us have been their victims — at work, through friendships or relationships — and not one of us can say, "A psychopath could never fool me."

Think you can spot one? Think again. In general, psychopaths aren't the product of broken homes or the casualties of a materialistic society. Rather they come from all walks of life and there is little evidence that their upbringing affects them. Elements of a psychopath's personality first become evident at a very early age, due to biological or genetic factors. Explains Michael Seto, a psychologist at the Centre for Addiction and Mental health in Toronto, by the time that a person hits their late teens, the disorder is almost certainly permanent. Although many clinicians use the terms psychopath and sociopath interchangeably, writes psychopath expert Robert Hare on his book 'Without Conscience,' a sociopath's criminal behavior is shaped by social forces and is the result of a dysfunctional environment.

Psychopaths have only a shallow range of emotions and lack guilt, says Hare. They often see themselves as victims, and lack remorse or the ability to empathize with others. 'Psychopaths play on the fact that most of us are trusting and forgiving people,' adds Seto. The warning signs are always there; it's just difficult to see them because once we trust someone, the friendship becomes a blinder.

Even lovers get taken for a ride by psychopaths. For a psychopath, a romantic relationship is just another opportunity to find a trusting partner who will buy into the lies. It's primarily why a psychopath rarely stays in a relationship for the long term, and often is involved with three or four partners at once, says Willson. To a psychopath, everything about a relationship is a game. Willson refers to the movie 'Sliding Doors' to illustrate her point. In the film, the main character comes home early after just having been fired from her job. Only moments ago, her boyfriend has let another woman out the front door. But in a matter of minutes he is the attentive and concerned boyfriend, taking her out to dinner and devoting the entire night to comforting her. All the while he's planning to leave the next day on a trip with the other woman.

The boyfriend displays typical psychopathic characteristics because he falsely displays deep emotion toward the relationship, says Willson. In reality, he's less concerned with his girlfriend's depression than with making sure she's clueless about the other woman's existence. In the romance department, psychopaths have an ability to gain your affection quickly, disarming you with words, intriguing you with grandiose plans. If they cheat you'll forgive them, and one day when they've gone too far, they'll leave you with a broken heart (and an empty wallet). By then they'll have a new player for their game.

Appendix A

The problem with their game is that we don't often play by their rules. Where we might occasionally tell a white lie, a psychopath's lying is compulsive. Most of us experience some degree of guilt about lying, preventing us from exhibiting such behavior on a regular basis. "Psychopaths don't discriminate who it is they lie to or cheat," says Seto. "There's no distinction between friend, family and sucker."

No one wants to be the sucker, so how do we prevent ourselves from becoming close friends or getting into a relationship with a psychopath? It's really almost impossible, say Seto and Willson. Unfortunately, laments Seto, one way is to become more suspicious and less trusting of others. Our tendency is to forgive when we catch a loved one in a lie. "Psychopaths play on this fact," he says. "However, I'm certainly not advocating a world where if someone lies once or twice, you never speak to them again." What you can do is look at how often someone lies and how they react when caught. Psychopaths will lie over and over again, and where other people would sincerely apologize, a psychopath may apologize but won't stop.

Psychopaths also tend to switch jobs as frequently as they switch partners, mainly because they don't have the qualities to maintain a job for the long haul. Their performance is generally erratic, with chronic absences, misuse of company resources and failed commitments. Often they aren't even qualified for the job and use fake credentials to get it. Seto talks of a patient who would get marketing jobs based on his image; he was a presentable and charming man who layered his conversations with educational and occupational references. But it became evident that the man hadn't a clue what he was talking about, and was unable to hold down a job.

How do you make sure you don't get fooled when you're hiring someone to baby-sit your child or for any other job? Hire based on reputation and not image, says Willson. Check references thoroughly. Psychopaths tend to give vague and inconsistent replies. Of course the best way to solve this problem would be to cure psychopaths of their 'illness.' But there's no recipe for treating them, say psychiatrists. Today's traditional methods of psychotherapy (psychoanalysis, group and one-on-one therapy) and drug treatments have failed. Therapy is more likely to work when an individual admits there's a problem and wants to change. The common problem with psychopaths, says Seto, "Is they don't see a problem with their behavior."

Psychopaths don't seek therapy willingly, says Seto. Rather, they're pushed into it by a desperate relative or by a court order. To a psychopath, a therapist is just one more person who must be conned, and the psychopath plays the part right until the therapist is convinced of his or her 'rehabilitation.'

Even though we can't treat psychopaths effectively with therapy, it doesn't mean we can't protect ourselves, writes Hare. Willson agrees, citing the most important factor in keeping psychopaths at bay is to know your vulnerabilities. We need to "realize our own potential and maximize our strengths" so that our insecurities don't overcome us. Because, she says, a psychopath is a chameleon who becomes "an image of what you haven't done for yourself." Over time, she says, "their appearance of perfection will begin to crack," but by that time you will have been emotionally and perhaps financially scathed. There comes a time when you realize there's no point in searching for answers; the only thing is to move on.

Taken in part from MW − By Caroline Konrad − September 1999

THE MALIGNANT PERSONALITY:

These people are mentally ill and extremely dangerous! The following precautions will help to protect you from the destructive acts of which they are capable.

First, to recognize them, keep the following guidelines in mind:

(1) They are habitual liars. They seem incapable of either knowing or telling the truth about anything.

(2) They are egotistical to the point of narcissism. They really believe they are set apart from the rest of humanity by some special grace.

(3) They scapegoat; they are incapable of either having the insight or willingness to accept responsibility for anything they do. Whatever the problem, it is always someone else's fault.

(4) They are remorselessly vindictive when thwarted or exposed.

(5) Genuine religious, moral, or other values play no part in their lives. They have no empathy for others and are capable of violence. Under older psychological terminology, they fall into the category of psychopath or sociopath, but unlike the typical psychopath, their behavior is masked by a superficial social facade.

If you have come into conflict with such a person or persons, do the following immediately!

(1) Notify your friends and relatives of what has happened.

Do not be vague. Name names, and specify dates and circumstances. Identify witnesses if possible and provide supporting documentation if any is available.

(2) Inform the police. The police will do nothing with this information except to keep it on file, since they are powerless to act until a crime has been committed. Unfortunately, that often is usually too late for the victim. Nevertheless, place the information in their hands.

Obviously, if you are assaulted or threatened before witnesses, you can get a restraining order, but those are palliative at best.

(3) Local law enforcement agencies are usually under pressure if wealthy or politically powerful individuals are involved, so include state and federal agencies as well and tell the

locals that you have. In my own experience, one agency that can help in a pinch is the Criminal Investigation Division of the Internal Revenue Service or (in Canada) Victims Services at your local police unit. It is not easy to think of the IRS as a potential friend, but a Swedish study showed that malignant types (the Swedes called them bullies) usually commit some felony or other by the age of twenty. If the family is wealthy, the fact may never come to light, but many felonies involve tax evasion, and in such cases, the IRS is interested indeed. If large amounts of money are involved, the IRS may solve all your problems for you. For obvious reasons the Drug Enforcement Agency may also be an appropriate agency to approach.

The FBI is an important agency to contact, because although the FBI does not have jurisdiction over murder or assault, if informed, they do have an active interest in any other law enforcement agencies that do not follow through with an honest investigation and prosecution should a murder occur. Civil rights are involved at that point. No local crooked lawyer, judge, or corrupt police official wants to be within a country mile if that comes to light! It is in such cases that wealthy psychopaths discover just how firm the "friends" they count on to cover up for them really are! Even some of the drug cartel biggies will scuttle for cover if someone picks up the brick their thugs hide under. Exposure is bad for business.

(4) Make sure that several of your friends have the information in the event something happens to you. That way, an appropriate investigation will follow if you are harmed. Don't tell other people who has the information, because then something bad could happen to them as well. Instruct friends to take such an incident to the newspapers and other media.

If you are dealing with someone who has considerable money, you must realize that they probably won't try to harm you themselves, they will contract with someone to make the hit. The malignant type is a coward and will not expose himself or herself to personal danger if he or she can avoid it."

Appendix B

Characteristics of a Sociopath and What We Can Do to Protect Ourselves from Such People

"According to the current bible of psychiatric labels, the *Diagnostic and Statistical Manual of Mental Disorders IV* of the American Psychiatric Association, the clinical diagnosis of "antisocial personality disorder" should be considered when an individual possesses at least three of the following seven characteristics:

(1) failure to conform to social norms;

(2) deceitfulness, manipulativeness;

(3) impulsivity, failure to plan ahead;

(4) irritability, aggressiveness;

(5) reckless disregard for the safety of self or others;

(6) consistent irresponsibility

(7) lack of remorse after having hurt, mistreated or stolen from another person.

The presence in an individual of any three of these "symptoms," taken together, is enough to make many psychiatrists suspect the disorder."[71]

"Other researchers and clinicians point to additional documented characteristics of sociopaths as a group. One of the more frequently observed of these traits is a glib and superficial charm that allows the true sociopath to seduce other people, figuratively or literally – a kind of glow or charisma that, initially, can make the sociopath seem more charming or more interesting than most normal people around him."[72]

"As a group, they are known for their pathological lying and conning, and their parasitic relationships with "friends." Their

---

[71] Martha Stout, Ph.D., *"The Sociopath Next Door,"* Broadway Books / Random House, USA, 2005. p. 6.

[72] Ibid. p. 7.

history "always includes a failure to acknowledge responsibility for any problems that occurred."

"And sociopaths are noted especially for their shallowness of emotion, the hollow and transient nature of any affectionate feelings they may claim to have, a certain breathtaking callousness. They have no trace of empathy and no genuine interest in bonding emotionally with a mate. Once the surface charm is scraped off, their marriages are loveless, one-sided, and almost always short-term. If a marriage partner has any value to the sociopath, it is because the partner is viewed as a possession, one the sociopath may feel *angry* to lose, but never sad or accountable.

All of these characteristics, along with the "symptoms" listed by the American Psychiatric Association, are the behavioral manifestations of what is for most of us an unfathomable psychological condition, the absence of our essential seventh sense – conscience."[73]

"Crazy, and frightening – and real, in about 4 percent of the population."[74]

"What sociopaths envy, and may seek to destroy as part of the game, is usually something in the character structure of a person with conscience, and strong characters are often specially targeted by sociopaths."[75]

"Being targeted by a sociopath is a very frightening experience, even when the sociopath is not of the violent variety. To suspect, and try to explain to others that one has been targeted by a sociopath is to be gas lighted." Here's how it works. "When a targeted person accuses a sociopath of a vicious act toward them or an unoffending other person, the natural question is "Why would a person like that do such a horrible thing?" This is the question others always ask, overtly or by intimation, and it is such a bewildering, unanswerable

---

[73] Ibid. pp 7-8.

[74] Ibid. p. 8.

[75] Ibid. p. 51.

question that the one who suspects the sociopath usually ends up asking it too, only to find that he has no rational sounding explanation. Such a person may come to lose faith, partially or completely, in his own perceptions. Certainly he will hesitate to tell his story again, since trying to expose the sociopath casts doubt on his own credibility and maybe even his sanity. These doubts, our own and other peoples,' are painful, and readily convince us to keep our mouths shut." Within an organization or community, in the event that a sociopath is finally revealed to all and sundry, the author, Martha Stout, reports that "it is not unusual to find that several people suspected all along, each one independently, each one in silence. Each one felt gas lighted, and so each one kept his crazy-sounding secret to himself."[76]

According to Stout, the answer she gives to the question, "How can I tell whom not to trust?" is that "the best clue is, of all things, the pity play. The most universal behavior of unscrupulous people is not directed, as one might imagine, at our fearfulness. It is, perversely, an appeal to our sympathy." [77] "The explanation [for this] is that good people will let pathetic individuals get by with murder, so to speak, and therefore any sociopath wishing to continue with his game, whatever it happens to be, should play for none other than pity.

More than admiration – more even than fear – pity from good people is carte blanche. When we pity, we are, at least for the moment, defenseless… and like so many other essentially positive human characteristics that bind us together in groups, our emotional vulnerability when we pity is used against us by those who have no conscience."[78]

"Sociopaths are not few and far between. On the contrary, they make up a significant portion of our population. For any individual living in the Western world to get all the way

---

[76] Ibid. p. 95.
[77] Ibid. p. 107.
[78] Ibid. p. 108.

through life without knowing at least one such person, in some capacity or other, is virtually impossible.

People without conscience experience emotions very differently from you and me, and they do not experience love at all, or any other kind of positive attachment to their fellow human beings. This deficit, which is hard even to ponder, reduces life to an endless game of attempted domination over other people. Sometimes sociopaths are physically violent. Often they are not, preferring to "win" over others by raiding the business world, or the professions, or government – or simply by exploiting one person at a time in parasitic relationships.

At present, sociopathy is "incurable;" furthermore sociopaths almost never wish to be "cured." In fact, it is likely that certain cultures, notably our Western one, actively encourage antisocial behaviors, including violence, murder, and warmongering.

These facts are difficult for most people to accept. They are offensive, non-egalitarian, and frightening. But understanding and accepting them as a real aspect of our world is rule number one of the "Thirteen Rules for Dealing with Sociopaths in Everyday Life" that Stout tells to patients and to other people who are interested in protecting themselves and the people they love.

Here are the thirteen rules:

THIRTEEN RULES FOR DEALING WITH SOCIOPATHS IN EVERYDAY LIFE

1. *The first rule involves the bitter pill of accepting that some people literally have no conscience.*

   These people do not often look like Charles Manson. They look like us.

2. *In a contest between your instincts and what is implied by the role a person has taken on — educator, doctor, leader, animal lover, parent — go with your instincts.*

457

Whether you want to be or not, you are a constant observer of human behavior, and your unfiltered impressions, although alarming and seemingly outlandish, may well help you out if you will let them. Your best self understands, without being told, that impressive and moral-sounding labels do not bestow conscience on anyone who did not have it to begin with.

3. *When considering a new relationship of any kind, practice the Rule of Threes regarding the claims and promises a person makes, and the responsibilities he or she has. Make the Rule of Threes your personal policy.*

One lie, one broken promise, or a single neglected responsibility may be a misunderstanding instead. Two may involve a serious mistake. But *three* lies says you're dealing with a liar, and deceit is the lynchpin of conscienceless behavior. Cut your losses and get out as soon as you can. Leaving, though it may be hard, will be easier now than later, and less costly.

Do not give your money, your work, your secrets, or your affection to a three-timer. Your valuable gifts will be wasted.

4. *Question authority.*

Once again – trust your own instincts and anxieties, especially those concerning people who claim that dominating others, violence, war or some other violation of your conscience is the grand solution to some problem. Do this even when, or especially when, everyone around you has completely *stopped* questioning authority. Recite to yourself what Stanley Milgram taught about obedience: At least six out of ten people will blindly obey to the bitter end an official-looking authority in their midst.

The good news is that having social support makes people somewhat more likely to challenge authority. Encourage those around you to question, too.

5. *Suspect flattery.*

Compliments are lovely, especially when they are sincere. In contrast, *flattery* is extreme and appeals to our egos in unrealistic ways. It is the material of counterfeit charm, and nearly always involves an intent to manipulate. Manipulation through flattery is sometimes innocuous and sometimes sinister. Peek over your massaged ego and remember to suspect flattery.

This "flattery rule" applies on an individual basis, and also at the level of groups and even whole nations. Throughout all of human history and to the present, the call to war has included the flattering claim that one's own forces are about to accomplish a victory that will change the world for the better, a triumph that is morally laudable, justified by its humane outcome, unique in human endeavor, righteous and worthy of enormous gratitude. Since we began to record the human story, all of our major wars have been framed in this way, on all sides of the conflict, and in all languages the adjective most often applied to the word war is *holy*. An argument can easily be made that humanity will have peace when nations of people are at least able to see through this masterful flattery.

Just as an individual pumped up on flattery of a manipulator is likely to behave in foolish ways, exaggerated patriotism that is flattery-fueled is a dangerous thing.

6. *If necessary, redefine your concept of respect.*

Too often, we mistake fear for respect, and the more fearful we are of someone, the more we view him or her as deserving of our respect.

Do not mistake fear for respect, because to do so would be to ensure your own victimization. Let us use our big human brains to overpower our animal tendency to bow to predators, so we can disentangle the reflexive confusion of anxiety and awe. In a perfect world, human respect would be an automatic reaction only to those who are strong, kind and morally courageous. The person who profits from frightening you is not likely to be any of these.

The resolve to keep respect separate from fear is even more crucial for groups and nations. The politician, small or lofty, who menaces the people with frequent reminders of the possibility of crime, violence or terrorism, and who then uses their magnified fear to gain allegiance, is more likely to be a successful con artist than a legitimate leader. This too has been true throughout history.

7. *Do not join the game.*

Intrigue is a sociopath's tool. Resist the temptation to compete with a seductive sociopath, to outsmart him, psychoanalyze, or even banter with him. In addition to reducing yourself to his level, you would be distracting yourself from what is really important, which is to protect yourself.

8. *The best way to protect yourself from a sociopath is to avoid him, to refuse any kind of contact or communication.*

Psychologists do not usually like to recommend avoidance, but in this case, Stout makes a very deliberate exception. The only truly effective method for dealing with a sociopath you have identified is to disallow him or her from your life altogether. Sociopaths live completely outside of the social contract, and therefore to include them in relationships or other social arrangements is perilous. Begin this exclusion of them in the context of your own relationships and social life. You will not hurt anyone's feelings. Strange as it seems, and though they may try to pretend otherwise, sociopaths do not have any such feelings to hurt.

You may never be able to make your family and friends understand why you are avoiding a particular individual. Sociopathy is surprisingly difficult to see, and even harder to explain. Avoid him anyway.

If total avoidance is impossible, make plans to come as close as you can to the goal of total avoidance.

9. *Question your tendency to pity too easily.*

Respect should be reserved for the kind and the morally courageous. *Pity* is another socially valuable response, and it should be reserved for innocent people who are in genuine pain or who have fallen on misfortune. If, instead, you find yourself often pitying someone who consistently hurts you or other people, and who actively campaigns for your sympathy, the chances are close to 100 percent that you are dealing with a sociopath.

Related to this – Stout recommends that you severely challenge your need to be *polite* in all situations. For normal adults in our culture, being what we think of as "civilized" is like a reflex, and often we find ourselves being automatically decorous **even when someone has enraged us, repeatedly lied to us, or figuratively stabbed us in the back.** Sociopaths take huge advantage of this automatic courtesy in exploitive situations.

10. *Do not try to redeem the unredeemable.*

Second (third, fourth, and fifth) chances are for people who possess conscience. If you are dealing with a person who has no conscience, know how to swallow hard and cut your losses.

At some point, most of us need to learn the important, if disappointing, life lesson, that no matter how good our intentions, we cannot control the behavior – let alone the character structures – of other people. Learn this fact of human life, and avoid the irony of getting caught up in the same ambition he has – to control.

If you do not desire to control, but instead want to *help* people, then help only those who truly want to be helped. Stout thinks you will find this does not include the person who has no conscience.

The sociopath's behavior is not your fault, not in any way whatsoever. It is also not your mission. *Your* mission is your own life.

11. *Never agree, out of pity or for any other reason, to help a sociopath conceal his or her true character.*

"Please don't tell," often spoken tearfully and with great gnashing of teeth, is the trademark plea of thieves, child abusers – and sociopaths. Do not listen to this siren song. Other people deserve to be warned more than the sociopaths deserve to have you keep their secrets.

If someone without conscience insists that you "owe" him or her, recall what you are about to read here: "You owe me" has been the standard line of sociopaths for thousands of years, quite literally, and is still so. It is what Rasputin told the empress of Russia.

We tend to experience "You owe me" as a compelling claim, but it is simply not true. Do not listen. Also, ignore the one that goes, "You are just like me." You are not.

12. *Defend your psyche.*

Do not allow someone without a conscience, or even a string of such people, to convince you that humanity is a failure. Most human beings *do* possess conscience. Most human beings are able to love.

13. *Living well is the best revenge."*[79]

The key aim here needs to be to discern what is true and what is false, act on what is true appropriately, and live life fully, love passionately and be fully ourselves with God and with other people who are safe and healthy for us to be around. Sociopaths are not such people.

---

[79] Ibid. pp. 155-162.

Appendix C

Personality Disorder of Evil[80]

- All personality disorders disavow responsibility for one's choices and actions
- This one is distinguished by:
  - Consistent destructive scapegoating behavior
  - Excessive, usually covert, intolerance to criticism
  - Pronounced concern with public and self-image
  - Intellectual deviousness with increased likelihood of evidencing a second personality under stress

---

[80] Peck, Scott, M.D. *The People of the Lie.* 1983. pp. 71-84.

Expulsions of the Impostors Posing as Jews Over the Past 2,000 Years[81]

The following is a list of 200 government entities from which impostors posing as Jews (designated as "jews" here) have been expelled over the past 2,000 years; while comprehensive, the list is by no means exhaustive.

This list of expulsions begs the question, what is it about the "jews" that has produced such widespread expulsions so many times for so many years by advanced, civilized, moral, refined, compassionate, Christian nations? The answer is plain as day: it is *not* because these impostors are "God's chosen people" as they falsely claim; and it is *not* because they are persecuted for no valid reason. It is because their conduct has been consistently evil, immoral, parasitic and subversive to their host cultures which they secretly hate and seek to destroy. This information has been actively suppressed and silenced by this very same group of psychopaths, religious zealots and fanatics who own and control all major media, publishing and education outlets worldwide and who secretly serve and worship the devil. If this evidence does not reveal the "jews" to be the Antichrist of the end times, nothing ever will.

Year	City or Principality	Country	By Whom	Until
250	Carthage	Roman Empire of North Africa		
415	Alexandria	Egypt	Cyril of Alexandria	

---

[81] Clèraubat, Brian Alois. *A Greater "Miracle" Than The Ten Lost Tribes Discovered . . . − The Dead "SIX MILLION" Uncovered . . . !* pp. 312-321, http://www.biblebelievers.org.au/expelled.htm, and http://www.subvertednation.net/jew-lists/jewish-expulsions-and-exiles/.

Appendix D

554	Diocese of Clement	France		
561	Diocese of Uzzes	France		
612		Visigoth Spain	King Sesbut	
642		Visigoth Empire		
855		Italy	Louis II	
876	Sens	France		
1012	Mainz	Germany	Emperor Henry II	
1066	[William "the Conqueror" brings first "jews" to England from France]			
1181		France	Phillip II Augustus	
1182		Germany		
1253	Vienna	Austria	Pope Innocent III	
1276	Upper Bavaria	Germany		
1288	Naples	Italy		
1290		England	Edward I	1655
1294	Berne	Switzerland		
1306		France	Phillip IV, the Fair	1682
1322		France	Charles IV	1359
1348	Basle	Switzerland		1869
1349	Burgsdorff, Zurich	Switzerland		

465

1349	Heilbronn	Germany		
1349	Saxony	Germany		
1349		Hungary		1364
1360		Hungary		1582
1360	Breslau	Germany-Poland		
1370	Brussels	Belgium		1700
1380		Slovakia		1745
1381	Strasbourg	France		
1384	Lucerne	France		
1388	Strasbourg	France		
1394		Germany		
1394		France	Charles VI	
1401	Berne	Switzerland		
1420	Lyons	France		
1420	Styria	Austria	Albrecht V	
1421	Vienna and Linz	Austria		
1421	Moravia	Czechoslovakia		
1424	Fribourg	Switzerland		
1424	Zurich	Switzerland		
1424	Cologne	France		
1427	Berne	Switzerland		
1428	Fribourg	Switzerland		
1430	Eger, Bohemia	Germany		
1430	Speyer	Germany		

Appendix D

1432	Savoy	France		
1436	Zurich	Switzerland		
1438	Mainz	Germany		
1439	Augsburg	Germany		
1442	Bavaria	Germany		
1442		Netherlands		
1442	Tivoli and Ravenna	Italy	Pope Eugenius IV	
1444		Netherlands		
1446	Bavaria	Germany		
1450	Bavaria	Germany	Ludwig IX	
1450		Sicily	Ferdinand II	
1453	Franconia	Germany-France		
1453	Breslau	Germany-Poland		
1454	Würzburg	Germany		
1454	Brunn, Moravia	Czechoslovakia	Ladislaus V	
1462	Mainz	Germany		
1475	Trent	Italy		
1479	Schlettstadt, Alsace	France	Frederick III	
1483	Mainz	Germany		
1484	Warsaw	Poland		
1485	Viscenza, Peruggia	Italy		
1486	Gubbio	Italy		

1490	Geneva	Switzerland		
1491	Ravenna	Italy		
1492		Spain	Ferdinand and Isabella	
1492		Sicily and Sardinia		
1492	Campo San Pietro and elsewhere	Italy		
1494	Florence, Tuscany	Italy		1513
1495		Lithuania	Grand Duke Alexander	1503
1496	Naples	Italy		
1496		Portugal	Manuel I	
1496	Carinthia	Austria		
1496	Styria	Austria		
1497		Portugal		
1497	Graz, Styria	Austria		
1498		Portugal		
1498	Nurnberg, Bavaria	Germany	Maximillian	
1498	Navarre	Spain		
1499		Germany		
1505	Orange, Burgundy	France	Philibert of Luxembourg	
1510	Brandenburg	Prussia		
1510	Colmar	Germany		

Appendix D

1510		Prussia		
1510	Naples	Italy		
1514	Strasbourg	France		
1515	Genoa	Italy		
1515	Laibach	Austria		
1519	Regensburg	Germany		
1526	Pressburg	Hungary	Maria of Hapsburg	
1527	Florence	Italy		
1533	Naples	Italy		
1539	Trnava	Czechoslovakia		
1540		Italy		
1541	Naples	Italy		1735
1542	Prague	Czechoslovakia		
1542	Bohemia	Germany		
1547		Russia	Ivan the Terrible	
1547	Ghent	Belgium		
1550	Genoa	Italy		
1551	Bavaria	Germany		
1553		Italy	Pope Julius III, burns 1000s of copies of Talmud in Rome, Bologna, Ferrara,	

			Venice and Mantua	
1555	Pesaro	Italy		
1557	Prague	Czechoslovakia		
1559		Austria		
1559	Milan	Italy	12,000 copies of Talmud burned	
1561	Prague	Czechoslovakia		
1563		France	Charles IX	
1563	Neutitschlin, Moravia	Czechoslovakia		
1567	Würzburg	Germany		
1567	Genoa	Italy		
1567		Brazil	Don Henrique	
1569	Papal States		Pope Pius V	
1571	Brandenburg	Prussia		
1571	Venice	Italy	Ordered but not fully enforced	
1582		Netherlands		
1582		Hungary		
1590	Lombardy	Italy	Phillip II of Spain	
1593	Brandenburg	Prussia		
1593		Austria		

1593	Papal States		Pope Clement VIII	
1597	Cremona, Pavia, Lodi, Milan	Italy		
1598	Genoa	Italy		
1614	Frankfurt	Germany		
1615	Worms	Germany		
1615		France	Louis XIII	
1619	Kiev	Ukraine		
1648		Ukraine		
1648		Poland		
1649	Hamburg	Germany		
1654	Little Russia	Ukraine		
1654		Brazil		
1656		Lithuania		
1669	Oran	North Africa		
1669	Vienna	Austria		
1670	Vienna	Austria	Leopold I	
1683	French possessions in America	France	Louis XIV	
1699	Lubeck	Germany		
1712	Sandomir	Poland		
1716	Brussels	Belgium		
1727		Russia	Catherine the Great	

1727		Ukraine	Catherine the Great	
1738	Württemburg	Germany		
1738	Breslau	Poland-Germany		
1740	Little Russia	Ukraine	Czarina Anna	
1742		Russia	Czarina Elizabeth Petrovna	
1744	Prague	Czechoslovakia		
1744	Breslau, Silesia	Germany-Poland	Frederick II the Great	
1744	Bohemia	Germany	Archduchess Maria Teresa	
1744		Slovakia		
1744	Livonia	Baltic		
1745	Moravia	Czechoslovakia	Maria Teresea	
1745	Prague	Czechoslovakia		
1753	Kovad	Lithuania		
1761	Bordeaux	France		
1761	Rhode Island	USA	Denies "jews" citizenship	
1774	Moravia	Czechoslovakia		
1774	Prague	Czechoslovakia		
1774	Bohemia	Germany		

1775	Warsaw	Poland		
1779		USA	General George Washington proposed expulsion of "jews" from the US	
1784	Warsaw	Poland	Marshall Mniszek	
1789	Alsace	France		
1791		Russia	Catherine II	
1792		Poland-Russia	Deported to the Pale of Settlement	
1804		Russia	Expelled from various villages	
1808		Russia	Expelled from various villages & the countryside	
1815	Lübeck, Bremen	Germany		
1815	Franconia, Schwaben & Bayem	Germany		
1816	Free city of Lubeck	Germany		
1820	Bremen	Germany		

1829	Nikolayev and Sevastopol	Russia		
1843		Russian border		
1843		Austria		
1843		Prussia		
1853		Austria	Forbade "jews" to own land	
1862	Areas under General Ulysses S. Grant's jurisdiction	USA		
1862	Areas under General William T. Sherman's jurisdiction	USA		
1866	Galatz	Romania	King Carol and Minister of the Interior Ion Bratianu	
1880s		Russia		
1881		Germany	250,000 petition to bar foreign "jews" from entering	
1882		Rural Romania	Czar Alexander III	

1891	Moscow	Russia		
1898	Kiev	Ukraine		
1905	Minsk	Byelorussia or White Russia	Took measures against	
1905	Brisk	Lithuania	Took measures against	
1914	Mitchenick	Poland		
1914	Tel Aviv	Palestine	Turkish authorities	
1915	Laibach	Austria		
1917	Jaffa, Tel Aviv	Palestine	Turkish authorities	
1919	Bavaria	Germany	Foreign born "jews"	
1929-38		Italy	Mussolini expelled "jews" from all public service and schools	
1938-39		Poland		
1938-45		Nazi controlled areas		
1941	Hungarian Ruthena	Ukraine		
1948		Arab countries		

Appendix E

Communist Democide 1900 - 1987[82]

STATE/QUASI-STATE/GROUP	START YEAR	END YEAR	LOW	MID	HIGH
Afghanistan	1978	1987	62	228	703
Albania	1944	1987	25	100	150
Angola	1975	1987	100	125	200
Bulgaria (Communists)	1944	1987	172	222	322
Cambodia (Khmer Rouge)	1975	1979	635	2,035	3,035
Cambodia (KR Guerillas)	1968	1987	222	362	462
Cambodia (Samrin)	1979	1987	68	230	383
China (Communists) (19)	1923	1949	1,838	3,466	11,692
China (PRC)	1949	1987	5,999	35,236	102,671
Cuba (Castro)	1959	1987	35	73	141
Cuba (Rebels)	1952	1959	-	1	1
Czechoslovakia (Communists)	1948	1968	24	65	181
El Salvador (Guerillas)	1979	1987	1	1	1
Ethiopia (Communists)	1974	1987	236	725	1,285
Ethiopia (Eritrea)	1974	1987	2	2	2
Ethiopia (Rebels) (23)	1976	1977	-	-	-
Germany (East)	1948	1987	70	70	70
Greece (ELAS)	1946	1949	14	20	25
Grenada (Coup)	1983	1983	-	-	-
Guatemala (Guerillas)	1954	1987	8	14	23
Hungary (Communists)	1948	1987	27	27	27
Indonesia (Communists)	1948	1948	2	2	2
Korea, North	1948	1987	710	1,663	3,549
Laos (Pathet Lao)	1960	1975	33	38	55
Laos (PDR)	1975	1987	46	56	70
Malayan (Communists)	1946	1951	3	3	3
Mongolia	1926	1987	35	100	200
Mozambique	1975	1987	153	198	350
Mozambique (Frelimo)	1964	1975	3	3	3
Nicaragua (Sandinistas)	1979	1987	4	5	7
Peru (Shining Path)	1980	1987	2	4	5
Phillipines (Communists)	1972	1986	5	5	5
Poland (Communists)	1948	1987	10	22	54
Rumania Communists)	1948	1987	245	435	920
USSR (27)	1917	1987	28,326	61,911	126,891
Vietnam (28)	1945	1987	721	1,670	3,664
Yemen, South	1967	1987	1	1	1
Yugoslavia (Partisans)	1941	1944	50	100	150
Yugoslavia (Tito)	1944	1987	585	1,072	2,130
TOTALS =			40,472	110,290	259,433

---

[82] https://www.hawaii.edu/powerkills/COM.TAB1.GIF.

Foods to Eat and Foods to Avoid to Achieve an Alkaline Body pH[83]

The Best: (always organically grown) Alkaline Forming:	The Worst: Acid Forming:
All fresh fruits	Alcohol **
All fresh salad greens	Barley
All sprouts	Black or white pepper
All vegetables (raw or cooked)	Bread, baked
Almonds & sunflower seeds, soaked *	Cake
Apple cider vinegar, balsamic vinegar	Canned or microwaved fruits & vegetables
Corn on the cob, fresh *	Carbonated beverages
Dates	Cereals, all
Dried fruits / unsulphured (not glazed)	Chocolate
Fresh berries	Coffee or caffeine
Fresh or dried seasoning herbs	Dairy
Fresh raw vegetable juice	Eggs
Garlic	Foods cooked with oil
Goat whey (raw) *	Grains, except quinoa and millet
Grapefruit	Legumes
Herbal teas (caffeine free)	Meat, fish, poultry, shellfish

---

[83] www.ariseandshine.com/cleansing/cleanse-guides.html

Honey (raw)	Nicotine
Lemons	Oatmeal
Lima beans *	Pasta
Maple syrup, organic	Popcorn
Melons	Preservatives
Millet *	Processed foods +
Molasses	Salt, including Celtic, sea and Himalayan
Potatoes *	Soda crackers
Quinoa *	Soft drinks
Raisins	Soy (tofu, tempeh, etc.)
Raw avocado, coconut, flaxseed, grape seed, olive, safflower, saffron, sunflower oils	Sugar, white and processed
Sauerkraut (unsalted)	Sweeteners, artificial
Vegetable broth	Tea, unless caffeine free
Vegetable soups	Vinegar, distilled
Wheat grass juice	Wheat, all forms
* Eat foods from this group no more than 3 times per week.	** Alcoholic beverages are highly acid forming and destroy friendly bacteria in the digestive system. + Processed and microwaved foods lack enzymes and minerals, making it hard for the body to get the nutrients it needs.

Appendix G

Already Fulfilled End Times Prophecies

#	End Times Prophecy	What It Says	Proof of its Fulfillment
1	Daniel 12:10	"Many shall be purified, and made white, and tried; but the wicked shall do wickedly: and none of the wicked shall understand; but the wise shall understand."	Go to Disqus, "follow" Watchman on the Wall, and read my blog posts teaching the unpleasant truth and examine the wicked, malicious, libelous, slandereous, defamatory lies made about me merely because I teach the truth which drives the wicked and the foolish totally insane. The attacks of the wicked and the foolish upon the rigtheous prove that the righteous are being sorely tried and that the wicked do wickedly and are incapble of understanding anything of the truth. I fully understand; do you?
2	Matthew 10:26-28	"Fear them not therefore: for there is nothing covered, that shall not be revealed; and hid that shall not be known. What I tell you in darkness, that speak ye in light: and what ye hear in the ear, that preach ye upon the housetops. And fear not them which kill the body, but are not able to kill the soul: but rather fear him which is able to destroy both soul and body in hell."	My book is a fulfillment of verse 26, and my obedience to verses 27-28. In my book, I reveal and expose the greatest lies that have been concealed and covered for the past 100 years and expose the hideous truth which God has revealed to me.
3	Matthew 24:15-16 & 21	"When ye therefore shall see the abomination of desolation, spoken of by Daniel the prophet, stand in the holy place, (whoso readeth, let him understand:) Then let them which be in Judaea flee into the mountains:... For then shall be tribulation, such as was not since the beginning of the world to this time, no, nor ever shall be,"	See Chapter 9 of my book which explains how all this has been fulfilled and what it conclusions we can and should draw from them.
4	2 Thessalonians 2:3	"Let no man deceive you by any means: for that day shall not come, except there come a falling away first, and that man of sin be revealed, the son of perdition."	"All forms of organized religion are, and always have been, demonic," YHWH revelaed to me in August 2013. My story, told in Chapter 7 of my book, proves it and Chapter 11 explains why, and provides numerous examples of how deceitful all organized forms of religion have become. Chapter 8 of my book reveals who is the Antichrist of these end times, who is the man of sin, the son of perdition, referred to in this prophecy.

479

Making Sense Out of a World Gone Mad

#	End Times Prophecy	What it Says	Proof of its Fulfillment
5	2 Thessalonians 2:10-12	And with all deceiveableness of unrighteousness in them that perish; because they received not the love of the truth, that they might be saved. And for this cause God shall send them strong delusion, that they should believe a lie: That they all might be damned who believed not the truth, but had pleasure in unrighteousness."	This clearly expalins why the wicked fools I encounter in my blogs as Watchman on the Wall are strongly deluded and cannot see the truths I reveal and expose in my book with hard evidence and simple logical reasoning. It explains why they are truly insane; totally disconnected from well-documented and objective reality.
6	2 Timothy 3:1-7	"This know also, that in the last days perilous times shall come. For men shall be lovers of their own selves, covetous, boasters, proud, blasphemers, disobedient to parents, unthankful, unholy, Without natural affection, trucebreakers, false accusers, incontinent, fierce, despisers of those that are good, Traitors, heady, highminded, lovers of pleasures more than lovers of God; Having a form of godliness, but denying the power thereof: from such turn away. For of this sort are they which creep into houses, and lead captive silly women laden with sins, led away with divers lusts, Ever learning, and never able to come to the knowledge of the truth."	Read my story in Chapter 7 of my book, along with the malicious and libelous slander to which I have been subjected to on Disqus when I teach the hideous and inconvenient truths revealed in my book.
7	2 Timothy 4:3-4	For the time will come when they will not endure sound doctrine; but after their own lusts shall they heap to themselves teachers, having itching ears; And they shall turn away their ears from the truth, and shall be turned unto fables."	Read my story in Chapter 7 and Chapter 11 which exposes the lies of all forms of organized religion today.
8	2 Peter 3:3-7	Knowing this first, that there shall come in the last days scoffers, walking after their own lusts, And saying, where is the promise of his coming? For since the days of the fathers fell asleep, all things continue as they were from the beginning of creation. For this they are willingly ignorant of, that by the word of God the heavens were of old, and the earth standing out of the water and in the water: Whereby the world that then was, being overflowed with water, perished: but the heavens and the earth, which are now, by the same word are kept in store, reserved unto fire against the day of judgment and perdition of ungodly men."	Read a number of the scoffers' ridulcules of my teachings on the blogosphere under Disqus of where we are in God's prophetic Biblicial timeline. All the evidence is there. Yet the fulfillment of 2 Thessalonians 2:10-12 explains why the obvious truth is concealed from those who rejected the the truth and found pleasure in unrighteousness.

Bibliography

Agenda: Grinding America Down. Curtis Bowers. DVD. AgendaDocumentary.com. 2010.

Alinsky, Saul D. *Rules for Radicals: A Practical Primer for Realistic Radicals*. Vintage Books, New York, NY, 1971. ISBN: 0-679-72113-4.

Allen, Gary. *None Dare Call It Conspiracy*. Buccaneer Books, Cutchogue, NY, 1971. ISBN-13: 978-0-8996617.

Ambassador Basic Curriculum, Courses 1, 2 & 3. Gregory Koukl. Stand to Reason. CDs. www.str.org. 2003.

Anderson, Rich. *Cleanse & Purify Thyself*. Christobe Publishing, Medford, OR, 1988.

Authentic Manhood: Winning at Work & Home. Lewis, Robert. DVDs. Lifeway Press, USA. 2006. ISBN: 1-4158-2823-7.

Bacque, James. *Other Losses: An Investigation into the Mass Deaths of German Prisoners at the Hands of the French and Americans after World War II*. Talonbooks, Vancouver, British Columbia, Canada. 2011 (first published in 1989). ISBN: 978-0-88922-665-4.

Balacius, Robert Alan. *Uncovering the Mysteries of Your Hidden Inheritance*. Sacred Truth Ministries, Mountain City, TN, 2001. ISBN: 1-58840-021-2.

Bennett, Todd D. *Names: The Father, the Son and the Importance of Names in Scriptures*. Shema Yisrael Publications, New York, NY, 2006. ISBN: 0-9768659-2-0.

Benson, Bill and Beckman, M.J. "Red." *The Law That Never Was Vol. I. – The fraud of the 16th Amendment and Personal Income Tax.* 1985.

Brown, Rebecca, M.D. *He Came to Set the Captives Free.* Whitaker House, New Kensington, PA, 1986. ISBN-13: 978-0-88368-323-1.

Brown, Rebecca, M.D. *Prepare For War.* Whitaker House, New Kensington, PA, 1987. ISBN-13: 978-0-88368-324-8.

Burns, Dr. Cathy. *Mormonism, Masonry, and Godhood: Can Angels Be Trusted?* Sharing, Mt. Carmel, PA, 1997. ISBN: 1-891117-01-7.

Clèraubat, Brian Alois. *A Greater "Miracle" Than The Ten Lost Tribes Discovered . . . – The Dead "SIX MILLION" Uncoverved . . . !* Institute for Historical Accuracy and Veracity, Mountain City, TN, 2007. ISBN: 1-58840-070-0.

Dalton, Thomas PhD. *Debating the Holocaust: A New Look at Both Sides.* Theses & Dissertations Press, New York, NY, 2009. ISBN: 978-1-59148-005-1.

Dice, Mark. *The Illuminati: Facts & Fiction.* The Resistance, San Diego, CA, 2009. ISBN: 0-9673466-5-7.

Dubay, Eric. *The Flat-Earth Conspiracy.* 2014. ISBN: 978-1-312-62716-1

Eldredge, John. *Waking the Dead.* Thomas Nelson, Inc., Nashville, TN, 2003. ISBN: 0-7852-6553-8.

Epperson, Ralph A. *The Unseen Hand: an Introduction to the Conspiratorial View of History.* Publius Press, Tucson, AZ, 1985. ISBN: 978-0-9614135-0-7.

Estulin, Daniel. *The True Story of the Bilderberg Group.* TrineDay LLC, Walterville, OR, 2009. ISBN-13: 978-0-9777953-4-5.

Hall, Marshall. *The Earth is Not Moving.* Fair Education Foundation, Inc., Cornelia, GA, 1991. ISBN: 0-932766-20-x.

Hendrie, Edward. *9/11 Enemies Foreign and Domestic: Secret Evidence Censored from the Official Record Proves Traitors Aided Israel in*

Attacking the USA. Great Mountain Publishing, Garrisonville, VA, 2010. ISBN: 978-0-9832627-3-2.

Hendrie, Edward. *Bloody Zion: Refuting the Jewish Fables That Sustain Israel's War Against God and Man*. Great Mountain Publishing, Garrisonville, VA, 2012. ISBN-13: 978-0-9832627-6-3.

Hendrie, Edward. *Solving the Mystery of Babylon the Great: Tracking the Beast from the Synagogue to the Vatican*. Great Mountain Publishing, Garrisonville, VA, 2010. ISBN: 978-0-9832627-0-1.

Hendrie, Edward. *The Anti-Gospel: The Perversion of Christ's Grace Gospel*. Great Mountain Publishing, Garrisonville, VA, 2005. ISBN: 978-0-9832627-4-9.

Hitchcock, Andrew Carrington. *The Synagogue of Satan*. RiverCrest Publishing, Austin, TX, 2007. ISBN: 978-1-930004-45-0.

Hoffman, Michael. *Judaism's Strange Gods*. Independent History and Research, Coeur d'Alene, ID, 2011. ISBN-13: 978-0-9703784-8-4.

Hoffman, Michael A. II. *Secret Societies and Psychological Warfare*. Independent History and Research, Coeur d'Alene, ID, 1989. ISBN-13: 978-0-9703784-1-5.

Kah, Gary H. *En Route to Global Occupation*. Huntington House Publishers, Lafayette, LA, 1992. ISBN: 0-910311-97-8.

Kah, Gary H. *The New World Religion*. Hope International Publishing, Inc., Noblesville, IN, 1999. ISBN: 0-9670098-0-4.

Koestler, Arthur. *The Thirteenth Tribe*. Pan Books Ltd., London, UK, 1976. ISBN: 0-330-25069-8.

Janov, Arthur, PhD. *The Primal Scream*. Perigree Books, New York, NY, 1970. ISBN: 0-399-50537-7.

Lewis, Robert. *The New Eve: Choosing God's Best for Your Life*. B&H Publishing Group, Nashville, TN, 2008. ISBN: 978-0-8054-4687-6.

Luther, Dr. Martin. *The Jews and Their Lies.* Liberty Bell Publications, York, SC, originally published 1543, reprinted 2004. ISBN: 1-59364-024-2.

Makow, Henry, PhD. *Cruel Hoax: Feminism and the New World Order.* Silas Green, USA, 2010. ISBN: 978-0-9687725-1-5.

Makow, Henry, PhD. *Illuminati: The Cult that Hijacked the World.* Silas Green, Winnipeg, Canada, 2011. ISBN: 1-4292-1148-5.

Makow, Henry, PhD. *Illuminati 2: Deceit and Seduction.* Silas Green, Winnipeg, Canada, 2010. ISBN: 1-4505-5311-7.

Makow, Henry, PhD. *Illuminati 3: Satanic Possession.* Silas Green, Winnipeg, Canada, 2014. ISBN: 978-0-9918211-2-9.

Marrs, Texe. *America Shattered.* Living Truth Publishers, Austin, TX, 1991. ISBN: 0-9620086-6-4.

Marrs, Texe. *Circle of Intrigue: The Hidden Inner Circle of the Global Illuminati Conspiracy.* RiverCrest Publishing, Austin, TX, 2010. ISBN-13: 978-1-930004-05-4.

Marrs, Texe. *Conspiracy of the Six-Pointed Star.* RiverCrest Publishing, Austin, TX, 2011. ISBN: 978-1-930004-57-3.

Marrs, Texe. *Dark Majesty: The Secret Brotherhood and the Magic of A Thousand Points of Light.* RiverCrest Publishing, Austin, TX, 2004. ISBN: 1-930004-16-8.

Marrs, Texe. *Dark Secrets of the New Age: Satan's Plan for a One World Religion.* RiverCrest Publishing, Austin, TX, 1999. ISBN: 0-9967421-4-1.

Marrs, Texe. *New Age Cults & Religions.* RiverCrest Publishing, Austin, TX, 2011. ISBN: 978-1-930004-58-0.

Marrs, Texe. *DNA Science and the Jewish Bloodline.* RiverCrest Publishing, Austin, TX, 2013. ISBN: 978-1-930004-81-8.

Marrs, Texe. *Ravaged by the New Age: Satan's Plan to Destroy Our Kids.* Living Truth Publishers, Austin, TX, 1989. ISBN: 0-9620086-1-3.

Marrs, Wanda. *New Age Lies to Women.* Living Truth Publishers, Austin, TX, 1989. ISBN: 0-9620086-3-X.

Bibliography

Marx, Karl and Engels, Friedrich. *The Communist Manifesto.* Tribeca Books, USA, originally published 1848. ISBN: 978-1936594436.

McCanney, James M. *Planet-X Comets & Earth Changes.* jmccanneyscience.com press, Minneapolis, MN, 1980. ISBN: 978-0-9722186-0-3.

McKenney, Tom C. *33 Degrees of Deception: An Expose of Freemasonry.* Bridge-Logos, Alachua, FL 2011. ISBN: 978-0-88270-438-8.

Meinig, George E. *Root Canal Cover-up.* Price-Pottinger Nutrition Foundation, Lemon Grove, CA, 1993. ISBN: 0-916764-09-8.

Montieth, Dr. Stanley. *Brotherhood of Darkness.* Hearthstone Publishing, Oklahoma City, OK, 2000. ISBN: 1-57558-063-2.

Mullins, Eustace. *The Secret Holocaust.* Sacred Truth Publishing, Mountain City, TN, 2000.

Mullins, Eustace. *The Secrets of the Federal Reserve.* Bridger House Publishers, Inc., Carson City, NV, 1991. ISBN: 978-0-9799176-5-3.

Noah Webster's 1828 First Edition of An American Dictionary of the English Language. Foundation for American Christian Education, San Francisco, CA, 1967. ISBN-13: 978-0-912498-03-4.

Pappe, Ilan. *The Ethnic Cleansing of Palestine.* Oneworld Publications Limited, New York, NY, 2006. ISBN: 978-1-85168-555-4.

Patrick, Daniel. *The Matrix of Gog.* RiverCrest Publishing, Austin, TX, 2014. ISBN: 978-1-930004-83-2.

Payne, Dr. Karl I. *Spiritual Warfare: Christians, Demonization and Deliverance.* WND Books, Washington, D.C., 2011. ISBN-13: 978-1-936488-33-9.

Peck, M. Scott, M.D. *The People of the Lie: The Hope for Healing Human Evil.* Touchstone, New York, NY, 1983. ISBN: 978-0-684-84859-4.

Peck, M. Scott, M.D. *The Road Less Travelled.* Touchstone, New York, NY, 1978. ISBN-13: 978-0-7432-4315-5.

Pitt-Rivers, George. *The World Significance of the Russian Revolution.* Sacred Truth Publishing, Mountain City, TN, 2006. ISBN: 1-58840-138-3.

Pranaitis, Rev. I.B. *The Talmud Unmasked: The Secret Rabbinical Teachings Concerning Christians.* Martino Publishing, Mansfield Centre, CT, 2010 (first printed in 1892 in St. Petersburg, Russia). ISBN: 1-891396-26-9.

Protocols of the Meetings of the Learned Elders of Zion. Pyramid Book Shop, Houston, TX 1934 (first published in Russian in 1905). ISBN: 978-1-162935133.

Rand, Jaysen Q., PhD. *The Return of Planet-X and Its Effects on Mother Earth.* Futureworld Publishing International, L.L.C., USA, 2007. ISBN: 978-0-9779209-1-4.

Reflections and Warnings: An Interview with Aaron Russo. Alex Jones. DVD. Infowars.com. 2009.

Sand, Shlomo. *The Invention of the Jewish People.* Verso, Brooklyn, NY, 2009. ISBN-13: 978-1-84467-623-1.

Shannan, Pat. *Everything They* Ever Told Me Was a Lie.* American Free Press, Washington, D.C., 2010. ISBN: 978-0-9823448-5-9.

Skousen, Cleon W. *The Naked Capitalist.* Buccaneer Books, Cutchogue, NY, 1970. ISBN: 0-89968-323-1.

Skousen, W. Cleon. *The Naked Communist.* The Ensign Publishing Company, Salt Lake City, UT, 1958.

Smith, Chuck. *Calvary Chapel Distinctives.* The Word for Today Publications, Costa Mesa, CA, 2000. ISBN-13: 978-0-936728-80-3.

Smith, Jerry E. *HAARP: the Ultimate Weapon of the Conspiracy.* Adventures Unlimited Press, Kempton, IL, 1998. ISBN: 0-932813-53-4.

Spiritual Warfare. Rebecca Brown, M.D., D.D. CDs. www.harvestwarriors.com. 2004.

Stout, Martha, PhD. *The Sociopath Next Door.* Broadway Books, New York, NY, 2005. ISBN: 0-7679-1582-8.

Strong, James, LL.D., S.T.D. *The New Strong's Exhaustive Concordance of the Bible.* Thomas Nelson, Inc., Nashville, TN, 1995. ISBN: 07852-5055-7.

Sussman, Brian. *Climategate.* WorldNetDaily, Washington D.C., 2010. ISBN: 978-1-935071-83-9.

Sutton, Anthony C. *America's Secret Establishment: An Introduction to the Order of Skull & Bones.* Liberty House Press, Billings, MT, 1986. ISBN: 0-937765-02-3.

The 1905 Revolution in Russia. Reproduced from National Geographic 1907. Lord's Covenant Church, Sandpoint, ID.

The Great Adventure. Lewis, Robert. DVDs. Lifeway Press, USA. 2005. ISBN: 1-4158-2296-4.

The Hebraic-Roots Version Scriptures. Institute for Scripture Research, Republic of South Africa, 2004. ISBN: 0-9584353-9-1.

The Human Cost of Communism in China. Committee on the Judiciary, United States Senate, U.S. Government Printing Office, Washington, D.C., 1971.

The Human Cost of Soviet Communism. Committee on the Judiciary, United States Senate, U.S. Government Printing Office, Washington, D.C., 1971.

The International Jew: The World's Foremost Problem. Martino Publishing, Mansfield Centre, CT, 2010, originally published in 1920 by The Dearborn Publishing Company. ISBN: 1-57898-928-0.

The New Oxford Annotated Apocrypha, New Revised Standard Version. Oxford University Press, Inc., New York, NY, 2010. ISBN: 978-0-19-528961-9.

The Quest for Authentic Manhood. Lewis, Robert. DVDs. Lifeway Press, USA. 2004. ISBN: 1-4158-2293-x.

The Truth Project. Del Tackett. Focus on the Family. DVDs. www.thetruthproject.org. 2006.

They Sold Their Souls For Rock N Roll. Joe Schimmel. Good Fight Ministries. DVD. www.goodfight.org.

Thorn, Victor. *Made in Israel: 9-11 and the Jewish Plot Against America.* Sisyphus Press, State College, PA 2011. ISBN: 978-1-61364-279-5.

U.S. War Department, 1919: The Power & Aims of International Jewry. Sacred Truth Publishing, Mountain City, TN, 2011.

Viola, Frank and Barna, George. *Pagan Christianity?* Tyndale House Publishers, Inc., USA, 2002. ISBN-13: 978-1-4143-1485-3.

Viola, Frank. *Finding Organic Church: A Comprehensive Guide to Starting and Sustaining Authentic Christian Communities.* David C. Cook, Colorado Springs, CO, 2009. ISBN: 978-1-4347-6866-7.

Viola, Frank. *Reimagining Church: Pursuing the Dream of Organic Christianity.* David C. Cook, Colorado Springs, CO, 2008 ISBN: 978-1-4347-6875-9.

Weiland, Ted R. *God's Covenant People: Yesterday, Today and Forever.* Mission to Israel Ministries, Scottsbluff, NE, 1994.

Weiland, Ted R. *Israel's Identity: IT MATTERS!.* Mission to Israel Ministries, Scottsbluff, NE, 2000. ISBN: 978-0-9679392-3-0.

Weiland, Ted R. *The Mystery of the Gentiles: Who Are They and Where Are They Now?* Mission to Israel Ministries, Scottsbluff, NE, 2005. ISBN: 0-9755943-0-3.

What in the World are they Spraying?: The Chemtrail/Geo-Engineering Cover-up. G. Edward Griffin, Michael Murphy and Paul Wittenberger. Truth Media Productions. DVD. 2010.

About the Author

Watchman on the Wall is a researcher, author and blogger on the global conspiracy and its obvious connections to the fulfillment of end times Bible prophecy, what it all means and what we can expect in the next 21 months. He has conducted research nearly full time for four years in support of this book.

Prior to his current career, Watchman was a business management consultant and turnaround Chief Financial Officer (CFO) and general manager for half a dozen smaller high and low tech companies in the San Francisco Bay Area over a 30 year career in a variety of challenging conditions. He was instrumental in the successful turnaround and sale of one of those companies in a mergers & acquisitions transaction and in turning around and taking a second company public in an Initial Public Offering (IPO) and remained as that company's public company CFO for five years thereafter.

Watchman holds a bachelor's degree in Economics from U.C. Davis with Highest Honors and Phi Beta Kappa and Phi Kappa Phi honors distinctions and an MBA degree from the Harvard Business School with second year honors. As part of his formal education and subsequent research on his own, he has a particular expertise in and understanding of world history, political science, economics, philosophy, psychology, finance, business strategy, organizational behavior, American sociology and Biblical theology, all of which were vitally important to the writing of this book.

For More Writings by the Author

Watchman on the Wall actively blogs under his Watchman on the Wall moniker on Disqus and maintains his own website at:

http://www.awatchmanonthewall.com